Friedrich Carl von Savigny

A Treatise on The Conflict of Laws

Salzwasser

Friedrich Carl von Savigny

A Treatise on The Conflict of Laws

1. Auflage | ISBN: 978-3-84605-380-5

Erscheinungsort: Frankfurt, Deutschland

Erscheinungsjahr: 2020

Salzwasser Verlag GmbH

Reprint of the original, first published in 1869.

Private International Law.

A TREATISE

ON

THE CONFLICT OF LAWS,

AND

THE LIMITS OF THEIR OPERATION IN RESPECT OF PLACE AND TIME.

BY

FRIEDRICH CARL VON SAVIGNY.

Translated, with Notes, by

WILLIAM GUTHRIE, ADVOCATE.

EDINBURGH:
T. & T. CLARK, LAW PUBLISHERS, 38, GEORGE STREET.
LONDON: STEVENS & SONS.
1869.

CONTENTS.

CHAPTER II.—LIMITS IN TIME OF THE AUTHORITY OF RULES OF LAW OVER LEGAL RELATIONS.

INTRODUCTION.

This volume, which is now offered to the English student, forms part of the System of Modern Roman Law, the most remarkable monument of Savigny's learning and genius. To translate the whole work into English would have been no unworthy or unprofitable labour, and I know that such a task has been contemplated by more than one admirer of the greatest of modern jurists. But in this country so few addict themselves to the study of scientific jurisprudence, that such a publication would almost certainly prove a commercial failure; nor could a translator hope for any professional or literary credit that might indemnify him for the absence of other reward. The eighth volume of that system, however, is a treatise on Private International Law, or the Conflict of Laws, complete within itself, and admitting of being detached from the earlier volumes without impairing its value as a legal authority, or even as a model of juridical style and reasoning. It deals with a subject of great practical importance, as to which the opinions of foreign jurists have always been respected in British courts. And not only has this eighth volume itself been cited as an authority in our tribunals, but English writers have borrowed or enforced its doctrines and arguments, with more or less exactness of reproduction. For a treatise, therefore, which even under the disadvantages of being written in a foreign language, and encumbered with the technicalities of a foreign jurisprudence, has obtained a distinct recognition and authority among British and American lawyers, the Publisher and Translator may reasonably expect a favourable reception in its English translation.

This volume, it has been said, is complete in itself, and is easily separable from the rest of the *System*. A survey of the foregoing volumes might therefore be spared, were it not that some technical terms, of everyday use in Continental systems of jurisprudence, but unfamiliar to the lawyers of this country, demand explanations which can be given most naturally and clearly in a brief review of the work.

The part which Savigny bore in the controversies of the last generation, and his position as the head of the 'historical school of jurisprudence,' occasioned misapprehensions which he endeavoured to remove by the eloquent preface to his first volume. This preface is the best introduction to the study of the great jurist.

'A department of science, cultivated as ours has been by the uninterrupted exertions of many ages, offers to the men of the present generation the enjoyment of a rich inheritance. It is not merely the mass of ascertained truth which descends to us; but every well-directed effort of the intellectual powers, all the endeavours of the past, whether they have been fruitful or have been failures, are useful to us as examples or as warnings, so that in a certain sense we are enabled to labour with the united strength of centuries past. To abandon from indolence or blind self-complacency this natural advantage of our position, carelessly to leave it to chance how much of that rich inheritance shall exert its educating and ennobling influence upon us, would be to renounce those most precious gifts which are inseparable from the very being of true science,—the community of scientific convictions, and the steady progress without which that community would become a dead letter. In order that this result may be averted, it is desirable from time to time to gather up and present in one view the particulars that have been sought out and won. For even contemporary searchers after scientific truth arrive at strikingly contradictory results; and such contrasts are still more prominent when we compare different ages with each other. Here it avails not to adopt the one and reject the other; but we must endeavour to resolve the contradictions which we discover into a higher unity, which is the only way to make certain progress in science. The proper frame of mind for such a comprehensive work is a disposition to reverence what is great in the achievements of our predecessors. But that this reverence may not degenerate into a narrow and weakening partiality, impairing our freedom of thought, it is necessary to fix the eye steadily on the great end of science, in comparison with which the utmost which an individual can accomplish must appear imperfect.

'But if the continuous development of our science through many generations offers us a rich possession, it is attended by great and peculiar dangers. In the mass of general ideas, rules, and technical terms which we have received from our predecessors, there will assuredly be included a large admixture of error, which operates on our minds with the traditional power of old prescription, and may easily obtain dominion over us. To avoid this danger, it is desirable that from time to time the whole body of what is handed down to us should be examined anew, questioned, traced to its origin. This is effected by placing ourselves in the position of those who have to communicate the doctrines so received to the ignorant, the sceptical, or the gainsaying. The proper spirit for such a work is one of intellectual freedom, of independence of all authority; but that this sense of freedom may not be perverted into arrogance, there must be added that wholesome feeling of humility which naturally results from an unbiassed contemplation of the restriction of our own individual powers.

'Thus, from opposite points of view, we are led to recognise the same necessity for the science of law, the necessity of a periodical revision of the labours of our predecessors, in order to reject the untrue, and to appropriate the true as a permanent possession that enables us, according to the measure of our strength, to approach nearer to the solution of our common problem. To effect such a revision for the present time, is the purpose of this work.

'It must not be ignored at starting how much the unprejudiced reception of this work may be endangered by recent events in the history of jurisprudence. Many will be led by the author's name to call in question the purpose of this book, which has just been stated, believing that it is designed less for the fair and honest service of science than for the advocacy of the historical school; that the work, therefore, has the character of a controversial writing, against which every one who does not belong to that school has to be on his guard.

'All success in our science depends on the co-operation of different mental energies. The phrase, "the historical school," was innocently used by me and others in former years to designate one of these energies, and the scientific tendencies specially arising from it. This side of legal science was then raised into prominent relief, not in order to destroy or to lessen the value of other forms of activity or other scientific tendencies, but because historical jurisprudence had long been neglected, and therefore at the time required particularly zealous and vigorous attention, in order that it might recover its just position. In connection with that designation there was a long and animated controversy, and even lately hard words have been spoken about it. A vindication against such attacks would be useless—to some extent impossible; for as the dissatisfaction arises more from personal feelings than from scientific disagreements, the opponents of the historical school are in the habit of using that name to express a collective condemnation of every literary production that is inconvenient or distasteful to them. Who, then, could attempt a refutation? One charge, however, on account of its more general character, must be excepted. It is often said that the members of the historical school, ignoring or renouncing the independence of the present time, sought to subject it to the dominion of the past; in particular, that they endeavoured unduly to extend the authority of the Roman law, not only as against the German law, but as against the new jurisprudence which scientific writers and practice have substituted for the pure Roman law. This is a charge of a general, scientific character, and cannot be passed over in silence.

'The historical view of jurisprudence is entirely misunderstood and distorted when it is regarded as setting up the law which has descended to us from the past as supreme, and requiring the maintenance of its unimpaired authority over the present and the future. The essential characteristic is rather the equal recognition of the value and independence of each age, and it merely lays the chief weight on the recognition of the organic connection between the present and the past, without the knowledge of which we can only perceive the external appearance of existing legal institutions, but cannot understand their true essence. In its special application to the Roman law, the historical view does not consist, as many assert, in ascribing to it an undue authority over us. Rather, on the one hand it seeks to discover and ascertain, in the whole body of our existing law, what is in truth of Roman origin, in order that we may not be unconsciously controlled by it; and on the other hand it strives, within the known sphere of the Roman elements of our law, to set aside and discard what is in fact dead, and retains only from our misapprehension a misleading show of life, in order that there may be free space for the development and healthy influence of the still living portions of those Roman elements. The present work, in particular, is so little intended to attribute an excessive authority to Roman law, that it rather disputes its applicability in not a few departments in which it has hitherto been received, even by those who have always declared themselves opponents of the historical school. The author cannot be charged with having changed his mind in this respect, as he has publicly expounded most of the views referred to for a period of from thirty to forty years,—a fact which proves the utter baselessness of the charge which has been made against the historical school in general, and against myself in particular. With unprejudiced persons the knowledge of this fact may result in the gradual discontinuance of the controversy and the party names connected with it, especially as the reasons which first gave rise to the name of a historical school have almost disappeared with the prevalent errors which it was then necessary to attack. A continuance of such a controversy may indeed serve more clearly to define many contrasted tendencies and doctrines; but this advantage is more than outweighed by the prevention of our unprejudiced judgment of the labours of others, and by the application to party strife of powers which might be more usefully devoted to the prosecution of our common science. I am far from ignoring the great benefit of scientific controversy, which is indeed a condition of scientific life; in the kind and direction of the intellectual powers of individuals, moreover, a great diversity will always be observed. Just from the co-operation of such opposite elements, however, the true life of the science is derived, and the possessors of such various powers ought never to cease to regard themselves as labourers on the same great building. If, on the contrary, we allow them to engage in hostile combat with each other, and if we seek, by the industrious application of party names, to make the controversy a personal one, our apprehension of the question soon becomes fundamentally false, and its consequences can only prove ruinous. The individual life and work of men vanishes from our eyes, while we defend or assail them chiefly as members of a party, and we lose the natural advantage for our own culture which might result from the undisturbed influence of their works upon us.

'While the design of asserting an excessive authority for the Roman law is thus distinctly repudiated, it must be as distinctly acknowledged, on the other hand, that a thorough acquaintance with it is of the highest value—nay, is indispensable—in the present state of our law. Even if this belief were not here expressed, it would yet be clearly manifested in my undertaking so comprehensive a work as the present. It remains to show the ground and the character of the high importance thus ascribed to the knowledge of that law.

'Not a few have the following notion of it:—In the countries where the Roman law is in force as a positive law, no conscientious lawyer can omit its careful study; but where new codes have been introduced, that necessity no longer exists, and the law must there be regarded as in an improved condition, because the jurist can bestow his time and energies on more practical and interesting matters. If this view were correct, the Roman law would have at most a very precarious value even for the former countries, for nothing would be easier for the legislature than to introduce such an improved state of the law by adopting an existing foreign code, if it should not be disposed to produce a new one of its own. Others have supposed the assertion of the peculiar merit of the Roman law to mean that its material contents, as stated in particular practical rules, are superior to similar rules appearing in the legal systems of the middle ages or of modern times. That the present work does not aim at any defence of this kind, itself will show. In truth the question lies deeper (very special cases excepted) than to allow of its being disposed of by such a choice between opposite practical rules; and a work which should attempt to follow out in details such a method of comparison, would remind us of the children's way of asking, when told stories of the wars, on which side were the good people, and on which the bad.

'The intellectual activity of individuals in regard to the law may exert itself in two different directions: by the reception and development of the consciousness of right in general, therefore by knowing, teaching, expounding; or by applying it to the events of actual life. The theoretical and the practical elements belong alike to the very nature of law itself. But in the course of the last centuries the two tendencies have diverged and been appropriated to different orders and callings, so that, with few exceptions, lawyers are exclusively addicted either to the theory or the practice of the law as their exclusive or preponderating vocation. As this has not been effected by any arbitrary arrangement, it is not a subject for indiscriminate praise or blame. But it is important to consider what is natural and expedient in this distinction, and how it may result in an injurious one-sidedness. No harm will ensue, if in this separation of functions every one keeps constantly in view the original unity,—if every theoretical lawyer in a certain degree maintains and develops in himself the practical spirit, and every practitioner the theoretical spirit. Where this is not done, where the separation of theory and practice is absolute, the theory of the law is inevitably degraded into a fruitless game of skill, and its practice into a mere handicraft.

'When I say that every theorist ought to cultivate in himself a practical element, I mean spiritually and intellectually, and not with respect to the mere nature of his employments; although in truth some practical occupation, rightly followed, is the surest way of promoting the practical spirit. Certainly many who have devoted themselves to legal science with zeal and affection, have found that some particular case has given them such a lively apprehension of a legal institution as they would never have attained by the study of books and solitary reflection. What we have gained in a single instance by accident may be conceived as the conscious aim of our labours, and applied to the whole extent of the science. Then he would be the perfect theoretical lawyer, whose theory is animated by complete and thoroughgoing apprehension of the whole of legal practice; all the morally religious, political, economical relations of actual life ought always to be before his eyes. It need scarcely be mentioned, that this requirement is not to be taken as implying a censure of those who do not altogether fulfil it; for every one who sets up such a standard for others, must admit how far he himself falls short of it. Yet it is good to have such a standard before our eyes for the united efforts of many different minds; chiefly that we may keep in the proper course, but also that we may be guarded against the seductions of self-conceit, from which no one is altogether safe. If we contemplate the actual condition of our theoretical jurisprudence as it is now, in comparison with its condition fifty, and still more a hundred years ago, we find advantages mingled with disadvantages. No-one can deny that much has now become possible, and has actually been accomplished, which could not formerly be thought of—nay, that the mass of actually ascertained and established truths stands very high in comparison with these former periods. But if we look to the practical spirit by which the science of individual theorizers ought to be animated, the comparison is less favourable for the present time. This deficiency of the present time is connected with the peculiar tendency which is now observable in the labours of theoretical jurists. Certainly nothing is more laudable than the desire to enrich science by new discoveries; yet this desire has often in our time taken a one-sided and unwholesome direction. An exaggerated value has been attached to the production of new views, in comparison with the honest and earnest improvement and exhaustive exposition of that which has already been investigated; although even in this, when it is done in earnest, existing materials will always assume a new form, and so will promote the real though less conspicuous advancement of science. But as the majority of men are not endowed with great creative power, that undue love of novelty has led many to expatiate in isolated detached thoughts and opinions, and in this distraction to let slip their hold of their science as a whole. In this respect we were surpassed by our predecessors, among whom there was in proportion a greater number of individuals capable of representing the totality of the science in a worthy manner. But whoever will look at the thing from a more general point of view, will easily be persuaded that such phenomena are not peculiar to jurisprudence, but stand in connection with the general course of our literary development.

'We have desiderated, on the other hand, that the practitioner should retain some theoretical element. It is not meant that he should be an active writer, or even that he should constantly prosecute an extensive study of books. In most cases both of these are made impossible by the demands of practical business. But amid his practical occupations he ought always to cherish a sense and feeling for the science of law,—he ought never to forget that that science, rightly apprehended, is nothing else than the generalization of the rules which it is his function to make known (zum Bewusstseyn bringen), and apply in detail. Nothing is more common, in estimating the merits of a practical lawyer, than to attach exclusive value to mere dexterity and quickness, although these very useful qualities are quite compatible with the most unconscientious superficiality. That our juridical practice is not altogether pervaded by the right spirit, is manifest from a comprehensive view of its results. If it were influenced by this spirit, practice itself would generate a steady progress in sound jurisprudence; it would support and sustain the efforts of theorists, and, where they err, restore them to the right path; but, in particular, it would so prepare the way for legislation, that the positive law and legal practice would advance together in perfect harmony, as the nature of things demands. And do we not in general find just the opposite of all this?

'If the radical evil of the present state of the law consists in a growing separation between theory and practice, the remedy must be sought only in the restoration of their natural unity. For this purpose the Roman law, rightly used, may render the most material service. In the Roman jurists that natural unity is seen still undisturbed, and in the most lively operation. It is no special merit of theirs, just as the opposite state of things in the present day has been brought about rather by the general course of development than by the fault of individuals. While, therefore, we earnestly and with unprejudiced minds penetrate into their method, so different from ours, we shall appropriate it to ourselves, and so regain the right path.

'But as a knowledge of the Roman law may be sought after in very different ways, it is necessary, if the wished-for end is to be attained, to state clearly what path ought to be pursued. Every one will assume that a thorough scientific method is demanded; but many may be alarmed by the erroneous idea, that every one who seeks to acquire such a knowledge of Roman law is expected also to undertake the whole labour of antiquarian research and critical examination of the law sources. But although that department of study is important, the wholesome principle of division of labour must not be ignored. Most persons, therefore, may content themselves in this matter with the results of the special investigations of individuals. On the other hand, it is wrong to imagine that the slightest progress has been made towards the end in view by a mere knowledge of the most general principles of the Roman law,—such a knowledge, for example, as is contained in a compend of the Institutions, or as is usually communicated in the French schools of law. Such a knowledge is sufficient to hand down a mere verbal memorial of the Roman law to a better future; but to the student who attempts no more, it hardly rewards the slender pains he bestows in acquiring it. If the knowledge of the Roman law is to be of any avail for the end we have here in view, there is but one way to it,—we must penetrate, by independent reading and reflection, into the writings of the old jurists. Then will the enormous mass of modern literature no longer terrify us. Judicious guidance may make us acquainted with what little of it can really aid our independent study; the bulk of it which remains we leave to the jurists who are theorists by profession, and who indeed cannot decline the laborious task.

'The present work is specially intended to promote this earnest and hearty study of the Roman law; especially, therefore, to diminish the difficulties which are wont to deter practical lawyers from a personal and independent study of the law sources. In consequence of these difficulties, an undue authority over practice is accorded to the opinions which are laid down in the most accessible modern handbooks. But if the purpose of the author of this work is fulfilled, something will also be effected towards the emancipation of practice from a spurious theory.

'These ideas certainly find their most direct application

in the countries where the Roman law still forms the basis of legal practice; but they are also applicable where new codes have taken its place. For in both, the defects in the state of the law are essentially the same, and therefore the evil and the nature of the remedy are less different than might be supposed. Hence, even in those countries which are provided with national codes, this manner of using the Roman law will both revive and reanimate theoretical jurisprudence, and guard it from subjective and arbitrary errors, but especially will bring it into closer connection with practice, which is most important of all. Such a change is indeed more difficult than in the countries of the common law; but it is not impossible. This is shown especially by the example of the modern French jurists, who frequently illustrate and supplement their code from the Roman law in a very clear and satisfactory way. In doing so, they act quite in conformity with the spirit of that code, and where they err, it is less from an improper method of applying the Roman law, than from defective knowledge of it. In this we are unquestionably superior to them; but in the manner of using it along with the national codes, we should do well to learn from them. Such a method of applying the Roman law in our Prussian fatherland is, it is true, more difficult than it is with them, because in our Landrecht the connection which really exists with the earlier law is often concealed, partly by the peculiar style of expression, partly by an excess of detail. It is not, however, impossible; and if it is restored, a very serious evil will be removed, which has arisen from the introduction of the code. This evil consists in that entire separation from the scientific cultivation of the common law, by which those engaged in the practice of the law have hitherto been deprived of one of the most important means of culture, —actual contact with the juridical thought of former ages and other countries. It cannot be ignored, that when the Prussian code was undertaken, German juridical literature was for the most part dull and inelegant, and hence had almost lost even the possibility of exerting a beneficial influence upon practice;

indeed, it was the very consciousness of this defective condition of the law which then led to the attempt to remove the evil by a national code entirely altering the groundwork of the practical law. If we should now succeed in restoring this lost connection with the literature of the common law, it would lead, in the altered state of jurisprudence, to a purely beneficial influence on practice, and those evils which formerly made themselves so perceptible would certainly not recur.

'Many regard the desire still to apply the Roman law as a means of advancing and improving our modern law as an injurious degradation of our age and country. They seem to imagine that we can in this way, under the most favourable circumstances, attain only to an imperfect imitation or restoration of the legal system of the Romans; while it would be far more dignified to produce, by our independent efforts, something new and original. This self-esteem, praiseworthy in itself, arises from the following mistake: With the great and manifold legal material which the centuries have handed down to us, our task has become incomparably more difficult than that of the Romans was; the standard we set up for ourselves is therefore higher; and if we succeed in reaching it, we shall not give a mere counterpart of the excellences of the Roman jurists, but something far greater than they achieved. If we have learned to use the materials at our command with the same free and ready handling which we admire in the Romans, then we shall be able to dispense with them as examples, and consign them to grateful remembrance in history. Till then, however, we must not be restrained, either by false pride or by indolence, from availing ourselves of a means of progress and culture for which we could hardly find any substitute by our own exertions. In this, too, we maintain a relation between our own time and antiquity, such as we observe in other departments of intellectual labour. It must not be supposed that by these words we seek to exalt the study of the Roman law, to the prejudice of those zealous Germanistic efforts which in our own times occasion such lively hope. Nothing is more frequent and more natural than to manifest our zeal in the field of our own inquiries, by depreciating a different but kindred sphere of labour. Yet it is an error which will infallibly injure only him who cherishes and practises it, and not the adversary who is so depreciated.

'It follows, from the plan thus proposed for the present work, that it will be chiefly of a critical character. Many will object to this because they only wish to have positive truth capable of immediate application, and are careless as to the mode of its attainment and the controversies that may exist concerning it. Our intellectual life would be easy and pleasant if we could but allow the clear and simple truth to work its effect upon us, and so advance without distraction or disturbance to ever new knowledge. But on every side we are surrounded and embarrassed by the *débris* of false and half-true ideas and opinions, through which we must make our way. Shall we expostulate with destiny for imposing on us such a useless labour? We must rather accommodate and adapt ourselves to it as a necessary condition of our mental being; but there is not wanting rich fruit, growing out of this necessity as a reward for our labour. Our intellectual powers have here their education; and every particular truth which we win in this conflict with error, becomes ours in a higher sense, and proves more fruitful than if we received it from others, passively and without trouble.

'The critical character of this work will appear chiefly in the following particulars: It will be conspicuously and indeed exclusively critical, in the purely negative results of some investigations in which we engage: whether these consist in proving that a Roman legal institution is extinct, and therefore foreign to our modern law, or in pointing out baseless ideas and theories foisted into our system by the mistakes of modern jurists. It is just such investigations with which many would least wish to be annoyed and delayed. But he who removes stones from the way, or warns against deviations from the highway by setting up finger-posts, materially improves the condition of those who come after; although, when advantages so gained have been confirmed by custom, it may soon be forgotten that there was ever a time when such difficulties were to be encountered.

'But the critical nature of the book appears not only in such purely negative results, but also where the simple, absolute contrast of the true and the false does not suffice to establish a positive truth, so that it becomes necessary to mark more exactly the degree of our convictions. For we may dispute the opinions of others in various manners. Often the feeling of absolute certainty accompanies our own convictions, because we see how our opponent's opinion has arisen from logical error, ignorance of facts, or a thoroughly wrong method. Then we hold such an opinion to be scientifically untenable, and our refutation necessarily involves a decided censure of our adversary. Not so in other cases, in which, after carefully weighing all the arguments, we give the preference to one opinion, yet without pronouncing so decided a condemnation on our opponent. In this probability, with which we must then be contented, degrees may be distinguished; and the precise indication, the scientific recognition of these degrees, concerns the moral as well as the scientific value of our labours (*a*). In other cases of conflicting opinions it is important to define exactly the limits of the matter in dispute, as well as the value and influence of diversities of opinion upon the science. The keenness of the controversy, and the exalted self-confidence which it often excites, easily seduce us into ascribing to it an exaggerated value, and thus cause us to mislead others

' (*a*) *Lebensnachrichten über B. G. Niebuhr*, ii. 208: "Above all things in the study of the sciences, we must preserve our truthfulness without spot, absolutely shunning every false appearance, writing down as certain not the slightest matter as to which we are not fully persuaded; and when we have to state conjectures or probabilities, using every effort to show the degree of our persuasion." Much in the admirable letter from which this passage is taken belongs not merely to philology (to which it immediately relates), but to science in general.'

also. Finally, great attention is due to what may be called the relative truth of the opinions which we dispute. In a view which we are compelled to reject as decidedly wrong, we often recognise an element of truth which has only been transformed into error by a mistaken treatment or one-sided exaggeration. This occurs especially in many cases where the error only consists in regarding the concrete in too universal, or the general in too concrete, an aspect. The separation and recognition of such a true element in the views which we dispute may be of great importance to science; it is particularly adapted, in the case of unprejudiced, truth-loving disputants, to bring about a mutual understanding, and so to effect the purest and most satisfactory determination of the controversy, by resolving the opposing views into a higher unity.

'We seek to attain these ends in the form of a *System;* and as this method is not understood by all in the same sense, it is necessary to premise a general explanation. I hold the essence of the systematic method to consist in the knowledge and exposition of the organic connection, or relationship, by which the particular legal conceptions and rules of law are united into one great whole. Such affinities are, in the first place, often latent, and their discovery will then enrich our understanding. Further, they are very manifold; and the more we succeed in discovering and following out the affinities of a legal institution in different directions, the more complete will be our insight into it. Finally, there is often a deceptive appearance of such relationship, where none really exists; and it is then our task to put an end to this.—The outward arrangement of a systematic work will naturally be determined by that organic connection which is to be mirrored in it; and not seldom this alone is thought of in speaking of systematic treatment. Here, however, many misapprehensions must be guarded against. In the rich, living reality, all legal relations form one organic whole; but in order successively to apprehend them with our mind's eye, and to communicate them to others, we are compelled to separate them into their various elements. Hence the order in which we place them can be fixed only by that affinity which we regard as the most important, and every other relationship which exists in reality can only be noticed by way of separate or collateral exposition. Here a degree of forbearance is required, and even some scope for the writer's subjective line of thought, which perhaps leads him to give special prominence to a particular aspect of a question, which he is thus able to treat with peculiar fulness of result.

'Many require that nothing shall occur in such a systematic exposition which has not had a satisfactory foundation in what goes before, that the contents of following portions shall be in no way anticipated. To such persons the following work will give the greatest shock, since I do not consider that such a rule is to be followed even by way of approximation in such a work as this. It is founded on the assumption that the subject-matter of the book is quite new to the reader, and it is no doubt correct when it is laid down for guidance in the earliest teaching of any subject. But no one will readily conceive the idea of first learning the science of jurisprudence from an extensive and detailed work like the present. Such a work will rather be used by those who are already acquainted with the matters treated of from lectures and other books, for the purpose of proving, purifying, founding more deeply, and further extending knowledge already acquired. Such persons may well be expected at every point of the treatise to recall to their consciousness what they already know, even if it becomes the subject of exposition only at a subsequent part of this work. If we desire to avoid this, we shall be compelled either entirely to give up the exposition of the most important and most fruitful relations of the legal institutions, or to take it up at places where it must be far less clear and effective. If, therefore, by the arrangement adopted we actually attain only the advantage of a more lifelike perspicuity, our choice of that arrangement needs no other justification. Those, however, who are not induced by this consideration to pass from the censure referred to, are reminded that in detailed monographies they are content to receive a multitude of assumptions, the proof of which is not to be found in the same book. Why, then, should the author of a comprehensive System have less right in this respect than the author of a monography?

'As I have mentioned monographies in order to anticipate an objection, and as in modern times we owe to works of that class the most important advances in our science, it is right to remove at the same time a misunderstanding as to the relation of such works to a comprehensive System of law. Many regard a monography as if it were an isolated section out of a complete system, which has by some accident been separately composed and published. According to this view, there is only needed a sufficient number of good monographies, in order, by adding them together, to make a satisfactory System. The essential distinction is, that the monography arbitrarily selects the standpoint of a single legal institution, in order to trace from this its relation to the whole; so that there is here quite a different selection and arrangement of the matter from the case in which the same legal institution is dealt with in the connection of a complete legal System. I have found it necessary to make this remark also, in order to explain why the doctrine of possession will assume in this work quite another form from that which it presents in the book in which I treated of it separately.

'Besides the *System* itself, there will be found in this work separate inquiries under the title of *Appendices* (Beylagen). I have found this arrangement necessary for various reasons. Sometimes a particular question demands such extensive investigation, that if it were taken in the course of the *System*, the just proportion would be far exceeded, and the natural connection of subjects disturbed. In other cases a legal conception presses so equally upon quite different parts of the *System*, that only a separate exposition of it admits of an exhaustive treatment: this is true, in particular, of a full appendix on the doctrine of error (Appendix VIII). Finally, antiquarian investigations lie quite beyond the plan of the work; but these are sometimes so interwoven with institutions of the most modern law, that the latter could not be fully understood unless the former were admitted to their modest place in an appendix. To draw a rigid line between the matter which ought to be assigned to the *System* and to the *Appendices* is impossible, and many will perhaps wish that more or less in different places had been relegated to the *Appendices*. But here also a somewhat wide scope may without danger be left to individual freedom.

'In former times a uniform method used to be applied in explaining the various legal institutions, the chief feature of which was, that the general definition was followed by a complete enumeration of all possible subdivisions of the subject. Many modern authors reject this arrangement as useless and pedantic, and confine themselves to noticing subdivisions, where they have to do with them in explaining particular rules of law. I can accept neither the one method nor the other as a general rule, because I do not approve of that mechanical uniformity, whether it consists in doing or omitting. Every form is good and expedient, the application of which promotes a clear and profound understanding of a legal institution, and in each case, therefore, that ought to be done which is most conducive to that end. Where, therefore, the idea of a legal institution includes contrasts which enter deeply into its very nature, it may become necessary to the clear and complete treatment of the subject, that the general definition should be immediately followed by the formal subdivisions in which these contrasts or antitheses find expression.

In the following work special care has been taken to use a technical language conformable to the law sources; and it is necessary to vindicate this course, because many believe that in modern times an exaggerated value has been attached to this matter. Its importance lies in this, that there is a dangerous action and reaction between inaccurate use of language and the erroneous combination of ideas. If, on the one side, the vicious use of language is a product and mark of error in thought, on the other hand the latter is confirmed, extended, propagated by the former. But if this source of error is destroyed by a demonstration of the ungenuine terminology, we must not refrain from using new technical terms where the technical language of the law sources is inadequate. In this respect purism is sometimes perhaps carried too far. Only it is always expedient to avoid those spurious expressions which have already proved dangerous from their connection with erroneous ideas.

'A special chapter (§§ 32–52) explains the manner in which the law sources are used in this work; yet a few general explanations will not here be out of place. Jurists are often reproached with prodigality in their citations from the law sources, inasmuch as they attempt to prove, by numerous texts, what every one already believes. If such quotations are regarded as merely defensive measures against doubts and contradictions which do not exist, this censure might have some reason. But they are to be regarded in another aspect. If the assertion be correct, that in the study of the old jurists we may gain life and nourishment for our own thought such as can be found nowhere else, and if this study is not without its own difficulties, a systematic guide to them must be welcome to us. This work is intended to afford such guidance; and from this point of view the passages cited from the law sources are not merely authorities for the propositions laid down in the text; but these propositions are at the same time an introduction to and commentary on the passages quoted, which in this selection, in this arrangement and connection with the general exposition of the *System*, are brought nearer to our modes of thought, and so made more accessible to us. It happens sometimes that two equally careful inquirers, labouring on the same materials, are led to very different results. This diversity will generally depend on what texts are made the central point of the whole inquiry, and what are brought into connection with these only as subordinate. An error in this distinction may give a wrong direction to the whole work. Here small security is gained by laying down rules. The study of good models will do good service; but we must, above all, by actual personal use, seek to get the tact which teaches us to find the right way.

'Others, on the contrary, may be disappointed in their expectation of finding a more abundant literary apparatus than has been used in the following work. I have purposely cited only those writers who can in some way or another be useful in accordance with the plan of the work above explained, if only by referring in turn to other authors. I have not, therefore, sought after completeness in enumerating all the treatises bearing on a subject even when they give us no appreciable aid. In such a case the reader would owe me little gratitude if I misled him to waste his time in useless researches. If I had come to this undertaking at an earlier age, I would have attempted an exhaustive use of juristic literature in another sense. We find in it two great and almost unmanageable masses, from which certainly much good might still be got. The one consists of exegetical writers, from the glossators downwards, and especially through the time of the French school; the other, of practical writers, the authors of the numerous *consilia*, *responsa*, etc., also reckoning from the glossators downwards. An exhaustive use of these in the compilation of a legal system such as I indicate, would involve a perusal of all these writers, with special reference to this *System*, *i.e.* by means of them to prove it, to amend it, to supplement it. By this labour very much might be unquestionably gained in details, but less in regard to the fundamental principles. Now, as I begin this work in the evening of my life, it would be folly to think of such a plan. But if one should regard this work as possessing an enduring value, he might acquire for himself some real and lasting credit by undertaking to complete it by the literary labour I have pointed out. There is nothing quixotic in the suggestion, as it might be done quite gradually, and bit by bit; if, for instance, the authors of a limited period, or even single works, were read through for the desired end. Perhaps, at the very beginning of this work, a general view of the various treatises which are useful and commendable for the study of our legal system will be missed. It seems to me preferable to meet this really important want by separate bibliographical writings; just as the historical connection of our law sources, their manuscripts and editions, is better accomplished in books of legal history than in the introduction of a legal system, where the foundation and the connection required for a satisfactory treatise of this kind are wanting.

'The materials for the present work have been gradually collected and elaborated in lectures which the author has delivered on the Roman law since the beginning of the century. But in the form in which it is here presented, it is an entirely new work, for which these lectures could only be used as a preparation. For prelections are intended for the unlearned: to them they are intended to make known new and unknown subjects, by seeking to bring this information into connection with the existing knowledge and general intellectual development of the audience. The writer, on the other hand, labours for the learned; he presupposes that his readers are acquainted with the science in its present form; he connects what he has to communicate with this knowledge, summons them to review along with him the ideas they already possess, in order that they may sift, confirm, extend them. Undeniable as this distinction is between the two forms of conveying instruction, transitions from the one to the other are at times not merely conceivable, but unobjectionable. The writer himself may at times so use his materials as to go back imperceptibly with his reader to the beginnings of scientific ideas, and make them rise up, as it were, afresh before his eyes. Such a method will often do good service in correcting ideas and principles which have been arbitrarily used and distorted; and an author will have a special inclination and capacity for it who has frequently had occasion to treat in lectures of the subject of his literary labours.—The plan of the work in its present shape was first sketched in spring 1835; in autumn of the same year its execution was begun; and when the printing of it was commenced, the four chapters of the first Book and the first three chapters of the second Book were finished.

'Now, when I send forth this work, I cannot repress the thought of the destiny which awaits it. It will encounter good and evil like every human effort and work. Very many will tell me how defective it is; but none can see its defects more fully or feel them more deeply than I do. Now, when a considerable portion lies before me completed, I might wish that much of it had been more exhaustive, plainer, and therefore different. Should such a knowledge paralyze the courage which every extensive enterprise requires? Even along with such a self-consciousness, we may rest satisfied with the reflection, that the truth is furthered, not merely as we ourselves know it and utter it, but also by our pointing out and paving the way to it, by our settling the questions and problems on the solution of which all success depends; for we help others to reach the goal which we are not permitted to attain. Thus, I am now satisfied with the consciousness that this work may contain fruitful seeds of truth, which shall perhaps find in others their full development, and bear rich fruit. If, then, in the presence of this full and rich fructification, the present work, which contained its germ, falls into the background, nay, is forgotten, it matters little. The individual work is as transient as the individual man in his visible form; but imperishable is the thought that ever waxes through the life of individuals,—the thought that unites all of us who labour with zeal and love into a greater and enduring community, and in which even the meanest contribution of the individual finds its permanent place.'

The subject of Savigny's *System* is the Roman private law, as it exists in modern times, and forms the largest portion of the common law of Germany and other countries of the European Continent. He begins with an inquiry into its sources, which involves a preliminary investigation into the sources of law in general.

The proper objects of law are rights,[1] which appear in a visible form when they are disputed, and when a judicial sentence recognises their existence and defines their extent. This, however, is but an accidental form which they assume, and their real existence is in the *relation of right*, or, as it is perhaps less accurately translated in the following pages, the *legal relation* (Rechtsverhältniss). This conception is entirely foreign to the English mind, and it is therefore necessary to attempt an explanation. Savigny[2] defines the legal relation as 'a relation of person to person determined by a rule of law, this rule of law assigning to each individual a sphere or territory within which his will is supreme and independent of the will of other persons.' In another passage,[3] the nature of the legal relation is illustrated by an example. 'The celebrated *L. Frater a fratre*[4] deals with the following case: Two brothers are subject to the paternal power. The one lends to the other a sum of money, which the borrower repays after the father's death. The question arises, Whether he can reclaim the money as having been paid in error. The only question for the judge to determine here, is whether there is any ground for the *condictio indebiti;* but in order to do this, he must take a comprehensive view of the whole legal relation. Its particular elements are, the paternal power over both brothers, a loan by the one to the other, a *peculium* which the debtor had received from the father. This complex legal relation has gradually developed itself by the father's death, the succession to him, the repayment of the loan. From these various elements the decision required of the judge is to be derived.'

'Legal relations,' says Puchta,[5] 'are relations of men to

[1] Savigny, *System*, § 4; cf. Stair, i. 1, 22.
[2] *System*, § 52.
[3] *System*, § 4.
[4] *Dig.* xii. 6, 38.
[5] *Pandekten*, § 29.

each other, which are to be regarded as emanations from legal freedom,—from that freedom which belongs to the will as such, and irrespective of moral qualification or limitation; in a word, relations in which men are in the position of persons.[1] The activity of the moral will consists in a determination for good or evil,—that of the legal will, *i.e.* the activity of the person as such, in subjecting to itself external objects. The result of this subjection, so far as it is an emanation from the legal freedom, and therefore is in conformity with legal rules, is a legal power over such an object—a right in it belonging to the person. These rights constitute the substance or kernel of legal relations. Legal relations are complexes of rights which arise in the intercourse of persons in their relations to and action upon one another; and the legal determination and analysis of these relations consists in ascertaining the rights comprised in them, and in defining their effects and modifications in this connection.'

In many passages it will be found that the word Rechtsverhältniss may practically be rendered by the English word 'case.' When I have so translated it, however, the phrase 'legal relation' is added in parentheses; for it cannot be said that in any use of the word 'case' it really includes the whole meaning of Rechtsverhältniss. A 'case,' in the familiar language of lawyers, is a combination of facts as they have occurred in actual life, which raises a question of conflicting right, and which is laid by the parties concerned before a court of law for its decision. The phrase has of late years been technically appropriated to a particular form in which such a question is laid before the judge. In a still more frequent use of the word, it means a reported judgment of a tribunal upon a question of right stated and argued before it, and therefore embraces within its signification both a series

[1] 'Personality is the subjective capability of a legal will, of a legal power; the capacity for rights; the quality whereby a man is the subject of juridical relations.'—Puchta, § 22.

or complex of facts, and the exposition of the law which governs the relation arising out of them. 'Case' is thus by no means an English equivalent for 'legal relation' in every application and every shade of meaning. I only mean to point out, that when we say, for example, 'This case differs from that of B. *v* C., where the element of C.'s bankruptcy was added to the other circumstances which occur here,' a German might appropriately say, 'that the legal relation was not the same, having been further developed by the bankruptcy,' etc.

Savigny[1] says, after giving the definition above cited: 'Thus every legal relation consists of two elements: first, the matter or substance, *i.e.* the relation itself; secondly, the legal determination or regulation of this matter. The former may be regarded as its material element—the simple facts; the second, as the formal element—that by which the facts are endowed with a legal form and significance.' He does not further analyze the material composition of the legal relation; but he would probably have stated these to be the *subjects*, or parties interested, the object, and the facts in which the relation of the parties to this object has originated.

The positive law which governs legal relations does not exist merely in detached and unconnected rules. As particular rights are actually presented to us in their organic connection in the legal relation, so the rules of law have a deeper foundation in the legal institution (Rechtsinstitut), 'the organic nature of which is manifested as well in the living connection of its constituent parts as in its progressive development . . . . Each element of every legal relation is subject to a corresponding legal institution as its type, and is governed by it in the same way as the particular judgment by the rule of law.' Thus, in the example formerly given, the legal institutions relating to the various elements of the legal relation are the acquisition by the father through his children; the ancient

[1] *System*, § 52.

peculium, and, in particular, the *deductio* connected with it; the transmission of obligations to heirs; confusion of debts and credits; the *condictio indebiti*.'[1] Between the legal relation and the legal institution this distinction is observable, that while the former is presented to us by the events of life in its actual construction and intricacy, the latter may be, in the first instance, separately constructed, and afterwards combined at pleasure.

Having explained these two fundamental ideas, which are equally available for every theory of law, Savigny proceeds to state his own views as to the origin of law. Upon these views, or upon the plan of the earlier part of the *System*, it would be out of place to dwell in detail. It is sufficient for our purpose to say, that it is the fundamental principle of his philosophy, that law grows with the life of the nation, and is inseparable from it. In primitive times, as now, every sentence of the judge was called forth by a specific outward relation, a particular conflict of interests. It arose from a certain series of facts resulting in a collision of individual claims; but that collision was adjudicated upon according to an existing rule or *Institution*. It is true that these rules could not be expressed in any form of words, and that the sentences of early rulers recommended themselves to their narrow public by their conformity to an *unconscious* sense of law in the mind of the nation. The concrete precedes the abstract; and as yet judges gave no reasons for their decisions.[2]

The first step in the development of law depended on the increasing self-consciousness that accompanies increasing civilisation. 'In order to have the conception of law,' says Hegel, 'a nation must be educated to think, and must no longer stop short at that which is merely sensible; it must fit on to out-

[1] *System*, § 5.

[2] 'Principes erant quasi animatæ leges,' says an old writer. 'Populi nullis legibus tenebantur; arbitria principum pro legibus erant.'—Justin. in *S. Aug. de civ. Dei*, iv. 6.

ward objects the form of generality, and must be consciously striving after something universal.' Hence Savigny places the origin of law, properly so called, in the consciousness (conscience) of nations. It is the simplest truth taught by the history of law, that its development has been in proportion to the wants of society, its rules widening, and its details becoming more numerous with the growth of wealth and population, and with the multiplication within each community of the occasions and the means of intercourse between different places and individuals. Law is thus in a state of perpetual growth; and the main and most influential condition of this growth is its generation within a community held together by a common spirit and common traditions. The character and whole outward circumstances of the nation in which it springs up, determine in a very great degree the nature and peculiarities of each system of law; and the rapidity of its growth, and the promptitude with which it is adapted to the necessities and opinions of those who live under it, are in some proportion to the perfection of the national organization. The state is the organ of the growth of law within the nation. As a family expands into a nation, the rudimental forms of law and of the state (which is itself the highest production of the spirit of law) are developed simultaneously, and go on to more perfection as the nation advances. In short, the birth of society and of law is one. *Ubi societas ibi jus est.*

The assumption that law is law only as it originates in man's formally expressed will, is directly at variance with the fact, that wherever a legal question arises, a rule for its decision exists, and has not to be sought out or made for the first time. This necessary existence of law, anterior to every possible case which can call for its application, entitles it to the name and character of positive law. And it is now a somewhat trite proposition, that the earliest form of positive law within the state is the somewhat vague and indeterminate mass known as common law, and which assumes a visible but not always a very consistent or intelligible form, as 'case-law.' It first appeared in the form of usage, which is not, in the first instance, a maker of law, but only its origin and mark. In process of time it became difficult to descry, in the multitude of decisions and the variety of customs, the original idea of justice from which they derived their authority. The violence of ruling castes, and the tendency to adhere to old use and wont, when their meaning was forgotten and their utility lost, gradually corrupted and obscured the positive law. Then, in the municipal law, codes, or at least regular systems of legislation, were introduced, and the assisting influences of equity and scientific jurisprudence were called into constant and powerful operation.

These three—national or consuetudinary law, legislation, scientific law or jurisprudence—are the originating causes of law,—the sources of law in general.

In the third chapter of the first Book (§ 17 sqq.) Savigny proceeds to apply his general doctrine of the law sources to the Roman law, and to show the position which legislation, custom, and jurisprudence assume in that system as law sources (Rechtsquellen). This chapter embraces a valuable exposition of the rules to be observed in the interpretation of statutory law.

The second Book of the *System* (§ 52) opens with a classification of the various kinds of possible legal relations, and the relative legal institutions or sets of rules. This results in the division of the *System* into four main divisions,—the Law of Things, embracing property, both in moveables and immoveables; the Law of Obligations; the Law of the Family, pure and applied; and the Law of Succession. Instead, however, of entering at once on the exposition of these various departments, the author finds himself in the midst of a 'general part' of the *System*, which is not, as in some treatises, a mere receptacle for legal institutions which cannot be fitted into a convenient place in the *System* itself. In a comprehensive survey of the legal institutions he finds many subjects which recur, possibly with some modifications, in each. 'Among these,' he says, 'are, first of all, the *subjects* of rights, *i.e.* the persons interested in them, and, in particular, their capacity for rights; then the origin and the extinction of legal relations; finally, the protection of rights from violation, and the consequent modifications of the rights themselves. Not merely for the sake of avoiding repetition, but in order to obtain a more perfect knowledge of the common element which exists in all these portions of the legal institutions, Savigny places his exposition of these subjects, which are common to all, before that of the particular departments. Accordingly, the second chapter of the second Book treats of persons as the subjects of the legal relations. It has to do with the capacity of persons to have rights, not with their capacity to act, *i.e.* to acquire or lose rights. It forms an exhaustive treatise on the person, in its legal sense, from the beginning of capacity for rights at birth until its termination by death, with all its limitations and modifications in respect of freedom, political rights, dependence arising from the family relations, and other causes of less extensive operation. This chapter includes a full discussion of the nature of juridical persons (corporations, etc.).

The third chapter is entitled, 'Of the Origin and Extinction of Legal Relations.' The beginning and the end of legal relations are determined by *juridical facts*.[1] To these the law attaches the acquisition or the loss of a right, and the constitution or dissolution of a legal relation. Such a fact may

[1] 'The German *juristisch*, which is formed from the low Latin word *jurista*, with a Gothic affix in *isch*, is not translateable by legal or lawful or rightful, but denotes a legality arising out of positive law, out of the *jus proprium ipsius civitatis*. See Hugo's *Lehrbuch eines civilistischen Cursus*, B. 1, p. 14, 8th ed. In English we do not distinguish between an act which is lawful, from having a definite legal character attached to it, and an act which is lawful, from being simply not contrary to law.'—Sir E. Perry's Transl. of Savigny *On Possession*, p. 2, note. Sir E. Perry accordingly appropriates the term juridical to the former meaning, as has also been done in this volume.

consist either in an event or in a human action, whether the action of a person who acquires a right, or of one who becomes subject to an obligation in favour of another. Preliminary to the consideration of the various kinds of juridical facts (which occupies the third and fourth volumes of the *System*), are discussions of the personal conditions of the capacity to act, such as nonage, insanity, interdiction; of the exclusion of freedom in juridical acts[1] (which form the largest class of juridical facts) by force and error; of their voluntary limitation by the condition, *modus, dies.* The fourth volume includes an exhaustive discussion of 'donation,' which is often ranked as a special juridical act, such as sale or loan, but has in truth, like contract, a general character, which may be assumed by the most different kinds of juridical acts.

The fourth chapter of the second Book, which commences with the fifth volume, treats of the violation of rights in general, and the remedies for this violation; that is, of the law of actions and exceptions, with the judicial sentence, its effects and its surrogates (judicial confession and reference to oath), and a full exposition of the doctrine of *Restitutio in integrum.* The sixth, seventh, and eighth volumes of the *System*, which comprise the fourth chapter of this Book, were published in 1847 and 1848, after an interruption of six years; and they bring us down to the subject with which we are here engaged. The Author's preface to this volume explains how it was that the great plan unfolded at the commencement of the work was not to be fulfilled. Of the portion of it which in 1849 Savigny still hoped to accomplish, only two volumes, containing the introductory sections of the Law of Obligations, were published in 1851.

[1] Juristische Handlungen = Acts having a legal effect: (1) Purposely = Rechtsgeschäfte, or Willenserklärungen (juridical acts, declarations of intention); (2) Independently of the purpose of the actor, and that either, (*a*) in Rechtsgeschäfte, so far as they have results beyond those in the view of the actor, or (*b*) in *unpermitted acts*, delicts, violations of right, in which the result is always independent of the intention of the actor. See Puchta, *Pand.* § 49; Savigny's *System*, § 104, etc.

He died in 1861. The English reader who desires to know more of his writings and of his life is referred for a specimen of the former to the treatise on Possession, excellently translated by Sir Erskine Perry, and to a paper in the *Law Magazine and Law Review* for May 1863, which was written by the Translator of this volume, and was almost entirely taken from a short memoir by his accomplished pupil and affectionate friend, Professor Rudorff.[1]

It was the Editor's hope at one time to offer this translation to the public in a more perfect state, and with a more complete apparatus of notes and references to British and American law than it now possesses. But he was prevented by various circumstances from accomplishing his original project. Recently, however, he has been urged by many admirers of Savigny,[2] and encouraged by the increasing appreciation of his genius which is manifested in various quarters, to publish the translation nearly as it was written six years ago, with a few notes which appeared likely to be convenient to the reader. He makes no pretension to profound or extensive acquaintance with German legal literature; and his only endeavour has been to make the Author intelligible to the student and useful to the practical lawyer.

The latter chapter of this volume treats of a subject, the retroactive effect of new laws, which has never in this country been brought into connection with private international law. It was for the sake of the latter subject only that the transla-

[1] *Friedrich Carl von Savigny: sein Wesen und Wirken.* Von Professor Rudorff. Weimar 1862. This acknowledgment was inadvertently omitted in the *Law Magazine.*

[2] Among these the names of Professors Lorimer and Muirhead, of the University of Edinburgh, and of Mr. Fraser (whose recommendation to translate Savigny, in the recent edition of his learned work on *The Law of Parent and Child*, ought to produce more fruit than this small volume), cannot be omitted. To many other professional brethren the Translator is indebted for much valuable suggestion, encouragement, and aid.

tion was undertaken ; but, irrespective of the importance of the doctrines explained in the latter half of the volume, it would have been inexpedient to divide it. These doctrines deserve the attentive consideration both of the jurist and the legislator ; and though they are here given almost without commentary or reference to our native authorities, the Editor may perhaps be allowed on another occasion to illustrate, more fully than he has done, Savigny's doctrines on both the subjects embraced in this volume.

8, Fettes Row, Edinburgh,
December 26, 1868.

ADDENDA ET CORRIGENDA.

Page 105, line 11, *for* 'regret,' *read* 'reject.'

Page 16, Note 3. The following cases may be referred to on the subject of this note: *Barber* v *Lamb*, 6 Jur. N. S. 981, 8 C. B. N. S. 95; *Papayanni* v *Russian Steam Navigation Co.*, 9 Jur. N. S. 1160 (P. C.); *The Laconia*, 32 L. J. Adm. 11 (P. C.); *Gladstone* v *Ottoman Bank*, 32 L. J. Ch. 228.

The Author's footnotes are indicated by letters, those of the Translator by numbers, or, where they are continuations of the Author's notes, by being enclosed in parentheses, thus [ ].

PREFACE.

This eighth volume differs materially in the nature of its contents from those which precede. In the first place, the influence of the Roman law is much less conspicuous than in the subjects that have hitherto occupied us. Moreover, the theory here presented is, in comparison with others, merely in a state of growth, incomplete and unfinished. Nor is this to be understood as a mere personal confession of an author, who feels his own powers insufficient to overcome the difficulties of the subject: it is a conviction arising from the consideration of the peculiar nature of the subject itself, of which we are now to give a more exact account.

In this branch of our treatise, and especially in its first half (chap. i.), the opinions of writers, as well as the judgments of tribunals, have hitherto been wildly confused and conflicting: Germans, Frenchmen, English, and Americans, often stand in marked opposition to one another;[1] but all agree in evincing the most lively interest in the questions which it embraces, in an effort after approximation and agreement, such as is found in no other department of jurisprudence. It may be said that this branch of jurisprudence is already the common property of civilised nations, not because they possess certain and universally admitted principles, but because they all share in the scientific investigations that tend to the establishment of such principles. A remarkable picture of this

[1] See per Porter, J., in *Saul v His Creditors*, 17 Martin (Louisiana), R. 595, 596, cited by Story, § 28, and 4 Phillimore 745.

imperfect but hopeful state of things is presented in the excellent work of STORY, which is also extremely useful, as a rich collection of materials, for every inquirer.

But it is not merely the spectacle of the development and formation of the juridical theory that is here so attractive and so stimulating: it is still more the noble prospect of a community of legal convictions and legal life, working out a universal practice.

Let us contemplate, in particular, the position of this branch of jurisprudence in regard to the controversies and parties of the most recent times.

The frequent antagonism of Germanists and Romanists[1] appears in this province less than elsewhere. In the most important questions the German jurists have generally attained to great unanimity, undisturbed by those controversies which often break out to the detriment of science. The Roman law operates by immediate positive rules less than in other departments. But the most exact acquaintance with it is here especially necessary, because the opinions of authors and of tribunals have in a great measure been determined, often unconsciously, by views true or false of Roman ideas and maxims.

Moreover, if it be one of the prevailing tendencies of these times, to bring into marked prominence the principle of nation-

[1] As the names imply, these were jurists who contended for the predominance, in the German law of the future, of the native and of the Roman elements of the law respectively. The controversy was quite distinct from that earlier one between the historical and non-historical schools; but it arose very much out of the clearer views of the nature of national law promulgated by the former, especially by Savigny, combined with the reaction against the dry and barren methods of the civilians of the seventeenth and eighteenth centuries, and the general resurrection of national life, dating from the commencement of the present century. Savigny himself, though his life was devoted to the study of the Roman law, would probably be ranked in this controversy as a Germanist; at least he would not have arrogated for the Roman law an undue dominion over the indigenous elements of the law of Germany. See *System*, Pref. vol. i. p. xv. See, for information as to modern legal schools and controversies in Germany, Bluntschli, *die Neueren Rechtschulen der Deutschen Juristen*, Zurich 1862.

ality, this tendency cannot find a place in a science which by its very nature aims at confounding national distinctions in a recognised community of different nations.

Thus we discover, on the one side, the noblest prospects for the future, and, on the other, the impossibility of obtaining as yet a complete solution of our problem, even irrespective of the personal ability of the individual labourer. The consideration of such a position may inspire as much courage as modesty. The writer must hold it an honour if he succeed in promoting the progress of the science by establishing some of its true principles, even although his work should one day be remembered only as a single preparatory step in its development.

Former writers appear to have specially erred in treating separately of the two subjects which in this volume appear in connection,—the local limits, and the limits in time, of the authority of the rules of law. The author thought himself bound to remedy this defect by combining the two parts of the subject, not only by placing them in external juxtaposition—which alone is not enough, and has often before been attempted without adequate results in the short outlines of elementary books,—but by investigating and explaining the intimate connection of the principles which govern both parts of the subject.

With the present volume, the general part of the system, the scope of which was explained at the commencement (i. § 58), is brought to a close. According to the summary prefixed to the first volume, the three first books, which contain this general portion, should have been immediately followed, in a continuous series of volumes, by the special portion, to which the following titles were assigned :—

Fourth Book : LAW OF THINGS.
Fifth Book : LAW OF OBLIGATIONS.
Sixth Book : FAMILY LAW (DOMESTIC RELATIONS).
Seventh Book : SUCCESSION.

A long interruption, occasioned by accidental circumstances, has, however, made the completion of the whole still more unlikely than it was at first. By this consideration I have been led to make the following alteration in the outward arrangement of the work, which must not be attributed to any change of opinion as to the fitness, in all essential points, of the plan itself.

I now regard the eight volumes already published as a complete and independent work, so that the title of each volume is to be supplemented in thought by the words, General Part.

The special part will not now be titled, as a continuation of the general, with a progressive numeration of the volumes, but will consist of separate works, among which the law of obligations (not, as was originally proposed, the law of things) will have the first place. These separate works will therefore take the form of monographs, but will not possess the essential character of such writings (i. p. 39); and they will be composed in precisely the same way as if the change of the original plan just indicated had not taken place.

WRITTEN IN JULY 1849.

AUTHORITY OF THE RULES OF LAW OVER THE LEGAL RELATIONS.

SECT. I.—(§ 344.)

INTRODUCTORY.

IT was the object of the first book of this System of Law to exhibit the law sources,[1] that is to say, the originating causes of the rules of law; of the second, to explain the general nature of the legal relations[1] which are governed by those rules. It still remains, under the general portion of the system, to determine the connection which exists between rules of law and legal relations,—a connection which appears, from one side, as the dominion of these rules over the legal relations; from the other, as the subordination of the legal relations to them.

In order, however, that this important and difficult part of our task may from the first be clearly apprehended, it is necessary to fix exactly in what sense this connection (dominion, subjection) is to be understood (*a*).

It is the function of the rules of law to govern legal relations. But what is the extent or sphere of their authority? what legal relations (cases) are brought under their control? The force and import of this question becomes apparent when we contemplate the nature of positive law, which does not happen to be one and the same all over the world, but varies

[1] These terms are explained in the Introduction.

(*a*) The basis of the present inquiry, and the explanation of the general terms here employed, will be found in vol. i. §§ 4-9, 15. [See Introduction. The reader is here reminded that 'legal relation' (*Rechtsverhältniss*) may often, though not always, be rendered, and in this translation sometimes is rendered, by the word 'case.']

with each nation and state; being derived in every community, partly from principles common to mankind, and partly from the operation of special agencies. It is this diversity of positive laws which makes it necessary to mark off for each, in sharp outline, the area of its authority, to fix the limits of different positive laws in respect to one another. Only by such demarcation does it become possible to decide all the conceivable questions arising from the conflict of different systems of positive law in reference to the decision of a given case.

The converse mode of procedure may also be followed, in order to the solution of such questions. When a legal relation presents itself for adjudication, we seek for a rule of law to which it is subject, and in accordance with which it is to be decided; and since we have to choose between several rules belonging to different positive systems, we come back to the sphere of action marked off for each, and to conflicts resulting from such limitation. The two modes of procedure differ only in the points from which they start. The question itself is the same, and the solution cannot turn out differently in the two cases.

Most writers on this subject beginning with the question of conflicts or collisions, deal with these as the only problems requiring solution. No satisfactory results can arise from this method of procedure. The natural sequence of thought is rather the following. As to the rules of law, the question is, what legal relations do they affect? As to legal relations, to what rules of law are they subject? Within what *limits* certain rules of law operate,—how far the province of each extends,—and when they come into collision, are, in their very nature, secondary and subordinate questions (*b*).

Besides the inquiry as to the bounds of each system of positive law, there arises another distinct yet analogous question. Hitherto we have regarded the rules of law as fixed, without taking into account the possibility of changes occurring in the course of time. Yet it is of the essence of positive law not to remain stationary, but to be in continual progress and de-

(*b*) Wächter, ii. 34, justly observes that many writers, by separating the question as to the application of laws from that as to collisions, are led to give contradictory answers to two identical questions. [See Note A at end of section.]

velopment (*c*); and hence secular variation is one of its recognised characteristics. Moreover, every case (legal relation) that occurs for decision necessarily originates in juridical facts (*d*), which are connected with a past more or less distant. But as the positive law may have undergone changes in the interval between the origin of the legal relation and the present time, it must be determined from what point of time we are to take the rule which governs the legal relation.

Here, then, is another sort of limitation of the authority of the rules of law, and another kind of possible conflicts, not less important and difficult than the limits and conflicts before contemplated. In the former case the rules of law were regarded as simultaneous, stationary, steady; in this latter they are regarded as not simultaneous, varying by progression, successive. For the sake of brevity and uniformity, I will use the following expressions:

Local Limits (*Oertliche Gränzen*) of the authority of Rules of Law.

Limits in Time (*Zeitliche Gränzen*) of Rules of Law.

The second of these terms needs no explanation. The first can be vindicated only in the course of the following inquiry.

The subject of the present work is the Roman Law. In what relation, then, does the Roman law stand to the questions here raised? We must allow that it has two very distinct relations.

In the first place, when the Roman law prevails in particular states and nations, and comes in contact with other positive laws, we must enter upon these questions, if we would secure for it any practical value. This would be indispensable, even if the Roman jurists had never thought of these questions, and had never been occupied with them. But, secondly, the Romans have, in point of fact, dealt with this subject; and we

(*c*) See above, vol. i. § 7. [See Introduction.]

(*d*) See above, vol. iii. § 104. ['Juridical facts are the events by which the beginning or the end of legal relations is effected. All juridical facts, therefore, have this in common, that they produce a change in the legal relations of particular persons.'—Savigny, *supra*, l. c. The most important juridical facts which Savigny reviews in the third and fourth volumes of this *System* are successions (changes in the *subject* of the legal relation), voluntary acts, declarations of will (*i.e.* voluntary acts immediately directed to the origination or the dissolution of a legal relation), contracts, donations, facts depending on the lapse of periods of time.]

must therefore investigate and verify their opinions. Although these opinions are to some extent one-sided and defective, so that we cannot always apply them as a matter of course even where we are justified in assuming the general authority of the Roman law, it is yet of great importance that we should be acquainted with them. It is so, because the doctrine of modern writers, and the practice connected with it, rest in great measure on the decisions of the Romans, though often on an erroneous apprehension of them; and thus a right understanding and criticism of modern principles and practice is only possible after a thorough examination of the doctrines of the Roman law.

The following inquiry, thus introduced, will have to establish in two chapters, (1) the local limits, (2) the limits in time, of the authority of rules of law over legal relations.

In regard, however, to these twofold limits, it is to be observed, that a certain reciprocal action may take place between them. If ever two rules of law come into collision with one another in respect of time, so that it is necessary to determine the authority of the one or the other by settling the boundary between them, the occurrence of an alteration is always presupposed. Such a change may happen in two ways.

It may be, first, in the rule of law. The simplest case is when the lawgiver, by enacting a new statute as to the given legal relation, alters the previous rule, and so makes new objective law.

But the change may also be in respect of the legal relation, if, the rule of law being unchanged, the facts which constitute, or are conditions of, the legal relation are altered. The capacity to act may serve as an example. This is judged of according to the law which prevails at the domicile of the person. If, then, this person change his domicile, the legal relation (case) may thereby be shifted under another rule of law; and the question may arise, whether the capacity of acting is henceforth to be determined according to the law of the earlier or of the later domicile.

It is evident that changes of the latter kind fall within the province of both sorts of collision. The local element, however, is predominant; and it is therefore proper and expedient to discuss all the relative questions in connection with the local limits of authority, and therefore to comprehend them within the first chapter (*e*).

Consequently, only changes of the first class—those which take place in the rule of law—remain for the investigation, in the second chapter, as to the limits in time of the authority of laws.

NOTE A, p. 6.

'That intercourse which trade has introduced, has given rise to nice questions of competition betwixt the laws of different nations, in which it is not always easy to determine by what law a contract is to be governed. Respectable authors have treated the question. A foreign writer of great reputation has given a treatise on the subject, which he calls "*conflictus legum*." He there treats some questions of nicety, but he has given his book a very wrong title: there can be no *conflictus legum* among civilised nations. A person may have a *forum* in different countries, and the same question may therefore fall to be determined in different states, but the decree will be the same in all of them; if the judgments be different, some of them must be wrong. Though much has been said about *comitas*, it is an improper term; there is no such thing as a decision from complaisance. Where judges determine by the law of another country, they do it *ex justitia;* they are bound to do it. In questions of succession, for instance, England and Scotland have different laws; but if a man dies intestate in Scotland, the English will not regard their own law, but ours, in deciding on his succession. They commit injustice if they determine by the English law. "What is the Scots law?" ought to be the very first question that they ask; if they do otherways, they do wrong. The judgment of English and Scots judges, in such a case, ought to be the same.'—Per Macqueen, J. C., in *Watson* v *Renton* (1791), Bell's 8vo Ca. 106. See § 348, note C. The terms 'Collision' and 'Conflict of Laws' assume 'that the laws of different states always conflict with one another, when their application in a particular case comes into question; whereas it is quite possible that they are all in perfect harmony, and all leave the decision to the same law and the same tribunal. . . . A collision of laws occurs not merely by reason of the diversity of the laws, which in a particular case may possibly be applicable, but only when the laws of different states, differing in themselves, seek to subject a single relation each to its own authority.'—Bar, § 1,

(*e*) The discussion of these questions occurs in § 365 (end of section), §§ 366–368, § 370 n., § 372, N. iii., § 379, N. 3. Under other subjects this question does not occur, because in these the influence of the naturally mutable relation of fact is fixed to a definite point of time, and thus all possibility of doubt is removed. So in Succession (§§ 374, 377), and in the rule *locus regit actum* (§ 381).

p. 7. The same writer objects to Savigny's phraseology, 'local limits,' on the ground that the very facts that certain laws follow the person everywhere, and that the laws of one state are often applied by the courts of another, are inconsistent with the term; and that the phrase is still more unsatisfactory, as embracing discussions on domicile and nationality, the objects of which are simply to fix whether a particular person—without reference to local residence—belongs to one or to another state. Some modern German writers on private law (Thöl., *Einl. in das Deutsch. Priv.;* Eichhorn, *D. Priv.* § 34) treat of this subject as 'The Relation of the Law Sources' (Verhältniss der Rechtsquellen),—a term which is sufficiently accurate, except in the law of procedure. It cannot properly be used to include questions as to the effect of foreign judgments (Bar, *ib.*).

CHAPTER I.

LOCAL LIMITS OF THE AUTHORITY OF THE RULES OF LAW OVER THE LEGAL RELATIONS.

Summary. Sect. II.—(§ 345.)

Authors (*a*).

Bartolus *in Codicem*, lib. i. *C. de summa trin.* (1, 1), Num. 13–51.

B. Argentræi, *Comment. ad patrias Britonum Leges, ed. oct.* Antwerp 1664 f. The 218th article of the *Coutume de Bretagne* ordains that no one shall leave away from his legal heirs more than one-third of his immoveable property. Thereupon arose the question, whether foreign immoveables should be included in this third; and so, in the sixth gloss upon the said article, D'Argentré came to explain the whole doctrine of the collision of laws, of which he here treats, pp. 601–620. The author died in 1590, and his work did not appear till after his death (1608).

Chr. Rodenburg, *de Jure Conjugum*. Traj. 1653. 4to. The *prœliminaria*, pp. 13–178, contain a detailed treatise on the collision of statutes. [This work is also printed at the end of Boullenois. See below.]

P. Voetius, *de Statutis eorumque concursu*. Leodii 1700. 4to (first at Amsterdam 1661). Only sections 4, 9, 10, 11 relate to the collision of statutes.

J. N. Hertius, *de Collisione Legum*. 1688. *Com. et Opuscula*, vol. i. pp. 118–154. Only section 4 (§§ 1–74) relates to this subject.

Ulr. Huber, *de Conflictu Legum* in the *Prœlect. ad Pand.*, as appended to lib. i. tit. 3, *de Legibus* (§§ 1–15).

J. Voetius, *de Statutis*. In the Commentary on the Pan-

(*a*) For the sake of brevity, I mention the writers here enumerated in future only by their names.

decta, after lib. i. tit. 4, *de Constit. Princ.*, as Pars 2, *de Statutis* (§§ 1–22).

L. BOULLENOIS, *Traité de la Personnalité et de la Realité des Loix, etc.* Paris 1776. 2 vols. in 4to. A French translation of the above-cited work of Rodenburg, with very extensive additions.

D. MEIER, *de Conflictu Legum Divers.* Bremæ 1810. 8vo.

G. VON STRUVE, *ueber das positive Rechtsgesetz in seiner Beziehung auf räumliche Verhältnisse.* Carlsruhe 1834. 8vo.

JOS. STORY, *Comment. on the Conflict of Laws.* Boston 1834. Second edition, greatly enlarged, Boston 1841. 8vo.

W. BURGE, *Commentaries on Colonial and Foreign Laws generally, and in their conflict with each other, and with the Law of England.* London 1838. 4 vols.

W. SCHAEFFNER, *Entwickelung des Internationalen Privatrechts.* Frankfort 1841. 8vo.

VON WAECHTER, *ueber die Collision der Privatrechtsgesetze, Archiv. für Civilistische Praxis*, vol. xxiv. pp. 230–311, vol. xxv. pp. 1–60, pp. 161–200, pp. 361–419—in all, 32 sections. 1841, 1842. For shortness of citation, I indicate the portion contained in vol. xxiv. as I., that in vol. xxv. as II.

NIC. ROCCO, *dell' uso e autorità delle leggi delle due Sicilie considerate nelle relazioni con le persone e col territorio degli Stranieri.* Napoli 1842. 8vo.

FŒLIX, *du Droit International Privé*, second edition, Paris 1847. 8vo. (First edition, 1843.) [Ed. Demangeat, 1856.]

[BAR, *Das Internationale Privat- und Strafrecht.* Hannover 1862.

PHILLIMORE (Sir Robert), *Commentaries upon International Law.* Vol. iv. *Private International Law or Comity.* London 1861.

WESTLAKE, *Treatise on Private International Law, or, The Conflict of Laws, with principal reference to its practice in the English and other Cognate Systems of Jurisprudence.* Lond. 1858.

KENT'S *Commentaries on American Law.*

Considerable additions may be made to this list, by reference to the lists of authorities prefixed to Bar, Story, Burge, and Schäffner, and the voluminous notes of Sir R. Phillimore's fourth volume.]

Every right presents itself in its primary aspect as a power belonging to the person (*b*), and, accordingly, as a quality of that person; and from this most direct and rudimentary standpoint we have to regard legal relations also as attributes of persons. In this way the question with which we are engaged would be viewed thus: Over what persons does each rule of law extend its authority? or, conversely (§ 344): What are the laws to which a given person is subject?

The following consideration, however, must at once convince us, that this statement of the question is not sufficient. In the region of the acquired rights (*c*), the individual extends himself after the objects of these acquired rights; and from this extension arises at least the possibility of his entrance into the territory of a rule of law originally alien to him. This bare possibility takes quite a new form, if we contemplate the nature of the objects of acquired rights. Among them we find, first of all, other *persons*, of whom, again, each is subject to a particular set of authoritative rules; and as it is quite accidental, whether two persons connected in the same legal relation belong to the same or to different legal territories, there arises a new and very prolific source of collisions between the rules of law which govern legal relations.

The following outline of the subjects of the rules of law will show in how many ways collisions may take place between the rules of different territories of positive law (*d*). Laws may have for their subject-matter:—

I. *Persons* themselves, their capacity for rights and capacity for acting, or the conditions under which they can *have* rights and *acquire* rights. It is this class of the rules of law with which we started at the beginning of the section.

(*b*) See above, Book I. § 4. [See Introduction. Some writers have therefore regarded the domicile of the person as the central principle regulating all questions of private international law. Eichhorn, *Deutsches Privatrecht*, §§ 27, 36; Thibaut, *Pandektenrecht*, § 38 (Lindley's Transl., p. 37); Göschen, *Civilrecht*, i. p. 111. A peculiar form of this theory is found in Mailher de Chassat, *Traité des Statuts*, 11, 53. See Bar, § 22.]

(*c*) Vol. i. § 53.

(*d*) This view is intended to serve only as a preliminary abstract. It will be given more in detail below (§ 361).

II. *The Legal Relations.*
1. Rights to specific things.
2. Obligations.
3. Rights to a whole estate, as an ideal object of indefinite extent (Succession).
4. Family relations.

From this summary, it is evident that the first and immediate object to which the rule of law applies is the person; and while it is, in the first instance, the person in its general character, as the subject and centre of all rights, it is also the person, in so far as, by its free actions in the most numerous and most important cases, it produces, or helps to produce, the legal relations.

But the person expands itself into artificial extensions of its being. It seeks to have dominion over things, and thus betakes itself to the place which these things occupy—possibly, therefore, enters the territory of a foreign law. This takes place most distinctly in respect of immoveables, the site of which is not accidental and changeable; but, in reality, it is not less true of things moveable. By means of obligations, a person seeks to control the actions of others, or to subject his own acts to another's will. He enters into particular forms of life by the family; and thus also in many ways, sometimes voluntarily, sometimes involuntarily, oversteps the limits of his original and purely personal rights.

It follows, from these considerations, that the rule of law applicable to every given case is determined and bounded, first and chiefly, by the subjection of the person concerned to the law of a certain territory;[1] but that, at the same time, there may be the most numerous and most important modifications, in consequence of the relation in which certain things or certain acts or relations of life stand towards the laws of other territories (*e*).

Our first task, then, will be to inquire what principles deter-

[1] More literally, "subjection to a certain legal territory," "stand towards other legal territories." Rechtsgebiet = territory of a system of law, *territorium legis;* Gerichtsgebiet = territory of a court, *territorium iudicis.*

(*e*) With this is connected the distinction, which formerly prevailed very extensively, of *statuta personalia, realia, mixta;* of which we shall speak below (§ 361).

mine the general connection of a person with a particular legal territory.

SECT. III.—(§ 346.)

RACE AND TERRITORIALITY AS GROUNDS OF THE SUBJECTION OF A PERSON TO A PARTICULAR POSITIVE LAW.

In order to discover the connection by which a person is attached to a particular positive law by subjection to it, we must remember that the positive law itself has its seat in the people as a great natural whole, or in an ethnical (volksmässig) subdivision of this whole. It is only another expression of the same truth, when we say that law has its seat in the state, or in a particular organic part of the state, because, as it is only in the state that the will of individuals is developed into a common will, it is there only that the nation has a realized existence (*a*). In pursuance of this general plan, we have then to determine more minutely how this whole is constituted, and how this unity is defined, within which the rules of law, as constituent parts of the positive law, have their seat. Thus we shall know by what tie individual persons are held together in the common possession of the same positive law.

If we seek to solve this problem historically, we find two causes by which such community of positive law has hitherto been mainly fixed and defined: NATIONALITY and TERRITORIALITY.

I. *Race or Nationality*, as the basis and limit of community of laws, has an entirely personal and invisible character. Although, by its very nature, it seems to exclude the arbitrary influence of choice, it is yet capable of extension by the free reception of individuals.[1]

Nationality appears in a greater extent as the ground and limit of legal community among wandering tribes, who have no fixed territory, as among the Germans in their nomadic era.

(*a*) Cf. *supra*, vol. i. §§ 8, 9.

[1] Among the German tribes referred to in the next paragraph, this seems to have been exceptional. Bar, § 3, p. 17. Gibbon, c. 38, vol. iv. p. 185 (ed. Bohn). See as to the *Professio Legis:* Savigny, *Gesch. d. R. R.* §§ 41, 42; Hegel, *Gesch. d. Städteverfassung von Italien*, i. p. 436, Leips. 1847.

Among them, however, even after their settlement on the old soil of the Roman empire, the same principle long retained its vitality in the system of personal laws, which were in force at the same time within the same state; and among which, along with the laws of the Franks, Lombards, etc., the Roman law also appears as the permanent personal law of the original inhabitants of the new states founded by conquest (*b*).

In modern times[2] we find still existing in the Turkish empire[3] the most complete example of this kind of community of laws. In the Christian states of Europe, a remnant of it has been longest preserved in the Jewish nation, the continuance of whose national law, and separate nationality itself, stands in connection with religion. But even this remnant is gradually vanishing away (*c*).

Analogous, yet not entirely identical with the ground of community of laws just described, is that which arises from the political rank of certain classes of persons. It appears, in a very complete and lasting form among the Romans, in the classes of *cives*, *latini*, *peregrini*, which again are connected with the systems of the *jus civile* and *jus gentium* (*d*). Yet, in regard to the subject with which alone we are here engaged, this distinction, in other respects very important, never obtained an influence which could be compared with that of nationality or territoriality.

(*b*) Savigny, *Geschichte des R. R. im Mittelalter*, vol. i. c. 3, §§ 30–33; [Montesquieu, *Esprit des Loix*, l. 28, c. 2; Bar, § 3; Gibbon, c. 38; Hallam, *Middle Ages*, vol. i. p. 144 seqq.; Story, § 2.]

[2] See Note A at end of section.

[3] The Act 6 and 7 Vict. c. 94 regulates the exercise of Her Majesty's power and jurisdiction which she has 'by treaty, capitulation, grant, usage, sufferance, and other lawful means, within divers countries and places out of Her Majesty's dominions.' See Miltitz, *Manuel des Consuls*, London 1839; Tuson's *British Consul's Manual*, p. 122 seqq., London 1856; *Papers relating to the Jurisdiction of Consuls in the Levant, presented to Parliament*, 1845; Order in Council, Nov. 30, 1864; Abdy's *Kent's International Law*, c. 3; Cornewall Lewis, *On Foreign Jurisdiction and Extradition*, London 1859, p. 15; Ortolan, *Régles International de la Mer*, 1853, vol. i. p. 317 seqq.; Wheaton, *International Law*, Part ii. c. 2, p. 215 seqq. (ed. Lawrence, 1863); Phillimore, *International Law*, vol. i. p. 361; *Maltass* v *Maltass*, 3 Curt. 231, 1 Rob. 67; *The Griefswald*, Swa. Adm. 430.

(*c*) In Prussia, *e.g.*, as early as 1812, the '*Judenedict*,' §§ 20, 21, established the common law of the other inhabitants as the rule for the Jews, and retained their peculiar national laws only in exceptional cases. [See Note B at end of section.]

(*d*) Cf. *supra*, vol. i. § 22; and *Geschichte des R. R. im Mittelalter*, vol. i. § 1.

II. *Country* or *Territoriality* is the second very important and extensive principle which determines and limits the community of positive law among individuals. It is distinguished from the preceding (nationality) by its less personal nature. It is connected with something outwardly cognisable, namely, the visible geographical frontiers; and the influence of human choice on its application is more extensive and immediate than in nationality, where this influence is merely exceptional.

This second source of community of laws has, in course of time, and with the advance of civilisation, more and more supplanted the first (nationality).[4] The more varied and more active intercourse between different nations, by which the rougher contrasts of nationalities were necessarily removed, chiefly contributed to this result. But the influence of Christianity must, least of all, be overlooked, which, as a common bond of spiritual life embracing the most diverse nations, has thrown their characteristic differences more and more into the background.

If we start from this second source of the community of law, the collision to which our attention must be constantly directed, relates to the *local* difference of laws; and our problem can now be stated, in all possible cases of collision, in the following question:

What *territorial law* is applicable in any given case?

Here, then, is the reason why the contemporaneous limits of the rules of law have hitherto been called *local* limits (§ 344).

Let us first endeavour to explain by example the meaning of collision or conflict between different local or territorial laws. At a particular place a lawsuit is to be decided as to the performance of a contract, or the ownership of a thing. But the contract was entered into at another place than that of the tribunal; the thing in dispute is situated elsewhere, and not in the country of the court; the two places have a different territorial law. Besides this, the parties to the cause may, in regard to their persons, belong to the place of the court, or both to a foreign place, or both to different places. Which of the different local laws with which the legal relation in dispute in any way comes in contact, is to be applied in the decision of

[4] See Note C at end of section.

the question? That is the meaning of the question of collision in respect to territorial laws (*e*).

NOTE A, p. 16.

The ground of the modern exceptions to the principle of territoriality is thus stated by Lord Stowell:—'In the western parts of the world, alien merchants mix in the society of the natives; access and intermixture are permitted, and they become incorporated to almost the full extent. But in the East, from the oldest times, an immiscible character has been kept up: foreigners are not admitted into the general mass of the society of the nation; they continue strangers and sojourners, as all their fathers were—*Doris amara suam non intermiscuit undam.*'—*The Indian Chief*, 3 Rob. 29. See Lawrence's *Wheaton*, 219–230. Lord Brougham in *Warrender* v *Warrender*, 2 S. and M'L. 204. Westlake (p. 131–147) treats of these exceptions under the title of 'The principle of the Law common to the Parties.' As to criminal law, see 6 and 7 Vict. c. 94; Phillim. i. 358, ii. 272, iv. 705; Sir G. C. Lewis, *On Foreign Jurisdiction and Extradition*, Lond. 1859; Bar, 512, 531. Englishmen settling in a newly discovered country, carry with them so much of the English law, 'which is the birthright of every subject,' as is applicable to the circumstances. Blackst. *Com.* i. 108; Stephen's *Com.* i. 104; *Ruding* v *Smith*, 2 Hagg. *Cons.* 371. It is an extension of this principle, that in Hindostan 'the English law is the dominant law for all those inhabitants who belong to the European family of nations.' *Maclean* v *Cristall*, Perry's Or. Ca. 85; *Mayor of Lyons* v *E. I. Co.*, 1 Moore, P.C. 573; *Adv.-Gen. of Bengal* v *Ranee Surnomoye*, 2 Moore, P.C., N.S. 22. Till recently, in British India, it was only within the three capital cities that any *lex loci* existed; and even there English law was applicable only under certain exceptions. Morley, *Digest of Indian Cases*, Introd. p. ix. seqq.; *First Report of Indian Law Commission*, 1856, App. p. 187 seqq. Beyond the limits of cities 'there is not (1855) in actual operation any *lex loci*, any substantive civil law for the various classes of persons who have not—like the main portions of the population, namely, the Hindus and Mohammedans—special laws of their own, which the judicatories are required to enforce.'—*Second Report of Indian Law Com.* 1856, p. 7; *First Rep. of do.*, App. pp. 189, 200, 202, 223, etc.; *First Rep. of Com. appointed to prepare a Body of Substantive Law*, 1864, App. p.

(*e*) The question of the collision of laws also arises, no doubt, where the community of law is based on nationality, and needs a solution there as well as in the case of territorial laws. To enter more minutely on this phase would here be out of place, because it could only be touched on at present on account of its historical connection, and has no importance for modern law. Compare Savigny, *Geschichte des R. R. im Mittelalter*, vol. i. § 40.

57 seqq.; Morley, Introd., especially pp. xxii. clii. clxxxi. It is only, however, in certain specified cases that Mohammedan and Gentoo law are authoritative. Lawsuits arising out of contracts are governed by 'justice, equity, and good conscience,' upon which basis a system has been framed by the Sudder and Mofussil courts, which may be regarded as an adaptation of the English law of contracts. *Sam* v *Lallah*, 6 L.T., N.S. 767, P.C. Macpherson, *Outlines of the Law of Contract in India*, Pref. (Lond. 1860). 'According to this system, the judge is frequently obliged to investigate the obscure and doubtful customs of Armenians and Indian Portuguese; and it is occasionally necessary to refer, for the decision of matters originating and terminating in India, to the systems of law prevalent in France, Holland, America, China, and every part of the world.'—Mr. Amos, in a minute appended to the *Report of Indian Substantive Law Com.* 1864, p. 63. The principle of personal laws was recognised by the laws of Menu, c. vii. v. 203; and was applied to India, nearly as it now exists or lately existed, in 1781, by 21 Geo. III. c. 70. See, in general, Mill, *Hist. of British India*, iv. 218, 374, *et al.*; v. 351 seqq., 376 seqq., etc. Strange, *Hindu Law*, Introd., Lond. 1830. *Westminster Review*, N.S., vol. xxi. 1–30 (Jan. 1862). Morley, *Administration of Justice in British India*, Lond. 1858. Campbell's *Modern India*, 464 seqq., 529, 546; Lond. 1852. Kaye's *Administration of East India Co.*, 318 seqq., 417 seqq.; Lond. 1854. Money's *Java*, vol. ii. 1–121, Lond. 1861. Sleeman's *Tour through Oude.* As to the law applicable to Parsees, see *Perozeboye* v *Ardaseer Cursetjee*, 10 Moore, P.C. 375; Perry's *Or. Ca.* 57; 2 Morley's *Anal. Dig.* 335; *Papers relating to Parsees of Bombay in App. C. to Report of Com. for Subst. Law*, 1864, p. 77 seqq. British India is now passing out of the condition in which laws are personal, by the gradual enactment of a series of codes. A penal code, prepared in 1837 by a commission of which Lord Macaulay was president, was enacted by Act XLV. of 1860; a code of civil procedure was enacted by Act VIII. of 1859; and the law of succession has been codified by Act X. of 1865. As to British subjects, etc., in China, see 6 and 7 Vict. c. 80; Order in Council, 13 June 1853; Phillim. i. 363; Wheaton, *l. c.;* Tuson, *Br. Cons. Man.* 176–275.

NOTE B, p. 16.

In England the ecclesiastical courts have exercised an anomalous jurisdiction in ascertaining the validity of Jewish marriages contracted in England by Jewish laws; as to which Dr. Lushington, in declining a similar jurisdiction as to Parsee marriages in India, observed (*Perozeboye* v *Ardaseer Cursetjee*, supra) that 'the very great difficulties attending such investigations, and the almost absurd consequences to which they lead, would not induce us to follow these precedents further than strict necessity requires.' Comp. Lord

Stowell's hesitation in the leading case of *Lindo* v *Belisario*, 1 Hagg. *Cons.* 216. These scruples relate only to the jurisdiction of *ecclesiastical* courts over marriages between persons not Christians, not to the applicability of the law. Cf. *Goldsmid* v. *Bromer*, 1 Hagg. *Cons.* 324; *Ruding* v *Smith*, 2 Hagg. *Cons.* 385; *Moss* v *Smith*, 1 Man. and Gr. 232; *Goodman* v *Goodman*, 4 Jur. N.S. 1220, and 5 Jur. 902; Stephen, *Com.* ii. 269, 422; Burn, *Eccl. Law*, ii. 336; Roper, *Husband and Wife* (ed. Jacob), ii. 476; Bishop, *On Marriage and Divorce*, s. 185 seq.; 6 and 7 Will. IV. c. 85, § 2; 10 and 11 Vict. c. 58. The canonists left the Jews in possession of their own marriage laws: 'de anima Judæi non se impedit ecclesia.' Maranta, *Spec. Aur.*, p. 3, s. 57; Friedberg, *Das Recht d. Eheschliessung*, p. 358; Covarruv. *de Matr.* ii. vi. 10, 7; Sanchez, vii. 3, 6. As to marriages contracted by British colonists according to the rites and customs of the savage tribes among which they settle, see *Armitage* v *Armitage*, L. R. 3, Eq. 343; *Connolly* v *Woolrich*, 11 Lower Can. Jur. 197, said to be appealed.

NOTE C, p. 17.

'A law which had distinct territorial limits was more or less strange to the ancient German tribes, whereas, with us, everything turns upon the fact that some action is performed, or some legal relation is realized, *in a place where* a certain law prevails. In the personality of the law there was a preference of that which is *personal*, whereas with us there is a conflict of the territorial with the territorial.'—Schaeffner, § 7, citing Laferriere, *Hist. du droit Franç.* i. 210, for the proposition that this change was due to the feudal system. See Maine's *Ancient Law*, pp. 97, 103–112; Westlake, § 28 seq., 149, 150, where this transition is shown to correspond in some sort with the transition from pure common law to legislation. 'When rights,' he says, 'are considered as proceeding from an external enactment by sovereign authority, the necessity, that in a very artificial state of society each such authority should have definite geographical limits assigned to its activity, leads to the conception of private rights as dependent on the law of the place where they originate, since, at that place, the local sovereign alone can issue the commands which are requisite to create them.' Historically, the change from personal to territorial laws was conditioned by different causes in different parts of Europe. In Northern France, *e.g.*, 'the system of feudal dependence and fealty changed the nation from a mass of popular communities into a mass of feudatories and vassals. As in the former, national common law (Volksrecht) prevailed, so in the latter, feudal law (Dienstrecht). This feudal law derived its substance, for the most part, from the old popular or common law; but it no longer distinguished according to race, for everybody was born merely subject to this or that feudal service, not to this or the other national law. As in the north of France the Germanic law had been predominant, the law of the *Cours des Seigneurs* was almost entirely founded upon it, and the Roman law, already rare, because it had kept its ground only from the nationality of a few individuals, of necessity almost disappeared. The converse took place in the south of France, where the Roman blood was by far the more numerous. For the same reason the Roman law disappeared in Germany, where, as late as the sixth and seventh centuries, it was the personal law of many inhabitants of the countries on the Rhine.'—Savigny, *Gesch.* i. 152. 'In Italy (in the twelfth century) the old principle of the personal laws had never indeed been destroyed, but its application became more and more rare, and finally was entirely forgotten as the national connection was gradually relaxed. This was necessarily effected by the mere local intermixture of different nations, but still more by frequent family connections, whereby national origin might often fall into oblivion, and always of course lost its importance. Most of all was this dissolution of the old tie of nationality promoted by the fact that a new bond, quite different from that of national descent, was attracting all attention to itself. In the civic union of the cities, men of all nations found themselves connected; and the closer and the more important the tie which bound the citizens of Milan, of Bologna, etc., to one another, the more was the Roman or the Lombard origin of these citizens lost sight of.'—Savigny, *Gesch.* iii. 77. Spain was much earlier subject to a territorial law, the Visigothic law prohibiting the use of foreign laws in practice, under severe penalties. Savigny, *Gesch.* ii. 76. Eichhorn, *Deutsche Staats und Rechtsgesch.* i. § 46, assigns to the latter cause—viz. the growth of municipal institutions—the chief influence in the formation of the territorial system. Bar (p. 19 seq.) observes that both causes (feudality, and the growth of municipal institutions) contributed to the downfall of the personal system, but do not fully explain the transition to the territorial system. He points out how the theory of personal, real, and mixed statutes, in truth, grew out of the old personal laws, and how in the middle ages the subjection of all foreigners to territorial laws was very incomplete. Laws were obligatory only on subjects, and the question whether a statute was binding on a clerk was discussed on the same principles as the collision of territorial laws.

Sect. IV.—(§ 347.)

CONFLICTING TERRITORIAL LAWS IN THE SAME STATE.

The conflicting territorial laws, for the collision of which we have now to lay down rules (§ 346), may have twofold relations to another; and although the principles by which their application is determined remain always the same, yet this difference has the greatest influence upon the mode of applying these principles.

Those territorial laws may be in force *either* in different districts of one and the same state, *or* in different independent states.

I. Different territorial laws within one and the same state have been noticed in a former part of this work under the name of *Particular Laws*, in contradistinction to the common law of such a state; and they may exist either in the form of positive statutes or in that of customs (*a*).

They differ greatly in their historical origin, as well as in the limits assigned by it to their authority. The most important instances of such laws during the subsistence of the German empire, arose from the relation of the individual German states to the empire embracing them all (*b*). A similar state of matters existed within each particular state of the German empire, and even still existed after its dissolution.

Such particular laws appear sometimes in entire provinces, sometimes in parts of provinces, sometimes, and principally, in particular parishes (*communes, Gemeinden*). They occur very frequently in townships (*Stadtgebieten*),—sometimes even in the separate local divisions of one and the same township (*c*).

(*a*) See above, vol. i. §§ 8, 18, 21.

(*b*) Vol. i. § 2.—A similar relation, yet not quite the same, existed among the little sovereign states composing the United Netherlands, which were not united, like the German states, by a common supreme government and legislation. By the cases of collision which very often arose there, the jurists of Holland (Rodenburg, P. Voet., J. Voet., Huber) were led to give great attention to this subject. The relation of the free states of North America is similar. [The supreme court of the United States administers international law or comity as between the independent states of the union. *Bank of Augusta* v *Earle*, 13 Curt. 277, 284, 13 Pet. 619. See below, p. 28, note 3.]

(*c*) Thus *e.g.* there co-existed in Breslau, until 1st Jan. 1840, five different particular laws and observances in regard to succession, the

In larger tracts of country (provinces, or parts of provinces), particular laws often arose from the fact that the district was formerly the territory of an independent state, or part of a different state from that with which it was afterwards incorporated.

In towns, special laws have often been enacted for the particular town, either by the sovereign, or by its own magistrates with permission or ratification of the sovereign.

We find this origin of particular municipal laws as far back as the time of the Roman empire, whose separate communities not only had the right of legislating for themselves before their union with the empire, but did not thereby entirely lose that right, although they were always subject to the new laws promulgated at Rome (*d*). It was entirely owing to these municipal laws that the Roman jurists had occasion to direct their attention to the questions we are here considering (*e*). They are contrasted, as particular laws, with the common law of Rome. Still more extensive and important were the municipal laws (*Stadtrechte*) which in the Middle Ages developed themselves in almost every town of Italy, and which, as particular laws, were there contrasted, not with the Roman law only, but also with the Lombardic, both regarded as common laws (*f*). It was in connection with them that the technical term *Statuta* was first used; and it was afterwards transferred to other countries; and the doctrine of *Statuta personalia, realia, mixta* was added (§ 345 f.).

Under the subject of collision of territorial laws within the same state, an attempt might perhaps be made to include the following case, which is really of quite a different nature, and does not fall within the present inquiry. In any state particular laws may occur in different gradation and subordination, from the narrowest local limits, in ever-increasing spheres of application, up to the common law of such a state. Here, too,

property of spouses, etc., the application of which was limited to certain territorial jurisdictions. Not unfrequently the law varied from house to house; and it even happened that one house was situated on the borders of different laws, to each of which, therefore, it belonged in part. Comp. the Law of 11th May 1839 (*Gesetzsammlung*, 1839, p. 166.)

(*d*) Savigny, *Geschichte des R. R. im Mittelalter*, vol. i. c. 2.

(*e*) See above, § 344.

(*f*) *Geschichte des R. R. im Mittelalter*, vol. iii. §§ 42, 189; vol. ii. § 76.

we may speak of a collision, inasmuch as at certain places each of these particular laws has in general practical authority; and therefore it may be asked in a given case, which of these, if they conflict, shall be the rule of decision. Here, however, the question of conflict, if the term is to be used at all, has a different meaning from that which it has in the case of particular co-ordinate laws of the same state. These are independent of one another, and do not therefore stand in the relation of dependence and subordination.

Where several laws are subordinate, one to another, the simple rule holds, that that law has always the preference which has the narrowest sphere of application. The only exception to this rule is the case in which the wider law above it contains special provisions of an absolute and imperative character (*g*).[1]

The collision between different independent particular laws is not governed by so simple a rule. For them a more searching examination is necessary; and this will be instituted in the sequel of the present chapter.

It has still to be noticed, while we are engaged with the particular laws of one and the same state (*h*), that it might be thought that the collision of these laws would itself be regulated by the general legislation of the state. But this is just what

(*g*) See above, vol. i. §§ 21, 45. Except in this special case, therefore, the rule holds: 'Stadtrecht bricht Landrecht, Landrecht bricht gemein Recht.' ['Le droit de la cité l'emporte sur le droit du pays; le droit du pays, sur le droit commun.'—Guenoux.]

[1] This doctrine of 'subordinate laws' appears to correspond to that of 'customs' in England, such as gavelkind in Kent, borough English, customs of the city of London and of particular manors. Gavelkind and borough English are recognised by the law, and require no proof of their existence, but merely that the lands in question are subject to them. Proof of this, and in other cases also of the existence of the custom, is taken before a jury. The custom of London is ascertained by certificate of the Recorder. Custom cannot prevail against express Act of Parliament. Stephen's *Com.* i. 54–61, 215–219; Pulling, *On the Laws and Customs of London*, p. 3 sqq., Lond. 1849; Robinson, *On Gavelkind*, ed. Norwood, Ashford 1858; *Hook* v *Hook*, 1 H. and M. 43; *Farley* v *Bonham*, 2 J. and H. 177; *Cox* v *Mayor of London*, 1 H. and C. 338, 2 H. and C. 401; *Muggleton* v *Barnett*, 2 H. and N. 653; *Birtwhistle* v *Vardell*, 9 Bligh 48. As to burgh usages, udal rights, etc., in Scotland, see Bankton, *Inst.* i. 1, 71, 72; Erskine, *Inst.* i. 1, 45, 46, ii. 3, 18; Bell, *Princ.* § 932 seq.; *Rendall* v *Robertson*, Dec. 15, 1836, 15 S. 265; *Mag. of Linlithgow* v. *Edin. and Glas. Ry. Co.*, 21 D. 1215, 3 Macq. 691.

(*h*) This is conceivable, whether there be one and the same common law over the various particular laws (as in Prussia the *Allgemeine Land-*

has not hitherto been carried out in any country in an exhaustive manner. On the contrary, the most numerous and important questions of this sort have been left to be settled by juridical science.[2]

Sect. V.—(§ 348.)

CONFLICTING TERRITORIAL LAWS IN DIFFERENT STATES.

II. The second possible case of conflict between different territorial laws is where these laws exist, not in the same state, but in different independent states (§ 347). If we revert to the examples above given (§ 346), to illustrate the whole question of collision, these now take the following shape:—A judge of our state has to decide upon a case (legal relation), which, owing to the facts which lie at its foundation (*e.g.* the place where a contract may be entered into, or where the thing in dispute is situated), comes in contact with the law of a foreign state, different from our positive law. Besides this, it is possible that both parties may be natives or both foreigners, or that the one may belong to the country of the judge, the other to the foreign country. Which of the different territorial laws here competing shall the judge apply?

Exactly the same question might be brought before the judge of that foreign state, if the lawsuit had happened to arise there.

recht is over the provincial laws of Brandenburg, Pomerania, East and West Prussia, etc.) or not; for even in the latter case, which occurs *e.g.* between the Rhenish and the other provinces of Prussia, it is quite conceivable that a Prussian general statute might have completely regulated the collision of these different laws.

[2] Cf. Story, § 24; *infra*, p. 32. Various British statutes regulate questions of this kind arising in regard to special points: *e.g.*, 45 Geo. III. c. 92; 54 Geo. III. c. 186 (Criminal Justice); 6 and 7 Vict. c. 82 (Power of Lord Chancellor to grant Commissions); 11 and 12 Vict. c. 42 (J. P. Warrants); 17 and 18 Vict. c. 34 (Witnesses); 19 and 20 Vict. c. 60, and c. 97 (Mercantile Law); 19 and 20 Vict. c. 79 (Bankruptcy, Scotland); 24 and 25 Vict. c. 134 (Bankruptcy, England); 20 and 21 Vict. c. 60 (Bankruptcy, Ireland); 21 and 22 Vict. c. 56 (Confirmation and Probate); 22 and 23 Vict. c. 63 (Ascertainment of Law); 24 and 25 Vict. c. 114 (Lord Kingsdown's Act as to Wills of British Subjects).

Many have attempted to determine these questions by the principle of independent sovereignty alone, laying down the two following postulates: (1) Every state is entitled to demand that its own laws only shall be recognised within its bounds; (2) No state can require the recognition of its law beyond its bounds (*a*).

I will not only admit the truth of these propositions, but even allow their extension to the utmost conceivable limits; yet I believe that they afford little help in the solution of our problem.

To carry out the principle of the independent sovereignty of the state to the utmost possible extent with regard to aliens, would lead to their complete exclusion from legal rights. Such a view is not strange to the international law of the Romans (*b*); and even where it was not enforced by them against foreign countries, a great distinction as to the capacity for rights was always maintained between Romans and foreigners (§ 346). Modern law, on the contrary, has gradually tended towards the recognition of complete legal equality between natives and foreigners (*c*).

But this legal equality of *persons* does not at all determine the question of collision between native and foreign laws. In the first place we must admit, that if the domestic laws give directions for the treatment of cases of conflict, these must be applied absolutely by the judges of our state (*d*). Nowhere, however, do such laws exist in any degree of completeness; in particular, not in the states where the German common law prevails (*e*).

The strict right of sovereignty might certainly, among other things, go so far as to require all judges of the land to decide

(*a*) Huber, § 2; Story, §§ 18–21. [This is very fully discussed by Schaeffner, §§ 25–29, with special reference to the theory of Zachariae founded on the independence of states.]

(*b*) The Roman law applies this principle, and that with reciprocal consequences, not only to *hostes*, of whom the very notion presupposes a declaration of war, but even to all citizens of states with which Rome had contracted neither *fœdus* nor *amicitia*. L. 5, § 2, *de capt.* (49, 15).

(*c*) Wächter, i. 253, ii. pp. 33, 34, 181; Puchta, *Pandekten*, §§ 45, 112; Eichhorn, *Deutsches Recht*, § 75. [See Note A at end of section.]

(*d*) Wächter, i. p. 237 f.; Story, § 23. Struve, §§ 9, 37, strangely contradicts this, declaring those laws to be null which proceed from erroneous principles as to conflict.

(*e*) It is the same here, therefore, as in the collision of particular laws.

the cases that come before them solely according to the national law, regardless of the perhaps different rules of some foreign law with whose territory the case in question may have come in contact. Such a rule, however, is not to be found in the legislation of any known state; and its absence is to be accounted for by the following consideration :—

The more multifarious and active the intercourse between different nations, the more will men be persuaded that it is not expedient to adhere to such a stringent rule, but rather to substitute for it the opposite principle. This has resulted from that reciprocity in dealing with cases which is so desirable, and the consequent equality in judging between natives and foreigners, which, on the whole, is dictated by the common interest of nations and of individuals. For it is the necessary consequence of this equality, in its full development, not only that in each particular state the foreigner is not postponed to the native (in which equality in the treatment of persons consists), but also that, in cases of *conflict of laws*, the same legal relations (cases) have to expect the same decision, whether the judgment be pronounced in this state or in that.[1]

The standpoint to which this consideration leads us, is that of an international common law of nations having intercourse with one another; and this view has in the course of time always obtained wider recognition, under the influence of a common Christian morality, and of the real advantage which results from it to all concerned.

In this way we come to apply to the conflict of territorial laws of independent states substantially the same principles which govern the collision of particular laws in the same state (§ 347);[2] and this co-ordination is preserved throughout the following inquiry.

In regard to both kinds of collision, then, the question may be stated thus :—

To ascertain for every legal relation (case) that law to which, in its proper nature, it belongs or is subject.

This equalization, as contrasted with the strict law above

[1] This was very early recognised in the brocard, 'diversitas fori non vitiat merita causæ.' See Phillimore, iv. 9.

[2] See Note B at end of section.

mentioned, may be designated a friendly concession among sovereign states; that is, an admission of statutes originally foreign among the sources from which native courts have to seek for their decision as to many cases (legal relations), (*f*).

Only this sufferance must not be regarded as the result of mere generosity or arbitrary will, which would imply that it was also uncertain and temporary. We must rather recognise in it a proper and progressive development of law, keeping pace with the treatment of cases of conflict between the particular laws of the same state (*g*).

But the assimilation of the two kinds of collision is subject to this qualification, that in the case of conflicting particular laws (§ 347), the question of collision may be decided by a common law of the land paramount to both.[3] Such a resource

(*f*) Huber, *de conflictu legum*, § 2. 'Rectores imperiorum id *comiter agunt*, ut jura cujusque populi . . . , teneant ubique suam vim.' J. Voet., *de Statutis*, §§ 1, 12, 17. Dein quid *ex comitate* gens genti . . . liberaliter et officiose indulgeat, permittat patiatur, ultra citroque.' Story, *Conflict of Laws*, §§ 24–38. [The classical passage in English law on this point is in Lord Stowell's judgment in *Dalrymple* v *Dalrymple*, 2 Hagg. *Cons.* 39; Dodson's *Rep.*, Lond. 1811; and in Clark's *Cabinet Library of Scarce Tracts*, p. 6, Edin. 1837. 'Being entertained in an English court, it must be adjudicated according to the principles of English law applicable to such a case. But the only principle applicable to such a case by the law of England is, that the validity of Miss Gordon's marriage rights must be tried by reference to the law of the country where, if they exist at all, they had their origin. Having furnished this principle, the law of England withdraws altogether, and leaves the legal question to the exclusive judgment of the law of Scotland.' Comp. Sir Ed. Simpson in *Scrimshire* v *Scrimshire*, 2 Hagg. *Cons.* 395; Turner, V. C., in *Caldwell* v *Vanvlissingen*, 9 Hare 425. 'A judge applies foreign law, not because it is enacted by a foreign legislator, but because his own law requires the particular question to be adjudicated according to the foreign law.']

(*g*) Hence I cannot agree with Wächter, i. p. 240, ii. pp. 12–15, when he warns so earnestly against confounding the judicial and legislative standpoint. What he assigns to the legislative standpoint certainly falls, in great measure, within the judicial, in a matter which legislation has left very much to scientific development. There is an approximation to the view here advocated in another passage of Wächter (i. 265), in which he bids the judge note the tendency and spirit of his national laws. [See Note C at end of section.]

[3] See an example in the cases of alienage and treason. See Note B, p. 32. Except where, as in these cases and others, the laws of England and Scotland have been assimilated by statute, they are to be regarded as 'independent foreign countries, unconnected with each other' (per Campbell, C., in *Stuart* v *Moore* (Bute Guardianship), 17 May 1861, 4 Macq. 1, 23 D. 902; cf. *Fenton* v *Livingstone*, 3 Macq. 467); though, it has been said, 'standing to one another in very peculiar and close bonds'—per Lord Ivory in *Fenton* v *Livingstone*, 1856, 18 D. 865, 896. A court of appellate jurisdiction can-

cannot be found at all in the case of conflicting laws of independent states.

This standpoint of a community of law among independent states, from which has arisen an approximate uniformity in the treatment of conflicts among different positive laws, was unknown to the Romans. The intercourse of nations had to receive the enormous impulse which we observe in modern times, before the felt want of such principles could bring them to recognition and development.

If this view has not been expressly adopted by modern writers, yet it lies in reality at the foundation of the universal customary law so often appealed to in inquiries of this kind (*h*). This customary law is, it is true, claimed especially for the domain of the German common law; but its derivation from the (constantly progressing) concurrence of writers and judicial decisions carries us irresistibly beyond these limits. Neither can it make any difference that there is a dispute as to the substance and the limits of that customary law. The general assumption that it exists, and the general attempt to determine its contents, are decisive in favour of our assertion. We cannot, however, be surprised to find wavering and conflicting opinions in a branch of jurisprudence, which, like that now before us, is presented to us only in a state of growth (*i*).

not rectify or redress conflicts between particular laws within its territory, which are administered by separate courts of original jurisdiction: Lord St. Leonards in *Geils* v *Geils*, 1852, 1 Macq. 255, 263; see per Inglis, J. C., in *Moore* v *Stuart*, 23 D. 913. It is bound by the law administered by the court of first instance. *Alex. ad Bartolum in Cod. de s. trin.* § 20; Bar, § 28, n. 12. The position of the supreme court of the United States is somewhat peculiar in this respect. By the Judiciary Act of 1789, § 34, it is bound to decide in ordinary appeals by the laws of the several states. But this is held to apply only to laws strictly local, *i.e.* to the positive statutes of the state and the construction thereof adopted by the local tribunals (see *Leffingwell* v *Warren*, 1862, 2 Black 599), and to 'rights and titles to things having a permanent locality, such as rights and titles to real estate and other matters immoveable and intraterritorial'—'not to questions of a more general nature not dependent on local statutes or local usages of a fixed and permanent operation, *e.g.* to construction of ordinary contracts or other written instruments, and especially to questions of general commercial law.' Per Story, J., in delivering judgment of supreme court, *Swift* v *Tyson*, 16 Pet. 1, 14 Curt. 166. See Kent, *Com.* i. 341 seqq.

(*h*) Wächter, i. p. 255-261; ii. pp. 175–177, 371. Schäffner, § 21.

(*i*) Compare as to this the Preface to this volume. [Schäffner, the purpose of whose work was 'to inquire in what points a settled practice has been formed,' and who regards such a settled practice as 'positive

The principles I have laid down as to the possibility and the advantages of a common system of rules in dealing with conflicts between territorial laws, are very greatly promoted by public treaties between neighbouring states, where cases of collision frequently occur. Such treaties are not only earnestly desired and recommended by jurists, but have long ago actually existed (*k*). It would be erroneous to suppose that these, where they exist, positively enact an entirely new law, so that, apart from them, and before their date, precisely the opposite rules may have prevailed. They are rather, in almost every case, to be regarded as the expression of the community of legal feeling above explained, and therefore as attempts to make it more clearly apprehended.

No state in modern times has contracted so many such treaties as Prussia; and in these treaties the point of view above indicated is unmistakeably predominant. I here give a view of the Prussian treaties with neighbouring states, for the sake of more easy reference in the sequel:

Treaty with Saxe-Weimar, 1824,	*Gesetz-Versammlung,*	1824, p. 149.
Treaty with Saxe-Altenburg, 1832,	,,	1832, p. 105.
Treaty with Saxe-Coburg Gotha, 1833,	,,	1834, p. 9.
Treaty with Reuss Gera, 1834,	,,	1834, p. 124.
Treaty with Kingdom of Saxony, 1839,	,,	1839, p. 353.
Treaty with Schwarzburg Rudolstadt, 1840,	,,	1840, p. 239.
Treaty with Anhalt Bernburg, 1840,	,,	1840, p. 250.
Treaty with Brunswick, 1841,	,,	1842, p. 1.

Note A, p. 26.

See Phillimore, i. 345–360, ii. 3 seq., iv. 2, 6 seq., 641 seq.; Story, §§ 29, 541 seq.; Bar, § 27; *Code Civil*, art. 3, 11, 13; *infra*, § 361 *fin.*; Heffter, *Eur. Völkerrecht*, § 60; *Ringer* v *Churchill*, 1840, 2 D. 307, 311 (per Lord President Hope). After stating this principle, Heffter observes, *l.c.*, that 'in modern times a distinction between national and

law,' fully admits the difficulty of the inquiry and the uncertainty of the rules of this branch of jurisprudence, *l.c.*, and pp. 4, 7, 14. He adopts the language of Porter, J., in *Saul* v *His Creditors*, 17 Mart. (5 Mart. N. S.) 569, cited at length in Phillimore, iv. 734, 743: 'A subject the most intricate and perplexed of any which has occupied the attention of lawyers and courts,—one on which scarcely any two writers are found entirely to agree, and on which it is rare to find one consistent with himself throughout. We know of no matter in jurisprudence so unsettled, or none that should more teach men distrust for their own opinions, and charity for those of others.']

(*k*) J. Voet., §§ i. xii. xvii.

general law, such as that between the *jus civile* and *jus gentium* of the Romans, can no longer be made, except in so far as, by a constitutional law, the acquisition of certain rights is made to depend on a certain political status. Modern legislation is entirely in this direction, and is defective only in a few special points. That foreigners, when suing, must find caution, is a rule justified by the circumstances; hence the universal practice. Where, on the contrary, legacies and successions are either entirely withheld from a foreigner, or are subjected to a deduction (*jus defractus, traite foraine*), this is a remnant of ancient prejudice, the retention of which is inconsistent with the principle of the free intercourse of nations, for which reason, also, the custom is being frequently, though not thoroughly, abolished by treaties.' See, as to France, Gaschon, *Code Dipl. des Aubains*, 1818; Gand, *Code des Etrangers*, 1853; *infra*, § 376, note *d*.

In Scotland every person abroad, *i.e.* out of the jurisdiction of the supreme court, whether a Scotsman or a foreigner, must sist a mandatory in order to entitle him to sue or defend. Shand's *Pract.* 154 seqq.; *Faulks* v *Whitehead*, 1854, 16 D. 718; *Overbury* v *Peek*, 1863, 1 Macph. 1058. In England all plaintiffs residing out of the jurisdiction of the court, without distinction, except in some few particulars, whether he be a native Englishman or a foreigner, must, if required, give security for costs. Lush's *Pract. of Superior Courts*, p. 929 (3d ed.); Daniell's *Chancery Pract.*, p. 27 seq. (4th ed.); Phillimore, iv. 469. As to France, where the courts violate this principle by refusing, except in commercial matters, to administer justice between foreigners, see Fœlix, ii. 2, 2, 1; Phillimore, iv. 645 seq., 651; Bar, § 27.

Both in England and Scotland aliens are incapable of acquiring real (heritable) property, either by purchase or succession. 7 and 8 Vict. c. 66, § 5; Ersk. iii. 10, 10; Bell, *Pr.* 2135; Stephen's *Com.* i. 138, 442, 482, ii. 423–429; Jarman *On Wills*, 37, 59 seqq. (3d ed. 1861); Tudor, L. C., *Real Pr.* 685 seq.; Kent, *Com.* ii. 61. But in most of the United States the disability of aliens in this respect is removed or modified. Kent, ii. 70. And even when naturalized, they remain incapable of becoming members of either House of Parliament, or of the Privy Council. 7 and 8 Vict. c. 66. Aliens may take advantage of the English and Scottish and American bankrupt laws—12 and 13 Vict. c. 106, s. 277; Griffith and Holmes *On Bankruptcy*, i. 91; 19 and 20 Vict. c. 79, s. 4; *Judd* v *Laurence*, 1 Cush. Mass. Rep. 531; and they enjoy the privilege of copyright, provided only they are within the British dominions (including colonies) at the date of publishing a book, etc. See *Low* v *Routledge*, 10 E. Jur. 922; on appeal, 11 E. Jur. 939, 1 Law Rep. Ch. Ap., where Turner, L. J., said: 'Every alien coming into a British colony becomes temporarily a subject of the Crown, bound by, subject to, and entitled to the benefit of the laws which affect all British subjects.' See Tudor, L. C., *Merc. Law*, 491, and Kent's *Com.* ii. 372 n., as to trade-marks.

NOTE B, p. 27.

The qualifications to which this statement is subject seem to be reducible to two heads:—I. Matters of constitutional law.—Thus in Great Britain it has been asserted that questions as to the inheritance and rights connected with British peerages must be ruled by the law of England, although the domicile and property of the party concerned may be in Scotland. *Strathmore Peerage Case*, 4 W. and S. Appendix, 89. See, however, *Moore* v *Stuart* (Bute Guardianship), 1861, 4 Macq. 1, 23 D. 902. But the chief instances of this are in regard to the law of treason and of national character. Where a province or country is incorporated with a country retaining its own laws in all other respects, its inhabitants become natural-born subjects of the new country. Their national character is determined by the jurisprudence of the dominant country, or by a constitutional law common to both; and hence this relation may be ascertained by the rules of a different system of law from that which, when it is fixed, governs the rights of parties. Thus British nationality is determined by the laws of England, though the rights of a party as a British subject may, in the particular case, be decided by the laws of the colony in which he resides. *Donegani* v *Donegani*, 3 Knapp, P. C. 63; *Re Adam*, 1 Mo. P. C. 460. See *Shedden* v *Patrick*, 1 Macq. 535, 612; Westlake, § 25; Bar, p. 71. In Scotland the decisions of English courts are followed in questions as to national character. *Dundas* v *Dundas*, 1839, 2 D. 31; *Macao* v *Officers of State*, 1822, 1 S. App. 138. See *Calvin's Case* (case of *Postnati*), 7 Co. Rep. 1, 2 St. Tr. 559, 683. The privileges conferred on Frenchmen in Scotland by treaty (see Mackenzie, *Obs. on St.*, *Works* i. 261) seem to have ceased with the Union. Bankton, i. 2, 61, 65. Some doubt has been introduced into the law by 10 and 11 Vict. c. 83, which declares that 7 and 8 Vict. c. 66, the existing statute as to naturalization of aliens, shall not apply to the colonies, and that all past and future colonial Acts imparting the privilege of naturalization shall, within the several colonies, have the same effect as other colonial statutes. See Westlake, *l.c.*; Phillimore, iv. 30. In the United States alienage is not subject to state laws, except as to consequences, but is, under the constitution, a matter of national jurisprudence. Kent, *Com.* ii. 1 seqq.

II. Cases of conflict for which a legislature common to both provinces has expressly laid down a special rule different from the ordinary rule of private international law. (The former case might perhaps be described as that in which the common legislature has *implicitly* enacted a special rule).—'If the law which we are bound to administer be opposed to the principles of international jurisprudence, the sequestration will receive no effect in foreign countries, though, of course, it must receive full effect in England, because the law is contained in and created by a statute of the Imperial Parliament.'—Per Inglis, J. C., in *Joel* v *Gill*, 1859, 21 D. 929; cf. *Young* v *Buckel*, 1864, 2 Macph. 1077; *Moyes* v *Whinney*, 1864, 3 Macph. 183. See p. 28, note 3.

NOTE C, p. 27.

'If one independent state allows commercial intercourse and contracts between its citizens and those of another, the rights of the parties and the relations between them would seem to have a higher claim than that of mere comity,—a claim of justice, though perhaps of imperfect obligation, under the laws of independent states, within their own territories.' Kent's *Com.* ii. 611. Comp. per Macqueen, J. C., in *Watson* v *Renton*, Bell's 8vo Ca. 106 (cited *supra*, § 344, p. 9); Lord Brougham in *Yates* v *Thomson*, 3 Cl. and Fin. 544, 586, and in *Warrender* v *Warrender*, 1835, 2 S. and M'L. 154, 198, 9 Bligh 89, 2 Cl. and Fin. 488; Story, § 226 c. note; per Lord Wensleydale in *Fenton* v *Livingstone*, 1858, 3 Macq. 497, 548.—'If we examine more nearly how the principle of the *comitas gentium* was carried out, we see with amazement that it was in truth nowhere properly applied, or at least that in most cases an appeal was made to something quite different from comity. How could any reasonable results be attained with an idea so infinitely vague and unlegal? In fact one cannot even approximate to a correct decision of the simplest case of private international law upon this principle. Where is the beginning of the end of comity? How can questions *of law* be solved according to views of policy, which are the most shifting and uncertain things in the world?' Schäffner, § 30. See Westlake, §§ 144, 160. Reddie's *Inquiries into Int. Law*, 435 seqq.; Bar, pp. 26, 57, etc.

SECT. VI.—(§ 349.)

CONFLICTING TERRITORIAL LAWS IN DIFFERENT STATES.

(CONTINUATION.)

Our inquiry has now brought us to this result, that in deciding cases (legal relations) which come in contact with different independent states, the judge has to apply that local law to which the case (legal relation) pertains, whether it is the law of his own country or the law of a foreign state (§ 348).

But this principle must be limited with respect to many kinds of laws, whose peculiar nature does not admit of so free an application of the community of law obtaining between different states. Where there are such statutes, the judge will have to apply the domestic law more exclusively than that principle allows, and must, on the other hand, leave the foreign law unapplied, even where that principle would justify its application. Thence arises an important class of exceptions, to determine the limits of which is perhaps the most difficult part of this subject. The often unconscious respect paid by writers to these exceptions has not a little contributed to hinder the unanimous recognition of the rules which are limited by them. If it were possible satisfactorily to establish and ascertain the extent of these exceptions, many disputes as to the rules themselves would be prevented or brought to an end.

I will endeavour to reduce such exceptions to two classes:

A. Laws of a strictly positive, imperative nature, which are consequently inconsistent with that freedom of application which pays no regard to the limits of particular states.

B. Legal institutions of a foreign state, of which the existence is not at all recognised in ours, and which, therefore, have no claim to the protection of our courts.

A. *Statutes of a strictly positive and absolute (coercitive, imperative) nature.*

Various contrasts in the nature and origin of rules of law have already been considered (*a*). To these distinctions it is necessary here to refer; still, they are not sufficient for our present purpose; and we must examine still more minutely the differences in the character of the rules of law.

It might be supposed that the distinctions of absolute and dispositive (suppletory) rules of law would here suffice (§ 16);[1]

(*a*) See above, vol. i. §§ 15, 16, 22.

[1] Absolute or imperative (absolute, gebietende) laws are those which 'are intended to rule with inflexible necessity, without allowing any play to individual will. This necessity may have its origin in the peculiar nature of the particular positive law; or in political or economical considerations; or may flow directly from moral considerations.' Dispositive, permissive, or suppletory (vermittelnde) laws are those which 'allow free scope to the individual will, and only step into its place where it has omitted to exercise its power, in order to give the necessary certainty and

but that would be a mistake. It is true that this distinction has some bearing upon the question, in so far as a merely dispositive rule of law can never be among these exceptional cases (*b*). It would, on the contrary, be quite incorrect to ascribe to all absolute laws such a positive and obligatory nature, that they must be classed among the exceptional cases. Thus *e.g.* every law as to the beginning of majority is an absolute statute, because it does not operate merely in defect of a private choice otherwise disposing; yet all are agreed that it can unquestionably take effect beyond the limits of the state in which it is enacted (§ 362).

Whether any law is to be reckoned among the exceptional cases, depends principally on the purpose of the legislator. If he has expressly declared his intention on this point, this declaration must receive effect; for it possesses the character of a *law as to collision*, which must always be unconditionally followed (§ 348, *d*). But such an express declaration is generally wanting, and then nothing remains but to have recourse to the differences among absolute laws themselves; and thus we arrive at the following distinction:—

One class of absolute laws has no other reason and end than to secure the administration of justice by certain fixed rules, so that they are enacted merely for the sake of persons who are the possessors of rights. Among these are laws which limit the capacity to act on account of age, sex, etc.; also those as to the transference of property (by mere contract or by tradition). In respect of all such statutes, there is no reason for including them among the exceptional cases. The conflicts occurring in regard to them can be better adjusted on the principle of the freest community of law; for every state can unquestionably allow foreign laws of this description to have effect within its bounds.

Another class of absolute statutes, on the contrary, has its

precision to the legal relation. The latter class of laws may therefore be regarded as interpreting the imperfectly expressed will.'—Savigny, *System*, vol. i. p. 57 (§ 16).

(*b*) Every statute as to intestate succession is dispositive or suppletory, because it operates only in defect of a last will. It is therefore generally admitted, that such statutes can take effect beyond the territory for which they are enacted; for the many dissentient opinions relate not to these statutes themselves, but only to their application to immoveable property, of which we shall speak in detail below (§ 376).

end and object beyond the province of pure law apprehended in its abstract existence (*c*), so that they are enacted *not* merely for the sake of the persons who are the possessors of rights. Laws of this class may rest on *moral* grounds. Such is every marriage law which excludes polygamy. They may also rest on reasons of *public interest* (*publica utilitas*), whether these relate to politics, police, or political economy.[2] Among these are many laws which restrict the acquisition of immoveable property by Jews.

All such statutes are among the exceptional cases, so that, in regard to their application, every state appears completely separate and distinct. If, therefore, the law of our state forbids polygamy,[3] our judges must refuse the protection of the law to the polygamous marriages of foreigners, to whom they are permitted by the law of their own country. If our law forbids to Jews the acquisition of landed property, our judges must forbid such acquisition not only to native Jews, but also to those foreign Jews in whose state there is no such prohibition; although, according to the general rules as to collisions, personal capacity for having rights and for acting must be determined according to the law of the domicile of the person. But, conversely, the foreign state whose law lays no such restriction upon Jews, will admit Jews belonging to our state to possess landed property, without respect to the restrictive laws of their personal domicile.

B. *Legal Institutions of a Foreign State of which the existence is not recognised at all in ours.*

The judges of a state in which the civil death of the French

(*c*) 'Contra rationem juris.' See above, vol. i. § 16, note *p*.

[2] See Note A at end of section.

[3] Westlake, § 197. Story, § 114. Lord Brougham in *Warrender* v *Warrender*, 2 S. and M'L. 200, 9 Bligh 112, 2 Cl. and Fin. 532,—where the *ratio* given is, that the infidel marriage is something radically different from the Christian. *Hyde* v *Hyde*, 35 L. J. Pr. and Matr. 57, 1 L. R. D. C. 130 (Mormon marriage). *Armitage* v *Armitage*, 3 L. R. Eq. 343 (New Zealand marriage). *Conolly* v *Woolrich and Johnson*, 11 L. Can. Jur. 197 (marriage with a Cree). A singular contradiction of this doctrine occurs in the North Carolina case of *Williams* v *Oates*, 5 Iredell 535, where Ruffin, C. J., is reported to have said: 'If a Turk with two wives were to come here, we would administer to them the justice due to the relations contracted by them at home.' Parsons (*Contracts*, ii. 107, 109) quotes this sentence twice without dissenting from it.

or Russian law is unknown, will not apply the legal incapacity arising from it to persons who have incurred it in these countries; although, according to the general rules as to collision, personal status must be determined according to the law of the domicile (*d*). So, in a state which does not recognise slavery, a negro slave who is found there cannot be treated as property of his master, nor as under general legal incapacity (*e*). In this last case, both the considerations here distinguished concur and lead to the same result. Slavery, as a legal institution, is foreign to our state, not recognised in it; and at the same time it is, from our point of view, totally immoral to treat a man as a thing. In the case of civil death, only the first principle could be brought to bear; not the second, because civil death is not more immoral than any other very severe punishment.[4]

These two clauses of absolute laws, however they may differ in other respects, agree in this: that they are withdrawn from that community of law between all states of which we have asserted the existence in regard to collisions; and they are therefore, in this respect, anomalous. It is to be expected, however, that these exceptional cases will gradually be diminished with the natural legal development of nations (*f*).

The exceptions to the general rules of collision treated of in these paragraphs relate to the conflicting territorial laws of

(*d*) Comp. above, vol. ii. § 75. Schäffner (§ 35) is of another opinion on this point, unless the efficacy abroad of a criminal sentence could be utterly denied. [In Great Britain and America the civil death of the French law would be disregarded, on the principle that 'the penal laws of foreign countries are strictly local,' and those of 'one country cannot be taken notice of in another.' *Folliott* v *Ogden*, 1 H. Bl. 135. *Ogden* v *Folliott*, 3 T. R. 733, 734. *Warrender* v *Warrender*, 2 S. and M'L. 205, 9 Bligh 119, 120, 2 Cl. and Fin. 538. Story, c. xvi. and §§ 91, 104. Hume, *Com.* ii. 355. *L. Adv.* v *Dempster*, 1862, 4 Irv. 143, 34 Sc. Jur. 140. *Commonwealth* v *Green*, 17 Mass. R. 540.]

(*e*) Wächter, ii. p. 172. Schäffner, § 34. [See Note B at end of section.]

[4] The concurrence of the two grounds of exception in many cases may be one reason why the second class (B) is rarely or never noticed by British judges or writers. Almost the only passage which can even be construed as recognising the second kind of exceptions as a separate class, is Lord Brougham's allusion to a Turkish marriage in *Warrender* v *Warrender*, *supra*; cf. *Hyde* v *Hyde*, *supra*.

(*f*) The most important and numerous applications of the rules here laid down will be found below, in the doctrine of capacity for rights and capacity to act (§ 365). What here appears in perhaps too abstract a form will there be more fully illustrated, and therefore more convincing.

different states. In the particular laws of one and the same state (§ 347), similar cases will be much more rare, as statutes of a strictly positive and coercitive nature are generally enacted for the whole extent of a state, without respect to the limits of particular laws. Yet such anomalous cases occur even within the same state; when, for instance, the diversity of local laws is derived from a time when many of the present constituent parts of the state did not yet belong to it. This is true, in particular, of the law of the Rhenish provinces of Prussia, with respect to that of the other Prussian provinces. In such a case, the special rules laid down in these paragraphs will be applicable within the limits of the same state.[5]

NOTE A, p. 36.

The word *utilitas*, in the Roman jurists, is not equivalent to 'utility' in the widest sense, but to that necessity or strong expediency which is the ground of those special and exceptional laws which the Romans designated as *jus singulare* and *privilegia*, and the distinctive character of which consists in their being deviations from the logical consistency of the legal system. 'Jus singulare est quod contra tenorem rationis' (*i.e.* contrary to general legal principle, or, as it is elsewhere expressed, L. 51, § 2, *ad L. Aq.* 9, 2, 'contra rationem disputandi'), 'propter aliquam utilitatem auctoritate constituentium introductum est.'—L. 16, *de leg.* i. 3. Savigny calls such rules of law *anomalous; supra*, § 16, vol. i. p. 61. Bar, pp. 109, 110, objects to the terms in which Savigny states this class of exceptions as too wide and indefinite. 'Most laws which are not logical consequences of general principles may be referred to reasons of this description (of politics, police, or political economy), and there would be really little room for the application of foreign law.' Bar probably errs on the other side when he says, 'All that can be granted is, that a court must never allow itself to realize a legal relation, which is regarded by the domestic laws as an immoral one, even if it should be permitted by the foreign law.' Practice, at least in British and American courts, recognises not only exceptions grounded on moral considerations, but also where foreign laws are contrary to the public policy, or in opposition to the laws of the country of the judge. But the grounds of exception have been so generally and vaguely expressed, that in many particular cases it is really left to judicial tact to draw

[5] See examples in *Fenton* v *Livingstone*, *supra*, *Birtwhistle* v *Vardill*, *supra;* and see § 348, Note B. An exception is asserted in matters of criminal law,—a conviction for theft in England being allowed to be charged as an aggravation in Scotland. *L. Adv.* v *Dempster*, 1862, 4 Irv. 143, 34 Sc. Jur. 140.

the line between the foreign laws which may, and those which may not, be applied. The terms used are, for example: 'When a court of justice in one country is called on to enforce a contract entered into in another country, the question is not only, whether or not the contract is valid according to the law of the country in which it was entered into, but whether or not it was consistent with the law and policy of the country in which it is to be enforced; and if it is opposed to these laws and that policy, the court cannot be called upon to enforce it.'—Turner, L. J., in *Hope* v *Hope*, 22 Beav. 351, 3 Jur. N.S. 454. Boyle, J. C., in *Edmonston* v *Edmonston* (Ferguson, *Cons. Rep.* 411, 1 June 1816, 19 F. C. 138, 164), based the exceptions on 'injustice,' and 'repugnance to the laws and institutions of our country.' See Lord Glenlee, *ib.* p. 404; Lord Robertson, p. 396. Lord Meadowbank, in *Gordon* v *Pye* (Ferguson, *Cons. Rep.* 361), takes a distinction similar to that in the text between laws affecting the contracting individuals only and those affecting the public; but he extends the compass of the latter class so far as to say, that 'the same principles which prescribe to nations the administration of their own criminal law, appear to require a like exclusive administration of law relative to the domestic relations.' Lord Ivory makes the exceptional considerations operate 'when the law is called in to enforce or give effect, directly or indirectly, to any act which infers either a scandal on society, or a breach of national morals and decency, or the commission of any crime,' and in other cases not specified. *Fenton* v *Livingstone*, 18 D. 805. Comp. Littledale, J., in *Birtwhistle* v *Vardill*, 5 B. and C. 455; Lord Brougham in *Fenton* v *Livingstone*, 3 Macq. 537. In a leading American case, Parsons, C. J. (p. 377), said: 'This rule is subject to two exceptions. One is, where the commonwealth or its citizens may be injured by giving legal effect to the contract by a judgment in our courts. Thus a contract for the sale and delivery of merchandise, in a state where such sale is not prohibited, may be sued in another state where such merchandise cannot be lawfully imported. But if the delivery was to be in a state where the importation was interdicted, there the contract could not be sued in the interdicting state; because the giving of legal effect to such a contract would be repugnant to its rights and interests. Another exception is, when the giving of legal effect to the contract would exhibit to the citizens of the state an example detestable and pernicious. Thus, if a foreign state allows of marriages incestuous by the law of nature, as between parent and child, such marriage could not be allowed to have any validity here, But marriages, not naturally unlawful, but prohibited by the law of one state and not of another, if celebrated where they are not prohibited, would be holden valid in a state where they are not allowed. As in this state, a marriage between a man and his deceased wife's sister is lawful; but it is not so in some states. Such a marriage celebrated here would be held valid in any other state, and the parties entitled to the benefits of the matrimonial contract. Another case may be stated as within this second exception, in an action on a contract made in a foreign state by a prostitute to recover the wages of her prostitution. This contract, if lawful where it was made, could not be the legal ground of an action here; for the consideration is confessedly immoral, and a judgment in support of it would be pernicious from its example. And perhaps all cases may be considered as within this second exception, which are founded on moral turpitude, in respect either of the consideration or the stipulation.' *Greenwood* v *Curtis*, 6 Mass. 358.

Taney, C. J., says, in *Bank of Augusta* v *Earle*, 13 Pet. 518, 589, 13 Curt. 277, 283: 'Courts of justice have always expounded and executed contracts made in a foreign country, according to the laws of the place in which they were made; provided that law was not repugnant to the laws or policy of their own country. The comity thus extended to other nations is no impeachment of sovereignty. It is the voluntary act of the nation by which it is offered, and is inadmissible when contrary to its policy or prejudicial to its interests.'

In *Forbes* v *Cochrane*, 2 B. and Cr. 448, Best, J. (Lord Wynford), said: 'The plaintiff must recover here upon what is called the *comitas inter communitates;* but it is a maxim, that that cannot prevail in any case where it violates the law of our own country, the law of nature, or the law of God. The proceedings in our courts are founded upon the law of England, and that law is, again, founded on the law of nature and the revealed law of God. If the right sought to be enforced is inconsistent with either of these, the English municipal courts cannot recognise it.'

This class of exceptions is sometimes expressed by the phrase 'prohibitory' laws. 'Where the positive laws of any state prohibit particular contracts from having effect, according to the rules of the country where they are made, the former should prevail, because that prohibition is supposed to be founded on some reason of utility or policy advantageous to the country that passes it; which utility or policy would be defeated if foreign laws were permitted to have a superior effect.' Porter, J., in *Saul* v *His Creditors*, 5 Mart. (La.) N.S. 569, Phillimore, iv. 742. Another maxim is often stated as creating an exception to the application of a foreign law, viz. 'that no nation will suffer the laws of another to interfere with her own, to the injury of her citizens.'—*Ib.* Phillimore, iv. 746; cf. Burge, iii. 778, 770. 'We always import,' says Lord Ellenborough, 'together with their persons, the existing relations of foreigners as between themselves, according to the laws of their respective countries, except, indeed, where those laws clash with the rights of our own subjects here, and one or other of the laws must necessarily give way, in which case our own is entitled to the preference.' *Potter* v *Brown*, 5 East. 124, 1 Ross, L. C. 786. This preference is said to be due to the *lex fori* in cases of 'irreconcilable conflict' (Phillim. iv. 529), —a doctrine derived, like so many others of English lawyers, from Huber, i. 3, 11. A particular instance, by far the most important, of laws which for reasons of utility or policy entirely exclude all foreign laws with which they come into collision, is to be found in laws relating to immoveable property. *Vide infra*, §§ 360, 366, etc. See the English rules as to laws of a positive and stringent character, and the principle of turpitude, in Westlake, § 196. The cases of *Birtwhistle* v *Vardill*, 5 B. and C. 438, 9 Bligh N. R. 32, 2 Cl. and Fin. 571, 1 Rob. Ap. 627, and *Fenton* v *Livingstone*, May 27, 1856, 18 D. 865, 3 Macq. 497, extend the exception to a very questionable extent in regard to succession to land, requiring legitimacy by the law of the situs, and disregarding the status impressed by the law of the domicile. See Westlake, § 90 seq. 'It is clear that a tribunal can never consent to give effect to (realisiren) a legal relation, which is regarded by the law of the land as an immoral one, even although it should be permitted by the law of the foreign country. Every further exception, however, is unjustifiable; and even a legal relation immoral, and therefore void in the eye of our law, must be recognised by our tribunals, when it is not to be realized within the territory of our state, but when its existence is only a prejudicial point for a claim otherwise maintained in our country. The institution of slavery must by common law be described as an immoral one; but if slavery is recognised in another country, and one there acquires property through his slaves, that acquisition, if he seeks to recover his property in our state, must be regarded as a just and rightful acquisition, even in our tribunals.'—Bar, § 33. Accordingly, even English judges have not refused to enforce gaming contracts, made where such contracts were not illegal; *e.g. Quarrier* v *Colston*, 1 Phillimore 147, Westlake, § 194. 'If we suppose a foreign contract not acknowledged by our law, we would distinguish between action for failure in the foreign country, and action to compel performance here. In some countries a game debt may be obligatory. If such a debt, contracted in such a country, were sued for here, we would decern for it. But suppose that a gaming copartnery were established, if that be allowed in any country, in an accounting between the parties, though we might decern here for sums which fell due before the adventurers came to Scotland, we would not decern for profits arising in Scotland, *e.g.* for bets at races in Scotland.'—Per Lord Glenlee in *Edmonstone* v *Edmonstone*, Ferg. *Cons. Dec.* 405.

NOTE B, p. 37.

'Slavery is a local law, and therefore, if a man wishes to preserve his slaves, let him attach them to him by affection, or make fast the bars of their prison, or rivet well their chains; for the instant they get beyond the limits where slavery is recognised by the local law, they have broken their chains, they have escaped from their prison, and are free.'—Per Best, C. J. (Lord Wynford), in *Forbes* v *Cochrane*, 2 B. and C. 448. It would be erroneous to suppose that the doctrine, 'as soon as a man sets foot on English ground he is free' (per Northington, C., in *Shanley* v *Harvey*, Eden's Ch. R. 126; cf. *Somersett's* case, Lofft R. 1, 20 St. Tr. 1; *Knight* v *Wedderburn*, 1778, M. 14,545, 20 St. Tr. 1; Hailes, D. 776), is peculiar to British jurisprudence. It was very early the law and custom of France. Bodin. *de Republ.* i. p. 41, ed. 1586. 'Les jurisconsultes Français disent que l'air de France est si bon et si bénin que dès qu'un esclave entre dans le roiaume, mesme à la suite d'un ambassadeur, il ne respire que liberté, et la recouvre aussitost.'—Wicquefort, *l'Ambassadeur*, i. 418; case of *Jean Borcaut*, Causes Celèbres, xiii. 562; case of *Francisque*, Denisart, iii. 406. So, as to Holland, see J. Voet. *ad Pand.* i. 5, 3; Grœnewegen, *ad Inst.* i. 8, 3. And the maxim has obtained almost universal recognition in international law. Heffter, § 14; Phillimore, i. 335 seq.; Story, § 96 seq., 259; Burge i. 735; *Commonwealth* v *Aves*, 18 Pick. 215. But see *Sandford* v *Dred Scott*, 19 How. 393; Kent, ii. 257 seq., and notes. Lord Stowell held a slave brought to England, and afterwards voluntarily returning to the country in which she had been held in slavery, to be reinstated in her condition of slavery; her liberty had been placed 'into a sort of parenthesis.' *The Slave Grace*, 2 Hagg. *Adm.* 94, 134. Cf. *Commonwealth* v *Aves*, *supra*. Bar (p. 164) asserts that it would be otherwise if the slave had acquired a domicile in the interval of freedom.

Sect. VII.—(§ 350.)

THE ROMAN DOCTRINE OF ORIGO AND DOMICILIUM.

INTRODUCTION.

The foregoing investigation leads us to this result, that the collision of different positive laws in the decision of a case (legal relation) is primarily to be regulated by the laws affecting the *person* concerned in the legal relation, and that even the numerous and important exceptions to this principle can be rightly understood only in connection with it, and as modifications of it (§ 345). It was further shown that the law governing the person, according to a rule long since universally recognised, is determined by territory, not by birth (§§ 346–348).

But even the result thus obtained has no more than a formal significance; for the question still remains: How is the individual person with its legal belongings (Rechtszustand) attached to the territory? What is it, therefore, that constitutes the connection between the person and the territorial law? We must next endeavour to answer this question. Two relations of fact may be the grounds of this connection,—*origo* and *domicilium*, origin and domicile. We have to explain the meaning of these, their juridical influence, and their relation to one another.

No one doubts that these terms, as well as the legal conceptions which they represent, have come to us through the Roman law; all who make use of them go back to the sources of the Roman law. We must therefore, first of all, ascertain what the Roman jurists understand by the phrases, and what influence they ascribe to the legal notions which they express. It is not, however, to be understood that the Roman conception of them is authoritative for us. It will rather appear in the sequel of this inquiry, that it is just here that our law shows the greatest deviations from the Roman law. We must begin, then, by seeking to secure ourselves against the mistaken use of words and ideas falsely supposed to be the technical terms and legal conceptions of the Roman law.

With one of the terms referred to, *domicilium*, there is little risk of mistake, since the state of the law is not essentially changed in regard to it, and daily practice sufficiently secures its right understanding. It is otherwise with *origo*; and that not because the Roman statements are obscure or ambiguous, but because our law is, in this respect, completely different from the Roman; and hence actual experience cannot protect against incorrect ideas. As, then, the term *origo* easily leads us to refer it to the *place of birth*, this last notion has often found acceptance with modern jurists, even with those who at the same time give the true meaning of *origo* from the sources of the Roman law (*a*). The mere place of birth, however, is

(*a*) Voet. *ad Pand.* v. 1, § 91: 'Est autem originis locus, in quo quis *natus est*, aut nasci debuit, licet forte re ipsa alibi natus esset, matre in

in itself a purely accidental circumstance, without any legal effect.

Before the true sense of these technical terms can be established, it must be observed that their practical importance is by no means limited to our question of collision, but rather that the decision of this question must be regarded as only part of a larger connection.

For, in the eye of the public law, every individual is in a position of dependence or obligation,—first, to the whole state to which he belongs as a citizen and subject; and, second, to some narrower local circle (according to the Roman system, to an urban community) which forms an organic member of that greater whole. A man's attachment to this narrower circle, and his connection with it, have many important consequences: in the Roman law, in liability to municipal burdens (*munera*), in obedience to municipal authorities, or in the positive municipal law, which is the personal law of the individual.

Obedience to local magistrates appears in the jurisdiction to which each individual is normally subject,—the *forum originis* and *forum domicilii.*

But the local positive law, as the personal law of each individual, is the reason for considering this matter here. It is necessary, in particular, to advert at the very beginning to the connection between the jurisdiction and the personal law,—*forum* and *lex originis; forum* and *lex domicilii* (*b*).

After this preliminary remark, I proceed to show the true meaning of *origo* and *domicilium* in the Roman law, and the practical bearing of these two notions on each other. *Origo* and *domicilium* determine for every person:

1. The liability to share in municipal burdens (*munera*).
2. The duty of obedience to municipal magistrates, particularly the personal jurisdiction arising therefrom.

peregrinatione parturiente.' The alternative certainly counteracts the injurious consequences of the fundamental mistake, but the references which follow show that opinions in this respect are conflicting. Glück, vol. vi. § 511, is likewise doubtful and confused,—the *place of birth* ever recurring in the midst of the correct statements.

(*b*) It must not be thought repulsive, that these things are here spoken of in such general and abstract terms. More minute definition and description, both as to the Roman and the modern law, is only possible in the further progress of this inquiry.

3. The special municipal law applicable to him, as a personal quality.

And these effects sometimes arise from both the relations (*origo* and *domicilium*) co-existing, so that they are found at two different places at the same time,—sometimes from one of them alone. All this is now to be more minutely explained.

SECT. VIII.—(§ 351.)

THE ROMAN DOCTRINE OF ORIGO AND DOMICILIUM.

I. ORIGO.

Common Sources for Origo and Domicilium.

Dig. L. 1. (*ad municipalem et de incolis*), and L. 4 (*de muneribus et honoribus*).

Cod. x. 38 (*de municipibus et originariis*), and x. 39 (*de incolis, et ubi quis domicilium habere videtur, et de his qui studiorum causa in alia civitate degunt*).

At the time of the complete development of the Roman constitution, towards the close of the republic and during the first centuries of the empire, the Roman empire consisted of the following constituent parts (*a*):—

All Italy beyond the city of Rome consisted of a great number of urban communities called, for the most part, *municipia* and *coloniæ*, with some subordinate classes of communities. Each of them had a more or less independent constitution, with its own magistrates, with jurisdiction, and even with its own legislation (§ 347, *d*). The whole soil of Italy, therefore, with the exception of the city of Rome and its territory, was included in the bounds of these towns, and every inhabitant of Italy belonged either to the city of Rome or to one or other of these urban communities. The provinces, on the contrary, had originally very various constitutions. They had, however, gradually approximated to the municipal system

(*a*) See Savigny, *Geschichte des R. R. in Mittelalter*, vol. i. c. 2.

of Italy; although in them this system was not carried out so completely and thoroughly. In the time of the great jurists, in the second and third centuries of our era, the proposition just now laid down in regard to Italy could almost be applied to the whole empire. The soil of the empire was almost entirely included in distinct urban territories, and the inhabitants of the empire appertained either to the city of Rome or to one or other urban community (*b*).

The urban communities bore the common name of *civitates* or *respublicæ* (*c*). The district attached to each town is called *territorium*, sometimes *regio* (*d*). Every urban territory, and the community pertaining to it, embraced as well the *vici* lying within its bounds (*e*) as the solitary farms in which at all times so great a proportion of the population of Italy was contained. Hence it may be asserted, that almost the whole soil of the empire was broken up into a great number of urban communities.

It is now to be determined in what way each individual comes to pertain to an urban community, and thus enters into a definite relation of dependence towards it. This takes place in two ways: (1) by citizenship of the community (*origo*); (2) by domicile in the urban territory (*domicilium*).

(1.) *Citizenship.*

Citizenship (Bürgerrecht) is acquired by the following facts: Birth, Adoption, Manumission, Election (*f*).

1. Birth (*origo, nativitas*). (Note *f*.)

This mode of constituting the relation is entirely in-

(*b*) How far they could, and afterwards must, belong to both at the same time, will be shown below.

(*c*) See above, vol. ii. § 87. *Municipes* also, as a collective expression, is often used to signify the community itself as a legal person; the word then stands for *municipium*;—which last, however, is not used precisely, in this abstract sense, for towns of every kind (§ 352, *f*, *g*).

(*d*) *Territorium*, L. 239, § 8 *de V. S.* (50, 16); L. 20 *de jurisd.* (2, 1); L. 20 *de jud.* (5, 1); L. 53 *C. de decur.* (10, 31). *Regio*, Siculus Flaccus, *de condicionibus agrorum*, at the beginning, p. 135 of the *Gromatici Veteres*, ed. Lachman, Berol. 1848.

(*e*) L. 30, *ad mun.* (50, 1). In older times there were also *vici* which had their own *respublica*. Festus, *v. Vici.*

(*f*) L. 1, *pr. ad mun.* (50, 1): Municipem aut nativitas facit, aut manumissio, aut adoptio. L. 7, *C. de incolis* (10, 39): Cives quidem origo, manumissis, allectio, vel adoptio, incolas vero, domicilium facit.

dependent of the free-will of the person who is thereby attached to the community.

It is the regular and most frequent origin of citizenship, and its name is therefore very commonly used to designate the civic relation itself so arising (*g*).

It indicates birth in a legal marriage when the father himself has the right of citizenship (*h*). The native place of the mother is, as a rule, without any influence; yet some communities had the peculiar privilege, that the citizenship of women belonging to them was transmitted to their legitimate children (*i*). Illegitimate children acquired by *origo* citizenship in the native place of the mother (*k*).

2. Adoption. (Note *f*.)

This does not extinguish the citizenship derived from birth; but the adopted son has then a double citizenship, which descends to his children (*l*). Emancipation of the adopted child, however, destroys every effect of adoption, and therefore also this effect, which pertains to public law (*m*).

3. Manumission. (Note *f*.)

The manumitted slave could have no right by birth. On the contrary, he acquired by manumission the right of citizenship in the native town of the patron, which also descended to his children. If the patron had citizenship in several places, or if the common slave of several masters was manumitted by them, then a plural citizenship might arise by manumission (*n*).

(*g*) L. 6, *pr.* § 1, 3; L. 9, *ad mun.* (50, 1); L. 15, § 3 *eod.* (*jus originis*). Other passages, certainly speaking more accurately, call the legal relation (of which *origo* is only the cause, and that not always) *patria* or *civitas*: L. 27, *pr.*; L. 30, *eod.*

(*h*) L. 1, § 2; L. 6, § 1 *ad mun.* (50, 1); L. 3, *C. de munic.* (10, 38).

(*i*) L. 1, § 2 *ad mun.* (50, 1). It is not clear whether the child was a citizen in the native town of the mother alone, or in both places. The latter opinion is in itself more probable.

(*k*) L. 1, § 2; L. 9 *ad mun.* (50, 1).

(*l*) L. 15, § 3; L. 17, § 9 *ad mun.* (50, 1).

(*m*) L. 16, *ad mun.* (50, 1).

(*n*) L. 6. § 3; L. 7; L. 22 *pr.*; L. 27 *pr.*; L. 37, § 1 *ad mun.* (50, 1); L. 3, § 8 *de mun.* (50, 4); L. 2, *C. de municip.* (10, 38). As to the text and meaning of L. 22 *pr. ad mun.*, comp. *Zeitschrift für Geschichtliche Rechtswissenschaft*, vol. ix. pp. 91–98. [Savigny, *Vermischte Schriften*, iii. 245.]

4. Election (Allectio) (*o*).

By this is to be understood the free gift of citizenship by the municipal magistrates, of the legality of which there could be no doubt, even if it were not expressly attested.

Citizenship, with its consequences, was not extinguished by the mere will of the persons who had acquired it in any one of the methods above described (*p*). By legal marriage in a foreign state, the wife, indeed, did not properly vacate her native citizenship, but she was relieved during the subsistence of the marriage from the personal burdens (*munera*) connected with it (*q*). A similar relief from personal burdens, without complete dissolution of the original citizenship, was also allowed to a citizen raised to the dignity of a senator of the Roman empire and to his descendants (*r*); also to every soldier as long as his service lasted (*s*).

From the rules here laid down, it follows that one person could possess at the same time citizenship in several cities of the Roman empire, and consequently often combined in his person the rights, and had to bear the burdens, pertaining to the citizens of all these places (*t*). So to the native citizenship a later one might be added by adoption or allection, and both subsisted together (note *b*). In like manner, the manumitted slave might be brought into several civic relations by manumission (note *n*).

The acquisition of citizenship by manumission could, however, be asserted only of a complete manumission. The *dedititii* were not citizens in the municipality of their patron (§ 356); and the same holds of the *Latini Juniani*.

(*o*) L. 7, *C. de incolis* (10–39), '*allectio vel adoptio.*' That in some MSS. *vel* is awanting, in others *atque* is found, does not affect the meaning. A more important variation is: 'allectio *id est* adoptio,' which Cujacius cites from MSS. without approving it (in iii. lib. *Opp.* ii. 737). This would entirely exclude allection as a particular mode of acquiring citizenship, although there is no reason whatever to doubt of it.

(*p*) L. 6 *pr. ad mun.* (50, 51); L. 4, 5, C. *de municip.* (10–38). Dismission by the municipal authorities must have been as necessary as allection by them.

(*q*) L. 37, § 2; L. 38, § 3 *ad mun.* (50, 51); L. 1 *C. de mun.* (10–62).

(*r*) L. 23 *pr.*; L. 22, § 4, 5, *ad mun.* (50, 1).

(*s*) L. 3, § 1; L. 4, § 3, *de muner.* (50, 4).

(*t*) This proposition appears to contradict Cicero, *pro Balbo*, cap. ii.: 'Duarum civitatum civis esse nostro jure civili nemo potest.' But in this passage he speaks of communities outside of the Roman state, which subsisted as sovereign states alongside of it. We speak of communities within the Roman empire.

On the other hand, however, it was conceivable that a person might have citizenship in no community, although certainly this case did not often occur. It necessarily took place when a foreigner was received as a resident into the Roman empire without becoming by allection a citizen of any municipality (note *o*); so, too, when the citizen of any town was released from its municipal connection (note *p*) without being received into another community; finally, among the freedmen of the lowest class, who were *dedititiorum numero*, and belonged to no community (*u*).

SECT. IX.—(§ 352.)

THE ROMAN DOCTRINE OF ORIGO AND DOMICILIUM.

I. ORIGO (*continuation*).

The great difference which originally existed between the constitution of the cities of Italy and of the provinces might easily lead to the erroneous supposition, that the rules here stated extended only to the municipal territories and citizenship in Italy, not in the provinces; but in fact there was hardly any difference.

The municipal territories (*territoria*) were just as clearly defined in almost all the provinces (*a*) as in Italy. Their

(*u*) Ulpian, xx. § 14. [Bar (pp. 75–77) disputes the correctness of these three categories of persons without *origo*, and argues that every inhabitant of the empire must have belonged as an 'active or a passive citizen' to some municipal territory. His remarks on the first two heads are inconclusive. He thinks it probable that the *dedititii* generally belonged to some *civitas*, 'if not as active, yet as passive citizens. Otherwise they would have enjoyed an immunity from municipal burdens, the existence of which cannot easily be admitted in regard to a class of persons in other respects under such serious disabilities. As they were reckoned among the freedmen (Puchta, *Inst.* ii. § 213), it is probable that they belonged to the *civitas* in which their patron had his special citizenship.']

(*a*) Egypt, which had a constitution distinguished in every respect by great restrictions, must be excepted. Thus it had no proconsul or proprætor, but only a *præfectus augustalis* of lower rank (Dio Cass. 51, 17; 53, 13; Tacitus, *Hist.* 1, 11; *Digest.* 1, 17). In like manner there were only districts (Nomes), no urban communities, and only in Alexandria was there a right of citizenship (Plinius, *Epist.* x. 5, 22, 23).

limits, as well as their influence on the liability to municipal burdens, particularly in the villages belonging to the cities, frequently gave occasion to lawsuits even in the provinces. In this respect only is a distinction noticed, that in many provinces, especially in Africa, the municipal territories did not exhaust the whole soil of the country; since there were there in the possession of many private persons, as well as of the Emperor, very extensive tracts of country devoted to pasture (*saltus*), which were quite independent districts, and belonged to no urban territory (*b*).

This doctrine of municipal citizenship arising by birth, manumission, etc., is laid down by the ancient jurists in regard to provincial towns, without distinguishing them in any way from those of Italy (*c*). The same may be said of the application of this law to municipal burdens, as well as to the exemptions from these burdens (*vacatio* and *immunitas*) (*d*).

Against so manifold and unambiguous testimonies, a passage of Ulpian is wrongly alleged, to prove that in the provinces no regard was paid to *jus originis*, but only to *domicilium* (*e*).

We may here make an observation (which is not unimportant for the understanding of our law sources) as to the meaning of the phrases *municipium* and *municeps*.—The original meaning of these words has been doubtful and controverted not merely in modern times; it was so among the Romans themselves. These doubts are partly of a verbal, partly of a real, and therefore of an historical nature (*f*).

(*b*) Agennius Urbicus, *de controversiis agrorum*, pp. 84, 85 of the *Gromatici veteres*, ed. Lachmann, Berol. 1848.

(*c*) L. 1, § 2; L. 37, *pr. ad mun.* (50, 1), (Ilium, Delphi, Pontus); L. 2, *C. de municip.* (10, 38), (*Aquitanian towns*); L. 7, § 10, *de interd. et releg.* (48, 22).

(*d*) L. 8, *pr.* L. 10, § 1, *de vacat.* (50, 5); L. 5, § 1, *de j. immunitatis* (50, 6).

(*e*) L. 190, *de V. S.* (50, 16): 'Provinciales eos accipere debemus, qui in provincia domicilium habent, *non eos, qui in provincia oriundi sunt.*' This passage, like so many others of the same title, has in the Digest a false appearance of generality, while originally it could have only a particular application, which cannot now be ascertained. Compare upon this passage, *Gundlingiana*, St. 31, N. 2, pp. 34–43; Conradi *Parerga*, pp. 488–506; Hollweg, *Versuche*, p. 6. In the prohibition of marriage between Roman provincial officials and the women of the province, the terms of L. 38 *pr. de ritu nupt.* (23, 2), are directly the reverse: 'inde oriundam, *vel* ibi domicilium habentem uxorem ducere non potest;' where it is quite an arbitrary proceeding to explain, as many do, the *vel* by *id est*.

(*f*) See especially Niebuhr, *Hist. of Rome*, ii. 36–88, 3d Engl. ed.

But for our purpose we may omit this difficult investigation, as the usage of the words was afterwards fixed beyond a doubt in the following way. After the *Lex Julia* conferring citizenship on all Italians, *municipium* was the regular designation of one principal class of Italian cities,—those, namely, which had not been first founded as communities from Rome, in contradistinction to the other principal class, the *coloniæ* (*g*). The name *municipium*, which is not rare even in the provinces, was by no means generally transferred to them at the time when citizenship was communicated to the whole empire, and consequently to all the communities. If, then, an urban community in general were to be indicated without distinguishing between *municipia* and *coloniæ*, between Italy and the provinces, the regular phrases for that were *respublica* and *civitas*. *Municeps*, however, appears in the ancient jurists as the common term for every citizen of such a community, without respect to the distinction just mentioned, and therefore has the same generality as the phrases *respublica* and *civitas* (*h*). For this difference in the extension of the two kindred phrases a satisfactory reason can be assigned. If only the inhabitants of the proper *municipia* had been called *municipes*, hardly

See also a programme of Rudorff, which is printed as preface to the Latin *Lectionskatalog* of the University of Berlin for the winter Semester of 1848.

(*g*) In the *Lex Julia Municipalis* the regular and repeated enumeration of the urban communities in Italy is as follows: *municipium, colonia, præfectura, forum, conciliabulum.* Haubold, *Monumenta Legalia*, N. xvi. It is nearly the same in the *Lex Rubria* (*ib.* N. xxi.).

(*h*) L. 1, § 1, *ad mun.* (50, 1). 'Et proprie quidem municipes appellantur muneris participes, recepti in civitatem, ut munera nobiscum facerent; sed *nunc abusive municipes dicimus suæ cujusque civitatis cives, utputa Campanos, Puteolanos.*' (In § 2 the same phraseology is applied to Ilium and Delphi.) So, too, in L. 23 *pr. eod.* The *abusive* has here a twofold meaning: First (and this is Ulpian's main intention), in contradistinction to the original, antiquated signification above referred to, which is indicated in Ulpian's preceding words. But, secondly, in this other meaning, that *municeps* was applied not merely to *municipia*, but also to colonies and provincial towns. These last occur in § 2; but Puteoli was certainly a colony since the time of Nero. Tacitus, *Ann.* xiv. 27. In the first reference, the abusive phraseology (*municeps* for *civis* in general) occurs as early as Cicero, *ad fam.* xiii. 11: 'meos municipes Arpinates;' *pro Cluentio*, 16: 'municipum suorum dissimillimus;' and *de legibus*, ii. 2. A very accurate distinction is made in the *Lex Julia Municipalis*, lin. 145 (Haubold, p. 129): 'municipes, coloni, et qui ejus præfecturæ erant' (comp. lin. 159–163). And yet this very law may have mainly conduced to the later general signification of the expression *municipes*, as it embraced the citizens of Italian towns of all classes without distinction, and at the same time bore the name, Lex Julia *Municipalis*.

another name would have remained for the inhabitants of the towns in general except *civis* (*i*), analogous with *civitas*, which, in fact, denoted every urban community without distinction. But the word *civis* was here less available, because in the classification of *cives*, *Latini*, *peregrini*, it had with the old jurists too important and indispensable a place to allow of its being employed for another purpose, which would have led to many ambiguities.

Municeps, therefore, became the general term for every possessor of any municipal citizenship out of Rome, and therefore for all those persons whose common connection with an urban community is very commonly expressed by *origo* or *patria*.

This kind of connection with an urban community received a very peculiar extension after the right of Roman citizenship had been given by the *Lex Julia* to all Italy, and by an ordinance of Caracalla to all the provinces also. For, as the Roman *civitas* in its original sense was the citizenship of the city of Rome, almost all municipal citizens in Italy and in the provinces, who, besides this, might happen to have already a plural citizenship (§ 351), had now at least two: that of their own city, and that of Rome. This double *patria* is also expressly recognised at very different periods (*k*). This relation, however, was of less importance than might at first be supposed. In regard to the citizenship of Rome, the municipal burdens and duties (*munera*), so heavy in other cities, came little into view, as these were mostly provided for there in a different manner. The jurisdiction founded upon citizenship (*forum originis*) before the courts of the city of Rome, certainly existed for the inhabitants of other cities, yet only under great limitations. It was sustained only when these municipals happened to be sojourning in Rome, and even then only with numerous reservations, which were included under the common name of the *jus revocandi domum* (*l*). Finally, the application of the local law of the city of Rome to the persons of the

(*i*) This expression actually occurs in L. 7, *C. de incolis* (10, 39).

(*k*) Cicero, *de legibus*, ii. 2: 'Omnibus municipibus duas esse censeo patrias, unam naturæ, alteram civitatis . . . habuit alteram loci patriam, alteram juris.' L. 33, *ad mun.* (50, 1), (Modestinus): 'Roma communis nostra patria est.' Cicero speaks only of *municipes* from Italy; Modestinus speaks quite generally (nostra); each according to the law of his time.

(*l*) L. 28, § 4, *ex quibus caus.* (4, 6); L. 2, §§ 3–6, *de jud.* (5, 1); L. 24–28, *eod.*

citizens of other places (the proper objects of our whole present inquiry), can only be fully treated of below (§ 357) in a wider connection.

It would, however, be incorrect to assume from this new combination that, in fact, all free inhabitants of the Roman empire must have had at least the citizenship of Rome (as *cives Romani*). For even after the ordinance of the Emperor Caracalla as to the *civitas*, there was still always no small number of persons who entered anew into lower classes, and by whom, therefore, these classes were constantly preserved; partly as new *Latini* and *peregrini* were created by incomplete manumission (*m*), partly by immigration of foreigners into the Roman empire, upon whom citizenship was not at once conferred when they were received as subjects.

The proposition above laid down (§ 351) is true, therefore, for all periods, that free inhabitants of the Roman empire could be without any right of citizenship in any municipality, although, indeed, its practical application became in course of time rarer and less important.

SECT. X.—(§ 353.)

THE ROMAN DOCTRINE OF ORIGO AND DOMICILIUM.

II. DOMICILIUM.

Sources (see above, § 350).

Authors.

LAUTERBACH, *de domicilio*, 1663 (Diss. vol. ii. N. 72).
THOMASIUS, *de vagabundo* (Diss. vol. i. N. 3).
GLUCK, vol. vi. §§ 512–515.
KIERULFF, vol. i. pp. 122–128.

The second reason whereby individuals became attached to an urban community was domicile (*domicilium*) (*a*).

(*m*) Justinian abolished these imperfect manumissions (*Cod.* vii. 5, 6), of which the effects had continued down to his times, not only in the slaves themselves who were so manumitted, but also in their descendants.

(*a*) I think *Wohnsitz* more expressive, and therefore better than

That place is to be regarded as a man's domicile which he has freely chosen for his permanent abode, and thus for the centre at once of his legal relations and his business (*b*). The term *permanent* abode, however, excludes neither a temporary absence nor a future change, the reservation of which faculty is plainly implied; it is only meant that the intention of mere transitory residence must not at present exist.

Domicilium, like *origo*, established a connection with a particular urban community. It therefore related to a definite urban territory (*c*), and embraced not only the inhabitants of the city itself, but also those of the villages and farms (*coloniæ*) belonging to this territory (*d*).

For persons who became attached in this way to an urban community the regular designation is *Incola* (*e*). The two different grounds, however, by which such a connection could be established (citizenship and domicile), are distinguished by the following contrasted terminology:

Wohnort; but I cannot admit a difference in the meaning of the two terms (Linde, § 88, note *l*). The distinction of mere residence will be immediately mentioned and more closely defined. The doctrine of *domicilium* is here, like that of *origo*, expounded chiefly in its connection with Roman law. But as it will appear below that in modern law domicile occupies in its leading principles the same position as in Roman law, it seemed proper even here to consider the modern law also.

(*b*) L. 7, *C. de incolis* (10, 39), (see above, § 350, *f*): 'Incolas vero . . . domicilium facit. Et in eo loco singulos habere domicilium non ambigitur, ubi quis larem rerumque ac fortunarum suarum summam constituit, unde rursus non sit discessurus, si nihil avocet, unde quum profectus est, peregrinari videtur, quo si rediit, peregrinari jam destitit.' L. 203, *de V. S.* (50, 16): '. . . sed de ea re constitutum esse, eam domum unicuique nostrum debere existimari, ubi quisque sedes et tabulas haberet, suarumque rerum constitutionem fecisset.' [See Note A at end of section.]

(*c*) L. 3, 5, 6, *C. de incolis* (10, 39).

(*d*) L. 239, § 2, *de V. S.* (50, 16): 'Nec tantum hi qui in oppido morantur, incolæ sunt, sed etiam qui alicujus oppidi finibus, ita agrum habent, ut in eum se quasi in aliquam sedem, recipiant.' An apparent contradiction is found in L. 27, § 1, L. 35, *ad mun.* (50, 1), which allow to the inhabitant of a *colonia* the domicile of the city, only when, by a more lengthened residence in the city, he enjoys its advantages and comforts. This limitation, however, is owing without doubt to an inaccuracy of expression, and does not extend to domicile itself, but only to a peculiar effect of it, the participation in certain kinds of municipal burdens. For, certainly, no one doubted that the inhabitants of the *coloniæ* had their *forum* (*f. domicilii*) before the municipal authorities. Comp. below, § 355, *m*.

(*e*) L. 5, 20, *ad mun.* (50, 1); L. 239, § 2, *de V. S.* (50, 16), (note *d*); L. 7, *de incolis* (10, 39), (note *b*).

Municipes and *Incolæ* (*f*).
Origo and *Domicilium* (*g*).
Jus originis and *Jus incolatus* (*h*).
Patria and *Domus* (*i*).

From this definition results the essential distinction between domicile and mere residence on the one hand, and the ownership of land on the other. Residence, not accompanied with the present intention that it is to be permanent and perpetual, does not constitute domicile, even if by accident it continues for a long time, and therefore is not merely transient.[1] Such, for instance, is the residence of students at an educational institution; only when this continued for ten years was it, according to an ordinance of Hadrian, to be regarded as permanent, and therefore as constituting domicile (*k*). Ownership of land in a territory is not required for domicile, and by itself is insufficient to constitute it (*l*).

The constitution of domicile, with its legal consequences, is the result of free will and the act corresponding therewith, not

(*f*) L. 6, § 5, *de mun.* (50, 4). As to the expression *municipes*, see above, § 352, *g*; as to *incolæ*, note *e*. The language of Paulus is inaccurate in L. 22, § 2, *ad mun.* (50, 1), where he names mere inhabitants *municipes* (instead of *incolæ*), only meaning to say that they also have to bear the municipal burdens.

(*g*) L. 7, § 10, *de interd. et releg.* (48, 22); L. 6, § 3; L. 22, § 2, *ad mun.* (50, 1).

(*h*) L. 15, § 3, *ad mun.* (50, 1); L. 5, *C. de incolis* (10, 39).

(*i*) L. 203, *de V. S.* (50, 16).

[1] See Note B at end of section.

(*k*) L. 5, § 5, *de injur.* (47, 10); L. 2, 3, *C. de incolis* (10, 39). The ten years are, indeed, only a presumption of a purpose of constant residence. Lauterbach, *de domicilio*, § 27; [Westlake, § 51; Phillimore, iv. 90; Opp. in *Munro* v *Munro*, 1 Rob. 500, 518, 522.]

(*l*) L. 17, § 13; L. 22, § 7, *ad mun.* (50, 1); L. 4, *C. de incolis* (10, 39). Many cities had the privilege that mere ownership of land, without domicile, rendered persons liable to undertake personal *munera*. L. 17, § 5, *ad mun.* (50, 1). [See per Lord Stowell in *The Dree Gebrœders*, 4 Rob. Ad. 235. *Forbes* v *Forbes*, Kay 341, 23 L. J. Ch. 724; *Lord Adv.* v *Lamont*, 1857, 19 D. 557; *Tulloh* v *Tulloh*, 1861, 23 D. 639; *Rose* v *Ross*, July 16, 1830, 4 W. and S. 289. But though this is so, the purchase of land, the prospect of succession to a family estate, especially at the domicile of origin, and still more the possession of family estate, by one residing in a different country, have been repeatedly regarded as, along with other circumstances, important criteria of the *animus manendi*. See *Aikman* v *Aikman*, 1859, 21 D. 757, 3 Macq. 852, 858, 878; *Udny* v *Udny*, Dec. 14, 1866, 5 Macph. 164; *Munro* v *Munro* and *Macdouall* v *Dalhousie*, 1837, 16 S. 7, 18; 1 Rob. 475, 492; *Moorhouse* v *Lord*, 10 H. of L. 272, 32 L. J. Ch. 295; *Somerville* v *Somerville*, 5 Ves. 750, 787; *Jopp* v *Wood*, 34 L. J. Ch. 212.]

therefore of a mere declaration of intention without any act (*m*). Freedom of choice is in this matter so strictly required, that it must not be at all restrained by provisions of private law, *e.g.* by the condition of a particular residence annexed to a legacy, which condition is generally to be regarded as not written (*n*). On the other hand, this freedom may in many ways be restricted by the public law. Thus every servant of the state, *e.g.* every soldier, has a necessary domicile at the place of his service (*o*); the exile at the place of his banishment (*p*). Conversely, a certain residence may be forbidden by way of punishment (*q*).

But further, domicile could be constituted in the following cases by the relation in which a person stood to another person and his domicile; and this may be called a relative domicile:

1. Wives have universally and necessarily the same domicile as their husbands (*r*). This domicile is retained by the widow so long as she does not enter into a new marriage, or otherwise voluntarily change her domicile (*s*).

2. Children born in wedlock have unquestionably from their birth the same domicile as their father. They may, however, afterwards freely choose another domicile, when their

(*m*) L. 20, *ad mun.* (50, 1): 'Domicilium re et facto transfertur, non nuda contestatione; sicut in his exigitur, qui negant se posse ad munera, ut incolas, vocari.' [See Note C at end of section.]

(*n*) L. 31, *ad mun.* (50, 1); L. 71, § 2, *de cond.* (35, 1). See above, vol. iii. p. 184.

(*o*) L. 23, § 1, *ad mun.* (50, 1). [See Note D at end of section.]

(*p*) L. 22, § 3, *ad mun.* (50, 1).

(*q*) L. 31, *ad mun.* (50, 1); L. 7, § 10, *de interd. et releg.* (48, 22). When it is said in L. 27, § 3, *ad mun.* (50, 1), that the *relegatus* retains his previous domicile, this means merely that he is not freed by the punishment from liability to his former burdens. [In modern law an exile does not acquire a domicile in the country in which he has lived as an emigrant with an intention of returning to his native country as soon as he may safely do so. *De Bonneval* v *De Bonneval*, 1 Curt. Ec. 856. As to the domicile of the prisoner, the exile, and the lunatic, see Phillimore, iv. 127, 128, 91; Westlake, §§ 38, 52, 53. On the subject of the lunatic's domicile, reference may be made to cases as to lunatics' settlement under the Poor Laws. See *The King* v *Much Cowarne*, 2 B. and Ad. 861. Scotch cases in Guthrie Smith, *On the Poor Law*, p. 221 sq.]

(*r*) L. 5 *de ritu nuptiarum* (23, 2); L. 65 *de jud.* (5, 1); L. 38, § 3, *ad mun.* (50, 1); L. 9, *C. de incolis* (10, 38); L. 13, *C. de dignit.* (12, 1). This domicile is called the *domicilium matrimonii.* An invalid marriage does not constitute it, nor mere betrothal (*sponsalia*). L. 37, § 2; L. 32, *ad mun.* (50, 1). [See Note E at end of section.]

(*s*) L. 22, § 1, *ad mun.* (50, 1).

original one ceases (*t*). It must, in like manner, be said of natural children, that the domicile of the mother is to be regarded as theirs.[2]

3. So is it with freedmen. Their domicile was originally that of the patron (*u*); but they could afterwards change it at will (*v*).

4. In our modern relations, it is the same with hired servants (*w*); likewise with day-labourers working permanently on a particular estate, and the journeymen working with a master workman.

The *extinction* of a previous domicile takes place, like its constitution, by the free choice of the party. Commonly, though not universally and necessarily, this extinction will coincide with the establishment of a new domicile, and therefore in our law sources the extinction is termed translation (*x*).

NOTE A, p. 54.

The more important definitions of domicile will be found collected in Story, ch. iii.; Burge, vol. i. ch. ii.; Phillimore, iv. p. 41 seqq.; Westlake, ch. iii. See also M'Laren, *Law of Wills and Succession*, ch. i. (Edin. 1868). The definition of the code above cited is criticised by Kindersley, V.C., in *Lord* v *Colvin* (*Moorhouse* v *Lord*), 4 Drew. 366, 373, 423. See 10 H. of L. 272; *Whicker* v *Hume*, 7 H. of L. 159, 164. 'Domicile is a place of residence that cannot be referred to an occasional and temporary purpose;' per Lord Loughborough in *Bempdé* v *Johnson*, 3 Ves. J. 201. Donellus, *Com.* l. xvii. c. 12, p. 978, *b*, ed. Frankf. 1626, characterizes the definition in the *Code* as 'majore venustate quam certitudine definitionis,' and desiderates in it some test or criterion, 'unde sedem alicubi ita constitutam intelligamus ex quo illa sequuntur quæ dixi-

(*t*) L. 3; L. 4; L. 6, § 1; L. 17, § 11, *ad mun.* (50, 1). So they unquestionably follow the father, if he establishes a new domicile after their birth, as long as they themselves still belong to his household.

[2] As to the domicile of minors, see Phillimore, iv. 73 sqq. The mother's domicile is that of a child who lives with her after the death of the father, at least where there is no suspicion of fraud. *Pottinger* v. *Wightman*, 3 Mer. 67; *Arnott* v. *Groom*, 1846, 9 D. 142; 2 Kent's Com. 227 *n*, 431 *n*; Robertson on *Pers. Succ.* 198, 275. See however Bar, § 31, pp. 96, 97.

(*u*) L. 6, § 3; L. 22, *pr. ad mun.* (50, 1). On this last passage, comp. the treatise already cited above, § 351 *n*.

(*v*) L. 22, § 2; L. 27 *pr.*; L. 37, § 1, *ad mun.* (50, 1).

(*w*) Comp. the Prussian *Allg. Gerichtsordnung*, i. 2, § 13.

(*x*) L. 20, *ad mun.* (see above, Note C); L. 1, *C. de incolis* (10, 39). This variability is indicated by the expression *domicilii ratio temporaria*. L. 17, § 11, *ad mun.* (50, 1). [See Note F at end of section.]

mus. Pressius igitur et certius sic domicilium cujusque privatum recte definietur: *ut sit locus in quo quis habitat eo animo ut ibi perpetuo consistat nisi quid avocet.*'

NOTE B, p. 55.

'The gradation from residence to domicile consists both of circumstances and intention' (per Dr. Lushington in *Maltass* v *Maltass*, 1 Rob. 75); and however long residence at a place may continue, the presumption thus raised of an intention to be domiciled there, may, it would appear, be rebutted by evidence of a contrary intention. See *Hodgson* v *De Beauchesne*, 12 Moo. P. C. 283, 328; *Jopp* v *Wood*, 34 L. J. Ch. 212; *Drevon* v *Drevon*, 34 L. J. Ch. 133; *Udny* v *Udny*, Dec. 14, 1866, 5 Macph. 164; and cases cited *infra*, p. 62. 'The long duration of residence in one place is a material ingredient from which intention may be collected; but a person may live fifty years in a place and not acquire a domicile, for he may have had all the time an intention to return to his own country.'—Per Sir J. Dodson in *Bremer* v *Freeman*, 1 Deane 192, 219. 'Nulla tempora constituunt domicilium aliud cogitanti.'—D'Argentré, *Com.*, art. 449; cf. Mascard. *Concl.* 559, § 13, p. 249. See, however, *The Harmony*, 2 Rob. Ad. 322, 324, where Lord Stowell said, 'Time is the grand ingredient in constituting domicile.' Cf. *Cockerell* v *Cockerell*, 25 L. J. Ch. 730. Domicile in private international law requires to be distinguished from the residence to which municipal law assigns certain effects for various purposes, such as payment of taxes, the exercise of political rights, relief under the poor laws, etc. Thus Inglis, J. C., distinguishes domicile and settlement under the Scotch Poor Law Acts: 'The law of settlement is the creature of statute, and is regulated by statute throughout; the law of domicile depends on general principles of jurisprudence. What shall be held to be a party's settlement depends on matter of fact, and on that only; and the poor law . . . pays no regard to the intention of the pauper, or to the interest of the pauper . . . Whether a pauper has a residential settlement is a question of fact; and it must be determined by the answer to this further question, whether the pauper having a birth settlement to fall back upon, as every person born in Scotland has, has acquired by the fact of residing five years within another parish a settlement there, or has, by the fact of residing one year out of each succeeding five years, retained that settlement. The question of domicile depends on entirely different considerations. It is essential to consider what was the intention and purpose of the party, and mere physical fact alone is of no avail. A man's domicile requires to be determined in order to regulate his succession, or for some such purpose; and the main question in such an inquiry is, To what law did the person intend to subject himself, so that it should regulate his succession, and the like?'—*Crawford and Petrie* v *Beattie*,

1862, 24 D. 367. But this wide distinction does not seem to be countenanced by the actual decision of certain cases. See *Greig* v *Miles and Simpson*, July 19, 1867, 5 Macph. 1132. Phillimore, iv. 162, 176.

NOTE C, p. 56.

The President, 5 Rob. Ad. 279; *The Falcon*, 6 Rob. 198; *Stanley* v *Bernes*, 3 Hag. Cons. 447; *De Bonneval* v *De Bonneval*, 1 Curt. Eccl. 856, 868; *Anderson* v *Laneuville*, 9 Moo. P. C. 335; *Re Steer*, 3 H. and N. 594, 28 L. J. Ex. 22; *Drevon* v *Drevon*, 34 L. J. Ch. 131; *Pitt* v *Pitt*, Dec. 5, 1862, 1 Macph. 106; H. of L. April 6, 1864, 2 Macph. 28, 4 Macq. 627, etc.; *The Venus*, 8 Cranch, 253, 279–283, 3 Curt. 116. But written or spoken declarations of intention, made at the time, are often important items of evidence. After stating that no stress can be laid on casual expressions of preference for one country above another, which depend on the feelings at the moment, Lord Chelmsford observes: 'But I do lay very considerable stress on declarations made to parties to whom he would be likely to reveal his intentions, those declarations not being casual and occasional, but repeated from time to time, and evincing a strong determination to carry into effect the objects which he states.'—*Moorhouse* v *Lord*, 10 H. of L. 272, 32 L. J. Ch. 295; *Aikman* v *Aikman*, *Udny* v *Udny*, *supra*; *Lowndes* v *Douglas*, July 18, 1862, 24 D. 1391. When the person whose domicile is in question is living, he may be examined as a witness. *Maxwell* v *M'Clure*, Dec. 18, 1857, 20 D. 307, 3 Macq. 853; *Kennedy* v *Bell*, July 17, 1863, 1 Macph. 1127, revd. H. of L., May 14, 1868: cf. *Clarke* v *Territory of Washington*, 1 Wash. T. 82, 2 Abbott's *Nat. Dig.* 182; *Brodie* v *Brodie*, 2 Sw. and Tr. 259.

NOTE D, p. 56.

The modern rule rather is, that a soldier or sailor has a domicile in the country in whose service he is employed, even though stationed abroad. Where there are different laws within the same empire, an officer belonging to one of its provinces does not change his domicile merely by being quartered in another province in the course of his service. *Dalhousie* v *M'Douall*, 1837, 16 S. 6, 1 Rob. Ap. 475, 7 Cl. and Fin. 817; *Brown* v *Smith*, 15 Beav. 444, 21 L. J. Ch. 356: comp. *Somerville* v *Somerville*, 5 Ves. 750. Yet 'it may happen, though a military appointment be the cause of residence, that the residence is of that fixed and permanent sort which excludes the idea of any other domicile remaining, and necessarily induces a new domicile in the country where the residence is established.'—Per L. Pres. Hope in *Clark* v *Newmarsh*, 1836, 14 S. 488, 500 (Governor Trapaud's case); comp. *Ommanney* v *Bingham*, 5 Ves. 757, 3 Pat. Ap. 448 (Sir C. Douglas's case). This was probably the original ratio of the cases which established the doctrine (now regarded as anomalous; see per Kindersley, V.C., in *Drevon* v *Drevon*, 34 L. J. Ch. 129; *In re Capdevielle*, 33 L. J. Ex. 212, 2 H. and C. 982; comp. *infra*, Note F), that service in India or other colonies, requiring residence there, creates an Indian domicile. *Bruce* v *Bruce*, 6 Bro. 566, 2 B. and P. 230 *n*, 3 Pat. Ap. 163; *Munroe* v *Douglas*, 5 Madd. 379; *Craigie* v *Lewin*, 3 Curt. 435; *Commrs. of Inl. Rev.* v *Gordon*, 1850, 12 D. 657. But that doctrine had its origin at a time when the East India Company's was an independent, and almost a foreign service. See *Hook* v *Hook*, Feb. 7, 1862, 24 D. 488.

NOTE E, p. 56.

'Her abode and domicil followeth his.'—Stair, i. 4, 9. A doctrine long prevailed in Scotland, supported by the authority of Lord Brougham, that this domicile might be different from the husband's domicile for purposes of succession, and that jurisdiction in matrimonial causes, for example, might be founded by a domicile acquired by a temporary residence irrespective of the proper domicile of either spouse, or even by a mere residence of forty days required by a rule of process, sometimes called improperly a domicile of citation. *Utterton* v *Tewsh*, and other cases in Ferguson's *Cons. Rep.* 23, 68, 209, 226, etc.; *Warrender* v *Warrender*, 1834, 12 S. 847, 2 S. and M'L. 220, 2 Cl. and Fin. 520; *Jack* v *Jack*, 1862, 24 D. 467; *Pitt* v *Pitt*, 1862, 1 Macph. 106. This was corrected, however, by the House of Lords in the last cited case (2 Macph., H. of L. 28, 4 Macq. 627: cf. *Ringer* v *Churchill*, 1840, 2 D. 307; *Dolphin* v *Robins*, 1859, 3 Macq. 563, H. of L.), and the rule fixed, apparently, that nothing short of an absolute domicile can confer jurisdiction (comp. per Lord Deas, 24 D. 487). But observe the doubts of Lord Westbury, whether in every case the wife's domicile is by attraction or construction so inevitably and inflexibly the same as the husband's as to make her subject, for the purpose of divorce, to the tribunals of any country which he may choose. This probably saves the decision in *Jack* v *Jack*, and is supported by *Dolphin* v *Robins*, *supra*. Westlake, § 42; Phillimore, iv. 70; *Hume* v *Hume*, 1862, 24 D. 1342; Bar, § 31, p. 95; Bishop on *Marriage and Divorce*, § 728 sq.; *Harteau* v *Harteau*, 14 Pick. Mass. R. 181. See especially Fraser, *Conflict of Laws in Cases of Divorce*, p. 58 sqq., Edin. 1858. The wife retains the domicile of the husband as a rule, even though living apart by mutual agreement, unless there be a *judicial* separation. *Warrender* v *Warrender*, and *Dolphin* v *Robins*, *supra*; *Williams* v *Dormer*, 2 Robertson 505; *Hook* v *Hook*, 1862, 24 D. 488; *Tulloh* v *Tulloh*, 1861, 23 D. 639; *Barber* v *Barber*, 1858, 21 How. U. S. 582; *Yelverton* v *Yelverton*, 1859, 1 Sw. and Tr. 574. Lord Kingsdown, in *Dolphin* v *Robins*, held it an open question whether even a judicial separation would enable a wife to acquire a different domicile from the husband. But the preponderance of authority is in favour of the proposition as stated above. A betrothal to an Englishman was held not to change the domicile of a Scotchwoman, although she also resided in England three years before her death. *Arnott* v *Groom*, 1846, 9 D. 142.

NOTE F, p. 57.

The proposition at the end of the section is affirmed in *Kennedy* v *Bell*, H. of L., May 14, 1868. The tendency of British courts in the later cases has been to give less weight to circumstances formerly considered of importance as indicating an intention to change the domicile. 'The *animus* to abandon one domicile for another imports an intention not only to relinquish those peculiar rights, privileges, and immunities which the law and constitution of the domicile confers,—in the domestic relations, in purchases and sales, and other business transactions, in political or municipal status, and in the daily affairs of common life,—but also the laws by which succession to property is regulated after death. The abandonment or change of a domicile is therefore a proceeding of a very serious nature, and an intention to make such a change requires to be proved by very satisfactory evidence.'—Per Lord Curriehill in *Donaldson* v *M'Clure*, 1857, 20 D. 307, 321, aff. 3 Macq. 852; cf. per Lord Fullerton in *Arnott* v *Groom*, 1846, 9 D. 146, 148. It is so especially where the change of domicile is into a foreign country. 'You may much more easily suppose that a person having originally been living in Scotland, a Scotchman, means permanently to quit it and come to England, or *vice versâ*, than that he is quitting the United Kingdom in order to make his permanent home where he must for ever be a foreigner, and where there must always be . . . a complication, and a conflict between the duties he owes to one country and the duties that he owes to the other. Circumstances may be so strong as to lead irresistibly to the inference that a person does mean *quatenus in illo exuere patriam*.'—Per Lord Cranworth in *Whicker* v *Hume*, 7 H. of L. 124, 159. 'In order to acquire a new domicile . . . a man must intend *quatenus in illo exuere patriam*. . . . You do not lose your domicile of origin, or your resumed (*sic: qu.* assumed?) domicile, merely because you go to some other place that suits your health better, unless, indeed, you mean, either on account of your health or for some other motive, to cease to be a Scotchman, and become an Englishman, or a Frenchman, or a German.'—*Moorhouse* v *Lord*, 10 H. of L. 272, 283. See also *Aikman* v *Aikman*, 1859, 21 D. 757, 3 Macq. 854; *Pitt* v *Pitt*, 1864, 1 Macph. 106, rev. 2 Macph. H. of L. 28, 4 Macq. 627; *Drevon* v *Drevon*, 34 L. J. Ch. 129; *Hodgson* v *De Beauchesne*, 12 Moo. P. C. 285; *Jopp* v *Wood*, 34 L. J. Ch. 212; *Bremer* v *Freeman*, 1 Deane 192; *Attorney-General* v *Blucher*, 34 L. J. Ex. 29, etc.; M'Laren, *Law of Wills and Succession*, vol. i. p. 7.

It has been made a question whether the doctrine thus recently laid down by the House of Lords overrules that of Story (§ 46), frequently adopted by the tribunals, that 'if a person has removed to another place, with an intention of remaining there for an indefinite time, and as a place of fixed present domicile, it is to be deemed his place of domicile, *notwithstanding he may entertain a floating intention to return at some future period*,' or even 'a constant contemplation of returning at some distant and undefined period to his native country' (per Lords Glenlee, Moncreiff, etc., in *Munro* v *Munro*, *infra*). *In re Capdevielle*, 2 H. and C. 982, 33 L. J. Ex. 212. The doubts as to the extent of the doctrine to be deduced from *Moorhouse* v *Lord*, there expressed by Pollock, C. B., and Bramwell, B., are supported by earlier cases, such as *Bruce* v *Bruce*, 1790, M. 4617, Rob. *Pers. Suc.* 119, 183, 3 Pat. 163; *Stanley* v *Bernes*, 3 Hag. *Cons.* 438, 465; *Anderson* v *Laneuville*, 9 Moore, P. C. 325; *In re Steer*, 28 L. J. Ex. 22; *Munro* v *Munro*, 1837, 16 S. 35, 1 Rob. Ap. 523; *Shedden* v *Patrick*, 1852, 14 D. 721, 733; *Lord Advocate* v *Lamont*, 19 D. 779; *Lowndes* v *Douglas*, 1862, 24 D. 1391. See Westl. § 38, and *supra*, Note D, p. 59. There can, however, be no doubt that the law is now as above stated. The true doctrine appears to be that stated in the text, p. 54, which is consistent with the rule laid down by Lord Alvanley, M. R., in *Somerville* v *Somerville*, 5 Ves. 750, 786, that 'the domicile of origin is to prevail until the party has not only acquired another, but has manifested and carried into execution an intention of abandoning his former domicile, and taking another as his sole domicile;' and this intention, it is now held, must be an intention not merely to change the residence, but to adopt a new country. As to the revival of the domicile of origin while *in itinere* from an acquired domicile with the intention of residing permanently in the country of birth, see Story, § 48; Westlake, § 40; Fraser, *Personal and Domestic Relations*, i. 723; *Munro* v *Munro*, 1 Rob. 606; *Munroe* v *Douglas*, 5 Madd. 379, 405; *Lyall* v *Paton*, 25 L. J. Ch. 746.

SECT. XI.—(§ 354.)

THE ROMAN DOCTRINE OF ORIGO AND DOMICILIUM.

II. DOMICILIUM (*continuation*).

Domicile, as an independent ground of connection with a particular community, can exist simultaneously in regard to several localities, if a person uses several places alike as centres of his connections and affairs, and distributes his actual residence among them according to need. Many of the Roman jurists doubted the possibility of this; but at last it was allowed, although it was not forgotten that such a case was to be regarded as of rare occurrence (*a*).

Conversely, a person can be without a domicile in the sense of the word above defined, although this is certainly one of the rarer cases (*b*). It must be admitted in the following circumstances, in themselves very dissimilar:—

1. When a previous domicile is renounced, in order to go in quest of a new one, until this is chosen and actually constituted (*c*). This case is of little importance, on account of the generally short endurance of such an interval.

2. When a person has for a long time made travelling his occupation, without having any home as the permanent centre of his affairs, and to which he is wont regularly to return. This case, too, is of little importance, because it seldom occurs.

3. In the case of vagabonds or wanderers, who rove about without any settled way of life, seeking their subsistence for the most part by means uncertain and dangerous to the public welfare and security. This class is numerous and important, and is one of the greatest evils of our time (*d*).

The idea of domicile above laid down (§ 353) relates to the life of the natural man, and is not, therefore, properly ap-

(*a*) L. 5; L. 6, § 2; L. 27, § 2, *ad mun.* (50 1); C. 2, *pr. de sepult. in* VI. (3, 12).

(*b*) L. 27, § 2, *ad mun.* (50, 1).

(*c*) L. 27, § 2, *ad mun.* (50, 1). To this category belongs very often the case of a hired servant, day-labourer, or journeyman tradesman changing his service or his work, when such a change is accompanied by a change of residence (§ 353, Num. 4). [See below, § 359.]

(*d*) It is remarkable that in the sources of the Roman law there is no special mention of this class. Even the fugitive slaves (*errones, fugitivi*, L. 225 *de V. S.* 50, 16), who are often mentioned, cannot be reckoned in it, since these have in the legal sense a certain domicile—that, namely, of their masters. The explanation of this remarkable fact is, that the persons who with us are vagabonds (together with the greatest part of our *proletaires*) were included by the Romans in the slave class.—Thomasius, *de Vagabundo*, § 79, 91, 112, calls *vagabundus* every one who has no *domicilium*, and distinguishes him from the wanderer of doubtful character, quite contrary to the prevailing usage, which regards these two expressions as equivalent. No one will call the merchant who has given up his domicile to seek a new one, or the respectable traveller by profession, a vagabond. [Van Haesten, *de Vagabundis*, Ultraj. 1773; Phillimore, iv. 55.]

plicable to legal persons (*e*). Yet even to these it may become necessary to assign something corresponding or similar to the domicile of natural persons,—as it were an artificial domicile, especially in order to fix their forum (*f*). In most cases all doubt will be removed by the natural connection of the legal person with the soil: so it is in the case of towns and villages, churches, schools, hospitals, etc. There may be doubt in the case of industrial associations, if their activity is either fixed to no locality, or extends over great distances, as *e.g.* the case of railway companies, or steamboat companies, or companies for the building of bridges over great rivers, whose banks are often subject to different jurisdictions, different legislatures, or even different states. In such cases it is advisable at the first establishment of such a legal person to fix its artificial or constructive domicile (*g*); if this is neglected, the judge must endeavour to discover by construction the centre of its affairs.[1]

If we here compare the two separate grounds of connection with a particular community, citizenship, and domicile, the following possible combinations follow from the principles laid down for both (§§ 351–354):—

An individual could have the right of citizenship in one city, in several, or in none (§ 351).

Together with this, the same person could have a domicile in one city, in several, or in none (§ 354).

But it was certainly the regular and most usual case that a person had citizenship in one city only, where he had also his domicile.

(*e*) See above, vol. ii. § 85 foll.

(*f*) Comp. Linde, *Lehrbuch*, § 88, note 14.

(*g*) Examples: *Statut der Berlin-Sächsischen* (*Anhaltischen*) *Eisenbalm-Gesellschaft*, § 1: 'Berlin is its domicile and the seat of its administration, and the royal court of the city of Berlin its forum.'—*Statut der Berlin-Stettiner Eisenbalm-Gesellschaft*, § 3: 'Stettin is the domicile of the company,' etc. (*Gesetzsamml. für die Preussischen Staaten*, 1839, p. 178; 1840, p. 306.)

[1] This and other questions relating to corporations will be considered below, under § 373.

SECT. XII.—(§ 355.)

THE ROMAN DOCTRINE OF ORIGO AND DOMICILIUM—EFFECT OF THESE RELATIONS.

After having described the two grounds of connection with a particular community, the practical side of this doctrine, or the legal effect of that connection, has to be examined.

One might expect it to have for its result an equal proportion of rights and duties; and it is somewhat striking that the law sources treat almost exclusively of the obligations it imposes, not of the rights it confers. This is to be explained in the following manner:—The right of citizenship (*origo*) certainly involved rights which were originally very valuable, especially the exclusive right of sharing in municipal government by being eligible to the senate and magisterial offices. But in the later ages of the empire, the membership of these senates was transformed from an honour into a burden and a means of oppression (*a*). As to the magistrates of the municipalities, our law sources give us very scanty information; which is to be accounted for by the fact, that these books were designed entirely for the use of Justinian's empire, *i.e.* the East (*b*). On the other hand, the obligations originally attached to citizenship remained unchanged in the course of time, so that in our law sources they could be, and necessarily were, treated of in their entirety. But in regard to domicile, as the second bond of connection, nothing was said of rights properly so called; since it could be established by the mere will of the individual (§ 353), with which the acquisition of such rights was hardly consistent. In fact, also, even where the statement of definite rights might be expected, mere matter of fact advantages and enjoyments are enumerated as practical results of domicile (*c*).

There remain, therefore, for more particular consideration, only the obligations arising from this connection. These have

(*a*) Savigny, *Geschichte des R. R. im Mittelalter*, vol. i. § 8.
(*b*) *Ib.* § 22.
(*c*) L. 27, § 1, *ad mun.* (50, 1): 'Si quis . . . in illo (municipio) vendit, emit, contrahit, in eo foro, balneo, spectaculis utitur, ibi festos dies celebrat, omnibus denique municipii commodis . . . fruitur, ibi magis habere domicilium.' Comp. as to this passage, § 353. *d.*

already been indicated in a general way: Municipal Burdens, Jurisdiction, the Local Law (§ 350); and these three branches are now to be more minutely developed and established by reference to our law sources.

I. MUNICIPAL BURDENS (*munera*).

By the term *munera*, burdens of every kind are generally understood. Here, however, only those burdens are taken into account which arise from the public law, consequently only *publica*, not *privata* (*d*), and, in particular, from the personal connection with an urban community; whence also they are called *civilia munera* (*e*). It is not to be supposed, however, that these burdens were necessarily borne for municipal ends and advantages alone; for a great portion of the local administration of the state was imposed on the municipalities, and many of the most oppressive municipal burdens were employed only for the purposes of the state, not of the municipalities themselves by whose members they were borne (*f*).

The Roman jurists distinguish *munus* and *honor*, in that the former was not, like the latter, connected with a personal dignity (dignitas) (*g*). It must not be supposed, however, that in this distinction they mean that *honor* is to be regarded merely as honour and right, without constraint and obligation. In regard to the *honor*, there was the same obligation to undertake it as for the *munus* (*h*): the two were alike regarded as municipal burdens, and that distinction, therefore, applied to the name only.

They distinguish, moreover, personal burdens and patrimonial burdens (*munera personalia* and *patrimonii*), according as, on the one hand, the trouble and labour involved was solely

(*d*) L. 239, § 3, *de V. S.* (50, 16); L. 18, § 28, *de mun.* (50, 4). If, therefore, the *munera* are elsewhere divided into *publica* and *privata* (L. 14, § 1, *de mun.*), that is not a division of the *municipal* burdens (which are always *publica*), but of burdens in general, which certainly may originate in relations of private law.

(*e*) L. 18, § 28, *de mun.* (50, 4).

(*f*) Comp. *e.g.* L. 18, §§ 3, 4, 8, 16, *de mun.* (50, 4).

(*g*) L. 14 *pr.* § 1; L. 6, § 3, *de mun.* (50, 4). The term *honor*, however, was applied not only to the magistrates, but also to the decurions. L. 5, *de vac.* (50, 5).

(*h*) L. 3, §§ 2, 3, 15, 17, *de mun.* (50, 4).

or chiefly considered; or, on the other hand, the expenditure or risk affecting the estate (*i*). This distinction, however, was fluctuating and of uncertain limits (*k*), as well as unimportant, since the two kinds of burdens affected uniformly the members of every municipality, and only them. On the other hand, it is important clearly to distinguish from these the burdens which attached only to landed property (such as land taxes), whether the possessors belonged personally to the city (by *origo* or *domicilium*) or not (*l*).

The obligation to undertake municipal burdens normally affected *all* members of a municipality, whether they had entered into this relation by *origo* or by domicile (*m*). Whoever, therefore, had by *origo* the citizenship of several towns at once, or, it might be, had also a domicile in several (§§ 351, 354), was in each of these towns obliged fully to participate in its burdens, and might thereby come into a very disadvantageous position.

But although this general and uniform obligation of all members was the rule, there were yet, by way of exception, many exemptions on different grounds, and under different names (*vacatio, excusatio, immunitas*)—some perpetual and some temporary (*n*).

II. JURISDICTION (*forum originis, domicilii*).

At the foundation of this subject lies the general rule, that every lawsuit is to be brought in the forum of the defendant,

(*i*) L. 1, §§ 1, 2, 3, 4, *de mun.* (50, 4); L. 6, §§ 3, 4, 5 *eod.*; L. 18 *pr.* §§ 1–17 *eod.* Among the personal burdens was the administration of the judicial office, as well as that of tutory. L. 1, § 4; L. 18, § 14 *eod.*; L. 8, § 4; L. 13 *pr.* §§ 2, 3, *de vac.* (50, 5).

(*k*) Wherefore many added an intermediate class, *mixta munera.* L. 18 *pr.* §§ 18–27, *de mun.* (50, 4).

(*l*) L. 6, § 5, *de mun.* (50, 4); L. 14, § 2; L. 18, § 21–25; L. 29, 30 *eod.*; L. 10, *pr. de vac.* (50, 5); L. 11 *eod.* Somewhat different is the language of a passage in which these burdens on the soil are called *patrimonii munera.* *L. un. C. de mulier.* (10, 62).

(*m*) L. 22, § 2; L. 29, *ad mun.* (50, 1); L. 6, § 5; L. 18, § 22, *de mun.* (50, 4); L. 1, *C. de municip.* (10, 38); L. 4, 6, *C. de incolis* (10, 39). The varying statements of many passages as to the domicile of farm-houses in municipal bounds (§ 353, *d*) may arise from this, that a different principle of apportionment was adopted for many kinds of burdens, perhaps according to local divisions.

(*n*) *Dig. L.* 5 and 6; *Cod.* x. 44–64. The more minute examination of these exemptions may here be omitted, as it is unimportant for our present purpose.

not of the plaintiff (*o*). If it be asked, then, where the defendant has his regular forum, the Roman law determines it thus: In every town, whose magistrate he is bound to obey, because he belongs to it. But the individual belongs to a town as well by *origo* as by *domicile;* and thus that principle is transformed into the practical rule: A person may be cited as defendant in every town in which he has citizenship by *origo*, and also in every town in which he has a domicile. This rule is enunciated precisely in these terms, and also referred to the higher principle above assigned, in the following passage of Gaius (*p*): 'Incola et his magistratibus parere debet, apud quos incola est, et illis apud quos civis erit; nec tantum municipali jurisdictioni in utroque municipio subjectus est, verum etiam omnibus publicis muneribus fungi debet.'

In this important passage it is recognised that the forum is in precisely the same position as the municipal burdens. It follows, therefore, that there could be jurisdiction over the same person in more than two towns at the same time; if, for instance, he had citizenship by *origo* in several towns, and at the same time domicile in several others. It was, then, in the free choice of the plaintiff in which of these *civitates* he would make a lawsuit depend, and the defendant was bound to answer in any place that might be selected.

In regard to this unambiguous enunciation as well of the rule itself as of its higher principle, and of its connection with the municipal burdens, it is remarkable that so little is said in other passages of the jurisdiction founded upon mere *origo* (*forum originis*), as distinguished from domicile. In many passages in which the personal forum is mentioned for particular cases and incidentally, only the *forum domicilii*, not the *forum originis*, is spoken of (*q*). Yet this need not make us doubtful as to the rule itself; it is rather to be explained by the following reasons:—In the first place, that rule had com-

(*o*) *Vat. Fragm.* 325, 326; L. 2, *C. de jurisd.* (3, 13); L. 3, *C. ubi in rem* (3, 19); L. 3, 4, *C. ubi causa status* (3, 22).

(*p*) L. 29, *ad mun.* (50, 1).

(*q*) L. 19, § 4, *de jud.* (5, 1); L. 29, § 4, *de inoff. test.* (5, 2); L. 1, 2, *de reb. auct. jud.* (42, 5); *Vat. Fragm.* 326; L. 2, *C. de jurisd.* (3, 13); L. 1, *C. ubi res her.* (3, 20); L. 4, *C. ubi causa status* (3, 22). On the other hand, several passages mention the choice of the plaintiff between the *forum domicilii* and the *forum contractus*. L. 19, § 4, *de jud.* (5, 1); L. 1, 2, 3, *de reb. auct. jud.* (42, 5).

plete application only in Italy, not in the provinces, in which there were no municipal magistrates with jurisdiction (*r*). Here, therefore, *origo* could found no jurisdiction; while, on the contrary, the abstract notion of domicile was just as applicable to the territory of a province, and therefore to the jurisdiction of the imperial governor, as to the territory of a particular town. But several of the passages cited expressly speak of the provinces only (*s*); and others may also have spoken of them, although in their present form it is not apparent. In the second place, perhaps, the application of the *forum originis* to one who had *origo* and *domicilium* in two different municipalities, was always limited to the case in which he happened to be found in the town to which he belonged by *origo* (*t*). But even if such a restrictive rule of law had not existed, the plaintiff must still, for his own interest, have preferred the *forum domicilii*, because the defendant was more easily and conveniently reached in the place of his domicile.

But, in conclusion, it must still be remarked, that the rules here laid down, although they have been established, for the most part, by the testimonies of the ancient jurists preserved in the Digests, can yet claim certain and universal authority only from the time when the confirmed and fully developed government of the emperors had introduced a high degree of uniformity into the various parts of the empire. It is therefore quite compatible with them, that many provinces in earlier times, soon after their subjection to the Roman empire, enjoyed peculiar privileges in the judiciary system, of which no trace is now to be found in our law sources (*u*).

(*r*) It was later that the *defensores* received here a kind of jurisdiction, which long remained very limited, and was first raised to somewhat greater importance by Justinian. Savigny, *Geschichte des R. R. im Mittelalter*, vol. ii. § 23.

(*s*) So *e.g.* among the passages cited in note *q*; L. 19, § 4, *de jud.* (5. 1); L. 29, § 4. *de inoff.* (5, 2): *Vat. Fragm.* 326.

(*t*) So was it with the *forum originis* in the city of Rome (§ 352. *k*); and it is perhaps only accidental that no mention is found of a similar rule for other cities.

(*u*) This is the case in regard to Sicily. Cicero, *in Verrem*, act. 2, lib. 2, c. 13, 24, 25, 37.

Sect. XIII.—(§ 356.)

THE ROMAN DOCTRINE OF ORIGO AND DOMICILIUM—EFFECT OF THESE RELATIONS.

(CONTINUATION.)

III. THE PARTICULAR LAW OF A COMMUNITY AS A QUALITY OF THE PERSONS BELONGING TO IT (*lex originis, domicilii*).

In our general statement, three effects of a person's connection with an urban community have been assigned (§ 350): Municipal Burdens, Jurisdiction, and, finally, the Law of the Community as a Quality of the Person. The first two effects have already been explained in detail (§ 355); and it still remains to examine the third, which alone belongs to our present subject, and for the sake of which the whole foregoing discussion was undertaken, since it is only in this way that the subordination of the person to the local law of a particular city can be understood in its true connection.

This inquiry arises out of the proposition, that every person is subject to a particular positive law (§ 345); but this law is to be regarded principally as local or territorial (§ 350), and, according to the Roman system, as connected with an urban territory (§ 351). Since, then, every person could belong to an urban territory either by citizenship (*origo*) or by domicile (§ 351), so in these two ways also could his subordination to the territorial law of a city be determined.

Hence an intimate connection between the three different effects above enumerated, and especially between the two last effects of attachment to an urban territory (jurisdiction and territorial law); because both are to be regarded only as different sides of the totality of the local law. But the recognition of this intimate connection is important for our whole task, and even reaches beyond the proper Roman system, so as to be applicable in the exposition of the modern law.

I will now endeavour to show the correctness of this assertion, as well as its more particular development, in the sources of the Roman law. Certainly the utterances of the Roman jurists upon this question are very scanty; and the more so, as on critical examination we are compelled to put aside, as belonging to other subjects, very many passages which apparently refer to it. Besides, these few sentences could scarcely suffice completely to discover the views of the Romans.

1. The oldest case belonging to this subject relates to the collision of a positive Roman law with the law of other sovereign, yet allied, states (§ 348) (*a*).

In the year of the city 561 (S. Cornelio Merula, Q. Minucio Thermo, Coss.), there was great distress in Rome among debtors oppressed by usury. There were, indeed, protective usury laws, but these were evaded by the usurers taking their obligations in the names of inhabitants of neighbouring states (*socii* and *Latini*); for as these were not bound by the positive law as to usury, debtors had no protection against them (*b*). To check this dishonest proceeding, a special law was passed, providing that the Roman laws as to usury should be binding also upon the *socii* and *Latini*, as creditors of Roman citizens (*c*).

2. Of a similar nature is the rule of law recognised in a *senatus consultum* of the age of Hadrian, that the child of a marriage contracted *secundum leges moresque peregrinorum* is born a foreigner (and therefore belongs to his father), even when the mother (but not the father) had obtained citizenship at the time of the birth. Here, therefore, the principle of the Roman law, that the status of the *legitime conceptus* was to be determined as at the time of conception, was applied with complete reciprocity to the citizens of foreign states (*d*).

The following cases relate to the collision of the positive laws of Italy with the law of the provinces; consequently to a collision of laws within the limits of the Roman state.

3. The obligation of a *fidepromissor* did not in most cases, like that of a *fidejussor*, pass to his heirs; but exceptionally this transmission took place when the *fidepromissor* was a foreigner,

(*a*) Livius, xxxv. 7.

(*b*) What usury law, according to date, is here meant, cannot be determined, in the great uncertainty in which the history of these laws is involved. It may be that as to *unciarium fœnus*, or that as to *semunciarium*. For our present purpose the question is unimportant.

(*c*) Livius, *l. c.*: 'Plebesque scivit, ut cum sociis et nomine Latino pecuniæ creditæ jus idem, quod cum civibus Romanis esset.'

(*d*) Gaius, i. § 92, compared with § 89.

and belonged to a provincial town whose positive law differed in this respect from the Roman law (*e*).

4. A *Lex Furia* had appointed that the obligation of the *sponsores* and *fidepromissores* should be extinguished by the lapse of two years, as well as that several co-sureties of this kind should only be bound in part, not for the whole debt. This law, however, applied only to Italy, not to the provinces (*f*); that is, it was binding only for the citizens of municipalities in Italy, not for the citizens of provincial towns, even when these had the Roman citizenship (*g*).

5. There was a class of freedmen who became by manumission neither *cives* nor *Latini*, but only *peregrini*, and that with quite peculiar restrictions (*dedititiorum numero*). Of these it is said that they could make no testament, neither as Roman citizens, because they had not that rank; nor as *peregrini*, because they were not citizens of any particular town, so as to be able to test according to its municipal law (*h*). The reason of this is to be found apparently in the following assumption :—If this *peregrinus* were the citizen of a provincial town which recognised the right of testing and prescribed certain rules for it, he could, by observing these rules, make a valid testament as well in Rome as in his native city. But he cannot do so, because he is not a citizen of any municipality (§ 351, *n*).

(*e*) Gaius, iii. § 120: 'Praeterea sponsoris et fidepromissoris heres non tenetur, nisi si de peregrino fidepromissore quaeramus, *et alio jure civitas ejus utatur*.' It might be remarked that, in stating the rule, the *sponsor*, as well as the *fidepromissor*, is named, but is not afterwards mentioned in the exception. This is explained by the circumstance, that *peregrini* could not be *sponsores* at all. Gaius, iii. § 93.

(*f*) Gaius, iii. §§ 121, 122.

(*g*) The *sponsores*, who are assumed to be provincials in §§ 121, 122, must necessarily have had the Roman *civitas*; see above, note *e*. Rudorff attempts to give the *Lex Furia* a narrower limitation (*Zeitschrift*, xiv. p. 441), according to which it would no longer belong to this place. The more minute investigation of this point would lead us too far.

(*h*) Ulpian, xx. § 14: 'Latinus Junianus, item is qui dedititiorum numero est, testamentum facere non potest . . . qui dedititiorum numero est, quoniam nec quasi civis Romanus testari potest, cum sit peregrinus, nec quasi peregrinus, *quoniam nullius certae civitatis civis est, ut adversus leges civitatis suae testetur*.' Instead of the evidently correct reading, *civis est*, the manuscript reads *sciens*, which many have tried to defend in a forced and unsatisfactory manner. *Adversus* means here not, 'against,' 'in violation of,' but, 'in conformity with,' 'in terms of,' these laws. Just so in L. 5, *de usurp.* (41, 3). Others would correct it to *secundum*. See Lachmann, *Zeitschrift*, ix. p. 203.

6. Finally, the well-known fact may still be mentioned, that the peculiar marriage law of the Latin cities was lost when these obtained the Roman citizenship (*i*).

It would be very rash to seek to deduce, from these few isolated sentences, exhaustive rules for the treatment of the collision of different territorial laws; yet the following leading points of view cannot be mistaken:—

A. In a contract between two citizens of different states, the purely positive law of the foreign state cannot be opposed to either of the parties; they are rather to be judged according to the *jus gentium* (*k*). Yet, for political reasons, the contrary may be prescribed in particular cases (No. 1).

B. The right of citizenship in a particular town usually determines for each individual to what positive law he is personally subject, and according to which, therefore, he must be judged (Nos. 3, 4, and 5).

There are two other kinds of dicta of the Roman jurists, which may easily be regarded as rules relating to the observance of the local law, but which are not so in fact; so that it is necessary to give a special warning against their employment in the present inquiry.

1. Those isolated passages which, in the interpretation and application of juridical facts, refer us to local *customs*, but which would be wrongly understood of local *rules of law*. So, in the interpretation of an indefinite or ambiguous contract, that is to be understood as the probable intention of the parties which is usually practised in the district (*l*). Yet by this is evidently meant, not the rule of law in that district, but rather that to which people are there actually accustomed, which they are in the habit of doing often. One important application of this general rule of construction is found in the warranties which sellers of valuable commodities have to give: these also must be in accordance with the custom of the country, *i.e.*

(*i*) Gellius, lib. 4, c. 4.
(*k*) Comp. above, § 348, *c*.
(*l*) L. 34, *de R. I.* (50, 17): '. . . id sequamur, quod in regione in qua actum est *frequentatur*.'

similar to the securities which it is the custom voluntarily to grant (*m*).

Further, the amount of moratory interest is to be determined according to the usual rate of interest in the locality at the time (*n*). Exactly in the same way, the amount of interest which a factor may charge on the cash he advances (*o*). In both passages it is not a local rule of law that is spoken of by which the rate of interest is there determined, but the rate of interest as it was at the moment in the money market of the place. The reason of this rule was, that that interest was intended to give the lender a real compensation for the use of his money; which compensation could only be measured by the profit he could otherwise have obtained from the actual possession of it.

2. But, secondly, those passages are much more important which speak of the three classes of free inhabitants of the Roman empire (*cives, Latini, peregrini*), and which might possibly be regarded as determining the subordination of individuals to a particular positive law. For from this division might arise the idea that the *jus civile* was administered to the first class (*cives*), and the *jus gentium* to the two inferior classes. But this idea must be entirely rejected. That classification was extremely important for the capacity of individuals to have rights, since the *cives* had *connubium* and *commercium*, the *Latinus* had *commercium* without *connubium*, the *peregrinus* neither of these two capacities (*p*). On the other hand, that classifica-

(*m*) L. 6, *de evict.* (21, 2). For the same reason such a guarantee, the *duplæ stipulatio*, was, at least in regard to important subjects of sale, universally imported into the obligations of the seller. L. 31, § 20, *de æd. ed.* (21, 1), L. 2, L. 37 *pr.* § 1, *de evict.* (21, 2). Other applications of the same rule of interpretation (as to Testaments) are found in L. 21, § 1, *qui test.* (28, 1), L. 50, § 3, *de leg.* 1 (30 *un.*), L. 18, § 3, *de instructo* (33, 7). It will be shown below (§ 372), however, that in the subject of this volume an indirect use is to be made of the passages here rejected.

(*n*) L. 1, *pr. de usuris* (22, 1): '. . . usurarum modus *ex more regionis*, ubi contractum est, constituitur.'

(*o*) L. 37, *de usuris* (22, 1): '. . . debere dici usuras venire, *eas autem, quæ in regione frequentantur* ut est in b. f. judiciis constitutum" (that is the same moratory interest that is mentioned in the preceding passage). Comp. also L. 10, § 3, *mand.* (17, 1), L. 7, § 10, *de admin.* (26, 7).

(*p*) See above, vol. ii. §§ 64, 66. To this subject of capacity for rights, and not to the system of territorial law applicable to individuals (with which alone we have here to do), belongs also the maxim, that the stipulation in the formula, *spondes? spondeo*, could be used only by Roman citizens, not by *peregrini*. Gaius, iii. § 93.

tion has no connection with the subject before us, viz. with the system of positive rules of law applicable to each individual. Some examples will put this beyond a doubt. The rules of the *jus gentium*, no less than those of the *jus civile*, were applied to the *cives*. The *Latinus Junianus*, although as *Latinus* he had *testamentifactio*, could make no testament, because this was specially forbidden to him (*q*). But his son was a free-born *Latinus*, who was not affected by this prohibition; and if he made a testament, as by his status as *Latinus* he was entitled to do (note *q*), his succession was governed by the rules of the *hereditas*, and so according to the strictest *jus civile*, which therefore was necessarily applicable to him.

Still less than the passages referred to can we use in our inquiry those texts of the Roman law which only mention quite generally the regard paid to a local customary law, without presupposing or indicating an opposition between different local laws (the case of a collision) (*r*).

SECT. XIV.—(§ 357.)

THE ROMAN DOCTRINE OF ORIGO AND DOMICILIUM—EFFECT OF THESE RELATIONS.

(CONTINUATION.)

It appears from the foregoing investigation, that the connection of an individual with a particular urban community had three effects,—the person so belonging to it being subject, (1) to the burdens, (2) to the forum, (3) to the particular positive law of this community. These three effects were intimately connected, and might therefore be regarded as being

(*q*) Ulpian. xx. § 14. Ulpian says expressly (§ 8 *ibid.*) that he was not without the right of *testamentifactio* (and consequently only that positive prohibition stood in the way). Besides, the testament depended on the form of mancipation: and thus the *testamentifactio* was equivalent to the *commercium*, or capacity for mancipation, which belonged to Latini of all sorts. Ulpian. xix. §§ 4. 5.

(*r*) Among these are perhaps the following passages: L. 1. § 15. *de inspic. ventre* (25. 4), L. 19. *C. de locato* (4. 65). To the same order belongs the mention of the *chirographa* and *syngrapha*, as a "genus obligationis proprium peregrinorum."—Gaius. iii. § 134. As to the special passages on the rule: *locus regit actum*, cf. below, § 382.

of the same kind. But we have now to point out an important difference between them.

When a person belonged to several municipalities, whether by origo or by domicile, he was liable to the municipal burdens, and subject to the jurisdiction of each of them; so that a real concurrence existed among the claims of these cities to the same person. Such a concurrence was impossible as to the subordination of the person to the municipal law of different places, for that implies a contradiction. The same person might be sued before different magistrates at the choice of the plaintiff, but he could not be judged according to different, and perhaps contradictory, rules of law. Subjection to one local law only was therefore possible; and it was necessary for this purpose to make a decisive election between the various cities.

I hold it to be indubitable that when a person had *origo* and domicile in two different cities, the local law to which that person was subject was determined by *origo*, and not by domicile. For this opinion there are the following grounds: First, the *origo* was the closer and in itself superior tie, compared with domicile, which depends on an arbitrary and capricious choice. Secondly, it was earlier in time, since it was constituted by birth, while the domicile elsewhere existing could have arisen only by a later act of will; but there is no reason whatever why the territorial law once established in respect to the person should be changed. In the third place, several of the texts of the Roman jurists already referred to point to this result, inasmuch as they say: 'Si . . . alio jure *civitas ejus* utatur' (§ 356, *c*), and 'quoniam nullius certæ civitatis civis est' (§ 356, *h*); which expressions plainly refer to *origo*, and not to domicile, as the test of the local law applicable to the person.

If we accept the rule here laid down, there still remain to be determined the following cases, which are not decided by it.

First, a person could have *origo* in several places at once: in one place by birth, in another by adoption, or by allection (§ 351). In such a case, without doubt, the earlier citizenship—consequently that arising from birth—was preferable, because there existed no ground for assuming a change of the personal law. The citizenship of the city of Rome, which every *municeps* had along with his particular citizenship (§ 352), was certainly not taken into account in determining the personal law; but rather the law of the latter was alone regarded.[1]

In the second place, a man could be entirely without a municipal citizenship (§ 351), while he had a domicile. In this case the domicile necessarily served as the test of the personal law to be applied to him.[2]

Lastly, the cases remain to be considered in which a person had citizenship in no city (§ 351), and at the same time had a domicile either in several cities or in none (§ 354). How the Romans may have determined such cases—with them certainly very rare—cannot be shown by direct evidence from our law sources. We shall return to this in the examination of the modern law (§ 359).

With regard to these rules relating to the territorial law, we must repeat the remark above made as to the judiciary system, that the universality of these rules must be asserted for the age of the old jurists; while in earlier times, in consequence of the peculiar constitution of many provinces, they are to be admitted only with exceptions (*a*).

[1] Bar, § 2, n. 6, questions this, so far as concerns the later period of the empire, when the more important consequences of the *civitas Romana* were entirely within the region of private law. He refers to the known object of the constitution of Caracalla, viz. to obtain from the successions of *peregrini* the taxes previously paid only by those of Roman citizens (Gibbon, c. vi.); and asks, 'How could the Roman law of succession be applied to the citizens of the *municipia*, unless their family relations, their capacity for rights, and their capacity to act were governed by Roman law? According to the view here taken by Savigny, collisions must have been frequent between the Roman law and the particular laws of these cities; and the absence of cases of such collision in the law sources, admitted by Savigny, would be quite unaccountable.' Gellius, N. A. iv. 4, mentions, that when the Roman *civitas* was conferred on the Latin cities, these lost their peculiar marriage law.

[2] Bar, § 29 *fin.*, contends that domicile could never in the Roman empire, after Caracalla, have any influence whatever on the personal law of individuals, both because no persons could, as he thinks, be without *origo* (see § 351, note *u*), and because no municipalities had then particular laws.

(*a*) This applies particularly to Sicily, according to the passages above cited from Cicero (§ 355, *u*). in which the courts and laws are named together as privileges of the Sicilians. Cap. 13: '*domi certet suis legibus.*' Cap. 24: 'postulant, ut se ad *leges suas* rejiciat.' Cap. 37: 'ut cives inter se *legibus suis* agerent.'

SECT. XV.—(§ 358.)

ORIGO AND DOMICILIUM IN MODERN LAW.

It is not difficult to show that this Roman doctrine of *origo* and *domicilium* is no longer applicable in our modern law, especially in the common law of Germany, and that at most some particular portions of it remain; for the doctrine had its foundation and condition in the urban territories, which were spread like a network over the whole soil of the Roman empire, and consequently in the urban communities, which were the means of connecting their individual inhabitants with the state; so that all individuals with few exceptions were subject, as citizens of municipalities, to manifold and permanent personal obligations (§ 351).

This fundamental principle of the Roman constitution with reference to the various parts of the state territory, no longer exists in modern times. In Germany, indeed, the towns have for many centuries formed an important element in the constitution, as well in the empire as in its particular provinces,—yet only an isolated portion, along with other constituents generally still more important; so that here the division of the whole country into nothing but urban territories and communities could never be asserted.[1] In this respect, other modern states are in the same position as Germany; in Italy only there is still to some extent a state of things which, though imperfectly, reminds us not only of the condition of the Roman empire, but is in fact to be regarded as a remnant of it.

If the foundation of that Roman doctrine of *origo* and *domicilium* has disappeared, the legal relations depending upon it (*munera*, *forum*, urban law as the law of the person) can no longer be spoken of in the Roman sense. This is particularly clear as to *origo*—that is, the municipal citizenship assumed to belong to every individual,—while a certain kind of survivance may be admitted for the more abstract nature of *domicilium*.

Modern writers have long ago perceived and admitted that

[1] See Eichhorn, *über den Ursprung der Städtischen Verfassung in Deutschland*, in the *Zeitschrift für geschichtliche Rechtswissenschaft*, i. 147-247; Savigny, *Vermischte Schriften*, v. 183 (*Das Preussische Städteordnung*).

in this matter the position of our jurisprudence is utterly different from that of the Romans. They have not indeed seen the whole extent of the change, because none of them have understood the true and complete connection of these Roman legal institutions; but in one respect—jurisdiction—they observed this; and here they unanimously admit that the Roman *forum originis*, in its primitive signification, has entirely disappeared, and that at most there remains in modern law something analogous, but subordinate in rank, and a mere subsidiary resource in rare cases (*a*). If any one had doubted whether a complete change had really taken place in the conditions of this subject, he must have been convinced of it by the fact, that even the conceptions and technical terms of the Romans appear quite obscure and confused to the moderns. For the reason of this is, not that the sources of the Roman law are here particularly indistinct or fragmentary (which is not the case), but simply that the contents of those law sources are so little adapted to the circumstances of our time.

The alteration that has taken place might be regarded as consisting only in the disappearance of the one half (the *origo*) from the Roman law, while the other half (the *domicilium*) has continued unchanged; but this view can be held as correct only in a very restricted sense.

The practical significance of the Roman *domicilium* was always referred back to the urban community and its territory; for domicile, as much as citizenship, could constitute membership of an urban community (§§ 351, 353). This exclusive practical significance no longer exists, or, rather, it has taken another form.

On the contrary, the way in which domicile arises, and is lost again (§§ 353, 354), is just the same with us as in the Roman law; and in this respect the rules of the Roman law are still quite applicable.

The line between what is and is not applicable in the whole teaching of the Romans on this subject will be made plainer,

(*a*) Lauterbach, *de domicilio*, §§ 13, 14, 50; Schilter, *ex.* 13, § 24; Stryk, v. 1, §§ 17, 18; Glück, vol. vi. p. 261. [See *Grant* v *Pedie*, 1825, 1 W. and S. 716. For the effect given by the French and some modern codes to national character in founding jurisdiction, see Demangeat's *Fœlix*, No. 149 seq., vol. i. p. 284 sq. *et al.*; Westlake, § 113 seqq., § 379; *infra*, § 359.]

by considering separately the three effects which Roman law attaches to domicile as well as to citizenship (§§ 355, 356).

1. Municipal burdens (*munera*) may here be put out of view altogether, as they related to exclusively Roman circumstances.

2. Jurisdiction (*forum domicilii*).—This effect of domicile not only remains in modern law, but it is still more important than it was among the Romans; for with them the *forum originis* very often co-existed with the *forum domicilii*, so that the plaintiff might choose between the two (§ 355). With us, *origo* in the Roman sense has vanished; and thus the *forum domicilii* is now the only ordinary and regular *forum* of every man.

But this jurisdiction, like domicile itself, upon which it depends, has now a signification different from what it had in the Roman law. It no longer relates, as it did there, universally and necessarily to the judicial authority over a municipal territory to which the domicile refers, but to a judicial territory and local jurisdiction which may have very various origins and limits, and may or may not coincide with the boundaries of a municipal territory.

3. The particular territorial law to which, as his personal law, every individual is subject.—Here we repeat the observation which has been made with respect to jurisdiction. This effect of domicile has not only remained, but has become still more exclusively applicable, and therefore more important, than it was among the Romans; but at the same time it has, like the *forum domicilii*, acquired with us a different meaning.

This subject is more important for the purpose of the present inquiry than all the rest; indeed it is on account of it alone that all the other questions here treated of have been brought within the limits of this investigation. It must, therefore, be the subject of a separate and independent examination (§ 359).

Before quitting the subject of this great and generally acknowledged difference that has arisen in the transition from the Roman state of things into ours, it must be mentioned as a singularity, that in a little European country the law has come to resemble the Roman law on this subject above described. There is an *origo* different from domicile, but with a decided preponderance over it, which is not a remnant of the Roman, and just as little an imitation of it; and has this peculiarity, that it depends not exclusively upon a municipal citizenship, but upon nativity or citizenship in some community or other, whether it be urban or rural. This state of things is found in most of the German cantons of Switzerland, where nativity (Heimathsrecht) in a particular commune, which is at the same time a condition for acquiring the citizenship of the canton, is decisive for many of the most important legal relations, in preference to the domicile which may have been chosen elsewhere. It is so, in particular, for the capacity to have rights, and the capacity for acting; it regulates the law of marriage, paternal power, guardianship, as well as that of testamentary and intestate succession. For many of these legal relations—not merely the local law, but also the forum—is determined by *origo* (citizenship of a *commune*), in preference to domicile; it is so with the actions of divorce, and those relating to successions. All these rules are founded partly upon old custom, partly on treaties concluded between many of the cantons (*b*).

Sect. XVI.—(§ 359.)

ORIGO AND DOMICILIUM IN MODERN LAW.

(CONTINUATION.)

In modern law, *domicile* is to be regarded as determining, in the ordinary case, the particular territorial law, to which, as his personal law, every individual is subject (§ 358); and this proposition has at all times found general acceptance (*a*). That, therefore, becomes for us the normal condition, which, in the

(*b*) *Offizielle Sammlung der das Schweizerische Staatsrecht betreffende Actenstücke*, vol. ii. pp. 34, 36, 39, Zurich 1822, 4to. I owe this information as to Switzerland to a friendly communication from Keller.

(*a*) Compare the writers referred to in § 358, note *a*, and Eichhorn, *Deutsches Recht*, § 34. For the concurrence of foreign lawyers, the following testimonies are to be noted: *Projet du Code Civil*, Paris 1801, 8vo, pp. lv. lvi.; Rocco, lib. ii. c. 8, where, likewise, mere domicile is recognised as the basis of the territorial law for individuals, quite in a different way from (political) naturalization, of which he treats in lib. i. c. 10. Story, c. 3 and 4.

Roman law, was necessarily admitted only exceptionally for those persons who happened to have proper citizenship in no city, and therefore were without *origo* (§ 357). In order to show its relation both to the Roman law and to the kindred rule as to jurisdiction above referred to, this principle of modern law may be thus stated: 1. Among the Romans, the *forum originis* subsisted alongside of the *forum domicilii*, both having equal authority; with us, the *forum originis*, in the Roman sense, has disappeared,—the *forum domicilii* alone remains. 2. With the Romans, the *lex originis* was the personal territorial law of individuals, and the *lex domicilii* only exceptionally for those who happened to have no *origo*;[1] with us, the *lex domicilii* is the only regular criterion of the territorial personal law of individuals (*b*).

Although, then, this exceedingly important principle, which furnishes the foundation for the whole of the following inquiry, is very generally admitted as a rule, it is still necessary to define it more minutely in two respects.

First, in modern times, domicile, in regard to territorial law, has another meaning and other limits than in Roman law, just as has been already observed in respect of jurisdiction (§ 358). With the Romans, the *lex originis*, as well as the *lex domicilii*, was always the local law of a definite territory (§ 356); with us, on the contrary, the unity of a territorial law, just like the jurisdiction, has very various sources and limits (*c*); and it is only by accident that the territorial law coincides with the boundaries of a municipal territory, and is the law of a city. If, therefore, we wish to obtain for this relation the advantage of a fitting designation, we must first give it a special technical name; and perhaps the word *Gesetzsprengel* (territory of a law, *ressort d' une loi*) might be suitable, and would be easily under-

[1] *V. supra*, § 351, note *u*, and 357, note 2.

(*b*) I have already (§ 356) noticed the connection between *forum* (*originis*, *domicilii*) and *lex* (*originis*, *domicilii*). This connection is manifest not only in Roman law, but also in many purely practical consequences of modern law, as *e.g.* in the rule that persons exempted from the ordinary local jurisdiction of a place are not subject to its laws. Eichhorn, *Deutsches Recht*, § 34. It would be wrong, however, to make an unqualified and exclusive assertion of this connection, which would be inconvenient on account of the frequent concurrence of different kinds of jurisdiction (*e.g.* *domicilii* and *rei sitæ*).

(*c*) These differences in the nature and demarcation of territorial laws have already been spoken of in § 347.

stood from its similarity to the common word Gerichtsprengel (territory of a court, *ressort d' un tribunal*). Only it is here to be understood that the word Gesetz (statute, positive law), as well as *lex domicilii*, is taken in a wide sense for every rule of the positive law, without distinguishing whether it may have originated by a proper statute or by customary law.

In the second place, we might be tempted to allow unlimited influence to this rule as to the *lex domicilii*, only in the case of collision between the particular laws of one and the same state (§ 347), but not in the collision between the laws of sovereign states (§ 348). It might be held that, in such collisions, not domicile, but rather the state connection—the relation of allegiance—would be the regulator; for in several great states minute provisions have been made as to the acquisition and loss of national character; and it might seem to follow, that in these states the application of the territorial law to individuals would from that time be determined by national character, and not by domicile; in which case a modified return to the Roman notion of *origo* (as different from *domicilium*) might occur.

This supposition is not without plausibility in the French law, which contains minute provisions as to the origin and extinction of the quality of a *Français* (*d*). To this is added the provision that the personal status of the *Français* (*l' état et la capacité*), even when he resides abroad, is to be determined according to French law (*e*); further, that every *Français* enjoys all *droits civils* (*f*). This last proposition might be supposed to mean that foreigners may not enjoy *droits civils* in France, and thus to revive the Roman distinction between *cives* and *peregrini* in the doctrine of capacity for rights. But, apart from the fact that the French jurists have very confused and erroneous notions of the *droits civils* (*g*), nearly the same rights are conceded to foreigners as to the *Français* (*h*). Hence the

(*d*) *Code Civil*, art. 9-13, 17-21. The *citoyen* is different from the *Français*, and the term indicates political rights, art. 7. Fœlix, too (pp. 36-39) [t. i. p. 52 sqq.], speaks first of *nationalité* as criterion of the local law to be applied, but then takes this word as equivalent to *domicile*. He is not, therefore, in antagonism with the view which prevails among the common law writers.

(*e*) *Code Civil*, art. 3. See below, § 363, at the end of the section.

(*f*) *Code Civil*, art. 8.

(*g*) See vol. ii. p. 154.

(*h*) *Code Civil*, art. 11, where the principle of reciprocity is established,

practical importance of the notion of a *Français* is much less than it seems at first sight, and appears chiefly in the doctrine of capacity for acting, under which head we shall return to this subject.

In Prussia a law has lately been passed as to the origin and extinction of the quality of a Prussian or Prussian subject (*i*); and in this case, too, we might be induced to regulate by this law, independently of domicile, the applicability of the Prussian law to individuals (*k*). But, in fact, there is even less ground for this than in French law. That enactment concerns only relations of public law; and according to the general laws of Prussia, the personal law of individuals is undoubtedly determined by domicile, without any distinction between natives and foreigners (*l*).

In the English law, too, and the American law founded on it, it might be imagined that the notion of state connection, in itself different from that of domicile, would be taken as the fundamental principle. But Story, who proceeds entirely on the notions of the English law, assumes, notwithstanding, the idea of domicile as fundamental, and that precisely in the sense in which it is applied by writers on Roman law (chap. 3 and 4).

Domicile, therefore, must be recognised as, in fact, the *universal* principle of determination; and so the writers referred to above (§ 358, *a*) have treated it as the true foundation of the subject-relation (in respect to private law).

The principle, that domicile determines as well jurisdiction (*forum domicilii*) as the local law of the person (*lex domicilii*), is insufficient for two possible cases, and for these cases, therefore, needs some addition. It may happen that the person

which is now tending almost everywhere to a complete equality of capacity for rights between natives and foreigners.

(*i*) *Gesetz* of 31 Dec. 1842 (G. S. 1843, p. 15).

(*k*) The law cited expressly says that the quality of Prussian is neither acquired nor lost by the fact of domicile alone.

(*l*) *Allg. Landrecht*, *Einleitung*, §§ 23, 24, 34. This is confirmed by the numerous treaties with neighbouring German states, in which domicile is recognised for the subjects of both parties as the only foundation of ordinary personal jurisdiction, without mentioning the possibility of a different relation as subjects. I refer, only as examples, to the treaties with Weimar, 1824, art. 8, and Saxony, 1839, art. 8 (G. S. 1824, p. 150; 1839, p. 354).

whose forum or whose local law we have to determine may either have several domiciles, or none at all (§ 354).

In the first case, no difficulty arises in respect to the forum. This is completely established at each of the different places of domicile, and the plaintiff has a free choice, just as in the Roman law (§ 355).

For the local law of the person a similar determination is not possible; but one of the several places where domicile simultaneously exists, must be selected as exclusively fixing the law. I have no hesitation in preferring for this purpose that place at which the domicile was first established, and that because there is no sufficient reason for supposing a change to have taken place in the local law to which the person has once subjected himself by acquiring the first domicile (*m*).

The second case for which the principle above established is insufficient, and therefore requires an addition, is when the person whose forum or whose local law we have to discover has, for the present, no domicile.

This will generally occur when the person has formerly had, demonstrably, a true domicile, but has lost it without choosing a new one. Then we have to regard this former domicile as fixing the question; and here, again, as in the previous case (Note *m*), for want of a sufficient reason for supposing a change. And from the same standpoint is to be decided the last remaining question—the case in which that person had at no previous time established any domicile; for in such a case we must go back to a period when he had a

(*m*) On the same principle, we arrived at a similar decision above, when in Roman law the same person had citizenship at several places (§ 357). Meier, *de Conflictu Legum*, p. 16, concurs with the assertion here made. [British courts require a longer period of residence, and stronger indicia of permanency, for the purpose of fixing the domicile of succession, *i.e.* generally the domicile which fixes the local law, than for the purpose of founding jurisdiction. Hence, in England at least, the word 'domicile' is confined to the former use; and the phrase 'domicile of jurisdiction' is regarded as an improper use of the word. The doctrine which has been laid down in cases of matrimonial jurisdiction appears to arise from a consideration of the hardship and anomaly of compelling a wife to defend in any foreign country in which a husband may take up his abode. See *Pitt* v *Pitt*, and other authorities, *supra*, p. 60. Perhaps that hardship might be prevented by the reservation suggested by Lord Westbury in that case. Certainly the principle of such decisions is not to be extended beyond this class of cases in which it is laid down. See generally Phillimore, iv. 46 seqq; Westlake, §§ 34, 316, 379.]

domicile without any choice of his own. This is the time of birth, at which the domicile of the legitimate child is that which the father has at the time (*n*).

This, then, is *origo*, in the sense of our modern law; and in respect of the *forum originis*, the matter has always been so apprehended by sound lawyers (*o*), although the confusion with the mere place of birth (§ 350, *a*), and often, too, an indistinct conception of the relation of this to the Roman notion of *origo*, have prevented it from being correctly understood. In order to guard against every future confusion in this last respect, I will here briefly repeat the distinction, as it results from the whole previous discussion. The Romans designate as *origo* the citizenship acquired by his birth. We call by the name of *origo* the fiction that a man has a domicile at the place where his father's domicile was at the time of his birth.

This idea, then, of *origo*, or of extraction (*Herkunft*) in the sense of the modern law, is to be applied alike to jurisdiction, as *forum originis*, and to the local law of the person, as *lex originis*.

In this assertion we are not contradicting the declarations of the Roman law, the determination of which upon this case I left for a time unsettled (§ 357). I rather believe that the Romans would have decided precisely thus, if such a case had occurred to them. There is a presumption for this, not only in the intrinsic reasonableness which has been above established in regard to modern law, and which they were just as able to recognise as we are, but also in a distinct decision on a kindred and exactly similar case, resting on the same principle. The freedman could freely choose his domicile, independently of the domicile of his patron (§ 353, *v*). Yet it is said that the domicile of the freedman is determined by that of his patron; and just so the domicile of the freedman's children, and even

(*n*) See above, § 353 (with the more precise exposition there added). Voet. (v. 1, § 92 fin.) agrees with this opinion, and assigns the proper reason. Meier, *de Conflictu Legum*, p. 14, looks to the place of birth, which as such is quite immaterial. In fact, however, the two places will generally be the same.

(*o*) The Prussian code correctly adopts this sense. There is, indeed, in the *Allg. Landrecht Einl.* § 25, the indefinite expression, 'Ort der Herkunft;' and it could be understood of the mere place of birth. But the *Allg. Ger. Ordnung*, i. 2, §§ 17, 18, explains the 'Herkunft' and the *forum originis* expressly as the *forum of the parents*.

that of the slaves whom he in his turn manumits (*p*). The apparent contradiction between these rules is thus to be reconciled. At the moment of manumission, the liberated slave has no other domicile than that of his patron, to whose family he has hitherto belonged. He retains this domicile until it is changed by his own free will; that is, so long as no such change can be proved. The same domicile therefore must, till then, continue to attach to all the persons dependent on him (children and freedmen), until these effect a change by acquiring a domicile of their own. These decisions of the Roman jurists evidently rest on the same principle which has been assigned above for the *origo* of the modern Roman law; and they leave hardly a doubt that the Romans would have given to the son of a freeborn man, if he had acquired no domicile of his own, that which his father had at his birth.

We must here notice particularly a singular, but among modern writers a very common technical, expression: *domicilium originis* (*q*). According to the Roman usage, this collocation of words is contradictory, as these expressions indicated two different, independent grounds of subjection. As used by the modern jurists, it means: the domicile of a man which is constituted not by his own free will, but by his descent, and which, therefore, in some sort rests on a fiction.

We might, indeed, advance a little further in casuistry, and ask, what law is applicable to a man for whom neither a self-elected nor a paternal domicile can be discovered? This question may arise when the man dies, and his intestate succession is to be determined. Scarcely any course will be possible but to assume his residence at the time to be the domicile, and therefore (if the question relates to succession) the place at which he has died.[2] In the case of foundlings, the

(*p*) See above, § 353, *u*. The passages which decide this are: L. 6, § 3. L. 22. *pr. ad mun.* (50. 1): and for the correct understanding of these passages, it is specially necessary to compare: *Zeitschrift für geschichtliche Rechtswissenschaft*, vol. ix. p. 98. [Savigny, *Vermischte Schriften*, iii. 245.]

(*q*) Schilter. ex. 13. § 24: Lauterbach. *de domicilio*, § 13. Thomasius, *de Vagabundo*, §§ 44–68, criticises this expression, but involves himself in insufferable and utterly fruitless subtleties.

[2] This is agreeable to the principle of Lord Thurlow, that residence is *prima facie* evidence of domicile. *Bruce* v *Bruce*, 3 Pat. Ap. 163: 6 Bro.

place where they were found may be held as their domicile, with reservation of a change if they acquire a permanent residence at another place for the purpose of education, whether it be in a public establishment or with private persons (*r*).

SECT. XVII.—(§ 360.)

TRANSITION TO THE LEGAL RELATIONS.

We have now reached a point of our inquiry which forms one of its larger sections, and at which a retrospect of the part we have traversed seems proper.

The course of our inquiry has been the following: A legal principle was sought for, from which to deduce the subordination of the individual to a particular local law, and consequently the relation of the person to a particular territory (§ 345). Such a legal principle was found in Roman law, in municipal citizenship (*origo*), and, in default of this, in domicile within a particular urban territory (§§ 350–357). Domicile in a particular territory (§§ 358, 359) came in place of this principle in modern law.

It was at the same time acknowledged that this principle can only form a foundation for the solution of our problem, and cannot be itself regarded as such a solution; for it is not enough, in order to this solution, to regard the person in its abstract existence (as in the rule above laid down); it must rather be contemplated in quite another point of view, as entering into a wide circle of acquired rights, as the possessor of these rights, and thus, it may be, coming under the authority of the most various laws (§ 345).

While, therefore, the object of our inquiry has hitherto been the *person* as to whom we sought out the tie connecting him with a particular locality, the territory of a special law, our attention must now be directed to the *legal relations*, for which we have to establish a similar connection with a definite

566; 2 B. and P. 230 *n*. Of course this principle is applicable only in the absence of every other indication.

(*r*) Linde, *Lehrbuch*, § 89.

locality—a particular legal territory. But in order to bring the two parts of the investigation nearer to one another by the analogies of language, we can say that, in the sequel, a definite *seat* is to be sought for each class of legal relations.

Following out this idea, I will here repeat the formula which has already been laid down in another connection (§ 348), and according to which the whole problem comes to be—

To discover for every legal relation (case) that legal territory to which, in its proper nature, it belongs or is subject (in which it has its seat).

This formula is, in essentials, equally applicable to the collision of local laws of the same state and of different states.

Only by the complete solution of this problem will it be possible to make a safe and exhaustive application to actual life of any principles that shall be established; and from this standpoint we can describe the previous investigation as the theoretical part of the whole subject,—the following as the practical part.

In this inquiry some general points of view must be frequently mentioned. A preliminary survey of these will greatly facilitate the future application of them.

1. Attention has already been called to the intimate connection between the forum and the territorial law which already existed among the Romans, and which has not been lost in modern law (§§ 356, 359). This connection depended, as to the person, on the obedience which was due as well to the magistrate as to the local law; consequently on an equal subjection of the person to the two powers over him. A similar twofold subjection must be established for the legal relations; yet this intimate connection must not be supposed to amount to complete identity. Such an idea is excluded by the fact, that in many cases a plurality of jurisdictions is admissible, while there can never be more than one local law applicable.

2. The local law for every legal relation is liable to be very extensively influenced by the freewill of the persons interested, who may voluntarily subject themselves to the authority of a particular law, although this influence must not be regarded as unlimited. This voluntary subjection is also efficacious in regard to the competent forum for particular legal relations.

Voluntary subjection to a local law is manifested in various kinds and degrees. Sometimes it consists in the free choice of a particular local law to regulate a matter where another law might have been preferred; as, for example, in obligatory contracts, in which the freely elected local law is itself to be regarded as a part of the contract. In other cases, that voluntary subjection is manifested in the mere acquisition of a right, —thus *e.g.* in the acquisition of a landed estate in a foreign territory, in which case the acquirer has indeed full power to abstain from the acquisition; but when he completes it, must necessarily recognise the local law as governing the estate.

Two questions are always to be attended to in the application of a local law, as a consequence of voluntary submission to it: With what conditions is it to be invested, since an express declaration will generally be wanting? In what cases is it admissible, or excluded by contrary absolute statutes?

The great influence of this voluntary submission to the territorial law has always been very generally recognised.[1] It might have been doubted in Roman law, according to which personal dependence on a particular local law was chiefly determined by municipal citizenship (§ 357), which every one nor-

[1] 'The regard which is paid to the *lex loci contractus* does not arise from any blind deference to the law of a foreign country, but it is founded on the legal presumption that the parties had in view the law of the country where the contract was executed, and intended to bind themselves accordingly,' except in 'contracts relative to real estate,' 'where the parties had the law of another kingdom in view,' 'or where the *lex loci* is in itself unjust, or *contra bonos mores*,' etc.—Lord Robertson in *Edmonstone* v *Edmonstone*, 1 June 1816; Ferg. Cons. Rep. 397, 19 F. C. 139, 147, 148. The effect given to the choice of a particular law by the parties, is exemplified in *Earl of Stair* v *Head*, 1844, 6 D. 904, where a marriage contract of Scotch spouses domiciled in England provided that 'the import and effect of this contract, and all matters and questions connected with the intended marriage, shall be construed and regulated by the law of Scotland.' The rights of parties on the predecease of the wife still domiciled in England, were accordingly regulated by Scotch law. It would seem also that the use of technical legal terms of a country different from the place of domicile or of execution, creates a presumption that a document was intended to be construed according to the rules of that country. At least this is so in the case of testamentary writings, when the technical language used is that of the forum of administration, or of the *situs* of real estate disposed of. *Rainsford* v *Maxwell*, 1852, 14 D. 450; *Ferguson* v *Marjoribanks*, 1853, 15 D. 637. So we shall see that the rules laid down for ascertaining the *lex contractus* are founded on the presumed intention of the parties. See Lord Mansfield in *Robinson* v *Bland*, 2 Burr. 1077, 1078; 2 Kent's Com. 575 (460); Story, § 489; *infra*, § 372, notes; Lord Brougham in *Don* v *Lipmann*, 1857, 2 S. and M'L. 724.

mally obtained, not by his own free will, but by birth (§ 352). But every possible doubt disappears in modern law, in which personal subjection to a particular local law is determined by domicile; for as domicile itself is fixed by perfectly free choice, so in regard to particular legal relations the normal faculty of subjecting oneself at will to any territorial law admits of no doubt.

This voluntary subjection appears sometimes as unilateral (as in acquiring property and other real rights)—sometimes takes place by the concurrence of several persons (as in obligatory contracts). One might be disposed to regard this last case as itself a contract—namely, a tacit one; but this view would not be strictly correct. A positive volition, with distinct consciousness, is presupposed in every contract. This does not always exist in the case of voluntary submission. It is rather presumed, by a general rule of law, that that which is required by the necessity of the case is intended, so long as a distinct intention to the contrary is not expressed. The distinction—certainly a somewhat subtle one—between this presumed subjection and the contract, will find an important application below (§ 379, No. 3), in which the distinction itself will be made still plainer.

Although great unanimity prevails as to the influence which voluntary submission to a particular local law actually exercises, I must yet object to a mode of expression which has lately come into use. Modern writers are accustomed to designate this very general effect of the free will as *autonomy* (*a*)—a technical expression which has been applied, from an early time, as indicating a very peculiar relation in the development of the German law; namely, the competence of the nobility and of many corporations independently to regulate their own relations by a kind of internal legislation (*b*). In this sense the expression is indispensable; and its usefulness in the proper meaning is impaired by its superfluous application to the entirely dissimilar relations of the subject with which we are here

(*a*) Wächter, ii. p. 35; Mittermaier, *Deutsches Recht*, §§ 30, 31; Eichhorn, *Deutsches Recht*, §§ 34, 37; Fœlix, p. 134 [i. 202].

(*b*) Eichhorn, *Deutsches Recht*, §§, 20, 25, 30; *Rechtsgeschichte*, vol. ii. § 346; Phillips, *Deutsches Recht*, vol. i. p. 89, vol. ii. p. 73; Puchta, *Gewohnheitsrecht*, vol. i. pp. 155-160, vol. ii. p. 107.

engaged, which gains nothing by it in clearness and distinctness. If this phase be justified by asserting that the parties subject themselves to a law (already subsisting), and in that sense assign a law to themselves, the same is true in a still higher degree of the free choice of domicile; and yet no one thinks of describing that as the result of autonomy. Accordingly it seems advisable, in regard to voluntary subjection to any local law, the choice of domicile, and the countless other voluntary actions from which legal consequences flow, to avoid the word autonomy (*c*).

3. If we contemplate from a general point of view the treatment of the questions before us, as it appears during several centuries in writers, in the practice of courts, and even in the legislation of different nations, we discover an evident change, and indeed an advance, in one and the same direction. A rigid separation between different states formerly prevailed, in place of which an ever-increasing approximation has been taking place. Corresponding with this, a remarkable diminution of previous differences of opinion has manifested itself among the writers of various nations. Two facts already mentioned (§ 348) testify to this altered tendency: the more general recognition of the equal legal capacity of natives and foreigners, and the increasing agreement as to many propositions of a universal customary law on the questions with which we are engaged. If the development of the law thus begun is not disturbed by unforeseen external circumstances, it may be expected that it will at length lead to a complete accord in the treatment of questions of collision in all states. Such an accord might be brought about by means of juridical science, and the practice of the tribunals guided by it. It could also be effected by a positive law, agreed to and enacted by all states, with respect to the collision of territorial laws. I do not say that this is likely, or even that it would be more convenient and salutary than mere scientific agreement; but the notion of such a law may serve as a standard to test every rule that we shall lay down as to collision. We have always to ask ourselves

(*c*) Comp. also Puchta, *Gewohnheitsrecht*, vol. i. p. 158, vol. ii. p. 107. In the phraseology here censured, there is a confusion similar to that by which the acts which originate legal relations are placed in the same rank with the law sources. Se above, vol. i. § 6, note *b*.

whether such a rule would be well adapted for reception into that common statute law of all nations.

In the midst of this approximation, one chief point remains, around which the strongest contradictions have continually clustered. The older German law starts from a sharp distinction between property in immoveable things, on the one side, and moveable corporeal property, together with all other means and estate (particularly obligations), on the other side. If this distinction is preserved, we shall be led to decide questions as to immoveable property altogether according to the law of the place where it is situated, and therefore, in many of the most important cases, to separate it entirely from the rest of the estate. If the distinction be given up, the estate of all kinds comes to be treated alike in many such cases. This very important difference will hereafter be more minutely dealt with, —first, in regard to real rights, but especially in succession, and in regard to the property of married persons. As the question is of a general nature, it seems to require a preliminary notice here.

On impartial consideration, it must be admitted that the great changes in respect of property and commerce which have taken place in modern times, tend to the abandonment of that sharp distinction. The opponents of this opinion do not indeed ignore the great difficulty as to details which now results from its retention; but they are accustomed to look somewhat contemptuously upon this circumstance, asserting that such an inconvenience ought not to hinder us from adhering to correct principles. This argument might be allowed if the question related to a mere difficulty of the judge, whose trouble and labour would be lessened by assimilating the two kinds of property. But the difficulties and disadvantages affect the parties themselves to whom the laws are to be applied; and we must never forget that rules of law are made for the parties, whose real interests it is their purpose impartially to further, and that the interests of parties are not to be made subservient to the uniformity or consistency of the rules of law.

Let us examine more closely what principle could possibly be endangered by removing that difficulty. We might suppose the interest of our own fellow-subjects to be imperilled, if in some cases a landed estate in our country were to fall by inheritance, according to the rules of a foreign country, to a foreigner, instead of to a native. But the opposite result might as probably occur, in the particular case, in applying the foreign rules of law; and besides, every such danger, if people will use that word, is completely removed by the reciprocity we have assumed to exist. Or it might be supposed that the dignity and independence of our country would be endangered, if foreign rules of law were applied to the succession to an estate on its soil. But this objection also is refuted by the supposed reciprocity, which, more generally viewed, resolves itself into an international community of law, as the foundation and highest aim of our whole doctrine (§ 348).

This conflict of opinions has, in fact, arisen thus: German writers have in modern times ever been more and more inclined to give up the strict separation between immoveable and other estates; so much so, that Romanists and Germanists are here quite agreed. The English writers, on the contrary, with the Americans (whose doctrine is founded on the same basis of the common law), adhere to the distinction with great tenacity (*d*), and the French writers appear to take the same side. The practice of the courts appears, by a very natural mutual action and reaction, to go everywhere hand in hand with the writers.

Sect. XVIII.—(§ 361.)

TRANSITION TO PARTICULAR LEGAL RELATIONS.

(CONTINUATION.)

We shall next endeavour to ascertain, for the legal relation of every class, to what territory it belongs, and therefore, as it were, to discover its seat (§ 360). A comparative view of the legal relations themselves must form the basis of this inquiry (*a*).

(*d*) The Norman feudal law, which still governs to a great extent the transference of landed property in England, has not been without influence on the continuance of this principle in that country. [See Westlake, §§ 69–74.]

(*a*) Compare above, § 345, and vol. i. §§ 53-58. Capacity for rights and capacity to act are expounded above, vols. ii. and iii.; the law of

The centre of every legal relation is the person as having the right or interest in it, and the legal position (status—Zustand) of the person itself must be fixed, first of all. This is effected by ascertaining two kinds of conditions: the conditions under which a person can *be* interested in legal relations (capacity for rights); and the conditions under which, by his own free will, he can *become* interested in legal relations (capacity to act). This twofold capacity is usually called the absolute status (Zustand) of the person.

Around this centre (the abstract person) the acquired rights arrange themselves in their manifold forms. They may be reduced to two principal classes, which are distinguished with reference to their objects: Family Law (Familienrecht), and Property Law (Vermögensrecht).

To property law, or the law of patrimonial rights, belong, in the first place, rights to particular *things* (real rights), then rights in particular actions of certain persons (law of obligations, of which the law of actions is to be regarded as one branch).

The rights constituting property (patrimonial rights) are found as a technical unity in *succession*, which has for its object the *estate* in its abstract conception and indefinite contents.

The family appears partly in its original nature as a permanent mode of life (pure family law), partly in the important influence which its various branches exercise upon property (applied family law). It is to be contemplated in the three forms which alone remain in modern Roman law—marriage, paternal power, guardianship—since the law of slavery, which was preserved to the latest period of Roman law, has long since disappeared.

From this view we obtain, as a guide for the sequel of this inquiry, the following series of legal relations:—

I. Status of the person in itself (capacity for rights, and capacity to act).
II. Law of things.
III. Law of obligations.

actions in vols. v. vi. and vii. It is of course understood that this inquiry, as well as the whole work, is confined to the substantive part of the private law, so that the law of procedure and criminal law must be excluded from it. See vol. i. § 1 [and Introduction].

IV. Succession.
V. Family law (Domestic Relations).
A. Marriage.
B. Paternal power.
C. Guardianship.

With regard to every legal relation belonging to one of these classes, we have now to determine by what rule the collision of different local laws is to be regulated. The formal principle to be applied to the solution of this problem has already (§ 360) been specified—viz. to ascertain the seat (the home) of every legal relation (which must be clearly distinguished from the domicile of the person): *this* territorial law must be applied in every case of collision. The relations of fact which *may* come into consideration in determining this, and among which, therefore, a choice will always be made when the seat of particular legal relations has to be fixed, are as follows:—

The *domicile* of any person concerned in the legal relation.
The *place* where a *thing* which is the object of the legal relation *is situated.*
The place of a juridical *act*, which has been or is to be done.
The place of the *tribunal* which has to decide a law-suit.

Attempts have been made at different times to find a material principle for the determination of all possible questions of collision. I will here compare the most important efforts of this kind. The test of each will be, whether it corresponds with the formal principle before laid down; that is to say, whether, in fact, the true seat of every legal relation can be certainly discovered by means of it. All these attempts, however, must appear beforehand to be of very doubtful augury, because the various legal relations are of such diverse nature, that they can hardly be reduced under a common absolute rule as to their seat.

1. The division of *statuta personalia, realia, mixta* (*b*).

This division is found in a very immature form as early as

(*b*) This has already been indicated at the end of § 345, and in § 347. Wächter treats of it at length, i. pp. 256–261, pp. 270–311; cf. also Fœlix, § 19 seq.; Story, § 12 seq.

Bartolus (*c*), and was more fully developed only towards the close of the sixteenth century (*d*).

By *personal statutes* are meant those which have for their object *principaliter* the person and its qualities, although they may contain besides rules relating to property.

Those are called *real statutes* which deal *principaliter* with things (that is to say, immoveable things), though persons may also be mentioned.

Mixed statutes, according to some, are those which have neither of the two (person or thing) for their object, but rather acts (*e*); according to others, those which include both person and thing at once. These two definitions are apparently conflicting, yet they run into one another.

The practical significance of these ideas is this: We start from the question, what statutes are to be applied even beyond the territory of the legislator; and it is answered in the following way:—Personal statutes are to be applied to all persons who have their domicile in the territory of the legislator, even if a foreign judge has to decide. Real statutes are applicable to all immoveables situated in the territory of the legislator, again without distinguishing whether a native or a foreign judge has to decide. Mixed statutes, finally, are applicable to all acts done in the territory of the legislator, whether the decision is given in the same country or not. Such is a general view of the whole matter; but in details there are innumerable differences of opinion, according as the limits of the classes themselves, as well as of their practical application, are drawn in one direction or another.

This doctrine cannot be rejected as entirely erroneous, since it admits of the most opposite constructions and applications, among which, no doubt, we may find some that are quite correct. On the other hand, it is quite unsatisfactory, because it is both incomplete and ambiguous, and therefore altogether useless as a foundation for this part of our subject.

Many modern writers have asserted that this doctrine has

(*c*) Bartolus in L. 1, *C. de summa trinitate*. The principal text is quoted in Wächter, i. pp. 272–274.

(*d*) Argentræus, N. 5, 6, 7, 8. There is a short and clear abridgment by J. Voet. §§ 2–4.

(*e*) Sometimes they are further limited to the form of acts.—J. Voet. § 4.

been definitively received as a universal customary law (*f*). The correctness of this assertion is not only without proof, but is entirely impossible, since the opinions of writers, with which the decisions of the courts are more or less in unison, are widely diverse, and can therefore afford no evidence of a general custom. The only part of this statement which we can admit as true, is the fact that almost all writers, even to a very recent period, make use of the technical terms in question (personal and real statutes along with mixed) in treating of this subject. But as they attach to them entirely different ideas and rules, the residuum of truth in the assertion is quite unimportant.

The sharp distinction between immoveable and other property above noticed (§ 360, No. 3) is usually placed in juxtaposition with this doctrine,—in this way, that the advocates of that distinction attach special importance[1] to the notion of real statutes, which has much less interest for their opponents.

2. Where there is doubt, every legal relation is to be determined, as a general rule, according to the law of the domicile of the person whom it concerns. This takes place, therefore, in all cases in which a special exception cannot be established (*g*).

At first sight this proposition seems to be connected with the very generally accepted rule, which I also have recognised, according to which domicile is the bond that connects a person with a particular legal territory (§ 359, *a*). On closer examination, it is found to be in a quite different position. The law that governs the person as such is not necessarily the law that governs the particular legal relation in which that person may be concerned, and through which he may come under the authority of the most different laws (§ 360). The local law of the

(*f*) Thibaut, *Pandekten*, § 38; Kierulff, pp. 75-82.

[1] Hence Schäffner observes (§ 20) that modern writers have ceased to attach importance to the ideas originally involved in the phrases 'real' and 'personal statutes,' and have used them merely as received technical terms. The expression 'personal statute' was employed to signify the laws in force at the domicile of a person, the term 'real statute' to signify the *lex rei (immobilis) sitæ;* and for brevity he uses them so in his treatise. It can hardly be said that his remark applies to the use of the terms in British and American law, although that is sufficiently loose.

(*g*) Eichhorn, *Deutsches Recht*, § 34; Göschen, *Vorlesungen*, vol. i. p. 111; Puchta, *Pandekten*, § 113, and *Vorlesungen über die Pandekten*, § 113. (Puchta adopts this principle only in collisions of local laws within the same state.) Wächter, ii. pp. 9-12, declares against this principle.

person may indeed be applicable for some of his legal relations, and thus that proposition is found in many cases to be correct. But such a coincidence is quite accidental, the principle has in itself no claim to be universally applicable to the particular legal relations, and we cannot escape from the necessity of ascertaining with complete impartiality to what law each of them is properly subject.

There is, besides, the important fact, that the larger number of legal relations concern not a single person, but several. In such cases this principle leaves us quite helpless, since we cannot find out from it which of the persons affected by the legal relation shall fix by his domicile the local law to be applied.

Lastly, we must entirely object to the form in which this alleged principle is presented to us. It is said to apply usually, or in cases of doubt; therefore, only when the authority of another local law cannot be established (*h*). Thus the conclusiveness of the principle appears to be assumed in advance for the numerous cases in which plausible reasons, weighty authorities, decisions in courts, are adduced for one opinion or the other. Here, therefore, the usage of the civil procedure is to some extent adopted, in which every one on whom the burden of proof lies loses his cause if he does not succeed in his proof. I cannot approve this method of dealing with the matter. On the contrary, the legal territory to which every case (legal relation) naturally belongs, must be independently sought out and ascertained, in such a way that no general presumption, for or against, shall be mixed up in the investigation. This objection is raised not only against the last-mentioned unsound principle, but it is equally applicable to that which follows.

3. Every legal relation is to be judged, in general, according to the place of the court, that is to say, by the laws of the land to which the judge belongs. This principle is applied only to the collision of the laws of different states, not to the collision of the particular laws of the same state (*i*). But if it be admitted as true, there is no reason why it should not be applied also to the conflicting particular laws of the same state.

(*h*) So especially Puchta, *Pandekten*, § 113, note *b*.

(*i*) Wächter, i. pp. 261–270 (whose whole work treats only of the laws of different states); Puchta, *Pandekten*, § 113, *Vorlesungen*, § 113. This view is contested by Schäffner, §§ 24–29; Kori, *Archiv*. vol. xxvii. p. 312. [Bar, §§ 24, 25.]

The apparent truth of this proposition consists in the fact that every lawgiver has exclusive authority over his country, and is therefore not obliged to suffer within that territory the intermixture of any foreign law; or, which is the same thing from another point of view, that every judge is called to administer the laws of his own state only (*k*). This ground would be decisive, if the prevailing view of modern legislation were the jealous maintenance of its own authority. But this is not a matter of course; but rather the question presents itself, in the first instance, whether the domestic legislation in its spirit and tendency forbids, as a rule, the application of any foreign law to legal relations that come in contact with more than one legal territory (*l*). A modern writer gives to this view the following very appropriate expression:—We will admit that every judge has to administer the laws of his own country; but then he must apply them only to the persons and the cases for which they are made. *Whether*, then, the legislator has intended his law to apply to cases (legal relations) in themselves doubtful, and in which there is a collision of territorial laws: *this*, says that writer, is the *only* difficult point (*m*).

If we consider without prejudice the question thus raised, we must be convinced that the leading principle of modern legislation and practice does *not* consist in the jealous maintenance of its own exclusive authority; nay, that there is rather a tendency to the promotion of a true community of law, and therefore to the treatment of cases of conflict according to the essence and requirements of each legal relation, without respect to the limits of states and the territory of their laws (§ 348).

But if we accept as correct this leading principle of the modern legal development (in legislation and practice), we must necessarily reject the proposition that the judge has, as a rule, to decide according to the laws of his own country when a collision occurs. This proposition disturbs and hinders the desirable and gradually approaching accord in deciding cases of conflict in different states. It could not possibly, therefore, be

(*k*) This proposition is also akin, apparently, to the affinity before established (§ 360) between the jurisdiction and the territorial law; but its advocates err in exaggerating this relationship into actual identity.

(*l*) This is also admitted to be correct by the advocate of the opinion which is here examined. Wächter, i. p. 262.

(*m*) Thöl. *Handelsrecht*, vol. i. p. 28.

admitted into a general statute of all states as to the collision of local laws, if such should ever be attempted (§ 360, p. 92).

There is also a special reason which makes the application of this principle very dangerous. In many cases of collision jurisdiction is equally competent at several places, so that the plaintiff in the particular suit has the choice of the forum. Thus, if this principle prevails, the territorial law to be administered in any case is made to depend not only on accidental circumstances, but even on the mere will of a single party. But a principle that leads to such results cannot possibly be regarded as correct. The hardships and arbitrariness to which the principle may lead is very striking, if we imagine it applied to the countries in which the *Landsassiat*[2] has full sway (*n*).

In conclusion, however, the true elements of the principle here contested must be noted, and the rather because the admission of them may perhaps facilitate the reconciliation of conflicting opinions.

A. If the judge finds a domestic law on the question of conflict, he must follow it unreservedly, even if it should not coincide with his own theoretical view (§§ 347, 348). The adoption of this rule will, however, seldom lead us very far, for the statutes as to the treatment of collisions are generally but the expression of an incomplete and unsatisfactory theory.

[2] The Landsassiat is a rule peculiar to certain German states, by which the acquisition of certain kinds of property, or of rights in such property, involves complete personal subjection to the law of the country, and the necessity of taking an oath of allegiance. See references in Heffter, *Europ. Völkerrecht*, § 61.

(*n*) Eichhorn, *Deutsches Recht*, § 75. There is also a special objection to the principle, in the fact that several local laws may exist within the territory of a judge, and that it would then remain undecided, in any case, which of them he should administer,—which of them should be the ruling one. Seuffert, *Archiv. für Entscheidungen der obersten Gerichtshöfe in den deutschen Staaten*, vol. ii. No. 4. [It has constantly been laid down that the law applicable to a case must be independent of the choice of the parties. 'Pluribus in locis nos aliquando defendere tenemur nec propterea negotium judicatur ex more loci ubi judicatur.'—Rodenburg, ii. 2, 4, § 5. See Bar, § 44. A partial reception of the view criticised in the text seems to have taken place in America. It was said by the court in a leading case: 'In the conflict of laws, it must often be a matter of doubt which should prevail; and whenever a doubt does exist, the court which decides will prefer the laws of its own country to that of the stranger.' *Saul* v *His Creditors*, 17 Mart. La. 569, 595; Story, § 28; *Olivier* v *Townes*, 2 Mart. La. N.S. 93. This is certainly very questionable, both in principle and in the practical consequences to which it may lead.]

B. The judge must never apply a foreign territorial law, if its application is excluded by the limits above fixed for the legal community of independent states (§ 349). The most important consequences of this rule will be exhibited below in § 365. Thereby it will become apparent that the practical difference between this theory and the view which I maintain is, in fact, not so great as it at first appears.

C. The judge must always apply the law of his own state, if the question concerns not a relation of the substantive law, but a point of legal procedure. To this category belong not only forms and rules of procedure proper, but also, in part, the rules of the law of actions. Here, however, as the demarcation is often very difficult, great caution must be used, and regard must always be had to the true nature and purpose of the particular legal institutes. Very many rules are only in appearance rules of procedure, and really concern the legal relation itself.[3]

4. Every legal relation must be judged according to the local law of that territory within which it has *come into existence* (*o*).

This principle is not only arbitrary, because the place of origin in itself, and irrespective of the circumstances in which the legal relation may have been brought into existence, cannot determine the local law to be applied; but it has only the appearance of a substantive principle, while it is in reality of a merely formal nature. For the place where each legal relation comes into existence, in the juridical sense, can only be known by more minute examination of its specific nature; and in this a predominant and capital regard paid to the place of origin will only obstruct us.

5. That local law should always be applied by which vested rights shall be kept intact (*p*).

This principle leads into a complete circle; for we can only

[3] An important example of this—laws as to prescription—will be discussed under § 374. See also Bar, § 64, p. 213.

(*o*) Schäffner, § 32. Compare on the other side, Wächter, ii. p. 32. [Bar, § 21.]

(*p*) Compare as to this proposition, Wächter, ii. pp. 1–9. [Bar, § 23.]

know what are vested rights, if we know beforehand by what local law we are to decide as to their complete acquisition.

In this general survey we must notice, lastly, some of the comprehensive codes that have been promulgated, in recent times, in the greater European states.

The *Allgemeine Landrecht* of Prussia (*q*) very distinctly recognises the principle of equality before the law, in its treatment of native subjects and foreigners (*r*); and where exceptions occur, these are not at all intended to secure for the domestic law an exclusive authority over foreigners, but they are rather benevolently directed to protect legal acts from the invalidity which might be derived from the collision of local laws (*s*). The general prevalence, at the time of its compilation, of the doctrine of real and personal statutes had a marked influence on the terms of these passages of the *Landrecht* (*t*); and it is just the imperfection of this theory that has mainly caused the doubts and disputes that have lately arisen on one of the most important practical points, of which we shall afterwards have to speak in treating of succession (§ 378).

The French code contains but a few rules that can be regarded as determining questions of collision; yet it also unambiguously recognises the equality as to legal rights of natives and foreigners (*u*).

The Austrian code is similar to the Prussian (*v*). It acknowledges the equal rights of foreigners and natives, and has well-intended provisions for the maintenance of legal acts, similar to those of the Prussian law (*w*).

(*q*) Compare *A. L. R. Einleitung*, §§ 23–35.
(*r*) *A. L. R. Einl.* § 34.
(*s*) *A. L. R. Einl.* §§ 27, 35.
(*t*) Bornemann, *Preuss. Recht*, 2d ed. vol. i. p. 52. Koch, *Preuss. Recht*, vol. i. p. 129.
(*u*) *Code Civil*, arts. 3, 11–13. Cf. above, § 358, notes *d* to *h*.
(*v*) *Oesterreich. Gesetzbuch*, §§ 4, 33–37.
(*w*) *Ibid.* §§ 33–35.

Sect. XIX.—(§ 362.)

I.—STATUS OF THE PERSON (CAPACITY TO HAVE RIGHTS AND CAPACITY TO ACT).

In judging of the various conditions and qualities (Zustände) of a person, whereby the capacity for rights and the capacity to act are determined, a pure and simple application of that local law to which the person himself belongs by his domicile, is the only possible course (§ 359).

This principle, it is true, has not remained uncontradicted (*a*). But the number of its supporters is so overwhelming, that it may, notwithstanding, be described as an almost universal opinion; it has even been confirmed by a universal consuetudinary law in Germany (*b*). This, too, is the proper signification of *personal* statutes, to which notion so much importance was attached in former times (§ 361, No. 1).

It would be a mistake, however, to estimate this accord as very complete; it is in great measure only apparent. The following distinction was very early attempted, and has lately been asserted with great emphasis (*c*). We are to distinguish between the mere abstract existence of the *legal qualities of a person* and the legal effects of these qualities; that is to say, the rights and limitations of the person arising out of them. The qualities themselves must be judged according to the local law of the domicile; but the legal consequences not according to it, but according to another local law. What law? Of this we have to speak afterwards. The advocates of this distinction, therefore, restrict to the abstract qualities or conditions themselves the generally received opinion, and the universal consuetudinary law depending on it.

The meaning of this distinction will become clear from the following instances:—Among the qualities themselves are those of the ward, the pupil, the minor, the prodigal; also of females, of the married woman, of legitimate or illegitimate children,

(*a*) So *e.g.* in J. Voet. § 7. See other opponents in Wächter, ii. pp. 162, 163; and Fœlix, p. 121 [i. 181].

(*b*) Wächter, ii. pp. 162, 163, 175, 177.

(*c*) Hert, §§ 5, 8, 11, 22; Meier, p. 14; Mittermaier, *Deutsches Recht*, § 30, p. 118 (7th ed.); but especially Wächter, ii. pp. 163, 175, 184.

etc. The question, therefore, whether any one is under age or not—that is to say, what is the limit of minority—is to be decided according to the law of the domicile. On the other hand, the rights and restrictions of the minor are among the juridical effects, and are therefore, by this doctrine, not to be judged according to the law of the domicile.[1]

At all times, however, many writers have made no such distinction, but have determined the legal effects as well as the qualities themselves, solely according to the law of the person's domicile (*d*). And in accordance with them, I too must altogether regret this distinction. I maintain it to be arbitrary and illogical; for any real ground for drawing such a line is entirely wanting. If we look into the matter closely, we find no other difference than this, that many personal qualities or states are known by specific names, while others are not. But this accidental and indifferent circumstance can afford no reason for applying to them different territorial laws.

We call him *major* who possesses the fullest capacity to act, attainable by age. It is therefore only a name for certain legal effects, for the negation of previous limitations of capacity. So we call him a *minor* who does *not yet* possess that full

[1] In the great scarcity of authority in British law on the subject of status properly so called, which in this country is almost always confounded with family law, it would be rash to say that either the one view or the other of this question has prevailed. In truth, the question has hardly been asked. In *Birtwhistle* v *Vardell*, the judges expressed opinions which seem to involve a recognition of the distinction of Hert and Wächter. Lord Tenterden said: 'We adopt the laws of all Christian countries as to marriage, but it by no means follows that we are to adopt all the consequences of such marriages which are recognised in foreign countries; it is sufficient if we admit all such consequences as follow from a lawful marriage solemnized in this country.'—5 B. and C. 452. This view was adopted by Tindal, C. J., giving the opinion of all the judges, 7 C. and F. 935; 1 Rob. App. 627; and cf. Alexander, C. B., 2 C. and F. 575. So in *Johnstone* v *Beattie*, 7 Cl. and F. 42, 114, etc., the law lords laid it down, that while the status of a foreign father would be recognised in England, he would be allowed to exercise his paternal authority only within the limits allowed by the law of England to English parents. These dicta, however, may be referred to the principle of laws affecting morals (*ante*, § 349); they are merely *obiter*, and they are spoken rather with reference to a question of family law, and not of status. See Bar, §§ 43, 44, pp. 143, 149; Westlake, §§ 70, 146, 400; Fraser, *On Parent and Child*, 589.

(*d*) Argentræus, N. 47, 48, 49; Rodenburg, tom. i. c. 3, §§ 4–10; Boullenois, tom. i. pp. 145–198; Huber, § 12; Fœlix, p. 126 [i. 187]. With regard to married women and the tutory of women, see many other supporters of this opinion in Wächter, ii. p. 167.

capacity. It is a name for the negation of the condition of perfect capacity. If a law lays down, in regard to minority itself, certain degrees of capacity, without affixing to them specific names, no ground can be discovered why these degrees of capacity, just as much as the commencement of complete capacity, should not be judged by the law of the domicile. This assertion will become still more evident by the following example: —The defenders of that distinction admit that a Frenchman twenty-one years old must be regarded as major and of full capacity in Prussia, where twenty-four years—and likewise in the countries of the Roman law, where twenty-five years—are the terms of full age; for by article 488 of the French code, he has received the rank of *majeur*, and has accordingly an essential quality to which the law of the domicile is to be applied. But the same code allows to minors, partly at sixteen, partly at fifteen and eighteen, years of age, certain more limited powers, without constituting them a special class with a specific name (*e*). This is therefore, according to that theory, no essential quality, but merely a legal effect,—a specially constituted restriction of the person; and the law of the domicile does not apply to it.

The following may serve as another example:—By many positive laws, women require the concurrence of a guardian in their juridical acts; by others, married women need the consent of the husband. If, therefore, a woman performs a juridical act abroad, then, as a logical result of that doctrine, only the existence of the mere personal quality would be judged by the law of the domicile; that is to say, the question whether she is a woman (as distinguished from a man), or a married woman (in contradistinction to a maiden or widow). On the contrary, the necessary concurrence of the guardian, or the consent of the husband, would not be judged of according to the law of the domicile, since these things are some of the legal consequences and limitations (*f*).

(*e*) *Code Civil*, art. 903, 904, 477, 478.

(*f*) This is in fact the opinion of Wächter, ii. p. 180, who is thereby led to apply to the acts of our countrywomen abroad quite different rules of collision from those which we allow to the acts of foreign women among us. [See *Ilderton* v *Ilderton*, 2 H. Bl. 145; *Birtwhistle* v *Vardell*, 2 C. and F. 571; 9 Bligh, N. R. 32. Bar, § 53, says that the diversity of opinion on this question arises from the fact that some writers have in

I now come to the question: What local law other than that of the domicile is applied by the assertors of that distinction, when the legal consequences of personal qualities are to be determined? As to this there are the following discordant opinions.

In former times an attempt was made to apply to this case the distinction of *real* statutes when immoveable property was in question, so that one and the same person might have a quite different capacity to act in respect of his foreign immoveables, and in respect of the rest of his estate. This opinion now obtains little credit in Germany (*g*).

Others hold that the *effects* of the personal qualities are to be judged by the law of the place where a juridical act is performed (*h*). This opinion must also be rejected on special grounds, irrespective of the general argument against the theory. If he who enters into a contract abroad has more extensive capacity to act at his domicile than at the place of the contract, it cannot be assumed that he has chosen, in this contract, to subject himself to a local law, according to which it would be invalid; but voluntary submission (the so-called autonomy) is the only ground on which the law prevailing at the place of the contract can be made applicable. But if, conversely, the contracting party has a more restricted capacity to act at his domicile than at the place of the contract, so that the contract, if entered into at the domicile, would be invalid, it would be illogical for the law of the domicile to disallow the contract, and yet to authorize it when made with the aid of a

view a curatory of women, which is merely a protective formality in more important transactions, in which case the *lex loci actus* is applicable; while others speak with reference to a real incapacity to act, where the guardian's consent 'supplements her will,' and is necessary to the validity of her acts.]

(*g*) Wächter, ii. pp. 163, 164. [This doctrine is applied in British courts. *Birtwhistle* v *Vardell*, *supra*; *Fenton* v *Livingstone*, 27 May 1856, 18 D. 865; rev. 15 July 1859, 3 Macq. 497. It has not only the effect, as Lord Brougham points out in *Birtwhistle* v *Vardell*, of making a man bastard in one country and legitimate in another; but in one and the same country he is regarded as bastard when he claims an estate in land, and legitimate when he seeks to obtain personal succession. See opp. in *Patrick* v *Shedden*, M. App. Foreign, 6; 5 Pat. App. 194; Story, § 93; and Westlake's argument against the English rule (§ 90 sqq.), from which the Scotch court, in *Fenton* v *Livingstone*, vainly strove to escape.]

(*h*) Meier, p. 14. Mittermaier takes the opposite view; *Deutsches Recht*, § 31, p. 120.

short journey; on the contrary, that law will prevent him as well from subjecting himself to the foreign law, as from entering into the contract. There is no need to mix up with this question the intention to evade the law (*in fraudem legis*).

The latest defender of this distinction maintains, on the other hand, that the consequences of the personal qualities are to be decided according to the territorial law of the judge who determines each case (Note *c*). I must, in the first place, urge against this opinion the reasons which have before been adduced against the whole distinction between the abstract qualities and their effects; and, in addition, the other reasons which pronounce against the territorial law of the deciding judge as an absolute and exhaustive rule (§ 361, No. 3). And here especially it must be remembered how harsh the application of that opinion appears in the countries where the *Landsassiat* is in full force; for every one who has a paltry land estate in such a country might be subjected, at the pleasure of his adversary, to a foreign law, for the determination of the legal consequences of his own personal qualities.

It is therefore my opinion, that every one is to be judged as to his personal status always by the law of his domicile, whether the judgment is at home or abroad, and whether the personal quality itself, or its legal effects, be the object of the judgment.[2]

The practical difficulties, however, that may be connected with the application of this principle in particular cases, must

[2] Notwithstanding the uncertainty and peculiarities of British law on this subject, the general rule, that the law of the domicile as to status follows the person everywhere (*personam sequitur sicut umbra*), has been frequently stated, subject to limitations; *e.g. Fenton* v *Livingstone*, and *Birtwhistle* v *Vardell*, *supra*. It is to be observed, however, that such dicta occur in cases of legitimacy in which the law of domicile (but not the actual but the birth domicile) admittedly furnishes the general rule. In regard to contracts, the *tendency* at least of English and American law is certainly in favour of the *lex loci contractus*, as regulating, for instance, the age of majority and the liabilities of minors. Story, §§ 82, 103; Burge, i. 125; Westlake, § 397 sqq. It is reasonable to expect, from a man who contracts in a country, a competent knowledge of the law of contracts of that country (Lord Stowell in *Dalrymple* v *Dalrymple*, 2 Hag. *Cons.* 61); but not that a person contracting with a foreigner, apparently of full age, shall satisfy himself of his capacity according to foreign law. But see Bar, § 45. Mr. Fraser (*Parent and Child*, p. 583) regards the applicability of a foreign law affording greater protection to minors than the law of the place of the contract, as a question of circumstances.

not be ignored. In contracting with a foreigner, it may sometimes be difficult to ascertain the territorial law of his domicile; but this difficulty is not removed, but only made less frequent, by the distinction which has been rejected. Nothing therefore remains but to make minute inquiries in such cases,—inquiries, indeed, which are necessary in regard to the individual circumstances of the foreigner, irrespective of the foreign territorial law. But if any one should desire more facility and certainty in this department of law, he must expect it only by means of positive legislation. What can be done in this way will immediately be shown in the survey of modern statutes on this subject.

Sect. XX.—(§ 363.)

STATUS OF THE PERSON (CAPACITY TO HAVE RIGHTS AND CAPACITY TO ACT).

(CONTINUATION.)

We have now to consider what is found in the most important modern codes as to this question.

I. The Prussian Allgemeine Landrecht gives the first place to the following proposition: 'The personal qualities and capacities (Eigenschäfte und Befugnisse) of a man are judged by the positive laws of the jurisdiction under which he has his proper domicile' (*a*). This rule relates to Prussian subjects, and does not distinguish whether they exercise their capacities (the chief of which is the capacity to act) at the domicile itself, or at another place in the native land, which has, it may be, another territorial law as to such capacities, or, lastly, abroad.

For foreigners this is the rule: 'Also subjects of foreign states, who live or carry on business in these lands, must be judged according to the preceding rule' (*b*).

So far all agrees with the principles above stated. A perfectly equal treatment of foreigners and natives, universal determination of the personal status, of the capacity to act,

(*a*) *A. L. R. Einl.* § 23. Detailed provisions follow in §§ 24–27.
(*b*) *L. R. Einl.* § 34.

according to the law of the domicile of the person, whether this be a domestic or a foreign law.

But two questions remain for discussion, which have been already thrown out in regard to the common law. *First*, Are only the abstract qualities here intended, or are their legal consequences also to be judged according to the law of the domicile? (§ 362). If it were merely said in § 23, 'the personal qualities,' the first or narrower meaning might be assigned to the words; but as there is added 'and capacities,' the rule must be referred also to the legal consequences of the qualities: it is to be decided for every one by the law of his domicile, not only whether or not he is minor, but also what, being minor, he can and cannot do. If any doubt remained, it would be entirely removed by some subsequent passages of the law, in which the subject-matter to be determined by the law of the domicile is designated as *capacity to act* (Fähigkeit zu handeln) (*c*), and in terms which show that nothing new is meant; but merely the same notion is expressed by a different but quite synonymous phrase. It is therefore beyond a doubt that the Prussian law includes the capacity to act among the personal qualities and capacities, and that it intends, therefore, not merely that the abstract qualities, but also that their legal effects, shall be judged according to the law of the domicile.

Secondly, we have already adverted to the practical difficulty that may arise as to the contracts of a foreigner in our country, because the law in force in the foreign country of his domicile happens to be unknown to us (§ 362). The Prussian law avoids this difficulty, by enacting that the foreigner's capacity to act shall be judged according to the most favourable law for the subsistence of the contract (therefore according to the most indulgent), provided always that the things which form the subject-matter of the contract are situated in our country (*d*). If, therefore, such a contract is made at Berlin by a Frenchman who is above twenty-one

(*c*) *L. R. Einl.* §§ 27, 35.

(*d*) *L. R. Einl.* § 35. 'But a foreigner, who enters into contracts in these lands as to things therein situated, is judged, in respect of his capacity to act, according to those laws by which the transaction may best subsist.' The 26th section contains a similar but far less important regulation. Both passages were wanting in the draft, and were first introduced with a view to the difficulty above indicated. Bornemann, *Preuss. Recht*, vol. i. p. 53, note *b*.

years of age, it is valid according to French law, which fixes majority at twenty-one years. If the contract is made at the same place by the inhabitant of a country subject to the Roman law, who is above twenty-four years old, the contract is valid according to Prussian law, which adopts twenty-four years as the term of minority. The first case is in conformity to the general principle; the second is a purely positive rule, laid down with the view of protecting subjects against the consequences of an innocent error, perhaps even of the dishonesty of their adversary. A similar regulation might be conceived as existing in the statutes of every state, and the identity of the rules for determining questions of collision, which is so desirable, would not thereby be impaired.

II. The Austrian civil code (1811) confines itself to two regulations on this subject, which are in harmony with the principles above laid down.

Citizens of the state, even in acts which are done beyond its jurisdiction, remain bound by these laws (*i.e.* by the laws of their domicile), 'in so far as their personal capacity to undertake them is thereby restricted' (*e*).

So likewise it is enacted as to foreigners: 'The personal capacity of foreigners for juridical acts is ordinarily to be determined by the laws of the place to which the foreigner is subject in virtue of his domicile' (*f*).

It undoubtedly follows from these passages, although they are couched in very general terms, that the personal status of subjects and foreigners shall be determined according to the same principle, namely, according to the local law of the domicile; further, that this determination is to extend not merely to the qualities in themselves (*e.g.* whether one is a minor or not), but also to the legal consequences of these qualities; for in both passages it is expressly said, 'the personal capacity to perform them' (the acts), 'the personal capacity . . . for juridical acts.'

On the other hand, there occurs here no special precaution with regard to the possibly unknown local law to which the foreigner may be subject (*g*).

(*e*) *Oesterreich. Gesetzbuch*, § 4.
(*f*) *Ibid.* § 34.
(*g*) We might indeed refer to this the 35th section, by taking it in a

III. The French code has only the following brief passage on this subject: 'Les lois concernant l'état et la capacité des personnes régissent les Français même résidant en pays étranger' (*h*). But it appears to follow indubitably, from the discussions which preceded this enactment, that it was assumed that also a foreigner's personal capacity to act must be determined by his domicile, and therefore by the foreign law. As to this, the decisions of writers and of courts are agreed (*i*).

The terms of the law clearly show that it must be referred not only to the abstract qualities (l'état), but also to the juridical consequences of these qualities (et la capacité) (*k*). It further follows very distinctly, that so long as the quality of a *Français* is not lost, this quality alone decides, even if the person removes his domicile to a foreign country (même résidant en pays étranger); so that the French law does not adhere rigidly to the domicile as the foundation of the capacity to have rights and to act (§ 359, *e*).

Sect. XXI.—(§ 364.)

STATUS OF THE PERSON (CAPACITY TO HAVE RIGHTS AND CAPACITY TO ACT).

(CONTINUATION.)

The principle has hitherto been discussed, that the abstract personal status, which consists chiefly in the capacity to act, must be determined according to the law of the domicile of the person. Not unfrequently, however, those who accept this as a general principle add to it various restrictions, which are now to be examined. Some of these have the nature of real exceptions, while others depend merely on the recognition of

similar sense to the rule of the Prussian law above referred to (note *d*). But on an impartial comparison of the 34th section with §§ 35–37, we must be convinced that § 34 speaks only of the personal capacity to act, while the three following sections speak of the objective nature and validity of juridical acts.

(*h*) *Code Civil*, art. 3.

(*i*) Fœlix, p. 44 [ed. Demangeat, i. 65].

(*k*) Fœlix, p. 126 [ed. Demangeat, i. 187], (*v. supra*, § 362, *d*).

natural limits, which may happen to be misunderstood. These restrictions we must partly accept as well founded, while in part they must be rejected.

In many quarters a distinction is asserted between a *general* and a *particular* capacity and incapacity for juridical acts. The first is said to refer to juridical acts of all kinds, and therein, it is said, the local law of the domicile should be applied. The second is said to extend only to certain peculiar transactions, and to these the law of the domicile is not applicable, but that local law within the bounds of which the particular juridical act has taken place. This distinction, however, is arbitrary and groundless, since the incapacity attached to a particular status of the person has in both cases the same nature; besides, a clear discrimination, and consequently a safe application, is here hardly possible (*a*). This distinction may be applied in the following cases:—

1. By the Roman law, women are incapacitated for effectually undertaking suretyships, simply by reason of their sex (*Sc. Vellejanum*). If, then, a woman becomes a surety in a foreign country, the question arises: According to what local law is the validity of the obligation to be judged? According to this distinction, it would be invalid if the Roman law were in force at the place of the contract, although another law should exist at the domicile of the woman. According to the correct opinion, the suretyship is ineffectual if the Roman law is in force at the domicile of the female surety, without respect to the law existing at the place of the contract. If we were to use here the technical term that formerly prevailed, we must say, The *Sc. Vellejanum* is a purely personal statute (*b*).

2. In like manner, by the Roman law every person subject to paternal power is incapable of contracting a valid loan of money without the knowledge of his father (*Sc. Macedonianum*). This rule is similar in its nature to that relative to guarantees by women: it is a purely personal statute. The validity of the loan will depend, therefore, on the question, whether at the

(*a*) Wächter also rejects this distinction on both grounds; ii. p. 172.

(*b*) This expression is in fact used by the following writers, who defend the view here stated (with confutation of its opponents): Boullenois, tom. i. p. 187; Chabot de l'Allier, *Questions Transitoires*, Paris 1809, tom. ii. p. 352.

domicile of the debtor the *Sc. Macedonianum* is the subsisting law. The law of the place where the loan is contracted is immaterial.

3. The most difficult and most important application of the distinction relates to bills of exchange. In regard to no act are so many different laws in existence as in regard to the personal capacity to make or indorse bills (Wechselfähigkeit), and no juridical act spreads its operation over so boundless an extent. At common law the matter stands thus: The advocates of this distinction must determine the general capacity of the drawer (*e.g.* majority) by the law of the domicile; his special capacity, by the law of the place where the bill is drawn (*c*). According to the correct view, the local law of the domicile alone decides.

The peculiar nature of bills of exchange might justify, as to this point, a facilitating interference of positive legislation, since it will very often be difficult, and even impossible, for the purchaser of a bill to know the various laws as to capacity for exchange, to which the various debtors on the bill (drawers, indorsers, acceptors) are subject by their domicile, as well as the personal relations of these debtors in regard to domicile (*d*). The difficulty, however, is less in reality than it may at first sight appear. The cautious purchaser of a drawn bill (*e*), although it has travelled through various parts of the world, and is covered with numerous signatures, will generally look only to a few subscriptions, which he knows from his own experience to be safe; and all besides these may be immaterial to him. Throughout Germany the difficulty has been greatly lessened by the new German law as to bills of exchange, 27th November 1848 (*f*), which, in its first article, declares

(*c*) Schäffner, p. 120, is here of a different opinion. According to him, the drawer must be capable of making a bill, (1) at the place of drawing, and (2) at his domicile, if he shall be sued there; because, otherwise, an absolute statute would bar the action. He has been led astray by a misapprehension of the rules of the Prussian law, of which we shall immediately have to speak.

(*d*) Hence in Prussian law a different rule as to personal capacity, facilitating dealings in bills (see below, notes *l*, *m*).

(*e*) In the case of promissory notes (*trockenen Wechsel*), the great simplicity of the transaction makes the ascertainment of capacity less difficult.

(*f*) Cf. the Prussian *Gesetzsammlung*, 1849, p. 51. The law has force in Prussia from 1st February 1849

every one who can enter into other contracts to have capacity for bills, and thus removes all previous special restrictions of such capacity (*g*). In respect to foreign countries, this law accepts the principle here laid down, that the personal capacity is to be decided according to the domicile of each obligant; only with the very judicious practical improvement, that he who enters into an obligation by bill abroad, is to be regarded by the courts of this country as possessing the requisite capacity, provided only the law of this country recognises him as capable (Art. 84).

It would be quite incorrect to assimilate the case of a debtor on a bill to whom the law of his domicile denies the capacity requisite for such an obligation, with the case in which the law of the domicile (or the place of drawing) does not recognise bills at all. In this case, the drawer, indorser, or acceptor is to be held of due capacity, if only he have capacity to act in general. But an *action* on a bill will certainly not lie against any one at a place where the law does not recognise bills of exchange, because in this action everything depends on the local procedure. The personal liability itself derived from the drawing of the bill is not thereby excluded, although it cannot (at least at the domicile of the drawer) be made available by an action on the bill.

In this matter the Prussian law deserves special notice. If its general rules as to personal capacity to act (§ 363, No. 1) be applied unconditionally to capacity in respect of bills, we have the following result:—The Prussian subject's capacity for bills is determined by Prussian law (the law of his domicile), whether he subscribes a bill in his own or in a foreign country. The foreigner who subscribes a bill in Prussia is judged by Prussian law or the law of his domicile, according as the one or the other is more favourable to the validity of the contract (§ 363, *d*). Our law, however, has not adhered to this simple application of its general principles to bills of exchange, yet without widely deviating from them. A modification might in fact be suggested, not only by the very peculiar nature of the con-

(*g*) The third article expressly declares that every subscription on a bill has of itself binding force, independently of the validity of the other subscriptions,—a regulation which is especially important with respect to personal capacity for bills.

tract of exchange, but also by the special limitations of the capacity for exchange which were found necessary, and in which Prussian legislation adopted a course of its own, different from that which obtains in other countries. Let us first consider these limitations as they stood, down to the latest date in the Prussian law.

Only the following classes of persons were held to have capacity for bills,—those who had the rights of merchants, possessors of manorial lands (Rittergutsbesitzer), tenants of demesne lands (Domänenpächter), and those on whom such capacity was specially conferred by their personal judge; all other inhabitants (and therefore the vast majority of the whole population) were held not to have this capacity (*h*). The ascertainment of that quality was especially difficult in consequence of the statutory rule, that where guilds of merchants existed, only their members should have the privileges of merchants, and consequently the capacity necessary for bills (*i*). This very peculiar restriction originated, doubtless, in a paternal care for those who might be disposed rashly to contract debts. On account of the strict execution connected with them, bills were considered particularly dangerous; and the use of these dangerous instruments for the enhancement of credit was denied to all to whom it was not indispensable on account of their special mercantile relations (*k*).

After this preliminary statement, I pass on to the rules as to the local law to be administered in judging of the capacity for bills. First, as to Prussian subjects. If these enter into contracts of exchange within the country, they are naturally liable to the restrictions of the Prussian law. If they do so

(*h*) *A. L. R.* ii. 8, §§ 715–747.

(*i*) *A. L. R.* ii. 8, § 480. This rule was abolished by the Gewerbegesetz (trades' law) of 7th September 1811, by which the trade licence was made sufficient for all mercantile privileges. On the other hand, it was restored for those towns which received a special statute for their traders,—as Berlin, Stettin, Danzig, Königsberg, Magdeburg, etc. Comp. *Ergänzungen des A. L. R.* by Gräff, Koch, Rönne, Simon, Wentzel (often called the *Fünfmännerbuch*), vol. iv. pp. 758–760, 2d ed.

(*k*) Koch, *Preuss. Recht*, vol. i. § 415, vol. ii. § 617, Nos. 2, 3, entirely separates the capacity of exchange from the general capacity to act. The former, he says, is in Prussian law a privilege of trade, a privilege of merchants. This view appears to me forced, nor does it at all explain the special rules as to territorial law in cases of capacity for bills (see below, note *q*).

abroad, they must be governed, according to the general principle, by the same law. They must be judged by the law of the domicile, and therefore by the Prussian law restricting the capacity of exchange. Here, however, the case is not so: their capacity of exchange is to be determined according to the place where the transaction has taken place (*l*), and only exceptionally according to Prussian law, namely, when both contracting parties are Prussians (*m*). How, then, is it to be explained that the *Landrecht* here departs from the general principle of the 23d section of the Introduction (§ 363, *a*), and now admits it only exceptionally for the case in which two Prussians enter into a contract of exchange with one another? The reason of this deviation is found, I believe, in the very peculiar character of the Prussian law as to the capacity of exchange. If a Berliner in Paris draws a bill on a Frenchman, it would certainly be extremely unfair to require of the Frenchman, in order to satisfy himself as to the future right of action on the bill at Berlin, not only to know the Prussian laws (which perhaps might be practicable), but also discover whether the drawer is a member of the Berlin corporation of merchants, or the possessor of manorial lands (Rittergutsbesitzer), or tenant of demesne lands,—qualities which are certainly not easily ascertainable. Such an injustice would, however, immediately meet with retribution, inasmuch as the credit of Prussians who happened to be abroad would be undermined, in respect at least to bills. It was therefore expedient, or almost necessary, to give up the general principle in this case (*n*). It was

(*l*) *A. L. R.* ii. 8, § 936. 'Contracts of exchange entered into abroad are to be judged according to the law of the place where they are concluded.' These words alone might be understood merely of the constitution of the bill, etc., and not of the personal capacity. Their reference to this last, however, is placed beyond doubt by the apparent contradiction in § 938: 'But if an inhabitant of this country has concluded a contract of exchange with another Prussian who has not capacity in respect of bills, then the same is to be judged just as if it had been concluded within the country.'

(*m*) *A. L. R.* ii. 8, § 938 (quoted in note *l*). The correctness of this view was formerly contested; now it is generally admitted. The authorities for it are, (1) a judgment of the Council of State (Staatsrath) in 1834; (2) a sentence of the supreme court (Ober Tribunal) of 21st November 1840. *Entscheidungen des Obertribunals*, by Simon, vol. vi. pp. 288–300, where an extract of the judgment of the Staatsrath referred to is also quoted, p. 289.

(*n*) This anomaly is differently explained in the opinion of the Staats-

necessary, however, to retain it exceptionally in the case of two Prussians dealing with each other abroad, since the Prussian law of limited capacity could otherwise be too easily evaded by a journey over the frontiers. It must still be added, that this deviation from general principles follows the analogy of another rule of our law, viz. of the 35th section of the Introduction to the *A. L. R.* What is here prescribed for foreigners in Prussia is there transferred to Prussians abroad, for which strong reasons existed, as already remarked in the law of bills. This transference, however, could have been generally effected for all legal relations, without too much derogating from principles.

I will now consider, further, the rules as to the capacity of foreigners who become obligants on bills within the Prussian state. The terms of the statute are as follows:—

§ 931. Foreigners travelling are not subject, in respect of their capacity to become liable on bills, to the restrictions of the law of this country.

§ 932. But in other respects, the liabilities on bills undertaken by them in this country are judged according to the rule contained in the Introduction (§§ 38, 39) (*o*).

It is owing only to its not very happy expression that § 931 appears, and has been understood by writers, to introduce a deviation from the general principles laid down in the Introduction to the *A. L. R.* No more is intended, however, than a mere application of these principles. Both the paragraphs might very well have been wanted, and without them the same result would have followed which is held to proceed from them. § 932 expressly says this as to the objective requirements for bills of exchange. But the same must also be asserted of the personal capacity of which § 931 speaks; for § 931 contains only the negative proposition that the restrictions of our law of

rath and the judgment of the supreme court (note *m*); for in both the distinction of the *general* and *particular* conditions of capacity to act is founded on, against which I have expressed an opinion in the beginning of this section. Koch gives still another explanation (note *k*), namely, that the exclusive capacity of merchants in our law being a *privilegium*, no application of it can be made in foreign countries.

(*o*) This reference is wrong; it must be 34, 35. Comp. Kamptz, *Jahrb.* vol. xliii. p. 445; *Ergänzungen*, etc., by Gräff, etc., vol. iv. p. 804. The error does not arise from a printer's blunder, but from the fact that the numbers of the paragraphs in the Gesetzbuch (1792) were retained, while in the *A. L. R.* (1794) they had here, as in some other passages, been altered.

exchange shall *not* affect the foreigner. But this does not imply that he should unconditionally have capacity for bills; rather (quite in conformity with § 35 of the Introduction) he is to be judged, in respect of capacity for bills, by that law which imposes the easiest conditions (*p*). This rule was in fact kept in view, and might without much hazard be expressed as has here been done, because it might be assumed as certain that no foreign law would go so far as the Prussian in curtailing the personal capacity of exchange. On this supposition the negative proposition of § 931 was quite sufficient for the practical end, although a simpler expression of the special purpose would have been desirable for preventing misunderstandings. If, then, the § 931 is, as I believe, no different rule, but only a simple application of general principles, it needs no special exposition and justification (*q*). At most it might be asked, why the paternal care that protects against the dangerous strictness of execution (on account of which the Landrecht denies to the majority of subjects the capacity for exchange) should not also be advantageous for foreigners. But this is sufficiently accounted for by the fact that the protective measures of each law giver are always limited intheir effects to his own subjects.[1] As, therefore, the Frenchman in Prussia is

(*p*) Comp. *Ergänzungen*, etc., by Gräff, etc., vol. iv. p. 804. There must, however, be this distinction as to § 35 of the Introduction, that that limitation of § 35, by which the transaction affects only things situated in this country, is not applicable to bills of exchange. This difference, however, arises from the nature and object of bills.

(*q*) The opinion of Koch (see above, note *k*) is not, I think, easily reconcilable with this rule. It is quite conceivable that the Prussian mercantile class had been allowed, as a privilege, and to the exclusion of the other inhabitants of the country, the advantage to be derived from bills of exchange, which could only have been done for the purpose of favouring that class. But in that case it would have been quite inconsistent to permit strangers (even those who are not merchants) coming into the country to enjoy the same advantage, while it is refused to native inhabitants of the same description.

[1] Bar, p. 179, while agreeing generally with the doctrine in the text, observes that the assertion of this sentence as to 'protective measures' is too wide, and refers to the duty of a court to name a temporary or provisional guardian in cases of need (*ib.* p. 368). 'Tutors may be given to strangers' pupils, in so far as concerns their lands, in Scotland.' Stair, i. 6, 11; *Brown* v *Donaldson*, 17 Dec. 1627, M. 4647; now judicial factors, *Ross* (*Petr.*), 11 Mar. 1857, 19 D. 699; *Hay* (*Petr.*), 16 July 1861, 23 D. 1291; or to a foreigner resident in Scotland who becomes insane, *Bonar* (*Petr.*), 18 June 1851, 12 D. 10. See Burge, iii. 1001; Westlake, § 398; *Johnstone* v *Beattie*, 10 Cl. and F. 42; *Nugent* v *Vetsera*, 35 L. J. Ch. 777; Fraser, *Parent and Child*, 604 sq.

acknowledged at twenty-one to be capable of making other contracts which may prove hurtful to him,—a capacity which we allow to the Prussian only at twenty-four,—we must, in consistency, hold the Frenchman capable to become an obligant by bills in Prussia without being a merchant, a possessor of manorial lands, or a tenant of demesne lands.

All these doubts and difficulties, however, were ended in Prussian law on 1st February 1849, when the new German *Wechselordnung* came into force in this country. That law declares every one who is of capacity to make contracts generally, to have also capacity for exchange (note *f*). (Note A.)

Note A.

'Although a law which professes to make any persons or class of persons incapable as to any act or contract is in fact a mere declaration that such act or contract, when attempted by them, is illegal and null, and is not therefore, on general international principles, necessarily to be respected by foreign sovereigns when the act or contract is attempted in their dominions, yet if such an artificial incapacity is contained in the jurisprudence of both of any two countries, they may reciprocally recognise it as though it were a natural one. Of this kind is the incapacity of nobles to engage in trade, and consequently to bind themselves by mercantile contracts, which existed in many European states, and may possibly exist still in some. Such an inability of each other's subjects would be reciprocally recognised in those countries, but would be disregarded elsewhere, as we disregard the native inability of a foreign slave to exercise any of the rights of freedom in these dominions. Another example is the inability which by many foreign laws attaches to persons in general to become parties to a bill of exchange, the peculiar obligations implied by such an instrument being regarded as so perilous that they are only allowed to be incurred by those classes, variously defined in different countries, for whose trading pursuits they are held to be necessary. Between such countries the capacity to become a party to a bill of exchange is decided by the domicile; but I know of no authority for supposing that the domicile would be referred to by our courts for such a purpose, if a foreigner drew, accepted, or indorsed a bill of exchange within their jurisdiction.'—Westlake, § 348, cf. § 403. 'It may be doubted whether the English courts would recognise this incapacity, though, according to all sound principles of comity, they ought to do so.'—Phillimore, iv. 607. 'A great proportion of writers have decided against the general acknowledgment of rules of the *lex domicilii* imposing such incapacity, and have maintained the validity of obligations on bills even where there is such an incapacity for exchange, provided only the obligation would be valid by the law of the place where it is entered into. It appears, indeed, intolerable for commercial interests, that one who binds himself by bill where the capacity for exchange is unlimited, should be allowed to escape from his obligation by appealing to an entirely exceptional law existing at his domicile. But it does not follow, from the rejection of the *lex domicilii* of the obligor in regard to capacity for bills, that it must always be ruled by the laws of the place where the obligation is undertaken. It is rather subject to the general laws which govern the obligation in other respects.'—Bar, pp. 182, 183.

SECT. XXII.—(§ 365.)

STATUS OF THE PERSON (CAPACITY TO HAVE RIGHTS, AND CAPACITY TO ACT).

(CONTINUATION.)

Hitherto the law of the domicile has been asserted as the general regulator of the capacity to act, and that even in those cases in which a different view is taken by many writers (§ 364). The limits to the application of that principle are now to be stated, and the cases in which it is not to be applied. The recognition of these cases may also perhaps facilitate reconciliation with many who have so far been my opponents, and who, in not a few instances, may have been made averse to the principle itself by the consideration of such cases.

These cases may be reduced to two classes.

A. When a law relating to personal status (capacity to have rights or capacity to act) is one of those absolute statutes which, by their anomalous nature, lie beyond the limits of the community of law subsisting between independent states, the judge has not to administer the law of the domicile of the person, but rather the law of his own country. This principle has been fully expounded (§ 349), and it is only requisite to mention here some of its most important applications to the capacity to have rights and the capacity to act, of which we are now speaking.

1. Where polygamy is recognised by law, he who is living in a subsisting marriage has the capacity, during its continu-

ance, of entering into a second marriage. But the judge of a Christian state will give him, in respect of this, no legal protection, and therefore will apply, in regard to this kind of capacity to act, not the law of the personal domicile, but the law of his own country.[1]

2. When one to whom the law of his own country refuses, as a heretic, the capacity to have rights, desires to acquire rights and perform juridical acts in a country which rejects as immoral such a law as to heresy,—perhaps even is of the same religion as this so-called heretic,—the judge of this country will not apply the law of the domicile of the person, but his own municipal law (*a*).

3. If the laws of a country restrict the capacity of ecclesiastical bodies to acquire property (mortmain), this limitation will then affect such bodies established in another country. Conversely, the ecclesiastical bodies which are under such laws in their own country are not subject to these limitations in a foreign country which has no such restrictive laws. Thus, in both cases, the capacity to act is judged by the law of the land to which the court belongs, not by the law in force at the domicile of such an institution.

4. If the law of a country declares Jews to be incapable of acquiring landed property, it affects foreign as well as native Jews; but native Jews are not thereby prevented from acquiring landed property in another country which has no such law. In neither case, therefore, is the law of the domicile of the person administered.

5. It is just the same with the well-known French law, which in some eastern departments (afterwards partly ceded to German states) declared Jews incapable of acquiring right to debts, except under certain very strict conditions. This law affects all Jews, native and foreign, within such a country (*b*):

[1] See above, p. 36.

(*a*) Hert, § 8, note 3. It is otherwise with the incapacity of foreign monks to succeed to property; which law of their domicile, as pertaining to the ordinary capacity to act, and also resting on the freewill of the person, is to be recognised in our state. Hert, § 13; Bornemann, *Preuss. Recht*, vol. i. p. 53, note 1.

(*b*) Wächter, ii. p. 173; Fœlix, p. 147 [ed. Demangeat, i. 219]. This is in accordance with a decision of the supreme court of Munich. Seuffert, *Archiv für Entscheidungen der Obersten Gerichte in den deutschen Staaten*, vol. i. n. 35.

native Jews in a foreign land are not affected by it. The law of the domicile, therefore, is not attended to in this case.

The preceding instances depend on the fact that the law as to the capacity to have rights, or the capacity to act, is of a strictly positive and compulsory nature (*c*). In the following cases a similar exception to the rule of the domicile must be asserted, because in one state a legal institution of another state has obtained no recognition at all.

6. This is the case with the legal incapacity arising from the civil death of the French and the Russian laws. The judge of a state in which the institution of civil death is unknown will make no application of it, and therefore cannot observe the law of the domicile (§ 349, *d*).

7. The same is true of the incapacity of a negro slave, if that comes into question in a state which does not recognise slavery as a legal institution (§ 349, *e*).

B. In other cases the applicability of our principle must be denied, on the ground that the question involved in them does not relate at all to the capacity to have rights or the capacity to act, of which alone we are here treating; and that therefore they lie beyond the limits of our doctrine, and can only be brought within it under false pretences. Among these I reckon the following cases:—

1. In many countries the nobility have certain peculiar rights in acquiring landed estate, or in succession. These privileges have no real connection with our subject. Whether they belong only to the nobility of the country, or also to foreign nobles, depends on the contents of the legal rules establishing the privilege. This question cannot be decided according to a general principle (*d*).

2. In the same position are the privileges in competition in bankruptcy, which in many laws belong to churches and convents, or, it may be, to the fisc. Particularly in regard to the fisc, it is not the abstract idea of a fisc that is meant, but in all cases only the fisc of the country. But all such rights do not belong to this place, but to the doctrine of bankruptcy (*e*).

(*c*) It is hardly necessary to mention that the merits or demerits of the laws here cited as examples are indifferent for our question, and therefore do not need to be discussed.

(*d*) Wächter, ii. p. 172. [Bar, § 51.]

(*e*) Wächter, ii. pp. 173, 181.

3. There is more doubt as to the restitution of minors, since it must be clearly fixed in what sense this right is itself understood by the legislator. Originally it was regarded as a limitation of the capacity to act, so that it would pass as a surrogate to minors for the complete incapacity that protects pupils. But since restitution has been applied to the acts of curators also, and in this form has been extended even to the tutors of pupils, it has lost that character (*f*). It does not now, therefore, rank among the limitations of the capacity to act, but it must rather be treated, in regard to the local law to be applied to it, in the same way as other grounds for impugning juridical acts (*g*).

4. In like manner, it must be asserted that the favour of minors, by which they are protected against all prescriptions under thirty years (and that even without restitution) (*h*), has no connection with the capacity to act, and therefore is to be judged, in respect of the local law, not by the rules here laid down (*i*), but by the rules as to prescription of actions.

In concluding this part of the inquiry, the two following remarks may be made :—

The subject of the inquiry related to the capacity *to have rights and the capacity to act* (§§ 362–365). Of these two relations, the highest rank belonged, in Roman law, to the capacity to have rights: it was paramount. In modern law the case is reversed; for of the Roman limitations of the capacity to have rights, some have entirely disappeared, and some have been diminished in importance. The influence of freedom and of *civitas* has disappeared; that of the paternal power has been diminished.

A second remark relates to domicile, here acknowledged as determining the local law of personal status applicable in every case. But domicile is of a changeable and unsteady nature, and consequently the legal status of the person will also be variable in consequence of changes of domicile; so that the legal status at any time is to be judged by the local law of the

(*f*) See above, vol. vii. § 322.
(*g*) Comp. Wächter, ii. pp. 174, 179. [Bar, § 56; *infra*, § 374, *r*.]
(*h*) See above, vol. vii. § 324, No. 1.
(*i*) Wächter, ii. p. 179.

present domicile, not by that of the former one, although this should have subsisted from birth (*k*).

This proposition is very generally recognised as the rule (*l*), and in particular it is confirmed, although only in an indirect way, by a passage of the Prussian Landrecht (*m*). In two respects, however, it needs closer examination.

First: This proposition will be easily and generally accepted by the tribunals of the new domicile; so also by the courts of any third place. On the other hand, opposition is not unfrequently encountered from the tribunals of the previous domicile, which seek to maintain their own local law even after the person has changed his domicile, although, in principle, this opposition cannot be vindicated (*n*).

Second: A very frequent and important application of that principle deserves special attention,—that, namely, to the legal period of majority. An unconditional application of the rule would here involve two contradictory results. The Prussian Landrecht fixes majority at twenty-four years; the French law in force at Cologne, at twenty-one. If, then, at the age of twenty-two a Berliner changed his domicile to Cologne, he would of necessity become major at that moment. On the contrary, if at the same age a native of Cologne changed his domicile to Berlin, he must become minor again, submit anew to guardianship, and remain under it for two years longer. The first of these two consequences is unquestionable, and can hardly admit of a denial; but the second consequence, although it likewise is defended by older writers (*o*), is to be rejected for the following reasons:—

For the minor who attains at his domicile the legal age of

(*k*) This whole question is one of those reserved above (§ 344, *e*).

(*l*) Story, § 69 sq. [Burge, i. 104; Bar, § 46.]

(*m*) *A L. R. Introd.* § 24. 'A mere withdrawal from his jurisdiction, in which the purpose of choosing another domicile is not yet perfectly evident, does not change the personal rights and duties of this man.' This implies the unquestionable converse, that the evident choice of a new domicile does in fact change the personal rights.

(*n*) Story, *l.c.*, adduces, for the one or the other opinion, both writers and English and American cases. In his detailed discussion, however, two very different questions are confounded,—the collision of the old and new domicile, and the collision of the domicile with the place where a legal act (*e.g.* a marriage) is entered into.

(*o*) Lauterbach, *de domicilio*, § 69, *Dissert.* vol. ii. p. 1353; Hert, § 5 *fin.*

majority, the independence thus obtained has the nature of a vested right, which cannot, therefore, be taken from him again by a merely accidental change of domicile.[2] This view is confirmed by comparison with the case in which the majority at the previous domicile is acquired, not by age, but by *venia actatis*, and the domicile is afterwards changed. The consequences of such a sovereign concession cannot possibly be withdrawn from him again (*p*); but it would be unnatural and arbitrary to ascribe to the majority founded on the law of the previous domicile, less strength and duration than to that which originated in a concession.

This doctrine is undoubtedly admitted in the Prussian law, both by the practice of the courts and by writers (*q*). (Note A.)

Note A. (Personal Status.)

The obscurity and uncertainty of this subject arise mainly from the want of a clear definition of what is meant by personal status. Many writers, such as Story and Fœlix, and in general English and American tribunals, include under this head (capacity of persons) a great part of the law of the family relations. Bar, § 44, attempts to supply this definition. He limits the term to the general or *proper* legal status of the person, which may differ in two ways: (1) as the person has a more or less extensive capacity to have or acquire rights; (2) as his general capacity to dispose *inter vivos* of his estate, or particular portions of it, is in question. All other legal propositions do not touch the essence of the person, but only affect particular rights

[2] Bar, § 51, disapproves of this reasoning,—first, because he rejects entirely the principle of vested rights in private international law, as involving a *petitio principii;* and secondly, because the capacity to act is not a vested right, in a juridical sense. He arrives, however, at the same practical result in this way: In order to a valid change of domicile, capacity to act is required both to quit the former and to acquire the new domicile. By acknowledging the competency of a minor (according to its laws) of his own will to transfer his domicile into its territory, a state implicitly recognises his full capacity to act, and thus tacitly confers on him the rights of majority. This argument does not apply to cases where a minor, without changing his domicile, enters into contracts in a foreign country; and does not therefore touch the reasons on which American and English authorities proceed in referring the age of majority to the *lex loci contractus.*

(*p*) This last is also admitted in the convention between Prussia and Saxony in 1821 (*Ges. Samml.* p. 39). It is likewise admitted by Hert, § 8, who, therefore, is here inconsistent (note *o*).

(*q*) Bornemann, *Preuss. Recht*, vol. i. p. 53, note 1, No. 2; Koch, *Preuss. Recht*, § 40, note 11. Both cite several rescripts of the ministry of justice, by which the practice of the courts is placed beyond a doubt.

incidentally belonging to the person. It is not necessary to the personality of the individual that he shall have certain concrete rights, but the first essential quality of personality is, that he shall be *capable* of having them. The second indispensable requisite is, that he shall have a legally effective will, *i.e.* that he be capable of acting. Rules of law, therefore, which only affirm or deny to a person certain concrete rights, do not touch the essence of his personality, but merely his incidental relations. If a person has disposing power *inter vivos* over all his means and estate, but is incapacitated to perform certain special juridical acts, that incapacitating rule does not touch the essence of the person whom it restrains. He has full power to transfer all his rights in another way. If a person so restricted in regard to a particular kind of act is regarded as limited in his proper capacity to act, the inhabitants of a whole country in which a particular juridical act is invalid, or is not recognised, must be regarded as so restricted. Thus in one country only women are disabled from contracting obligations by bills; in another no one can so bind himself. Properly speaking, a limitation of the capacity to act occurs only when the person in question can in no way dispose of his estate as a whole or of a part of it, or of particular patrimonial rights belonging to him. The limitation of the principle to juridical acts *inter vivos* arises from the fact that personality ceases with life. In the strict sense, the testator does not dispose of his property. He can only, by a declaration of his will, effect that some person shall or shall not acquire a complex mass of property, and shall or shall not undertake a complex mass of obligations, hitherto united in his person. Capacity for testamentary dispositions, therefore, is neither one of the essential properties necessarily belonging to every individual person, nor of those which belong to persons, as a general rule. Testamentary dispositions may be entirely invalid in any country, as they were by the older German law; dispositions *inter vivos* are indispensable for the intercourse of life.

Incapacity for special juridical acts is not a limitation of general capacity to act, when the person retains the power of disposing upon his whole estate by other acts *inter vivos.* Thus it is no limitation of capacity to act when women are prevented from binding themselves in security for others, sons unforisfamiliated by loans, country people or officials by bills, or when one is disabled from making a will till he reaches a certain age. Bar concludes by saying, that though the instances of true and only apparent incapacity to act coincide with the instances commonly given of general and special incapacity, the distinction is not identical in its meaning and force. The ideas of general and special incapacity, as used by Wächter and others, are relative, and do not allow of any boundary being drawn between them; and no reason can be assigned, in fact, for judging the special, otherwise than the general incapacity in international law. General incapacity to act is only a collective term, designating all special incapacities to act in the ordinary sense.

Bar points out (§ 45) that the rules on which the capacity of individuals to have rights depend, rest essentially on the political and moral convictions of a nation. Thus, if the law of the domicile of foreigners were to decide in this respect, the very facts which with us give full or partial capacity for rights would be a ground of postponement or inferiority: in one country, for instance, only Roman Catholics, in another only Protestants, can acquire land. Again, certain rules affecting this kind of capacity can be realized only because particular regulations actually exist in a state, which do not exist at all, or are not applied to the particular case in another state in which the person concerned actually lives—*e.g.* civil death. He concludes, therefore, that when the validity of a juridical act stands in question because an individual is not regarded as a person at all by the law of his domicile, that is decided by the law of the place where the individual actually was at the time of entering into the obligation; for at this moment the will of the contracting parties was directed towards the origination of the obligation, and it cannot be affected by afterwards coming in contact with the law of a different place. According to the opposite view, the judge must assume the authority of his law over the whole earth, and a legal reciprocity and comity would be hardly conceivable. Hence it follows, that one who by the law of his actual residence does not possess a legal personality, cannot, so long as he resides there, exercise rights and emit valid declarations of will (as by letters). Considerations of expediency also justify this result. In such cases an independent *cura absentis* is to be created. Rules as to capacity to act have a different purpose: they do not deprive of the enjoyment of certain rights, but they protect certain persons from loss by their own acts. This protective care extends to all persons domiciled in the state, and cannot be conceived as extending to foreigners, unless we imagine the impracticable measure to be adopted of establishing a guardianship for strangers temporarily residing in a country. Hence the necessity which lies on the tribunals of foreign countries of regarding as capable of acting, those who are so by the law of their domicile. The converse of this proposition cannot be regarded as logically necessary. From the purpose of laws as to capacity to act, we can only infer that foreigners capable to act according to the *lex loci actus*, but not by the law of their domicile, must be regarded as so capable by all other courts except those of the domicile, and of countries whose laws are the same as those of the domicile. No law can be supposed to have a greater anxiety to protect foreigners from the consequences of their acts than its own subjects. (See *Saul* v *His Creditors*, and other Louisiana cases on the age of majority; Story, §§ 75, 76.) Bar, however, admits that even in this case a universal customary law, at least on the continent of Europe, has made the law of the domicile the universal rule for the capacity to act. The rule to which English and American practice tends is founded on a principle—'Qui cum alio contrahit vel est vel esse debet non ignarus conditionis ejus'—which cannot equitably be applied to personal qualities determined by unknown foreign laws. When the tribunals themselves are not bound to know foreign law, and in every case require evidence of them, how should this knowledge be presumed in the case of private persons?—Bar, §§ 44, 45.

Sect. XXIII.—(§ 366.)

II. LAW OF THINGS.—GENERAL RULES.

In now passing on to rights in particular things, or to real rights, in order to ascertain the legal territory to which they belong, we are led, by the very nature of their object, to the determination of this territory. For since their object is perceived by the senses, and therefore occupies a definite space, the locality in space at which they are situated is naturally the seat of every legal relation into which they can enter. He who wishes to acquire, to have, to exercise a right to a thing, goes for that purpose to its locality, and voluntarily submits himself, as to this particular legal relation, to the local law that governs in that region. When, therefore, it is said that real rights are to be judged by the law of the place where the thing is situated (*lex rei sitæ*), this assertion rests on the same ground as the application of the *lex domicilii* to the personal status. Both arise from voluntary submission.[1]

[1] This, says Bar, § 57, is a *petitio principii*. It must first be shown, on the one hand, that the laws of the place where the thing is situated claim exclusive authority over all rights in it, without which voluntary submission would not suffice to warrant the application of the *lex rei sitæ*; and if it is true, on the other hand, that he who seeks, in point of fact, to exercise a right over a thing must go to the place where it is situated, and therefore may become subject to the laws of that place, it does not follow that other states are obliged to recognise this subjection,—*e.g.* if a moveable thing is afterwards brought into the territory of another state, etc. Bar agrees with Thöl. (*Deutsches Privatrecht*, § 84, Göttingen 1851), and Wächter, ii. 199, in referring the authority of the *lex rei sitæ* simply to the intention of the local legislator, without assigning any deeper reason. The defect of the prevailing theory—that moveable things follow the domicile of the person interested in them—is, that in ascertaining who has a particular right in the thing, it is assumed that some person already has some right or another;

Here, also, we discover the intimate connection of the forum with the local law (*a*). In the older Roman law, indeed, the *forum rei sitæ* was quite unknown (*b*); but it was early introduced in the *rei vindicatio* (*c*), and was afterwards extended to other actions *in rem* (*d*). It is not, however, held as the exclusive forum, but the plaintiff has an election between the (special) *forum rei sitæ*, and the (general) *forum domicilii*. But such an uncertainty, depending on the will of one party, was not available for the determination of the local law, which requires a fixed rule. For this end, therefore, one of the two must be exclusively adopted; and this can only be the local law of the place where the thing is situated (*lex rei sitæ*),—a selection which is justified by the special will directed to this particular legal relation. This preference is also supported by another reason. Several persons may be concerned in the same right to a particular thing, of whom each may have a different domicile. If, then, the law of the domicile is to regulate as to real rights, it would remain doubtful in such a case which domicile should determine. This doubt vanishes at once by the preference of the *lex rei sitæ*, which is always of a simple and exclusive nature.

This principle has been generally accepted from a very early time, and it stands in connection with the notion before mentioned of Real Statutes (§ 361, No. 1). That phrase was intended to indicate that the laws which primarily regulate the right to things are to be applied to all the things situated in the territory of the lawgiver, whether native or foreign persons may be concerned with them. Yet for a long time the recogni-

and although one or another real right—*e.g.* property or possession—is chosen, always arbitrarily, as the principal and decisive element, there is always wanting a *regula regulans* when two persons come to be at issue with regard to that right itself. *Infra*, p. 133.

(*a*) See above, § 360, No. 1. As to the *forum rei sitæ*, compare in general Bethmann Hollweg, *Versuche*, pp. 69-77, where the propositions which here follow are more fully treated.

(*b*) *Vatic. Fragm.* § 326. The contrary does not follow from L. 24, § 2. *de jud.* (5, 1); which passage does not speak of the *forum rei sitæ*, but of the *forum originis*, which every Roman citizen had in the city of Rome, along with his own domicile, but from which the *Legati* could withdraw themselves (§ 352, *k*).

(*c*) L. 3, *C. ubi in rem* (3, 19).

(*d*) *Nov.* 69. Whether this extension was here introduced as new law, or was only recognised, while it had before found its way into practice, cannot be determined in the defective state of the law sources. Mühlenbruch, *Archiv*, vol. xix. p. 377, maintains too decidedly that that law contains nothing new.

tion of this true doctrine was hindered by an arbitrary distinction which deprived it of all inherent force and consistency. The principle was held to apply only to immoveable things, while moveables were judged, not by the *lex rei sitæ*, but by the *lex domicilii;* and for this purpose it was necessary to assume by a fiction, that moveable things, even when they were situated elsewhere, must yet be regarded as if they were at the domicile of the person (*e*).

This distinction naturally arose in the law of succession, where a very important and erroneous use has been made of it.[2] Thence it was first transferred to rights to particular things, to which, however, in most cases it is so little suited, that its consistent application to real rights is often quite untenable, and indeed will hardly find defenders. In principle, the distinction is to be rejected in both these departments, so that everywhere one and the same local law is to be applied to moveable and immoveable things. It must, however, be observed here, that in these two applications party opinions stand towards one another in quite different, and indeed antagonistic, positions. In succession, the local law of the domicile, according to the correct opinion, is applicable to things of all kinds. Our opponents admit this as to moveables, but wish to apply to immoveables another law, the *lex rei sitæ*. Conversely, in the law of things, the local law of the place where the thing is situated, and that in regard to things of all kinds, is applicable according to the correct view. Our op-

(*e*) Modern writers often indicate this principle by the formula, *mobilia ossibus inhærent;* and that in such a way that we might suppose the formula to occur in the ancients on every side. Thus Story, § 362; Schäffner, § 65. This, however, is not correct; and I do not know what origin to assign to that formula.

[2] The maxim in question is always employed, both in the older writers, with whom it originated, and in the decisions cited by Story, with reference to questions of succession or conjugal property; and there resort was had to it in order to escape from the inconveniences of referring to a different law to regulate the disposal of the separate things belonging to a succession or to a *communio bonorum*, without sufficiently considering how far the particular law adopted the notion of a succession as a *universitas juris*. See Westlake, § 265 sqq; Bar, § 59. 'The maxim, *mobilia ossibus inhærent*, is correct, if it be understood to mean that the totality of moveables must be governed as a separate and distinct unity by the law of the place where the owner has or had his domicile . . . . . If, on the other hand, it be understood to mean, as many have understood it, that rights to moveables, as individual objects, are invariably to be determined by the *lex domicilii*, perhaps there never was a more unfounded assertion.'—Schäffner, § 66.

ponents admit this in regard to immoveable things, but seek to apply to moveable things the law of the domicile of the person.

In the present inquiry as to the value of that distinction (for the law of things), we shall first consider to what side the legislation of different ages inclines. And here we cannot dispute that the older German law-books, the *Sachsenspiegel* and the *Schwabenspiegel*, certainly seem to have a particular regard to immoveable things, and so far, therefore, appear to favour the distinction here contested (*f*). The passages relating to it are, however, so ambiguous and indistinct, and it remains, besides, so doubtful what contradictions are implied in the background, that no conclusive assertion whatever can be made on the subject.

The Bavarian legislation, from the middle of the eighteenth century, declares itself decidedly against the distinction, and, both as to moveables and immoveables, allows authority to the local law of the place where the thing is situated (*g*).

On the other hand, the codes of later times have adopted the distinction that prevailed at the time of their compilation, yet in so abstract and indefinite a way that a clear conclusion, especially as to the manner in which they intend to deal with real rights, cannot be drawn from them at all. This is true of the Prussian law (*h*), and in a still higher degree of the Austrian (*i*). The French code indicates its assent to the prevailing distinction only tacitly, in ordering for immoveable things the application of the *lex rei sitæ*, while it says nothing at all of moveable things (*k*). All these codes only say that certain things are to be judged according to these or the other

(*f*) *Sachsenspiegel*, i. 30, iii. 33; *Schwabenspiegel*, c. 87, 130, 405.

(*g*) *Cod. Bavar. Maximil.* P. i. C. 2, § 17. 'Rights *in loco rei sitæ*, without distinguishing whether the things are moveable or immoveable, shall be regarded and recognised *in realibus vel mixtis*.' The whole passage is quoted in Eichhorn, *Deutsches Recht*, § 34, note *a*.

(*h*) *A. L. R. Einleitung*, § 28. 'The moveable estate of a man *is judged* . . . . by the laws of his ordinary jurisdiction' (*i.e.* by the domicile, § 23). § 32: 'In respect of immoveable estate, *the laws* of the jurisdiction under which it is situated *are applicable* without respect to the person of the proprietor.'

(*i*) *Oesterr. Gesetzb.* § 300. 'Immoveable things are subject to the laws of the district in which they are situated; all other things are subject to *the same laws* as the person of their owner.'

(*k*) *Code Civil*, art. 3. 'Les immeubles, même ceux possédés des étrangers, *sont régis* par la loi Française.'

laws, *are subject to them*, etc. Such general expressions, however, are reconcilable with the most opposite intentions in respect to the mode and the limits of such judgment or subjection.

I now pass to the opinions of authors on this subject.

In more ancient times, the most numerous and most esteemed of these declare themselves decidedly *for* the distinction of moveable and immoveable things (*l*), and this opinion has maintained its ground till a very late date (*m*). It is to be met with, indeed, in several of the most recent writers more in appearance than in reality. They present that doctrine in the same general terms as their predecessors, and apparently follow their footsteps (*n*); but when they come to its actual application to rights to particular things, they turn away from it again, and become unfaithful to their own principle (*o*).

On the other hand, this distinction is entirely rejected by most modern writers, and the same rule asserted for moveable and immoveable things (the *lex rei sitæ*) (*p*), in favour of which opinion I have already expressed myself.

The weakest side of that distinction which applies to moveable things not the *lex rei sitæ*, but the *lex domicilii*, is generally evaded or concealed by its defenders. It is said that the domicile *of the person* is to determine the local law to be administered; but what person is thereby meant? (*q*).

Without doubt, the person interested in the legal relation to this thing. But this is a very ambiguous notion; and thereby the whole doctrine, even if it were admitted, becomes extremely

(*l*) Argentræus, Num. 30; Rodenburg, tit. i. c. 2; P. Voet, sect. 4, c. 2, § 8; J. Voet, § 11—(the last, however, with the very remarkable exception, that laws of the nature of police regulations—*e.g.* as to the exportation of grain—have necessarily a strictly territorial effect, even on moveables within the country).

(*m*) Story, c. 9, 10, and § 362; Fœlix, pp. 72–75, 80 [Demangeat, i. 111–131]; Schäffner, §§ 54–56, 65–68. Story, § 386, remarks, however, that the courts of Louisiana regard the *lex rei sitæ* (not *domicilii*) as applicable even to moveable things.

(*n*) Fœlix and Schäffner (note *m*).

(*o*) Fœlix, p. 78 [Demang. i. 120]; Schäffner, § 66, who expressly asserts that there is no general rule at all for rights to particular things.

(*p*) Mühlenbruch, *Doctrina Pandect.* § 72; Meissner, *Vom Stillschweigenden Pfandrecht.* But especially Wächter, i. pp. 292–298, ii. pp. 199, 200, 383–389,—where also in i. 293, note 130, other advocates of this opinion are cited. [Bar, § 57 sqq.; Westlake, c. viii.]

(*q*) Wächter urges this objection very well.

indeterminate and uncertain. By the party interested we may understand the owner (*r*); but then it remains doubtful whether, in a transference of property, the old or the new owner is meant; so, too, in a dispute as to property, which of the two competing parties, each of whom claims for himself the property. But we may also entirely give up thinking of the owner, and take the possessor as the party interested, by which, certainly, the matter is made simpler and easier. Besides property, various other real rights come under consideration; and each of these, when it exists or is even asserted, leads back to a new person interested in the thing. Thus the doctrine that directs us to the domicile *of the person*, even if it were in itself well founded, is yet a very ambiguous one, since each of the persons here named may have a different domicile; and therefore the alleged rule is not adapted to effect a practical solution of the question.

The main question, however, remains always this: Whether there is any valid reason for judging real rights to moveable things by a different local law from immoveables? This must be utterly denied. Perhaps an agreement upon the whole matter has hitherto been hindered chiefly by the too abstract view taken of the question. I will try to make it plain how the thing takes quite a different shape in actual life. This discussion will also tend to explain the origin of the opinion which I hold to be erroneous, and to point out the true element contained in it.

If we consider the position in space of moveable things, we can therein distinguish two extreme and perfectly opposite cases, between which lie many other cases with manifold gradations.

In the first place, the position in space of moveables may be so indeterminate and fluctuating as entirely to preclude any definite knowledge of this position, as well as of the territory in which the local law subsists; consequently also the assumption of a voluntary subjection under this local law. To this head belong the following cases:—A traveller with his baggage can pass, in a coach or on a railway, through several territories in one day, without even thinking of the one in which he happens for the moment to be. The same case occurs when a

(*r*) This is the view of the legislations of Prussia and of Austria. See above, notes *h* and *i*. [It is the view evidently taken by most writers, and expressly by Story, § 383.]

merchant sends goods to a great distance, as long as these goods are on their way,—more especially when they are sent by sea to different ports, perhaps to different parts of the world, in order that a profitable sale may be effected. In such cases it is evident that no application can be made of the *lex rei sitæ*. We are rather obliged to seek, in thought, for some resting-place at which such things are destined to remain for a longer, perhaps an indefinite time. Such a resting-place may perhaps be indicated beyond a doubt by the clearly demonstrated intention of the owner; in other cases it will coincide with the domicile of the owner. This last will be admitted, among others, in the case of the traveller's portmanteau, which at the end of his journey he usually brings home; often, too, in the case of the goods that have been shipped, and which the owner, when no sale takes place, perhaps causes to be brought to his domicile, there to await a more favourable season. A one-sided consideration of such cases seems to have occasioned or supported the doctrine, that the local law of the domicile is universally applicable to moveables (*s*).

The second case, which is the opposite of the first, is that in which moveables are devoted to a purpose which binds them as fixtures in a particular place. This happens with the furniture of a house, with a library or collection of works of art, and the stocking (Inventar) of a land estate. It is true that the purpose may be changed even in respect to these things,—they may be taken to another place or another country; but such changes are accidental, and are beyond the present intention and will of the owner (*t*). The relation here is exactly similar to that between the person and the domicile, which is considered as permanent, and yet always remains capable of change in the future (§ 353). No plausible reason really exists for dealing with things of this sort otherwise than with immoveable things; they ought rather, beyond all doubt, to be judged like these by that local law which is determined by their actual position, and

(*s*) This explains why American courts and writers (Story, for example) are much attached to this opinion, for they naturally have a pre-eminent regard to maritime commerce.

(*t*) Such a permanent local destination of moveable things is often mentioned in Roman law, although on different juridical occasions from that now before us. L. 35, *pr.* §§ 3–5; *de her. instit.* (28, 5); L. 17, *de act. emt.* (19, 1); L. 32, *de pign.* (20, 1); L. 203, *de V. S.* (50, 16).

not by the domicile of the owner or possessor. This is indeed acknowledged by many writers, who otherwise maintain the principle of the distinction between moveables and immoveables, but who assert for this class of things an exception from their general rule, and in so far represent an intermediate opinion (*u*).

Between the classes of moveable things which have been discussed, there are, finally, many intermediate ones in the greatest variety of gradations. For example, the merchandise which the owner keeps in reserve for an indefinite time at another place than his domicile; the travelling baggage during a transient residence of the owner in a strange place, etc. In these cases it will depend on circumstances whether the things belong to the first or second class. This will not depend merely on the shorter or longer time during which such things remain, but also on the nature of the rule of law, the application of which is in question. Thus, *e.g.* in the question as to the form of alienation (tradition or simple contract), a very short stay at a particular place will suffice to justify the application of the *lex rei sitæ*, while perhaps the question of prescription will be otherwise regarded. In general, however, we must hold fast to the application of the law of the place where the thing is situated, as the rule; so that a different treatment of the first of the classes of things above considered must be regarded only as a comparatively rare exception.

SECT. XXIV.—(§ 367.)

II. LAW OF THINGS.—PROPERTY.

I will here consider in their order the particular questions relating to property, in which the point at issue is the applicability of different local laws.

1. The capacity of a person to acquire property, and likewise

(*u*) J. Voet, *ad Pand.* i. 8, § 14; Story, § 382, and several others cited in Wächter, i. p. 296, note 133. [The question whether a thing or a debt is moveable or immoveable, is determined by the *lex rei sitæ*. Story, § 447; and a series of Scotch cases, of which the latest is *Downie* v *Downie's Trs.*, 1866, 4 Macph. 1066. See Bar, § 62; *Robinson* v *Bland*, 2 Burr. 1079, 1 W. Bl. 259.]

the capacity of a person to dispose of the property belonging to him, is to be judged by the local law of the domicile of the one or the other person (§ 362), and therefore not by the law of the place where the thing is situated, because each of these capacities is only a particular branch of the general capacity to have rights and to act, and therefore pertains to the personal status.

This rule has been disputed from the following erroneous points of view, which have already been disposed of. Many say that these capacities belong, not to the abstract qualities of the person, but to the legal effects of these qualities; and that as to these it is not the law of the domicile that is applicable, but the law of the judge who determines in each case (*a*).

Others admit that the law of the domicile is generally applicable, but make an exception for the case of immoveable things. Here, they say, the personal capacity is to be judged by the *lex rei sitæ*,—that is to say, the real statute comes to be applied (*b*).

An exception to this rule must certainly be admitted, when a limitation of the capacity to acquire is prescribed by strictly positive and compulsory laws, such as those which have the

(*a*) This opinion has been fully discussed above, § 362.

(*b*) Comp. above, § 362, note *g*. This erroneous opinion is adopted by Story, §§ 430–434, who quotes a number of writers. Huber, § 12, has the correct opinion. [With regard to the capacity to acquire property in land, Bar comes to the same result as Story upon a different ground, which would seem to support also the judgments in *Birtwhistle* v *Vardell* and *Fenton* v *Livingstone*, *ante*, pp. 106, 107. He says: 'The incapacity to acquire the property of land is a restriction not of the capacity to act, but of the capacity for rights, and therefore (*ante*, § 365, Note A) depends, not on the *lex domicilii* of the acquirer, but on the law to which the case is subject in other respects.' 'The capacity to act, on the other hand, is to be determined, even with respect to immoveables, by the law of the domicile. The opinion of many writers which makes the *lex rei sitæ* decisive, originates in too wide an extension of the notion of capacity to act, by which the capacity to test (which in certain circumstances depends entirely on the *lex rei sitæ*) is confounded with the capacity to act in the true and narrower sense. If a person who is still minor by the *lex rei sitæ* would be major by the *lex domicilii*, he would still be able to incur a personal obligation in respect of his property situated abroad, and the purchaser would then only need to sue upon the obligation, to put the matter in the same position as if the alienation had from the first been validly effected by the seller. The application of the *lex rei sitæ* is therefore, in this case, practically inoperative; and in the converse case, where the seller is by the *lex rei sitæ* major, and by the *lex domicilii* minor, it leads to the absurdity, that one who is incapable of binding himself by a personal obligation to transfer a real right, is in a position to alienate this right directly.'—Bar, § 64.]

nature of police laws. Such statutes are applicable to all things situated within the territory of the lawgiver, and no regard is paid to the law of the domicile of the person who wishes to acquire (§ 365).

2. The capacity of a thing to become subject to private property, and therefore not to belong to the *res quarum commercium non est*, is to be judged by the law of the place at which the thing is situated.

3. The same rule applies as to the extent of the class of things *sine domino*, and therefore as to the admissibility or restriction of the acquisition by occupation of property in things of many kinds. Of this character are laws as to the royalty on amber, and on many kinds of minerals. No one doubts that here the *lex rei sitæ* alone determines, and is therefore to be applied even to moveable things. If under this law the property in such a thing has once been acquired, it must be acknowledged in every other state, even if the latter state would not acknowledge a similar acquisition within its limits.

4. In the forms of alienation—*i.e.* of the voluntary transmission of property to another person—very different rules of law occur; and on the principle above considered, we must apply the rule of law in force at the place where the thing is situated, without regard to the domicile of the one or of the other person, and without regard to the place where the contract is entered into.[1]

Thus, in Roman law, alienation depends on the delivery of

[1] As to land, there is no dispute upon this point. The apparent contradictions referred to by Story, § 439 sq., occur in writers who are discussing the validity of a will, executed in conformity with the *lex loci actus*, to transmit foreign immoveables. This question may receive an affirmative answer in countries where the distinction of moveable and immoveable property is not admitted; but in this country and America, where the theory of universal succession has never been accepted with regard to immoveables, it is of course negatived. See Bar, § 61. The doctrine of certain cases in Louisiana (*Olivier* v *Townes*, 14 Mar. 97, etc.), applying the *lex rei sitæ*, which required tradition in order to the transfer of property in moveables, and rejecting the *lex loci contractus*, which was the law of the owner's domicile, has been strongly controverted by Story (§ 385 sqq.; see Burge, iii. 763) and others; but no authority is cited against it except the cases which establish the *lex domicilii* as the law regulating succession. On the contrary, the application of the *lex rei sitæ* appears to be *assumed* in all the numerous cases in which conflicts have arisen in regard to the transmission by sale of property in moveables, between the law of Scotland, which requires delivery, and that of England, which does not.

the thing; in the Prussian law, likewise, on delivery (*c*). In the French law, on the contrary, the transference of the property is effected by the mere contract (*d*).

The application of these rules will be made plainer by the following examples:—If a Parisian sells his furniture situated in Berlin, to a Parisian in Paris, the property is transferred only by tradition; but if, conversely, a Berliner sells his goods situated in Paris, to a Berliner in Berlin, the mere contract transfers the property. It will be just the same if in these examples we put the city of Cologne in the place of Paris.

It will suffice to bring this rule into operation, if the continuance of the things at a place should be only transient and very short (*e*); for in every case the transference of the property depends on a momentary act, and therefore fills no long space of time. It will be different in the exceptional cases, in which the present situation of the things is so indeterminate that the persons acting cannot be held to have any certain knowledge of it. In such cases we shall have to regard as the place where the thing is situated that at which it is destined first to remain, which will often be the domicile of the present owner (the seller) (*f*) [2]

In all the cases here distinguished, everything depends, undoubtedly, on the place where the thing is situated at the time of transference. If the transmission has once taken place, every subsequent change of the locality of the thing is immaterial for the destiny of the property, since the right of property once acquired cannot be affected by such a change of place.[3]

(*c*) *A. L. R.* i. 10, § 1. Comp. Koch, *Preuss. Recht*, vol. i., §§ 252, 255, 174. Even the important practical facilities in the tradition effected by transmission between absent persons (i. 11, §§ 128–133) make no difference in this principle.

(*d*) *Code Civil*, art. 1138. This is law also in the Rhenish provinces of Prussia.

(*e*) See above, § 366, p. 136.

(*f*) See above, § 366, p. 135. In the alienation of merchandise there are also to be considered the very doubtful questions of trade-marks, and (if the goods are stopped *in transitu*) of the effect of the transferred bill of lading. Comp. Thöl. *Handelsrecht*, §§ 79, 80.

[2] See *contra*, *Thuret* v *Jenkins*, 7 Mar. La. 318; Story, § 391; Westlake, § 270.

[3] 'Property in a moveable or immoveable thing situated in a country where the common Roman law prevails, is not transferred by a contract made in France, even between Frenchmen. But when the will of the contracting parties remains the same, and the thing in the meantime, and

5. The acquisition of property by prescription is essentially different from the acquisition by tradition, in being effected, not by a momentary fact, but by one extending over a longer period of time.

In regard to immoveable things, the application of the law of the place where the thing is situated is quite undisputed. On the contrary, opinions are very much divided in respect to the prescription of moveables (*g*). But here the question is specially important, because the laws of different countries vary exceedingly. The Roman law requires possession for three years, the Prussian for ten (*h*). The French requires no continued possession, but excludes with the very beginning of it the vindication of the former owner, with an exception in the case of lost and stolen things, the protection of which, however, ceases with the expiry of three years (*i*). By this last rule the French law, in its practical results, approximates to the Roman.

It is here precisely that the application of the *lex rei sitæ* appears especially certain, from the circumstance that the foundation of all prescription is continuing possession; but possession, as being essentially a relation of facts, is, with even less doubt than any real right, to be judged by the *lex rei sitæ* (§ 368).

A question may still arise where the situation of the moveable things, during the period of prescription, has been within different territories. There can be no doubt that all these periods of possession must be added together. The term of the prescription, however, and the complete acquisition of the property, must be judged by the law of the place at which the thing is last found, because it is only at the expiry of the whole period that the change of property takes place; before, it has only been in preparation (*k*). When property has been ac-

before a third party has become its owner by delivery, has been brought to France, the property is transferred at the moment it passes into the territory of the French law. Conversely, if the thing is in France, and the contract is made *e.g.* in Hanover, the property passes without tradition only when that was the intention of the contracting parties.'—Bar, § 64.

(*g*) Mühlenbruch, *Doctrina Pand.* § 73, correctly adopts the *lex rei sitæ*; Meier, p. 37, the *lex domicilii*, that is, of the domicile of the person taking by prescription, because he has already prætorian ownership during the course of prescription. Schäffner, § 67, leaves all uncertain.

(*h*) *A. L. R.* i. 9, § 620.

(*i*) *Code Civil*, art. 2279.

(*k*) Here, therefore, we follow the same principle as in the collision in time of laws as to usucapion (§ 391, *b*).

quired by prescription according to this law, it must be recognised in every other country, although the law of that country should require a longer period.

6. The vindication of property by action, with all the minute regulations concerning it, is to be judged by the law of the place at which the action is brought (*l*).

This *may* be the place where the thing is situated, on account of the jurisdiction constituted at that place (§ 366, *a*); then the *lex rei sitæ* is applicable. But it may also be the domicile of the defender, because at common law the two kinds of jurisdiction so concur, that the plaintiff has a choice between them; then the *lex domicilii* of the defendant is to be applied to all questions of law touching the action. It is true that, by this alternative rule, an objectionable latitude is allowed to the choice of the plaintiff; but it is here unavoidable.

There is a great diversity between the laws of different countries in respect of the restrictions applicable to the *rei vindicatio.* The Roman law admits the action unconditionally against every possessor who is not the owner, and that without any claim of this possessor for restitution of the purchase money. The Prussian law likewise admits the unconditional vindication, but reserving such restitution to the *bona fide* possessor (*m*). The French law admits, as a rule, no vindication of moveables, and allows only a few exceptions,—in the case of things stolen or lost, within three years; and things sold, but still unpaid for, which can be vindicated against the purchaser within eight days (*n*). The one or the other of these rules will necessarily be applicable according as the Roman, the Prussian, or the French law is in force at the place where the court sits before which the process is carried on.

The process as to property, once begun, may involve peculiar consequences, particularly in respect of the fruits, the claim for damages founded on the loss or the deterioration of the thing vindicated, etc. (*o*). All such questions are also to be decided by the law of the place where the court sits.[4]

(*l*) See above, § 361, No. 3, C.
(*m*) *A. L. R.* i. 15, §§ 1, 26.
(*n*) *Code Civil*, arts. 2279, 2102, N. 4.
(*o*) See above, vol. vi. § 260 foll.
[4] See Bar, § 64, for a statement of views upon the last two heads differing in some respects from those in the text.

SECT. XXV.—(§ 368.)

II. LAW OF THINGS.—*JURA IN RE.*

Real rights, besides property (*jura in re*), are for the most part governed by principles similar to those which we have discussed in regard to property.

1. That the prædial servitudes can only be judged by the *lex rei sitæ*, is nowhere disputed.

The same is true as to personal servitudes of which the object is an immoveable thing.

If the object is a moveable thing, the *lex domicilii* is wrongly held by many to be applicable, just as in the case of property in moveables. The controversy upon this general question has already been fully discussed (§ 366).

2. *Emphyteusis* and *Superficies* are subject to no doubt, since they can only occur in the case of immoveable things; and therefore, as all parties agree, are to be judged by the law of the place where the thing is situated.

3. The Prussian law gives to the hirer, tenant, and similar occupiers or holders, for their own use, of things belonging to others, a real right, with an action *in rem* against a third party in possession, provided that the thing has been delivered to them (*a*). In Roman law, of course, there is no such real right.

A real right of this kind undoubtedly arises when the thing, whether it be moveable or immoveable, is within the Prussian state at the time of delivery; if at that time it is within a country where the Roman law prevails, the real right does not arise.

But supposing that this real right is constituted in the Prussian state by delivery of a hired moveable, and the possessor brings the thing into a country where Roman law prevails, it might be thought that he could even here make the right which he had acquired effectual against a third party in possession. I believe, however, that this must be denied, because his claim rests upon an entirely peculiar legal institution

(*a*) *A. L. R.* i. 2, §§ 135–137; i. 7, §§ 169, 170. Comp. Koch, *Preuss. Recht*, vol. i. §§ 317, 318.

which is not recognised at all in the latter country (*b*). This question, however, is not of practical interest, because such a real right is attended with important consequences only in the case of immoveable things.

4. The right of pledge is not only of more extensive operation than the foregoing *jura in re*, but is also the subject of greater doubts and disputes in the question before us.

Here also the law of the place where the thing is situated must be held to rule, and most of the difficulties raised against it are merely apparent.

I will begin by giving a view of the most important general differences that occur in German states concerning this legal institution.

The Roman law rests on the following principles :—(a) The right of pledge becomes a real right, actionable against every third party in possession, by mere contract without delivery (*c*); (b) The contract may even be concluded tacitly, since, in the case of several obligatory acts, it is feigned, by a general rule of law, that a pledge has been at the same time stipulated in security of the obligation (*d*); (c) Moveable and immoveable things are not distinguished as objects of impignoration; (d) The express as well as the tacit contract may refer not only to particular things, but also to a whole estate. Impignoration of the last kind embraces all the things belonging to that estate at the time, and all afterwards coming into it; therefore those which are not specially mentioned, and which cannot even be brought to the knowledge of the parties. It has been erroneously supposed that the object of such impignoration is the estate in its ideal notion, irrespective of its contents; and hence the juridical notion of *universitas* and *successio per universitatem*

(*b*) See above, § 349, *b*. Wächter, ii. pp. 388, 389, is also of this opinion; not indeed in this very case, but in the similar case of the right of pledge, of which we are immediately to speak.

(*c*) I here confine myself purposely to the right of pledge in its proper sense, as *jus in re*, that is, a detached portion of the right of property, passing over the more artificial application of it to obligations, etc.

(*d*) L. 3, *in quib. caus.* (20, 2) : '. . . . *tacitam conventionem* de invectis . . . ;' L. 4, *pr. eod.*: '. . . . *quasi id tacite convenerit* . . . ;' L. 6, *eod.*: '. . . . tacite solet *conventum accipi*, ut perinde teneantur invecta et illata, *ac si specialiter convenisset* . . . ;' L. 7, *pr. eod.*: '. . . *tacite* intelliguntur pignori esse . . . . etiamsi nominatim id non convenerit.' The expression 'legal pledge' (*pignus legale*), in use with modern writers, obscures the true nature of the legal institution.

has been applied to it according to the analogy of the law of succession (*e*). In truth, however, it is only an indirect designation and definition of the individual things which are liable to the right of pledge.

Among the various countries which follow in general the Roman law, many subordinate differences occur in the law of pledge, while they still preserve the common foundation above described. The differences chiefly relate to the extent of the tacit pledge which, according to the codes of the various countries, is attached sometimes to more and sometimes to fewer kinds of obligations, which are held to be secured by a contract of pledge founded on the legal fiction referred to.

Suppose, then, the question to arise as to two countries that follow in general the Roman law. In the one, the rule of the Roman law is received, by which the promise to give a *dos* is always secured by tacit hypothecation of the whole estate (*f*); in the other country this rule is abolished. If, then, two inhabitants of the first country enter into such a contract, but the debtor possesses a landed estate in the second country, the question arises whether this estate is subject to the tacit hypothec. One might be disposed to answer this in the negative by applying the *lex rei sitæ*, but incorrectly. For the second state also recognises the possibility of hypothecation by mere contract, and even by tacit contract. Whether, then, in the case before us, such a contract exists, is a question of fact, which can only be determined by that law to which the juridical act is subject (*g*). But by a legal fiction established by this law, an express hypothecation of the whole patrimonial estate, and therefore of that foreign real estate, has taken place, and therefore the latter must be included in the hypothec (*h*). If the dotal contract had been entered into in the second country by inhabitants of it, neither the real estate nor the other property of the debtor would fall under the hypothec.

(*e*) As to these notions, comp. above, vol. iii. § 105.

(*f*) L. *un.* § 1, *C. de rei ux. act.* (5, 13).

(*g*) What that law is, will be established in the next section (the Law of Obligations, § 374, *d*).

(*h*) This decision is given by Meier, pp. 39–41; Meissner, *Vom Stillschweigenden Pfandrecht*, §§ 23, 24; but on a ground which I hold to be incorrect. The law of the domicile, as such, determines, according to them, just as in questions of succession, because here the ideal estate, the *universitas*, is the object of hypothecation.

An immensely greater difference exists between the German countries which recognise the Roman law of pledge generally, and those which place the law of pledge upon a quite new foundation. I will take the Prussian code as a type of the last, as it seems to have most completely created such a new law. Some of its provisions are found in other countries also, and it will not be difficult to apply the following rules to them :—

The Prussian law, without any exception, denies to the mere contract the power of originating a pledge as a real right. It also distinguishes between moveable and immoveable things. In immoveables, the real right arises only by entry in the register of mortgages (Hypothekenbuch) (*i*). A contract as to the registration of a particular landed estate is a title on the ground of which registration may be demanded ; a general contract of hypothec over the whole estate gives no such claim in respect to particular lands (*k*). A real right of pledge in moveables arises only by delivery (*l*) ; a contract for the impignoration of certain definite things entitles to claim such delivery (*m*).

If, then, in a country where the Roman law prevails, an hypothecation is effected by contract, expressly or tacitly, it can give rise to no right of pledge over things belonging to the debtor situated in Prussia. It can, at farthest, serve as a title to demand the constitution of an hypothec over these things (by registration or delivery), and even that only under the special conditions above mentioned (Notes *k*, *m*). But if, conversely, a contract of pledge of particular things, or of a whole estate, is entered into in Prussia, and portions of the debtor's estate are in a country where the Roman law prevails, there is nothing to prevent such property from being dealt with as duly hypothecated, since the Roman law makes hypothecation by contract dependent neither on the conclusion of the contract at a particular place, nor on a particular domicile of the debtor. Thus the *lex rei sitæ* must here receive undisturbed effect (*n*).

(*i*) *A. L. R.* i. 20, §§ 411, 412.

(*k*) *Ibid.* §§ 402, 403.

(*l*) *Ibid.* § 111.

(*m*) *Ibid.* §§ 109, 110. A contract of general hypothec gives this claim only in the special cases in which a security can also be demanded. *Ibid.* § 112.

(*n*) A literal construction of the *Allg. Landrecht Einl.* § 28, would make a Berliner at Stralsund (where the Roman law is in force) incapable of

The following case remains to be considered:—If in a country of the Roman law a moveable thing be validly impledged, whether expressly or tacitly, by mere contract, and the thing is afterwards brought to Prussia, does the hypothecation continue, so that the thing can here be vindicated by an action against every possessor (whether the debtor or a third party), and can likewise be alienated by the person in right of the pledge, if he obtains possession by accident without tradition? One might be inclined to answer this question in the affirmative, because, apparently, the vested right cannot lose its force by the change of place.

Yet I believe the question must be answered in the negative. For in such a case the question is not in regard to one and the same right of pledge, which may be acquired in different countries in different ways, somewhat as property is acquired here by tradition, and there by mere contract, and yet is everywhere alike recognised and operative as property. Rather, hypothecation by mere contract is quite another legal institution from that which can be constituted only by delivery, and the two can only have their names and general purpose in common. If, therefore, the moveable thing above referred to is brought within the territory of the Prussian code, and it is attempted to enforce the right of pledge elsewhere constituted by simple contract, the alleged creditor appeals to a legal institution not recognised in the Prussian state; and such a proceeding has above been shown to be inadmissible (*o*). On the

impledging his moveable property by mere contract, so that this hypothecation should be effectual at Stralsund (§ 366, *h*). The absurdity of this becomes very clear if we imagine the opposite case; for the Stralsunder would necessarily be able to hypothecate his moveable property by mere contract at Berlin, so that the hypothecation would be valid at Berlin. The last assertion will hardly find any supporters, and yet it results from the strict literal application of § 28.

(*o*) See above, § 349, B. The same view is maintained in the *Ergänzungen zum A. L. R.* by Gräff, etc., vol. i. p. 116. So also by Wächter, ii. pp. 386, 388, 389, with regard to the law of Würtemburg, which here agrees with the Prussian law. He gives as the reason, that the law here recognises hypothecation of moveables in origin and *in continuance* only in the form of *Faustpfand* [*i.e.* pledge, *pignus*, as distinguished from hypothec, *hypotheca*; *Inst.* iv. 67]. This principle is substantially the same as that proposed by me, and only different in the mode of expression. [Bar, § 65, p. 227, points out that the practical result of this reasoning is, that *e.g.* if the law of a country permits a ship to be validly mortgaged only by writing, an hypothecation validly effected by verbal bargain in another state, within whose territory the ship was at the time, could not be recognised in the

contrary, the creditor in a right of pledge, to whom a moveable thing has been impignorated by tradition in Prussia, can enforce his right also in a country where Roman law prevails; for he unites in himself all the conditions which are there required for an effectual right of pledge.

The priority of several rights of pledge constituted in the same thing, is judged by the *lex rei sitæ*. This priority may come into question especially in bankruptcy; and of this case we shall treat below (§ 374).

5. What has here been said of the real rights belonging to the Roman law, and of those formed in imitation of them by modern legislation, must be equally true of those which are purely Germanic. The rights to feuda or fiefs (*Lehen*) and entails or family substitutions (*Fideicommissen*) is always a right to particular immoveables, and is therefore governed by the law of the place where they are situated.

In the course of this inquiry as to the law to which real rights are subject, I have at every suitable place interpolated the question above reserved (§ 344, *e*), how far the law to be applied must be determined in one way or in another by a change in the situation of the moveable thing which is the object of a real right.

Possession is not one of the real rights; yet the question as to the local law applicable to it may be treated of here, along with real rights, more fitly than at any other place.

Possession itself is, in its nature, purely a relation of fact (*p*),

former state. The whole train of reasoning rests, moreover, on the very dubious proposition, that a right which, under the given circumstances, could not have originated in our country, must not be recognised there. Answering to the legal institutions existing in one country, analogous, yet in details materially different, legal institutions will always be found in another country. Are these the same, or are they quite different institutions, which must not be recognised? It cannot be said that, where there is the least difference, the latter case is to be assumed,—an assumption which would involve the rejection of all foreign rules of law. It is impossible to discover wherein the distinction consists between this case and that in which the right of property is passed in one country only by delivery, and in the other by informal contract; in which latter case Savigny (p. 146) regards a right of property acquired in the latter country by mere contract, as effectual in the former also. In both cases the question is as to different forms of constituting a real right.]

(*p*) Savigny, *Recht des Besitzes*, § 5.

and as such it can only be subject to the law of the place where the thing is situated, whether it relate to moveable or immoveable things. By this law alone, therefore, must be decided the question as to the acquisition or loss of any possession, and therefore as to its existence, without considering for what purpose or with what result this question may be raised. Two legal effects, however, are connected with possession,—usucapion and the possessory interdicts. The first has no independent nature, but rather coincides with property, and, like it, belongs to the *lex rei sitæ* (§ 367, No. 5). The possessory interdicts, as the second result of possession, have their place among the *obligationes ex delicto* (*q*), and are thus subject to the local law of the court before which the lawsuit is brought (*r*). This proposition, however, is of far less importance than might at first sight be assigned to it; for it concerns only the proper element of delict in the possessory actions, and therefore their penal nature, which is by far the less important part of their juridical contents. The more important constituent—the question as to the existence and recognition of the possession—is to be judged by every court, as just observed, only according to the *lex rei sitæ*.

SECT. XXVI.—(§ 369.)

III. LAW OF OBLIGATIONS.

(INTRODUCTION.)

In the law of obligations, as in real rights, a person emerges from his abstract personality into the local dominion of the law which governs a particular legal relation (§§ 345, 360, 366). Here, again, we have to find an answer to the ever-recurring question: Where is the true seat of each obligation; at what

(*q*) Savigny, *l.c.* §§ 6, 37.

(*r*) See below, § 374, *c*. This may, indeed, be the *forum rei sitæ*, which is certainly always competent for possessory actions. *L. un. C. ubi de poss.* (3, 16); *Nov.* 69, c. i. It *may* also, however, be the *forum domicilii* (which may happen to be different), since there is an election between them (§ 371, notes *n* and *p*).

place is its *home?* For from this seat of the obligation, from this its home, shall we discover the particular jurisdiction, as well as the local law, by which it is to be judged.

In the law of obligations the reply to this question is, more than in other parts of the law, difficult and doubtful, for the following reasons :—

First, the obligation has an object of an invisible nature in comparison with the real right, which is connected with an object perceptible by the senses,—a thing. We must therefore, first, try to realize that invisible object in the obligation.

Further, the obligation necessarily relates to two different persons: in the one it appears as an enlargement of liberty, as dominion over another will; in the other, as a restriction of liberty, as dependence on another's will (*a*). According to which of these closely connected yet different relations are we to fix the seat of the obligation? Undoubtedly according to the relation of the debtor, since the necessity of acting that exists in the person of the debtor constitutes the very essence of the obligation. This view is confirmed by the great and indisputable influence of the place of fulfilment on the jurisdiction, since fulfilment chiefly consists in an activity of the debtor, along with which an activity of the creditor occurs either not at all, or only in a subordinate and auxiliary manner. Further, by the intrinsic connection of the local law with the forum, which last always has a relation to the person of the defendant, that is, of the debtor.

Lastly, another difficulty arises from the reciprocity that is found, not in all, but in many obligations. Where this exists, each of the two persons is to be regarded as debtor, but with reference to different acts; for which reason, the rule that the debtor is to be chiefly regarded appears no longer to be sufficient. But in every mutual obligation the two separate debts always admit of being dealt with separately; so that even here nothing hinders us from fixing, according to the person of the debtor, the jurisdiction and the local law for each of the two halves produced by this separation. Nay, more, this division is to be regarded as the original and natural treatment,—the combination of the two obligations under one head and designation, as a secondary and artificial result, justified by their inti-

(*a*) See above, vol. i. § 56.

mate connection. The correctness of this view is confirmed by the ordinary practice among the Romans, of concluding a contract of sale, etc., by two distinct stipulations (*b*).

In the case of obligations we find, again, the often noticed connection between the forum and the law (§ 360, No. 1). But it is here more important and influential than elsewhere, because in the Roman law the doctrine as to the particular forum of obligations is carefully wrought out, while the local law is hardly mentioned. Yet the reasons determining the forum are perfectly applicable to the local law, since each depends on the equal obedience due to different branches of the public institutions of the place. We are able, therefore, safely to deduce, from the decisions of the Romans as to the forum of obligations, the sense in which the local law of obligations is to be regarded.

The particular jurisdiction, as well as the local law of obligations, depends on a voluntary subjection (§ 360, No. 2), which in most cases is not expressly declared, but is only to be inferred from circumstances, and for that reason is excluded by an express declaration to the contrary (*c*). The circumstances, therefore, under which an obligation arises may often excite in others a definite and well-founded *expectation*, and in such a case this expectation is not to be disappointed. That is the point of view from which not only the forum of obligations, but the local law governing them, must be considered.

Voluntary subjection is also the ground of prorogated jurisdiction; and there is thus, undoubtedly, a relation between it and the forum of obligations, although the latter has a more objective, prorogated jurisdiction a more subjective, character in consideration of a particular court, often of particular judges. To regard the jurisdiction of the obligation as a mere application of the prorogated jurisdiction, as a particular case of prorogation, is indeed not to be justified (*d*). The peculiar interest

(*b*) It cannot be denied that in many cases this separation of the two halves of a bilateral obligation may cause doubts and perplexities, especially in regard to the local law. But in principle it is not less correct, and it is asserted by others also for several cases. Comp. Wächter, ii. p. 45. [Story, § 291, commenting on *Arnott* v *Redfern*, 2 C. and P. 88; Bar, § 66, p. 236.]

(*c*) L. 19, § 2, *de jud.* (5, 1): '. . . nisi alio loci, ut defenderet, convenit.'

(*d*) As to this question, there is a controversy between Bethmann Hollweg, *Versuche*, pp. 20–27, 50, and Linde, *Abhandlungen*, vol. ii. p. 75 foll.

of this question may perhaps arise from its being uncertain whether, by Roman law, prorogation is strictly binding (*e*). The forum of the obligation, on the contrary, is certainly binding for the defendant, and just as certainly not so for the plaintiff, who has a free choice between this special forum and the *forum domicilii* of the defendant (*f*).

SECT. XXVII.—(§ 370.)

THE LAW OF OBLIGATIONS.—FORUM OF THE OBLIGATION.

Authors.

LINDE, *Archiv für civilistische Praxis*, vol. vii. pp. 59–79 (1824).

—— *Abhandlungen*, vol. ii. pp. 75-121 (1829).

VON BETHMANN HOLLWEG, *Versuche*, No. 1, pp. 1–77 (1827).

MUEHLENBRUCH, *Archiv*, vol. xix. pp. 337–384 (1836).

ALBRECHT, *Programme über das Motiv des forum contractus.* Würzburg 1845.

Three intimately connected questions have been raised above (§ 369): Where is the seat of an obligation? Where is its forum? Where are we to seek for the local law that is to be applied to it? The first of the three questions is of a theo-

But the latter is clearly wrong in rejecting, for obligations, not merely the expression 'prorogated' jurisdiction, but even voluntary submission, as a legal foundation. The leading texts on prorogated jurisdiction are: L. 1, L. 2, *pr.* § 1, *de jud.* (5, 1); L. 15, *de jurisd.* (2, 1); L. 1, *C. de jurisd.* (3, 13). [Donell. *Com.* xvii. cc. 10, 14.]

(*e*) According to L. 29, *C. de pact.* (2, 3), it seems binding; according to L. 18, *de jurisd.* (2, 1), revocable. The latter passage, indeed, presupposes a *nudum pactum;* so that the stipulation was certainly binding, as well as the *pactum adjectum* in a *b. f. contractus* (Cato, *de re rustica*, 149). Comp. also Hollweg, *Versuche*, p. 12.

(*f*) Comp. below, § 371. The ground of the special jurisdiction for obligations is therefore certainly not to favour the defendant (as Linde assumes, *Archiv*, vii. p. 67), but the plaintiff. To him the proof and the execution are to be facilitated,—perhaps also the conduct of the process itself,—since he is thus enabled often to sue at his own domicile, not merely at that of the defendant.

retical nature, and serves only as a foundation for the correct solution of the other two; for which reason it may be considered along with the second. This question, which relates to the forum of the obligation, has led in Roman law to a series of practical and very minute decisions: hence the differences in opinion among modern writers relate less to the substance of the rules of law than to their order and foundation, and are therefore more of a theoretical than practical nature.

The forum of the obligation (which coincides with the true seat of the obligation) depends on the voluntary submission of the parties, which, however, is generally indicated, not in an express, but in a tacit declaration of will, and is thus always excluded by an express declaration to the contrary (§ 369). We have therefore to inquire to what place the expectation of the parties was directed,—what place they had in their minds as the seat of the obligation. At this place we must fix the forum of the obligation, in virtue of their voluntary submission. But as the obligation itself, as a legal relation, is incorporeal and has no locality, we must seek, in its natural process of development, for some visible phenomena to which we may attach the essence of the obligation, in order to give it, as it were, a body.

In every obligation, then, we find principally and uniformly two such visible phenomena, which we might take as our guides. Every obligation arises out of visible facts; every obligation is also fulfilled by visible facts: both of these must happen at some place or another. We can therefore select either *the place where the obligation has originated*, or *the place where it is fulfilled*, as determining its seat and its forum,—either the beginning or the end of the obligation. To which of the two points shall we give the preference upon general principles?

Not to the origin. This is in itself accidental, transitory, foreign to the substance of the obligation and to its further development and efficacy. If in the eyes of the parties a permanent influence reaching into the future were to be ascribed to the place where the obligation arose, this certainly could not flow from the mere constituent act, but only from the connection of that act with extrinsic circumstances, by which a definite expectation of the parties was directed to that place.

The case is quite different with respect to the fulfilment, which is indeed the very essence of the obligation. For the obligation consists just in this, that something which was previously in the free choice of a person, is now changed into something necessary,—that which was hitherto uncertain, into a certainty; and when this necessary and certain thing has come to pass, that is just the fulfilment. To this, therefore, the whole expectation of the parties is directed; and it is therefore part of the essence of the obligation that the place of fulfilment is conceived as the seat of the obligation, that the special forum of the obligation is fixed at this place by voluntary submission. Before, however, this idea is carried out in detail, it seems proper to cast a preliminary glance upon the views which prevail among modern writers as to this question.

From an early period most writers have fixed the forum of the obligation at the place where it has arisen. But since most obligations arise out of contracts, the place at which the contract was concluded was held to determine the forum; and this explains the very widespread technical term, which is not justified by the law sources, *forum contractus*, for the special forum of obligations. The explanation and apparent justification of the doctrine of writers on this subject is found in some leading texts of the Roman law, in which, by a superficial interpretation, the true relation of the rule to the exception, of the central point to the subordinate rules, is mistaken, and thrust out of sight. The practical errors to which the principle in question might lead were averted by appending a series of exceptions, which in great measure resolved the principle itself into a mere phantom (*a*). According to the view we have adopted, this doctrine must be entirely rejected, because it altogether wants any substantial reason, which could only be derived from the essence of the obligation. What

(*a*) See above, vol. i. Pref. p. xlv. Those passages are: L. 3, *de reb. auct. jud.* (42, 5); L. 21, *de O. et A.* (44, 7); but particularly L. 19, § 2, *de jud.* (5, 1), which certainly seems at first glance to place, as is commonly done by the moderns, rule and exception alongside of one another; whereas in fact it only lays down tentatively an apparently general proposition, and then, by adding limitations, leads the reader to find by abstraction the true rule, which it does not directly enunciate;—all quite in accordance with the method of the old jurists.

partial truth, however, is contained in it, will find its true position in the following discussion of the subject, and will be duly acknowledged.

Other writers have in later times abandoned that doctrine, and have sought to attach the forum of the obligation rather to the place of fulfilment. I have already stated my general agreement with this opinion. The success, however, of this procedure depends on the way in which the place of fulfilment shall be fixed. This may be done, first, by the will of the parties expressed with reference to a particular obligation. It has never been doubted that the forum of the obligation shall be assumed to be at such a place. But the case here supposed is the less common one; and it has still to be ascertained in most instances what place, in defect of such an express declaration of intention, is to be taken as the place of fulfilment, and therefore as the special forum of the obligation.

The following principle is laid down by many writers:—In defect of private intention, the positive law determines. For every obligation, therefore, there is a firmly settled place of fulfilment. This depends either on the expressed will of the parties, or, in its absence, on the direction of the law. The one as well as the other determines the special forum of the obligation.

In my opinion, this theory is entirely to be rejected; but I shall not attempt to refute it until I have fully explained another, which may be thus expressed in a few words:

The place of fulfilment is always determined by the direct intention of the parties; but this may be either *express* or *tacit*. In both cases alike it determines the forum of the obligation, which therefore always depends on voluntary submission (§ 369) (*b*).

This view differs from that before mentioned and rejected, in substituting for the place of fulfilment fixed by law one determined by tacit agreement.

I pass now to the more minute exposition of this doctrine.

1. The first possible case which we have to consider pre-

(*b*) Albrecht, pp. 13–27, substantially agrees with this, and his exposition I accept as quite correct. In the subsequent part of his treatise, however (pp. 28–35), he returns to the erroneous theory above referred to, and of which we are again to speak below (note *aa*).

supposes that the direct intention of the parties has happened to fix a place of performance. This may be done by the contract, in which the payment of a sum of money is promised, with express mention of the place where this act shall be done. That in such a case this place shall be the forum of the obligation is so clearly and so often stated in our law sources (*c*), that no doubt has ever been raised about it (*d*).

Yet this case would be restricted within too narrow limits, if it were confined to the form which has just been illustrated by an example. To make this plain, it is necessary to observe the natural distinction among the acts which may become the object of obligations. Some of these—indeed the greatest number of them—are of such a nature that they can be performed at any place. Among these are prestations of personal service, also work to be done on moveable things, the transference of the possession of moveable things, and especially the payment of money. For these acts a definite place of fulfilment can be fixed only in the way mentioned in the example above given, namely, by verbal indication of the place where they are to be done. Other acts, on the contrary, are by their very nature so exclusively fixed down to one place, that they can only be conceived of as at that place. Among these are, all labour on a particular piece of land; the erection or improvement of a house; the letting, hiring, or sale of a house or lands. For in every sale the obligation of the seller lies in the transference of possession (*e*); and in the case of a piece of land, this is only conceivable at the place where it is

(*c*) L. 19, § 4, *de jud.* (5, 1); L. 1, 2, 3, *de reb. auct. jud.* (42, 5); L. 21, *de O. et A.* (44, 7), '*contraxisse* . . . . in eo loco *intelligitur*;' C. 17, x. *de foro comp.* (2, 2). In the same class is also L. 1, *de eo quod certo loco* (13, 4). For as this passage says that naturally (that is to say, irrespective of the *actio arbitraria*) an action lies at no other place than the stipulated place of fulfilment, it certainly implies, in the first instance, as the rule, that the action is admissible at this place.

(*d*) Many have obscured the true view by designating this case as *forum solutionis*, and thus have made it appear essentially different from the following cases. Others have carried out this very questionable distinction so far as to fall into the practical error of assuming, along with this forum, and co-existing with it, a second *forum contractus* at the place where the contract was concluded. Thus Linde, *Abhandl.* ii. pp. 112–114 (comp. Hollweg, p. 46). It is true that the universal *forum domicilii* subsists along with this special forum, so that the plaintiff has his choice between the two (§ 371). [Savigny, *Obligationenrecht*, i. 510 sqq.]

(*e*) L. 11, § 2, *de act. emti* (19, 1).

situated (*f*). It would therefore be an idle and superfluous formality to promise in the sale, that the delivery of the house sold should take place in the city in which it is situated. There is no reason at all for making the application of our principle depend on this formality; and we must therefore maintain that the place of performance, with its consequences, is fixed, not by verbal designation alone, but also by the nature of an act which can be conceived as occurring only at a certain spot (*g*). Nay, it would even be inexact to assume, in this case, a tacit expression of intention. For by this we understand the constructive inference from an act directed to other purposes than the expression of intention, which inference may always be excluded by a contrary express declaration (*h*). But if any one sells a house, that is, promises to deliver it, the circumstance that this delivery shall take place just where the house is situated is implied in the promise itself, for delivery at another place is impossible; so that even a contrary express declaration as to this accessory circumstance would be quite absurd.

We now pass to the far more frequent and very various cases in which no settled place of performance exists; these cases, however, can only relate to acts which are naturally capable of being done everywhere, and are not connected with a particular locality, because otherwise, as has just been shown, this very connection would involve the place of fulfilment. For all these places, then, we inquire at what place the fulfilment may be thought of and expected by the parties. This place we must regard as the true seat of the obligation and as its special forum, since that expectation, based on the circumstances, implies a *tacit* appointment of the place of fulfilment, and therefore also a tacit submission of the defendant to the jurisdiction of that place. From this assumption of a tacit agreement and submission, it follows, as a matter of course, that the special forum of the obligation to be established by the following considerations, can always be excluded by an expressed intention to the contrary (§ 369, *b*). This principle, indeed, is

(*f*) Apprehension is only possible if the acquirer of possession is present (Savigny, *Recht des Besitzes*, § 15), whereas the former possessor may be absent (*ibid.* p. 239).

(*g*) Bethmann Hollweg, pp. 47–50, is here of a different opinion.

(*h*) *V. supra*, vol. iii. § 131.

nowhere expressly enunciated in the Roman law; but all the particular decisions of the Roman jurists admit, without any forced construction, of being referred to it, and only to it; and it also stands in unmistakeable connection with the voluntary submission which, in all this doctrine, is everywhere to be regarded as decisive.

We are thus brought back to the facts in which the obligation has originated, and we have to specify in order those outward circumstances which lead to the inference that the place where the obligation arose was expected by the parties to be also the place of its fulfilment. If in this inquiry we closely follow the statements of the Roman law, the correctness and consistency of which, from the standpoint of the common law, cannot be questioned, we must not forget of what character these statements are. They do not contain rules of positive law, but leading points of view from which the probable and natural thought of the parties is to be discovered, and along with which, therefore, the special circumstances of each case are to be attended to. Where, therefore, the circumstances might lead to another decision, we act entirely in the spirit of these texts of the Roman jurists, if we do not practically apply them. This remark, however, will certainly not be of frequent importance.

II. In order to elucidate the first case of this kind, it is necessary to take a preliminary view of the diverse nature and outward form of the facts from which obligations arise. Most obligations arise from single transient acts. This is the nature of the most frequent of all their originating causes, the contract, which, though it is often long prepared for, is always instantaneous in its actual conclusion, and occupies a scarcely perceptible space of time. On the other hand, there are other, but fewer, obligations which arise from a continued, connected activity of the debtor,—an activity which always occupies a considerable space of time, and is connected with a particular locality. We may designate such an activity, out of which, in the course of time, a greater or less number of obligations is wont to spring, by the common name of *a course of business*. A survey of the most important cases of this kind, as they are mentioned in our law sources, with a notice of the jurisdiction thereby established, will make the matter plain (*i*).

(*i*) L. 19, § 1, *de jud.* (5, 1); L. 36, § 1; L. 45, *pr. eod.*; L. 4, § 5,

Among such cases are the following :—The tutory of pupils, and every kind of curatory. Further, the management of another person's affairs, whether it be of all his affairs (general mandate or agency), or of a certain class of them, such as a manufactory, trading establishment, etc.; and whether it be in consequence of a contract (mandate or *operæ locatæ*), or proceeding from the will of one party only (*negotiorum gestio*) (*k*). Finally, one's own continuing banking and commission business (*argentaria*). It follows from this review that one's own business, as well as that carried on for others, can found this jurisdiction; also a contract, as well as a quasi-contract, which lies at the foundation of the management of another's business. The essential condition consists only in this, that the continuing business is permanently fixed to a certain locality (*l*). In most cases this jurisdiction does not appear prominently, because the business coincides with the domicile; but the two can be separate, and then this jurisdiction shows itself effective (Note *l*).

Many authors have regarded this jurisdiction as a distinct and peculiar one, under the name *forum gestæ administrationis*, apart from the so-called *forum contractus*. This is quite wrong, since both rest upon the same ground,—on the expectation of the parties, founded on the circumstances, that the obligations arising from the course of business will be satisfied at the place where it is carried on. For this expectation the permanent nature of such business affords a quite sufficient ground; because in this course of business the totality of the obligations arising out of it has obtained, as it were, a local and visible existence, and is embodied in it. If, then, the technical term *forum contractus* is to be applied at all, this case must be completely included under it. Only it must not be supposed that the obligation arises at the place where the contract for undertaking the business has been concluded; nor even where the

de ed. (2, 13); L. 54, § 1, *de proc.* (3, 3); L. 1, 2, *C. ubi de ratiocin.* (3, 21). Voluntary submission is expressly assigned as the reason in *negotiorum gestio*, in L. 36, § 1, *de jud.* (5, 1): 'non debet judicium recusare . . . cum sua sponte sibi hanc obligationem contraxerit.'

(*k*) Not every mandate, and not every *negotiorum gestio*, belongs to this category; for both can also have for their object a single transient transaction, of which we are not here speaking.

(*l*) L. 19, § 1, *de jud.* (5, 1): 'Si quis tutelam . . . vel quid aliud, unde obligatio oritur, *certo loci administravit*, etsi ibi domicilium non habuit, ibi se debebit defendere.'

particular contracts of sale, the payments of money, etc., have taken place, in consequence of which the parties carrying on the business may become responsible to their principal. Both these places here vanish out of sight as subordinate, and the business itself, as a permanent whole, must be regarded as the common foundation of the particular obligations arising out of it (*m*). To the permanent seat of this business, the thoughts, the expectation, the voluntary submission of the parties were directed.

III. Those obligations still remain, in which neither a definite place of fulfilment is specified (No. I.), nor a continued activity at a determinate place serves as their foundation (No. II.). These must therefore have as their objects, acts which may take place everywhere alike; and they must arise from single transient acts, for otherwise they would come under the previous categories. In regard to them, therefore, we have to inquire under what conditions a contemplation of the place where they originate founds the expectation that it shall also be the place of fulfilment, and therefore the true seat of the obligation.

The first case which suggests itself is that in which a debtor enters into an obligation at his personal domicile. He thus subjects himself to the court of that place as the special forum of this obligation. It seems at first sight superfluous, and even contradictory, that that which is already established for this person as his general forum should now be regarded as something new, as a special jurisdiction, for in such a case it might appear sufficient simply to recognise the ordinary effect of the *forum domicilii.*

But this distinction becomes of practical importance in the case of possible alterations. If that debtor capriciously changes his domicile, or if he dies, his previous *forum domicilii* has, as such, entirely ceased. But in the quality here established, as the special forum of the obligation, it still continues: it follows the emigrant in his new domicile; it binds the heir in case of death, although he should have a different domicile (*n*).

(*m*) Cf. Albrecht, p. 23.

(*n*) L. 19, *pr. de jud.* (5, 1); L. 2, *C. de jurisd.* (3, 13). [See Donell. *Com.* xvii. c. 12: 'Reus ejus loci forum sequi debet . . . non quia ibi domicilium habuit; sed quia cum haberet (ibi) contraxit.' See also Donell. *Com.* xvii. c. 19; *infra*, § 371, note *s*.] Cf. Bethmann Hollweg, p. 24. This important proposition stands in connection with the reservation above

The reason of this peculiar rule is, that the debtor, by undertaking the obligation here, creates an *expectation* that he will also submit to its consequences at the same place (§ 369). This expectation must not be disappointed, neither ought the debtor to be prevented from changing his domicile at pleasure; but he must fulfil at his old domicile the obligations there undertaken.

IV. But even away from his domicile, one may enter into an obligation as debtor, in circumstances which raise a natural expectation that the place where the obligation originates shall also be that of its fulfilment.

Such an expectation is created by one who establishes away from his domicile a commercial business of some duration, and in doing so, makes arrangements from which it may be inferred that he will deliver the goods which he there sells in the same place. He thus subjects himself to the special forum of the obligation at the place where the contract is entered into. This is laid down minutely by Ulpian; and that while warning against the unconditional assumption of jurisdiction merely because a contract is concluded at any place. He justifies this warning by mentioning the case of a person who enters into a contract while on a journey, and of whom it certainly will not be asserted that he subjects himself to jurisdiction at the place of the contract (*o*).

But such a trading relation is to be regarded only as an example, not as the exclusive condition, of a forum of the obligation. For if contracts are concluded during a residence away from the domicile, it is necessary to deduce from the substance of them what notions as to their fulfilment the parties

made (§ 344, *e*). This proposition explains L. 45, *de jud.* (5, 1), which refers to the following case:—A female inhabitant of Rome obtains a loan at her domicile. After her death she is succeeded by her daughter, whose domicile is in a province, where the tutors have judgment given against them in the name of their ward. Yet, says Ulpian, the *judicati actio* belongs to Rome, because the testatrix had established there the forum of the obligation.

(*o*) L. 19, § 2, *de jud.* (5, 1): '. . . durissimum est, quotquot locis quis navigans, vel iter faciens, delatus est, tot locis se defendi. At si quo constitit, non dico jure domicilii sed tabernulam . . . officinam conduxit, ibique distraxit, egit; defendere se eo loco debebit.' L. 19, § 3, *eod.* L. *un. C. de nund.* (4, 60), denies the *forum contractus* only as against those who visit as travellers a public market for particular mercantile affairs, not as against those in whom the marks specified above by Ulpian are found. [See Donell. *Com.* xvii. c. 14, whose whole discussion on the *forum contractus* should be compared with the text.]

may probably have entertained. If, therefore, a public officer, in consequence of his official duties, or a deputy to a legislative assembly, stays for months at the same place, and there contracts debts connected with his daily subsistence, there is no doubt as to the establishment of the special forum of the obligation. So likewise, if debts are contracted for similar purposes during a residence at a watering-place. If, on the contrary, during such a residence at baths or a watering-place, contracts as to mercantile affairs are entered into, of which the further development can be expected only at the domicile, such a jurisdiction at the place where the contract is entered into must be denied (*p*). As all here depends on the probable purpose of the parties, a very short residence may, in some circumstances, suffice to found that jurisdiction. It will be held to exist as against a traveller, who refuses to pay his reckoning in a tavern, since in such matters immediate payment is the universal practice, and may therefore be expected by every one. Thus everything depends on the relation in which the nature and length of the residence stand to the substance of the obligation.

If we compare the foregoing rules (Nos. II., III., IV.) with the opinion above stated and rejected, the two views appear to stand in the following relation: That opinion regarded the place of the obligatory act itself as the ground of the jurisdiction of the obligation (but with exceptions). The rules and principles now laid down attach this effect, not to the obligatory act in itself, but only in connection with other circumstances originating and preceding it (*q*).

V. Finally, it remains to determine the seat of the obligation in those cases to which none of the conditions previously assigned extend, inasmuch as there is not a definite place of fulfilment (No. I.), and we are precluded, by the attending circumstances, from regarding the place where the obligation arises as that intended by the parties to be also the place of ful-

(*p*) Bethmann Hollweg, pp. 24, 25. Cf. Seuffert, *Archiv*, vol. ii. No. 119.

(*q*) Mühlenbruch deals with the cases collected under No. IV. correctly, and with practical insight into the relations of actual life (pp. 355–357, 360, 361, 365–375); but he errs in the theoretical foundation, for he assumes in these cases a quasi-domicile or a temporary domicile, and therefore connects them with the case No. III. This connection is forced and useless.

filment (Nos. II., III., IV.). Among these cases will be reckoned in particular that cited by Ulpian, in which a traveller, during his temporary residence concludes a contract (Note *o*). In the total absence of every indication of a definite place of fulfilment, it must be assumed that the domicile of the debtor, to which he always returns, was conceived to be the place of fulfilment. Such a case is to be judged, therefore, as if the contract had been entered into by the debtor, not on the journey, but at his own domicile (No. III.).

This case will most frequently present itself in the following form, which demands special mention on account of the ambiguity of the subject-matter of the obligation. If the owner of a manufactory or a commercial establishment travels about, or causes his servants to travel to collect orders, and so to conclude contracts for delivery of merchandise, it may seem doubtful what is the exact import of the obligation undertaken by him; and yet on this the place of fulfilment will depend. For the delivery is a complex transaction, occupying a space of time. The merchandise is first despatched by the seller, then remains for some time on the way, and finally comes into the possession of the purchaser. Here we might regard as the true subject-matter of the obligation, either the despatching, so that the receiving would be merely a later consequence of the completed performance; or, again, the receiving, so that the despatching could be no more than the preparation for the actual fulfilment. In the first case, the domicile of the seller would be the place of fulfilment; in the second case, the domicile of the purchaser. Which of these views, then, is to be preferred on general principles? I hold the first opinion to be the correct one. The proper fulfilment of the obligation consists in the despatching of the goods, and the place of fulfilment is therefore to be fixed at the domicile of the *seller*. Two rules of the Roman law are, as I believe, in favour of this. *First*, the transference of the risk of accidental loss to the buyer from the moment of the conclusion of the sale, and therefore before he acquires the property by delivery (*r*). *Second*, the rule by which in most cases the promised delivery of a moveable can be demanded only at the place where it is already situated (*s*).

(*r*) § 3, *Inst. de emt.* (3, 23).

(*s*) L. 12, § 1, *de pos.* (16, 3). We shall immediately speak more fully

In the Prussian law this view is still more unquestionably recognised; for by that law, not merely the risk, but the property, passes to the buyer when the goods are sent away, provided that the mode of despatch was either directed by the buyer, or approved by his silence (*t*).

I believe that we must place under the same category the case, in L. 65 *de judiciis* (5, 1), of a *dos*, as to which the future husband enters into a written contract away from his domicile (for example, at the domicile of the bride or of her father). The action for restitution of the *dos*, says Ulpian, is in future to be raised, not at the place where the dotal contract was concluded, but at the domicile of the husband. For this is also the seat of the marriage, and therefore the locality of the *dos*, and at this place accordingly must its future restitution be looked for.

For the sake of convenience, I will shortly recapitulate the rules that have just been discussed in detail as to the forum of the obligation. This jurisdiction is to be held as founded in the following cases:—

I. At the place which is specially fixed for the fulfilment of the obligation by the intention of the parties, whether it be so fixed by the verbal indication of some place or other, or because the act which is to be brought about by the obligation can possibly be performed only at a single place.

II. Failing the appointment of a place of fulfilment, this jurisdiction may be founded by the fact that the obligation arises out of the debtor's course of business, which is fixed at a particular place.

III. The jurisdiction is also fixed by the place where the obligation arises, if that coincides with the domicile of the debtor.

IV. The place where the obligation arises can found jurisdiction even if it be away from the domicile of the debtor, if the circumstances create an expectation that its fulfilment shall also be at the same place.

of this proposition. In connection with it, Thöl, *Handelsrecht*, § 78, notes 5, 6, asserts that the delivery of merchandise must, as a rule, take place where the seller has his ordinary warehouse.

(*t*) *A. L. R.* i. 11, §§ 128–133.

V. If none of these conditions exists, the forum of the obligation is at the domicile of the debtor.

All these cases, however various they appear, and however accidental their connection may seem, yet admit of being reduced to a common principle. It is always the place of fulfilment that determines the jurisdiction, either that expressly fixed (No. I.), or that which depends upon a tacit expectation (Nos. II.–V.). In both cases a voluntary submission of the defendant to this jurisdiction is to be assumed, unless an express declaration to the contrary excludes it.

The theory here proposed was compared with another partly similar, which must now be examined and refuted (p. 154). This other theory, carried to its logical result, may be thus stated: For every obligation a certain place may be assigned, at which it must be fulfilled. This may be fixed by the intention of the parties; failing such appointment, the law provides for a definite place of fulfilment. In both cases, the forum of the obligation is fixed at this place of fulfilment.

This whole theory stands and falls with the assertion, that for every obligation there is a place of fulfilment ordained by positive law. Let us first examine into the correctness of this assertion. It may be conceived, that by a rule of positive law every obligation must be fulfilled where it has arisen; then the *forum contractus*, in its literal sense, would be founded by the appointment of the place where the contract is concluded, as the place of fulfilment (*u*); and that doctrine would then not be wanting in internal consistency. But neither this nor any similar rule as to a legal place of fulfilment is true.

The true rule is, that, failing a place of fulfilment fixed by the contract, the debtor must fulfil just where he is sued (*ubi petitur*) (*v*); so that it depends entirely on the choice of the plaintiff at what place he will enforce performance, provided, of course, that he finds at the place where he chooses to enforce performance a forum which the defendant is bound to recognise.

(*u*) This was formerly Linde's opinion (*Archiv*, pp. 61–63, 75), but he afterwards himself departed from this principle (*Abhandlungen*, ii. p. 111). It will be immediately shown that he has partially adhered to it.

(*v*) L. 1, *de ann. leg.* (33, 1); L. 38, *de jud.* (5, 1); L. 47, § 1, *de leg.* 1 (30, *un.*); L. 4, *de cond. trit.* (13, 3); L. 22, *de reb. cred.* (12, 1).

Instead, therefore, of the legal place of fulfilment determining the forum, as that theory maintains, it is, conversely, the legal place of fulfilment that is fixed by any competent jurisdiction, so soon as the creditor determines to avail himself of it. By the Roman law, the *forum originis* existed for every debtor, as well as the *forum domicilii*, and the two might be different; nay, the debtor might be a citizen of several towns, and also have a true domicile in several towns. Then the plaintiff had a free choice at which of these many places he would sue; and wherever he sued, there also was the legal place of fulfilment. Thus that theory entirely reverses the true order of things; for by the actual doctrine of the Roman law, the place of fulfilment is not that which determines the forum, but it is itself dependent on the forum.

If, then, this rule of the Roman law stood alone, so palpable a circle would not have been unobserved, and the erroneous doctrine in question would hardly have found defenders. But in Roman law a limitation has been added to the rule, and this limitation has caused the whole mistake. In its complete form the matter stands thus:—

As a rule, every creditor can certainly enforce the fulfilment of an obligation at every place where he finds a jurisdiction over the debtor. But if the obligation is for delivery of a certain individual moveable of a *certa species*, there is this alleviation for the debtor, that he can free himself by delivery at the place where the thing happens to be at the time, and therefore he is not bound to bring it at his own cost and risk to the place where the action is raised. But he loses this advantage if the thing is elsewhere not by accident, but by his dishonest conduct. Moreover, this alleviation does not apply to all actions on debts, but only to actions on *bonæ fidei* contracts (*w*), or on a testament for payment of a legacy (*x*); not,

(*w*) L. 12, § 1, *depos.* (16, 3).

(*x*) L. 38, *de jud.* (5, 1); L. 47, *pr.* § 1, *de leg.* 1 (30, *un.*). It may strike us as remarkable that the personal action for a legacy is here classed with the *b. f. actiones*, since it was itself a *condictio*. (See above, vol. v. p. 540.) Probably those passages originally referred merely to the *sinendi modo legatum*, the principle of which involved this favour, and which was also dealt with by Julian as in other respects the same with the *fideicommissa*, and therefore as entitled to liberal treatment (Gaius, ii. § 280). With the disputed question now before us this doubtful point has no connection.

therefore, to the condiction arising out of a stipulation (*y*). On the contrary, these principles hold in actions *in rem*,—for instance, the *rei vindicatio*,—and likewise in the action *ad exhibendum*, both of which are arbitrary actions (*z*).

If we take this exceptional rule, as it has here been stated, as a mere equitable favour to the debtor, it is clear that it has nothing at all to do with the place of fulfilment and a jurisdiction founded upon that; for these, on the contrary, are binding and restrictive to the debtor. The correctness of my view, however, is shown by the fact that the *dolus* of the debtor excludes the exceptional provision,—a proposition which only means anything if that provision is regarded as a favour to the debtor. Whence it follows that the advocates of the theory here contested are in error when they see in this rule a legally appointed place of fulfilment, and seek to establish upon that a special forum of the obligation,—namely, one at the place where the moveable thing happens to be situated (*aa*). Besides, this last inference (on which all here depends) is entirely inadmissible—for this reason, if for no other, that it would create a *forum rei sitæ* for personal actions, which certainly no one will maintain.

The opinion we are disputing is further supported by the following circumstance: In regard to *fideicommissa* (by which certainly the *fideicommissum hæreditatis* is meant), there is a rule, based on equitable consideration for the burdened heir, that he is required to pay them only at the place where the greater part of the inheritance is situated. At this place, then, a special forum is said to be founded for that purpose (*bb*). A

(*y*) L. 137, § 4, *de V. O.* (45, 1): '. . . ut sic non multum referre videatur, *Ephesi daturum se*, an (quod Ephesi sit, cum ipse Romæ sit) *dare spondeat*. . . .'

(*z*) L. 10, 11, 12, *de rei vind.* (6, 1); L. 38, *in f.*, *de jud.* (5, 1); L. 11, § 1, *ad exhib.* (10, 4).

(*aa*) Linde, *Abhandlungen*, ii. p. 118; Albrecht, pp. 29–32. The latter wrongly lays stress on such expressions as 'ibi *dari debet*, ubi est,' in L. 38, *de jud.* (5, 1). Taken in its whole connection, that means, 'he is *only* bound to deliver it *at this place*,' as the exception which immediately follows clearly shows; he does not need, therefore, to pay the expenses of carriage: 'nisi dolo malo hæredis subductum fuerit, tunc enim ibi dari debet, ubi petitur.' So too in L. 38, *de jud.* (5, 1): 'Per in rem actionem . . . ibi *peti debet*, ubi res est.' And yet the plaintiff has always his choice between the *forum rei sitæ* and the *forum domicilii*. Bethmann Hollweg, p. 70.

(*bb*) L. 50, *pr. de jud.* (5, 1); L. *un. C. ubi fideicom.* (3, 17).

similar equitable consideration must also be had for the benefit of the *hæres fideicommissarius*, who is sued for the debts of the ancestor (*cc*). These rules, which are of a very positive nature as regards the jurisdiction, have quite erroneously been so connected with the rule already discussed as to the delivery of moveable things at the place where they are situated, that an attempt has been made to deduce from them a special jurisdiction for moveables also (*dd*). It was a still greater mistake to seek to apply these very arbitrary rules to support a general legal principle as to the forum of obligations. Their positive and solitary nature results partly from the very indeterminate notion of the *major pars hæreditatis*, which certainly does not point to any origin in general legal principles, partly from the historical development of the *fideicommissa*, which, protected by *extraordinaria cognitio*, were always subject to a much freer and more penetrating influence of legislation than obligations (*ee*).

Sect. XXVIII.—(§ 371.)

LAW OF OBLIGATIONS.—FORUM OF THE OBLIGATION.

(CONTINUATION.)

The rules here laid down as to the forum of the obligation still need some additions and more minute explications, which shall now be given.

According to an opinion formerly very widely diffused, and which lies at the basis of the technical expression, *forum contractus*, that forum is to be assumed, as a rule, to be at the place where the obligatory act—and therefore the fact in which the obligation has its origin—has taken place (§ 370). This opinion, indeed, was necessarily rejected, since that fact is not in itself, but only in connection with other circumstances preceding it and producing it, fitted to found such a jurisdiction (p. 153).

(*cc*) L. 66, § 4, *ad Sc. Trebell.* (36, 1).
(*dd*) Albrecht, p. 29.
(*ee*) Cf. Bethmann Hollweg, pp. 32–35, 48.

Still, even according to this modified view, an important influence on the establishment of that jurisdiction must be allowed to the obligatory act. And this question still appears to us to be important: Where is the true place of an obligatory act? or, in other words, Where does an obligation arise? The answer to this question, which is often difficult, will here be attempted with reference to the three most important kinds of obligatory acts: Contracts, Unilateral Permitted Acts, Delicts.

A. CONTRACTS.—These are mostly entered into at a personal meeting of the two parties; then the place of this meeting is also the place where the obligation originates. But the following deviations from this simplest and most usual course of events may occur:—

First, the validity of the contract may, by a regulation of positive law, or by the will of the parties, be made to depend on the observance of a particular form—it may be of a written, notarial, or judicial style. Then the place at which this form is completed is the true place of the contract, because, until such completion, no party is bound (*a*).

But it is a much more frequent and more difficult case when the contract is not entered into at a personal meeting of the parties, but by a messenger, by a document signed by the parties at different places, or, which is most usual, by a simple correspondence. In such cases the true place of the contract has been most keenly disputed. Three different questions naturally arise, although most jurists do not discriminate them: Where is the contract made? What place is to fix the forum? What the local law? To the first I answer, without hesitation, that the contract is concluded where the first letter is received and the assenting answer is despatched by the receiver; for at this place a concurrent declaration of intention has been arrived at. The sender of the first letter is therefore to be regarded as if he had gone to meet the other, and had received his consent (*b*). This opinion has been adopted by several (*c*). But many have

(*a*) L. 17, *C. de fide instr.* (4, 21). Cf. Meier, p. 58.

(*b*) The same is to be assumed in the case of the messenger as at the place where the assent is declared to him; in the case of the document subscribed by both parties at the place where the last subscription is affixed; in the case of a bill, at every place where any one accepts or indorses it.

(*c*) Hommel, *Obs.* 409, N. 17, 18; Meier, p. 159—(both in dealing with the question as to the local law); Wening, *Archiv f. civ. Praxis*, vol. ii. p. 267–271 (who speaks chiefly of the *time* when the contract is concluded,

suggested the following doubts:—The assenting letter, they think, may be recovered before its arrival, or annulled by a revocation; therefore the contract is first completed at the place where the sender of the first letter has received the answer, and has thus become aware of the other's agreement (*d*). But it is quite wrong to reject the true principle in consideration of such very rare cases. In far the greater number of instances both intentions will be declared without such a wavering of resolution; but where that does happen, the question can only be decided by taking into account a multitude of particular circumstances, so that, even then, the arbitrary rule proposed by our opponents is by no means sufficient (*e*).

I now pass to the second question: Where is the forum of the obligation in a contract concluded by correspondence? It might be supposed, in accordance with the doctrine just asserted,

yet in such a way that his decision is to be referred also to the *place*); Lauterbach, *de nuncio*, § 25 (*Diss.* T. 3, N. 107), where the discussion is chiefly as to the messenger, but he is placed quite on the same footing with the letter. [Puchta, *Pand.* § 251, *Vorles.* § 251; Savigny, *Obligationenrecht*, § 81. Comp. Bell, *Com.* i. 326, 327 (Shaw's ed. p. 41): 'It is the act of acceptance that binds the bargain; and in the common case it is not necessary that the acceptance shall have reached the person who makes the offer.' *Adams* v *Lindsell*, 1 B. and Ab. 681; *Higgins* v *Dunlop*, 2 July 1847, 9 D. 1407; aff. 6 Bell's Ap. 195, 12 Jur. 295, 1 H. L. Ca. 381; *Taylor* v *Merchants' Fire Ins. Co.* 1849, 9 How. 390, 18 Curt. 191; Parsons, *On Contr.* 406, 440; Chitty, *On Contr.* 10–13,—all which refer to the *punctum temporis* at which the contract is concluded. In the American case of *M'Intyre* v *Parks*, 3 Metc. 307, *cit.* Parsons, *Contr.* 440 n., the same principle was applied in regard to time as would be applied in this country. In *Thomson* v *James*, 13 Nov. 1855, 18 D. 1, it was decided that a contract was complete where an offer sent by post was accepted by a letter posted on the same day on which a retractation of the offer was posted. Lord Ivory said (p. 15): 'The question is, When does this *concursus* (*consensus in idem placitum*) take place? Now, naturally speaking, there is no offer *quoad* the acceptor until the letter containing it reaches him. An offer by letter is in some sort *ad longum manum*, and until it reaches its destination, there is only one will at work. If acceptance is then made, there is an instant *concursus*, and the offer hitherto in suspense takes effect,—the acceptance, when the offer comes to hand, merging with it into the completed contract.' In this case the question as to the *time* when the contract is complete was fully discussed, and the opinion of Pardessus (*Dr. Com.* §. 250), Toullier (t. vi. §. 29), Warnkœnig (*Com.* t. ii. pp. 69, 70), and many civilians, requiring the offerer's knowledge of the acceptance in order to complete the contract, was rejected.]

(*d*) Hert, *de commeatu literarum*, §§ 16–19, *in Comment.* vol. i. p. 243; Hasse, *Rhein. Museum*, ii. 371-382; Wächter, *Archiv*, vol. xix. p. 116. J. Voet, v. i. § 73, is somewhat ambiguous.

(*e*) Wening, *l.c.*, proposes some practical rules for this matter. The rules of the *A. L. R.* i. 5, § 90 foll., on a separate but analogous question, could not here be applied.

at the place where the first letter was received and an assenting answer returned. But this must be decidedly denied (*f*). For the sender of the first letter can at the utmost be compared to a passing traveller, certainly not to one who has set up a permanent abode at the domicile of the other party; and therefore he has not voluntarily subjected himself to the jurisdiction of this place (§ 370, *o*). The contract entered into by correspondence is rather to be viewed, in respect to each of the parties, as entered into at his own domicile; and here he must recognise the special forum of the obligation itself (§ 370, No. V.). But if a certain place of fulfilment is fixed in the contract, this will settle the forum of the obligation.[1] The peculiarity of bills of exchange (Note *b*) may justify great modifications of these principles as to the forum. Thus it is laid down in the Prussian ordinance introducing the late German 'Wechselordnung' (*g*), that not only the place of payment and the domicile found jurisdiction, but also that at the place where an action on a bill has once been raised, other debtors on the bill may be cited as defendants.

The third question as to the local law governing a contract by correspondence, can only be answered below (§ 373).

B. Unilateral Permitted Acts.—That these are in this respect to be regarded in the same way as contracts, is distinctly said in our law sources (*h*). An application of this proposition has already been made to the important obligations which arise out of a course of business, etc. (§ 370, No. II.). Only one case still needs special mention.

The heir who enters on an inheritance thereby undertakes obligations of different kinds, particularly towards the creditors of the *hæreditas*, and towards the legatees. These obligations are described in the law sources as similar to contracts (*i*). For this reason some writers have assumed for such a case a *forum contractus*, which is placed by some at the place where the heir's acceptance of the succession has been declared, by

(*f*) This is the opinion of Mühlenbruch, pp. 348, 351.
[1] See Notes to §§ 373, 374.
(*g*) § 5. *V. Gesetzsamml.* 1849, p. 50.
(*h*) L. 20, *de jud.* (5, 1): 'Omnem obligationem pro contractu habendam, existimandum est;' so said, undoubtedly, with respect to the jurisdiction. [Donell. *Com.* xvii. 14, p. 982; ed. Franc. 1626.]
(*i*) § 5, *J. de obl. quasi ex contractu* (3, 27); L. 3, § 3; L. 4, *quib. ex caus.* (42, 4); L. 5, § 2, *de O. et A.* (44, 7); L. 19, *pr. de R. J.* (50, 17). [See Donell. *Com.* xvii. cc. 14 and 15.]

some at that where the succession is situated, and by some at the domicile of the deceased (*k*). But this opinion is to be rejected, and such a forum cannot be admitted. Only exceptionally, by an altogether positive rule, is such a jurisdiction founded for *fideicommissa*, and that at the place where the greatest part of the succession is situated (*l*). The expression of the law sources above referred to relates only to the personal entrance of the heir into the obligatory relation towards creditors and legatees, not to its proper origin and juridical character.

C. DELICTS.—The special jurisdiction founded by a delict is unknown to the earlier Roman law, and first arose under the empire (*m*). It then found such general acceptance that it was afterwards, even in positive enactments, placed in the same rank as the *forum domicilii, contractus, rei sitæ* (*n*). It would be a mistake, however, to regard this forum as merely a particular form of the forum of the obligation, of the so-called *forum contractus* (*o*). For the *forum delicti* does not arise by a presumptive voluntary subjection, and therefore the limitations above laid down for the forum of the obligation (§ 370) do not hold good in respect to this. To found this jurisdiction, neither domicile nor any other external accessory circumstance is necessary; but it arises from the commission of the delict itself, even at an accidental and temporary residence. This jurisdiction is thus of a very peculiar character, since it is established, not by voluntary, but by necessary subjection, which, however, is an immediate consequence of the violation of right of which the delinquent has been guilty. The jurisdiction of the delict is, moreover, just as little exclusive as that of the contract; but the plaintiff has always his choice between this special one and the general jurisdiction founded on the domicile of the debtor. This is implied in the words in which that jurisdiction is mentioned in the passages cited (Note *n*); but it is a necessary result of its being introduced for the advantage, certainly not of the defendant, but of the plaintiff (*o*[2]).

(*k*) Linde, *Abhandlungen*, vol. ii. pp. 101-109; Mühlenbruch, §§ 379-382.
(*l*) Bethmann Hollweg, *Versuche*, pp. 32-35, 48. Comp. above, § 379 fin.
(*m*) Bethmann Hollweg, *Versuche*, pp. 29, 52.
(*n*) *Nov.* 69, C. 1; C. 20, *X. de foro comp.* (2, 2).
(*o*) In the passage quoted from the Canon Law, the two are expressly distinguished, and made co-ordinate.
(*o*[2]) Linde, *Lehrbuch des Prozesses*, § 93, note 10.

The question has been raised, whether the forum of the obligation extends merely to those actions which arise out of the natural development of the obligation, and therefore lead to its fulfilment; or also to those which have the opposite direction, seeking the dissolution of the obligation, or to reverse that which has already taken place towards its fulfilment. As a general rule, the first and more limited application of this jurisdiction can alone be admitted (*p*). The second and more extensive application can occur only exceptionally and in the smaller number of cases, in which the dissolution of the obligation has a common origin with its beginning, as when the dissolution of an obligation created by contract is derived from a collateral contract added to it (*q*).

The special forum of the obligation does not exclude the general jurisdiction arising from domicile, but it lies in the free choice of the plaintiff to raise an action before the one court or the other (*r*). Many have erroneously attempted to restrict this election to the case in which the jurisdiction is founded by a specially stipulated place of fulfilment. But it exists also when the jurisdiction is founded on the contract itself (without place of fulfilment) (*s*), or on a course of business (*t*).

Originally the very opposite had to be maintained as to a place of fulfilment fixed by stipulation, viz. that an action

(*p*) L. 2, *C. ubi et apud quem* (2, 47).

(*q*) Glück, vol. vi. pp. 301-303. This application of the jurisdiction receives an unqualified denial from Linde, *Archiv*, vol. vii. pp. 67–69.

(*r*) L. 19, § 4, *de jud.* (5, 1), (where we must read *habeat* instead of *habuit*; see Hollweg, p. 46); L. 1, 2, 3, *de reb. auct. jud.* (42, 5); L. *un. C. ubi conv.* (3, 18); C. 17, *X. de foro comp.* (2, 2). In Roman law the plaintiff could sue also in the *forum originis* (§ 355).

(*s*) L. 2, *C. de jurisd.* (3, 13). In the words, 'ubi domicilium reus habet,' the emphasis is not on *domicilium*, but on *reus*. The meaning therefore is, that the domicile of the defendant (not of the plaintiff) fixes the jurisdiction. This is shown by the words at the beginning of the passage. The plaintiff, however, is not thereby deprived of the right to prefer the *forum contractus*, where such a forum is established.

(*t*) The so-called *forum gestæ administrationis* has no special character at all (§ 370, II.). The right of election is also expressly recognised in the case of the *Argentarius*. L. 4, § 5, *de ed.* (2, 13). And for this case it has been denied on the authority of L. 45, *pr. de jud.* (5, 1). But here '*conveniri oportet*' means: he must submit to be sued. Of the correct opinion are Struben, *Bedenken*, iii. 96; Gönner, *Handbuch*, vol. i., *Abh.* xi. Of the erroneous opinion, Leyser, 73, 8; Weber, *Beiträge*, vol. ii. p. 35; Linde, *Archiv*, vol. vii. p. 73.

could *only* be brought at this place; because, by the special subject-matter of this stipulation, the creditor had renounced his right to select for the action the general personal forum of his debtor. But because this might lead to a complete denial of justice,—if, for instance, the debtor used the precaution not to appear at the stipulated place of fulfilment,—a special action was introduced, which could also be brought at the personal forum, only taking into account the possible difference in the rate of interest at the two places (*u*). This action, therefore, gives the plaintiff a right of election even in such a case.

On the contrary, there is no justification for the opinion of many who give the plaintiff an election between the forum founded on express, and that founded on tacit agreement as to a place of fulfilment (*v*); for the assumption of such a tacit agreement is always excluded by the existence of an express one.

The jurisdiction of the obligation can be made effective only if the debtor is *either* present in its territory, or possesses property there;[2] in which last case the decree against him will be enforced by *missio in possessionem.* By the older Roman law this alternative condition is unquestionable (*w*). By the

(*u*) L. 1, *de eo quod certo loco* (13, 4): 'Alio loco quam in quem sibi dari quisque stipulatus esset, non videbatur agendi facultas competere. Sed quia iniquum erat, si promissor ad eum locum, in quem daturum se promisisset, nunquam accederet, quod vel data opera faceret, vel quia aliis locis necessario distringeretur, non posse stipulatorem ad suum pervenire, ideo visum est utilem actionem in eam rem comparare.' What is here said of the stipulation is also true of every other obligation concerned with definite place of fulfilment, as soon as this produces a condiction (as loan and legacy), but not of the *b. f. obligationes*, in which the action on the contract was always of itself sufficient. L. 7, *eod.*

(*v*) So that the plaintiff could at pleasure constitute a *forum contractus*, either at the stipulated place of fulfilment, or at the place where the contract had been concluded (§ 370).

[[2] This is the rule in Scotland. *M'Arthur* v *M'Arthur*, 1842, 4 D. 354; *Sinclair* v *Smith*, 1860, 22 D. 1475. And in respect to presence in the territory, substantially it is so in England also, though there rules of venue have an important influence on questions of jurisdiction. See *Mostyn* v *Fabrigas*, 1 Cowp. 161, 1 Sm. L. C.; Westlake, § 120 sqq. See 15 and 16 Vict. c. 76, §§ 18, 19 (Common Law Proc. Act). The law of England and Scotland as to jurisdiction is too extensive a subject to be treated of in these notes, especially as the author here touches on it only incidentally.]

(*w*) L. 1, *de eo qui certo loco* (note *u*): '. . . si unquam accederet;' L. 19, *pr. de jud.* (5, 1): 'si ibi inveniatur;' § 1, *eod.*: 'si non defendat . . . bona possideri patietur.' In similar terms is the rule for the *forum rei sitæ* in L. 2, *Cod. ubi in rem* (3, 19).

terms of a law of Justinian we might regard it as abolished (*x*). But this law is expressed so generally and indefinitely, and mixes up the various jurisdictions so indiscriminately, that the intention to change the former law cannot with any certainty be inferred. Hence, too, a Decretal has paid no regard to it, but adheres to the older Roman law, even to the very phrases (*y*). The preponderance of modern practice has followed this opinion (*z*), so that the jurisdiction of the obligation cannot be made effectual against an absent person by the mere requisition of a foreign court. It is not to be denied that by this restrictive condition the forum of the obligation loses a great deal of its importance.

In the modern codes the forum of the obligation has, as was to be expected, taken the form which was in favour among writers at the time of their compilation; and it is therefore to some extent not in harmony with the present Roman law, with which, however, it was intended to be in accordance. Thus the Prussian law places that forum, in the first instance, at the place of the stipulated fulfilment, and where there is none such, at the place *where the contract is concluded* (*aa*), without regarding the restrictive conditions under which alone the Roman law holds the place where the contract is concluded to be decisive. The plaintiff's right of election is also admitted here; and at the same time the defendant, in the spirit of the modern practice (Note *z*), is only bound to that forum when he allows himself to be found within its territory.

(*x*) *Nov.* 69, C. 1, 2.

(*y*) C. 1, § 3, *de foro comp. in VI.* (2, 2): '. . . . nisi inveniantur ibidem (comp. note *w*) trahere coram se non debent invitos, licet in possessionem bonorum, quæ ibi habent . . . possint missionem facere.' From many this passage receives the very forced interpretation, that the judge is not directly to constrain the absent person by his own power, but only by requisition of his own judge. Cocceii, *Jus Controv.* v. 1 qu. 15; Glück, vi. p. 304; Linde, *Archiv*, vii. pp. 69, 70.

(*z*) This preponderance of practice is admitted even by its adversaries: Cocceii *l.c.*; Glück, vi. pp. 304–306; Linde, p. 69.

(*aa*) *Allgem. Ger. Ordn.* i. 2, §§ 148–152. This forum is also recognised in treaties with many neighbouring states, *e.g.* Weimar, 1824, art. 29, *Gesetzsammlung*, 1824, p. 153.

SECT. XXIX.—(§ 372.)

LAW OF OBLIGATIONS.—LOCAL LAW.

The doctrine of the forum of the obligation has been so minutely explained in its details (§§ 370, 371), because it affords the only safe basis for the inquiry as to the territorial law applicable to obligations, for which question there is naturally a total want of rules in the sources of the Roman law. Just in this way is the intimate connection between the forum and the territorial law as rich and fruitful as it is well founded; because the same voluntary submission which determines the seat of the obligation, and with it the jurisdiction, must also be accepted as determining the local law to be administered (*a*).

I hold, without hesitation, that the whole series of practical rules, as they have just been laid down in regard to the forum, also regulate the local law to be administered (§ 370). That therefore is, according to the different cases, to be referred to the following places (p. 163):—

I. When the obligation has a firmly-settled place of fulfilment,—to that place of fulfilment.

II. When the obligation has arisen out of a continuous course of business carried on by the debtor,—to the place where this course of business has its permanent seat.

III. When the obligation has arisen from a single act of the debtor at his domicile,—to the place of this act, so that a future change of domicile makes no difference.

IV. When the obligation has arisen from a single act of the debtor away from his domicile, but under circumstances which lead to expect the fulfilment in the same place,—to the place of this act.

V. When none of these conditions exist,—to the domicile of the debtor (*b*).

(*a*) Eichhorn also (*Deutsches Recht*, § 37, *b*) applies the passages of the Roman law which speak of the forum directly to the territorial law.

(*b*) It might seem as if I here meant to assent to the principle above rejected (§ 361, *g*), according to which the local law of the domicile is held to have a subsidiary authority for all cases in which another territorial law has not been specially indicated. But this is not the case; for we have

So far, therefore, the determination of the territorial law entirely coincides with the determination of the jurisdiction. Only in this respect is an important distinction to be observed, that, along with the special forum of the obligation, the general forum of the domicile also remains effectual, with a right of free election on the part of the plaintiff; whereas the local law to be administered cannot be subject to such election by one of the parties, but must be determined exclusively by the appointed place of fulfilment, failing which, by the place where the obligation arises, or by the domicile of the debtor, as the case may be.

The derivation of the rules here laid down from the presumed voluntary submission of the debtor to a particular territorial law, has some weighty practical results which must here be reviewed.

A. This territorial law ceases to be applicable when it is at variance with an absolute, strictly positive rule of law in force at the place of the court which decides the question (§ 349); for in such cases the free-will of the parties can have no influence at all (b^2).

B. The territorial law likewise ceases to apply when the presumption of voluntary submission is excluded by an expressed contrary intention (*c*).

C. It has been asserted in many quarters, that of several local laws in themselves conceivable, that must always be applied according to which the juridical act in question can best be supported (*d*). This proposition, in such generality, cannot indeed be established from the subsisting law; on the contrary, one might be led to state it as new positive law (*e*). But in

here recourse to the law of the domicile, not because no other law can be established, but because in this case the parties naturally expect the fulfilment of the obligation at the domicile of the debtor, rather than at any other place. This reason, however, which is merely one application of the general rule as to the seat of the obligation, applies to the jurisdiction (§ 370, No. V.) no more and no less than to the territorial law.

(b^2) Cf. Wächter, ii. pp. 397-405; Fœlix, p. 145 [ed. Demangeat, i. 216].

(*c*) L. 19, § 2, *de jud.* (5, 1): '. . . nisi alio loci, ut defenderet, convenit.' What is here said as to jurisdiction applies equally to the local law, so far as its rules can be altered by the will of parties. Comp. above, §§ 369, *b*, and 370.

(*d*) Eichhorn, *Deutsches Recht*, § 37, notes *f*, *g*.

(*e*) It is laid down for a single case by the Prussian code (*A. L. R.* i. 5-13), namely, for the case of different legal forms where a contract is concluded by correspondence.

the following sense the proposition may be defended:—If the application of the rules above laid down would lead us to subject the contract to a law (*e.g.* that of the place of fulfilment), according to which it would be invalid, while it would be valid by the law of the domicile, it is then certainly not to be presumed that the parties intended to subject themselves to a local law which is entirely opposed to their purpose (*e*[2]).

Although the seat of the obligation, and, at the same time, the local law that governs it, may upon the whole be determined with certainty by the rules here laid down, yet it must not be asserted that all possible questions of law occasioned by an obligation must be determined only by this local law. A more thorough investigation of such questions of law, in their whole connection, is required to settle this point; but that must be reserved for the sequel of this inquiry (§ 374) (*f*).

The opinions of writers differ from the doctrine here laid down as to the local law applicable to obligations, in the two following chief points:—

First, nearly all connect the local law to be administered with the place of the obligatory act itself, without taking into account the special conditions added in the Roman law (§ 370), although in general most of them imagine that they proceed on the principles of the Roman law. This is the more objectionable, because these conditions of the Roman law, which give the matter a new shape, do not rest on arbitrary, positive rules, but rather on considerations arising from the nature of things, on the circumstances which indicate whether a voluntary submission to a particular local law can or can not be assumed with probability.

Second, there is a very frequent objection to the opinion here adopted, according to which a stipulated place of fulfilment preferably determines the local law to be adminis-

(*e*[2]) So understood, the principle is in full harmony with a well-known rule of interpretation in ambiguous juridical acts. L. 13, *de reb. dub.* (34, 5). [This proposition would justify the decision in *Depau* v *Humphreys*, 20 Mart. La. 1; Story, § 298 sqq. See below, p. 203, note 2.]

(*f*) The different ways of judging such questions of law have already been pointed out by Leyser, 73, 3; Fœlix, p. 142-145 [ed. Demangeat, i. 212-216]. I cannot therefore regard these writers as my opponents in regard to this proposition; the object must be to arrive at a common understanding on the particular questions. A similar course has already been adopted in the doctrine of property (§ 367).

tered. In this respect, however, opinions are very much divided. One party of writers, and that the most numerous, agrees with the doctrine here presented (*g*). Another party, on the contrary, maintains that the local law must be determined only by the place of the obligatory act; that the stipulated place of fulfilment has no influence on it at all, because the passages of the Roman law speaking of such agreements are to be referred only to the jurisdiction, and not at all to the territorial law (*h*).

This controversy depends on the explanation of the passages of the Roman law relating to this subject, which, for the sake of convenience, I here prefix:—

1. L. 6, *de evict.* (21, 2): 'Si fundus venierit, ex consuetudine ejus regionis, in qua negotium gestum est, pro evictione caveri oportet.'
2. L. 21, *de oblig. et act.* (44, 7): 'Contraxisse unusquisque in eo loco intelligitur, in quo, ut solveret, se obligavit.'
3. L. 1, 2, 3, *de reb. auct. jud.* (42, 5): 'Venire bona ibi oportet, ubi quisque defendi debet, id est—ubi domicilium habet—aut ubi quisque contraxerit. Contractum autem non utique eo loco intelligitur, quo negotium gestum sit, sed quo solvenda est pecunia.'

These passages are explained by our opponents in the following way. The first, they say, speaks only of the territorial law, and directs that, in respect to it, that place shall be exclusively regarded at which the obligatory act has taken place (*in qua negotium gestum est*), whereby, therefore, all consideration of the place of fulfilment is excluded. The second and third passages, on the other hand, are held to speak only of the jurisdiction, not of the local law; but as to the jurisdiction, they require the place of contract to be regarded; and they indicate as the place of the contract, not the place of the obligatory act, but that of the fulfilment. Thus, say they, the forum and the local law are sharply distinguished in these passages, and dealt with according to opposite rules.

This explanation has plausibility, but no truth. The third

(*g*) Christinæus, vol. i. Dec. 283, n. 8, 11; P. Voet, sect. 9, c. 2, §§ 12, 15; Mühlenbruch, *Doctr. Pand.* § 73, note 17; Fœlix, pp. 142-145 [ed. Demangeat, i. 212-215]; Story, §§ 280, 299. [See Note A at end of section.]

(*h*) Hert, § 10, *ampl.* 2; Meier, pp. 57, 58; Wächter, ii. pp. 41-47.

passage certainly speaks of the forum, and not of the local law; but the second speaks so generally that it is applicable just as much to the one as to the other. If, then, the reasons above assigned for the intimate connection of the territorial law with the forum are convincing, a practical difference in the treatment of the two questions must be denied, so long as no distinct testimonies can be brought forward in support of this difference. These are said to be found in the passages above cited, and it will now be our chief endeavour to show, by the explanation of the first of them, that it does not in truth contain that practical contradiction of the two other passages which some find in it.

As to the first passage, the L. 6, *de evict.*, it has already been remarked that it does not speak of the territorial law to be administered, but of customs as matters of fact, which do not found rules of law (§ 356, *m*). We may, however, pass over this objection, and willingly allow that an indirect use of this passage may be made in the subject before us. For the same probability that the parties tacitly intended to follow certain actual local customs, may be alleged in favour of their voluntary submission to the law of the same place. We shall therefore deal with the passage just as if it decided as to the territorial law, and only ask for what particular place it decides. In the words, *ejus regionis in qua negotium gestum est*, it is intended apparently to exclude any other conceivable place. What, then, is the place so excluded? In order to make clear the various possibilities that may here come under consideration, I will select the following example: Two inhabitants of Puteoli, one of whom possesses a piece of land in that town, meet at the baths of Baiæ, and there enter into a contract for the sale of that piece of land; thereafter a dispute arises as to making good the warranty against eviction, and the question is, what local law is to be applied? According to the view of our opponents, it must be the law of Baiæ (*regionis, in qua negotium gestum est*), not that of Puteoli, and the latter must be held as excluded, on the authority of this text of the jurist. I admit that the old jurist may possibly have thought of the contradiction resulting from so complicated a case, and may have meant to give a decision thereon; but in the passage itself there is not the remotest hint of this, and an unprejudiced interpretation of it must rather lead us to suppose the following much simpler case. The two inhabitants of Puteoli have concluded the sale in their native town itself (*i*); but in the territory of this town there is a peculiar custom about eviction, which is different from that elsewhere observed. For, while the universal custom of other places provided for the payment of double the purchase price in case of eviction (*k*), it was usual in Puteoli to allow of another compensation, it may be the price and a half more, or three times the price. The words of the jurist, therefore, have the effect, not of making exigible the amount of compensation usual elsewhere, but that in use at the place; because probably this will have floated before the minds of the parties. Suppose, then, the further question had been laid before him, how the matter should stand if the contract had been entered into, not at Puteoli, but at Baiæ (of which, however, the passage certainly has no trace), then he would unquestionably have referred back to the custom of Puteoli, because the contract was to be fulfilled in that town, and not in Baiæ; only in the latter case he would not have used the phrase *in qua negotium gestum est*, because if there had been such a contract, this must almost necessarily have been misunderstood. If, then, this explanation of the passage is adopted—an explanation which strictly adheres to its words, and forces on it no extraneous suppositions —it contains no reason whatever for determining the local law by another rule than the forum.

Note A.

The law of England is: 'The place in which it is made is presumed to be that in which it is to be performed, unless the contract expresses that it is to be performed in some other place. Hence the law of the country in which the contract is made is that by which it is entirely to be governed, unless its performance is to take place elsewhere.'—Burge, iii. 758; Addison, *on Contr.* 1034; *Robinson* v *Bland*, 2 Burr. 1084, 1 W. Bl. 234; Story, §§ 232, 280; Westlake, §§ 110, 163-169; *Consequa* v *Fanning*, 3 Johns. Ch. 587, 17 Johns.

(*i*) The passage is thus explained by C. Molinæus also, *Conclusiones de Statutis* in the *Comm. in Cod.* after L. 1, *C. de Summa Trin.* (pp. 6, 7, ed. Hanov. 1604 f.): 'Quod est intelligendum non de loco contractus fortuiti, sed domicilii, prout crebrius usu venit, immobilia non vendi peregre, sed in loco domicilii. Lex autem debet adaptari ad casus vel hypotheses, quæ solent frequenter accidere: nec extendi ad casus raro accidentes.' [Cf. *supra*, § 356, notes *l*, *m*; *infra*, § 374, note *e*.]

(*k*) L. 31, § 20, *de ædil. ed.* (21, 1); L. 2; L. 37, *de evict.* (21, 2).

518. 'Contracts made in one place to be performed in another, are to be governed by the law of the place of performance.'—*Andrews* v *Pond*, 13 Pet. 65, 13 Curt. 42. 'Though the debt be contracted in England, if it be performable in Scotland, there is a presumed reference to the Scotch judges (law ?) whether or not it be well performed. It is a debt which is to be judged of by the law of Scotland.' —Lord Eskgrove in *Watson* v *Renton*, 1792, Bell's 8vo Ca. 103, M. 4582; cf. *Armour* v *Campbell*, 1792, *ibid.* 109, M. 4476; *Royal Bank* v *Scott, etc.*, 20 Jan. 1813, 17 F. C. 90, 2 Bell *Com.* 690; *Robertson* v *Burdekin*, 1843, 6 D. 17, 1 Ross L. C. 812. 'The general principle is, that the rights of the parties to a contract are to be judged of by the law by which they intended, or rather by which they may justly be presumed, to have bound themselves.' 'It is generally agreed that the law of the place where the contract is made is, *primâ facie*, that which the parties intended, or ought to be presumed, to have adopted as the footing upon which they dealt, and that such law ought therefore to prevail in the absence of circumstances indicating a different intention; as, for instance, that the contract is to be entirely performed elsewhere, or that the subject-matter is immoveable property situated in another country, and so forth,—which latter, though sometimes treated as distinct rules, appear more properly to be classed as exceptions to the more general one, by reason of the circumstances indicating an intention to be bound by a law different from that of the place where the contract is made, which intention is inferred from the subject-matter and from the surrounding circumstances.'—Per Curiam (Ex. Ch.) in *Lloyd* v *Guibert*, 35 L. J. Q. B. 74, where it was held that a charter-party between persons, both foreigners at the *locus contractus*, but of different nationalities, to be performed at places of different countries, was to be governed by the law of the nation of the ship. Bar, in treating of the general principles applicable to obligations, reasons somewhat as follows:—The possible laws which may come into consideration in regard to an obligation are, (1) the *lex fori*, which he dismisses on general grounds; (2) the law of the place where the obligation originated, which, although he recognises that it is frequently applicable on grounds of expediency and fairness, he rejects on principle, because it admits of evasion of the laws by subjects by means of a short journey, and because, as in the case of contracts entered into on a railway journey, it is often difficult to ascertain where a contract was made. Thus, to find the place of the contract is a question to be answered by means of a legal rule, which, when the law applicable is not fixed, is to argue in a circle. (3) The place of fulfilment; but the parties' knowledge of the law is not to be assumed; a conventional change of the place of fulfilment, after the conclusion of the contract, would involve a change of the law regulating the contract; and there would be no *regula regulans* if there were more places of performance

than the one. It remains, therefore, according to Bar, only to choose between the domicile of the creditor and that of the debtor, the latter of which must of course be preferred. The state allows its subjects to enter into obligations with foreigners and in foreign countries, but only in conformity with its own laws. The rules of the law of obligations are absolute, and are for the protection of the debtor; their vigour cannot be supposed to cease merely because an obligation is entered into with a foreigner, or in a foreign country. A party's intention is naturally construed according to the law of his domicile, as is generally admitted in regard to testaments. Action is almost always raised on an obligation with a view to execution at the domicile of the debtor; and finally, a change of domicile does not effect any change in the law, as no one would attribute to the law of the new domicile a retroactive effect on an old contract. To the objection that the contracting parties may have different domiciles (see Merlin, *s. v. Loi;* Fœlix, i. 208 sq.; Wächter, ii. 44), Bar answers, that every bilateral contract or transaction is divisible into two unilateral obligations. Each party is to be understood to bind himself in the sense and to the effect provided by the laws to which he is himself subject. If the laws of the parties are irreconcilably at variance, and a reconciliation cannot be effected by judicial construction, the plaintiff fails to establish his case, and the defender must prevail. Exceptions to the application of the *lex domicilii debitoris* must, however, be allowed, (1) in the case of rules of law which depend on purely local circumstances, as in laws as to the rate of interest (Stephen's *Com.* ii. 82); (2) where *bona fides* requires the application of another law, *e.g.* the *lex loci* rules in contracts made at fairs and markets, in contracts made at a foreign business establishment, or with a foreign railway company for the carriage of goods, etc.; (3) where the parties, as they frequently do, clearly indicate an intention to be governed by the law of the place of fulfilment; (4) in the case of contracts as to immoveables; (5) in obligations *ex delicto.* But while the places of the origin and the performance of obligations may have some influence in regard to the subject-matter of obligations, such institutions relating to their extinction, as prescription and discharge in bankruptcy, require, according to Bar, the unconditional application of the law of the debtor's domicile. Bar, § 66.

Sect. XXX.—(§ 373.)

III. LAW OF OBLIGATIONS.—LOCAL LAW.

(continuation.)

There remain to be discussed some subsidiary questions as to the territorial law of the obligation, mostly connected with similar subsidiary questions as to the forum of the obligation, which have already been examined (§ 371).

For in several cases the local law, just as the forum, is fixed by the place where the obligation arises (§ 372, No. III., IV), and thus the more exact determination of this place may be important, and sometimes doubtful. In regard to such doubts, several special cases are here given and subjected to scrutiny, as has already been done in reference to the forum.

A. Contracts.—The most doubtful and most disputed case is that of a contract concluded by correspondence. But we must place on the very same line with this case the contract which is completed by a document signed at different places, or by oral expression of intention through a messenger (§ 370, *b*).[1] On this point what has already been said (p. 168) as to jurisdiction in such cases, can only be repeated. The contract by correspondence can only be regarded as concluded at the place where the letter is received, and answered affirmatively.[2] If this were alone decisive, the same place must also determine the local law, and in fact this is the opinion of various writers (*a*). But it must be rejected, since the writer of the letter is at the utmost to be compared to a traveller who for a moment has gone to the receiver to enter into the contract; but by such a temporary abode, even if a contract is made during its continuance, the seat of the obligation, with its legal consequences, is not fixed. Here, therefore, the local law of the obligation is to be judged, in the first instance, according to the place of fulfilment, if that be firmly settled; failing such an appointment, the law of his domicile governs each

[1] See Note A at end of section.

[2] 'Eo loci quo ultimus in contrahendo assentitur.'—Casaregis, *Disc.* 179, n. 1; Story, § 319.

(*a*) Hommel, *Rhaps.* obs. 409, N. 17, 18; Meier, p. 59.

party (*b*). Differing entirely from these views, other writers have maintained that the contract concluded by correspondence must be judged by the law of nature (*c*); in regard to which it is only to be lamented that they have not also given us the system of natural law which they wish to be applied. The Prussian code determines this question only for the case in which a different law as to the *form* of contract prevails at the domicile of the two parties; then that law is to be applied according to which the contract may best be supported (*d*). But it is implied in the spirit of this rule, that the law of the domicile should decide as to the liability of each party in other respects also (where the question is not as to the subsistence of the contract, but the nature of its effects).

The most important application of this question is to the law of exchange. According to the principles we have laid down, it must be assumed that the obligation of every individual subscriber of a bill is to be judged by the law of his domicile.[3] But the peculiar necessity of this kind of contract may well justify a different positive rule. The latest German law of exchange provides as follows in art. 85 foll.:—Every liability arising from a bill is to be judged by the law of the place where it originates. If, however, it is defective by this law, but the requirements of the German law are satisfied, the subscriptions afterwards placed on the bill in Germany are valid. So also are the subscriptions which an inhabitant of that country gives to another abroad, if only they conform to the laws of Germany (*e*).

B. Unilateral Permitted Acts.—Under this category we have chiefly to consider the manifold obligations arising

(*b*) Wächter, ii. p. 45, adopts the law of the domicile universally without respect to the place of fulfilment. [The law of the place of final assent was held to govern in a New York case quoted by Westlake, § 221, where an insurance policy, illegal by the law of the insured's domicile, was sustained in conformity with that of the company's domicile, where the letter of proposal was received, and the policy executed. But the legality of a note given for the premium was held to depend on the law of the place where it was made.—Westlake, *ib.* See Notes, *ante*, p. 168, and *infra*, p. 196; *Church of England Assurance Co.* v *Hodges*, 1857, 19 D. 414.]

(*c*) Grotius, *de j. belli*, lib. 2, c. 11, § 5, n. 3; Hert, *de commeatu literarum*, §§ 16-19 (*Com.* vol. i. p. 243).

(*d*) *A. L. R.* i. 5, §§ 113, 114.

[3] See Note B at end of section.

(*e*) *Preussische Gesetz-sammlung*, 1849, p. 68. The *A. L. R.* ii. 8, §§ 936-938, has similar rules.

from the law of actions, especially from litiscontestation (Anstellung der Klage), judicial confession, the judicial sentence. In this matter many doubts and differences of opinion were formerly observable, which, however, have gradually approximated more and more to the true principle, that the law subsisting at the place of the court (*i.e.* the court of first instance) must be applicable, even if the question afterwards comes before other tribunals (*f*).

It must, however, be observed that, properly speaking, two questions, in themselves different, although related, have to be decided, of which the meaning will become most evident if I bring them to their most important practical application,—the judicial sentence. The first and certainly the most important question is, Whether the judicial sentence, once pronounced, is to be recognised elsewhere, even in another country? The second question relates to modalities in the conditions and effects of the judicial sentence, which may be differently defined in the positive laws of different countries. Most of our writers attend only to the first question; but whoever answers this in favour of the authority of the judicial sentence, must in logical consistency apply also to these modalities the law of the place where the judgment was given, since it can only be enforced in the sense in which the judge has pronounced it.

This distinction appears prominently in the terms of many treaties concluded with neighbouring states by the Prussian government (*g*). By the terms of these treaties it might be supposed that, if a judgment pronounced in Weimar were produced in a Prussian court, the *exceptio rei judicatæ* must be applied in conformity with the Prussian rules as to that exception, not according to the law of Weimar (common law). This somewhat delicate distinction can hardly have been thought of; and it is the less probable, because in these treaties the varieties which may occur in the theory of the *exceptio rei judicatæ* have certainly not been considered. On the contrary, the meaning

(*f*) Huber, § 6; Meier, p. 29; Story, § 584 foll.

(*g*) *Treaty with Weimar*, art. 3 (*v. supra*, § 348): 'A judicial sentence pronounced by a competent court founds before the courts of the other state the exception of the judicial sentence (*exceptio rei judicatæ*), *with the same effects* as if the judgment had been pronounced by a court of the same state in which such exception is pleaded and admitted.' So with several other neighbouring states.

unquestionably was, that the exception founded on a foreign judgment might be made effectual *just as certainly* as that arising from one pronounced in the country, and therefore could not be dismissed, because the former judge was a foreigner.[4]

C. Delicts.—The forum at the place where the delict has been committed is subject to no doubt, according to positive laws and to practice, although it must be founded in another way than the forum of other obligations (§ 371, *c*). But another rule must be maintained in respect of the local law. It will, however, be more appropriate to deal with this question in another connection (§ 374, *c*), for which reason it is here reserved.

The modern codes contain only very imperfect regulations as to the local law of obligations. The Prussian Landrecht gives a direction as to contracts entered into by correspondence (note *d*). Further, it recognises, in the question as to measures and weights, as well as the kind of money that may be intended in a contract, the principle that the usage of the place of fulfilment is applicable (*h*); this direction, indeed, refers properly not to the territorial law, but to the interpretation of contracts, which is a different matter (§ 374, *f*). But I hold it quite correct to apply, in the spirit of the code, the principle thus recognised also to the local law as to the effects of contracts, because the authors of the code can hardly be assumed to have had that distinction in view.

In determining the local law applicable, the Austrian code lays weight especially on the place where a contract is entered into, and only adds the natural exception, when the parties have had in view the application of another local law (*i*).

Note A. (Agency.)

By a detailed comparison of the various degrees of authority which an agent or messenger may possibly hold in regard to a dis-

[4] See Note C at end of section.

(*h*) *A. L. R.* i. 5, §§ 256, 257. Koch, *Preuss. Recht*, vol. i. p. 133, lays down the true principle, that the local law to which the parties have intended to subject themselves must govern; but assumes, without sufficient reason, that this will mostly be the *locus contractus*. Bornemann, vol. i. p. 65, adopts this place as the prevailing rule. The form of contracts will be further discussed below, under the rule *locus regit actum*. Comp. also the passages of statutes above cited in note *e*.

(*i*) *Oesterreichisches Gesetzbuch*, §§ 36, 37.

closed principal, Savigny shows elsewhere that a letter, and all agents acting within the limits of their authority, 'have, in a juridical point of view, essentially the same nature. It is immaterial whether the agent conveys to the other party my simple resolution, or, according to his own free selection, one of several resolutions which I have conceived. It is also immaterial whether the agent appears in the transaction to exercise more or less discretion. It is quite impossible to draw a sharp distinction between these very various cases, and there is no real ground for allowing any influence to such a distinction. For in all these cases alike the contract is completed by me by my will, and the agent is merely the medium through which my will is conveyed. Thus neither rights nor obligations arise for him out of the contract, but these arise for me directly.'—*Obligationenrecht*, ii. 55-60, § 57; cf. Westlake, § 219.

The British and American decisions upon international questions of agency have not been numerous, nor are all the points that have arisen clearly settled. It seems (1) that an agent in a foreign country, expressly employed to carry on a business there, binds his principal as if the latter were personally present. 'If I send an agent to reside in Scotland, and he, in my name, enters into a contract in Scotland, the contract is to be considered as mine where it is actually made. It is not an English contract because I actually reside in England. If my agent executes it in Scotland, it is the same as if I were myself on the spot, and executed it in Scotland.'—Per Lyndhurst, C., in *Albion Insurance Co.* v *Mills*, 3 W. and S. 233; 1 Dow and Cl. 342; Westlake, § 212. Cases cited, *infra*, § 374, note A. This is in accordance with the second general rule of § 372; cf. § 370, II. (2) When an agent's employment is special, that is, when 'his mandate, or *negotiorum gestio*, has for its object a single momentary transaction' (*supra*, § 370, note *k*), the local law of the contracts which he makes will be determined by the general rules which determine that question in other cases. 'Every authority given to an agent or attorney to transact his business for his principal, must, in the absence of any counter proofs, be construed to be to transact it according to the laws of the place where it is to be done.'—Per Story, J., in *Owings* v *Hull*, 9 Pet. 607, 11 Curt. 497 (case of special agency). Those two propositions relate to questions between the principal and third parties, where no question arises as to the authority of the agent, or the liability of the principal for his acts. Such questions depend on the contract of mandate, which requires attention in two points of view. (3) As between a principal and agent residing in different countries, the law of the contract would seem to be that of the agent's domicile, in the case of fixed agency involving a course of business there. There are few cases on the subject; but there seems to be a tendency to hold, in the case of other transactions not involving a course of business, that the obligations of principals and agents will be regulated by the domicile of the parties respectively, as the principle is stated in the text, or perhaps (which is nearly the same thing) by the law of the place where each party 'transacts affairs connected with the contract of agency.'—Westlake, § 231. The contract is thus broken up into two parts. Story, § 291, note, commenting on *Arnott* v *Redfearn*, 2 Car. and P. 88. See Bar, § 66, p. 236; *supra*, p. 182. Where goods were consigned by a Chinese merchant to factors in New York for sale, the obligations of the consignees were held to be subject to the law of New York, for the contract, though made at Canton, was to be executed there. 'The parties had express reference to the law of this country as the theatre of operations under the contract.' 'The contract did not oblige the consignees to pay the avails of the cargoes to Consequa at Canton. On the contrary, this country was the sphere of their duties; the *res gesta* was here, and they were not bound to do anything but with a reference to our laws.'—*Consequa* v *Fanning*, 1818, 3 Johns. Ch. 587; in error, rev. judgment of Chancellor Kent, 17 Johns. 518. Lord Ivory's opinion in *Ritchie and M'Cormick* v *Fraser*, Dec. 11, 1852, 15 D. 205, points to a forum contractus at the domicile of the agent, even against the principal. But (4) where questions arise as to an agent's authority to bind his principal to third parties, there is a wide distinction between an agent permanently established in a foreign country, and one who makes a transient visit for a special purpose, or who is called on by circumstances to exercise abroad powers conferred on him by a contract of agency (mandate), entered into where different rules prevail. In the former case the law of the place where the agency or branch establishment is fixed seems to determine the liability of the principal. In the latter case the agent's powers will be regulated, as to constitution and extent, by the law of the place contemplated in the contract, *i.e.* in general the place of his and his principal's domicile. Thus in *Kerslake* v *Clark*, July 1820, More's Notes, p. 6, the authority of an attorney to sue for a debt and grant a discharge was held as governed by the law of his and his principal's domicile, even when he was compelled by the removal of the debtor to apply for execution in the courts of Scotland.

The question what law shall decide as to the agent's authority to bind the principal to third parties in questions between them and the principal, has been the subject of much discussion in the case of shipmasters contracting abroad. The greater weight of authority is in favour of the law of the owner's domicile, or, to speak more correctly, of the law of the country to which the ship belongs, as fixing the limits of the liability of the principal to parties contracting abroad with a shipmaster.

'Any shipmaster in a foreign country is for some purposes the agent of the owners, and for some purposes the agent of the freighters. The agency is devolved upon him by the law of his flag. The same law that confers this authority ascertains its limits; and the flag at the masthead is notice to all the world of the extent of such power to bind the owners or the freighters by his acts.' If it were not so, the municipal maritime law 'is all but a nullity in point of national purpose and effect, since three-fourths of the maritime traffic of the country are by supposition beyond its compass.'—Maclachlan, *Law of Merchant Shipping*, p. 156; cf. *The Osmanli*, 3 W. Rob. Adm. 198, Tudor L. C. 61; *The North Star*, 29 L. J. Adm. 73, 76; *Lloyd* v *Guibert*, 35 L. J. Q. B. 74 (Ex. Ch.); Story, § 286; *The Nelson*, 1 Hag. Adm.; *Pope* v *Nickerson*, 3 Story, R. 465; Brodie's *Stair*, Sup. 956. The recent English cases of *The Eliza Cornish*, 1 Eccl. and Adm. Rep. 36, 17 Jur. 738, in which the general maritime law, and *Cammel* v *Sewell*, 3 H. and N. 617, 27 L. J. Exch. 447,—in error, 5 H. and N. 728, 29 L. J. Exch. 350,—in which the *lex loci* of the agent's contract was held to govern, seem to be at variance with this view. Mr. Westlake holds the first opinion in § 213, and the second in § 216; Phillimore, iv. 584–591, argues in favour of the *lex loci contractus* as controlling the authority of the shipmaster. The Louisiana cases of *Malpica* v *M'Kown*, 1 Lou. R. 249, and *Arago* v *Currell*, 1 Lou. R. 528, are also cited in favour of the *lex loci contractus*. Story, § 286 sq. In the latter case it was said: 'Every contract which by the general maritime law the master can make, is binding on the owner. By putting the former in command, and sending him abroad, the latter invests him with the general powers masters have as such; and those who contract with him have nothing to do with any private instructions by which the general power may have been limited. If the limitation arises, not from the owner's instructions, but from the particular laws of the country from which the vessel has sailed, must not the consequence be the same? Can these laws limit the master's power more effectually than the owners could? or can they extend further? We think not. They have no force in a foreign country, where they are presumed to be equally unknown.' This, however, was not actually decided, as 'the case did not present the question of the owner's responsibility in relation to the contract of mandate, the agent having confined himself within his powers.'—Westlake, § 212. Bar, p. 262, is opposed to this argument: 'He who contracts with a person who holds himself forth as the representative of one residing in another state, has clearly occasion to acquaint himself with the laws in force at the place where the mandate is granted. If he neglects this, he deserves no more indulgence than if he had contracted without any inquiry at all as to the authority . . . On closer examination, the regulation of the agent's authority by the *lex loci contractus* appears to be incompatible with the security of trade. Not only the ordinary mandatary or agent, but also the legal administrator of a juridical person, and one who represents another in virtue of a family relationship, could, by merely contracting abroad where the law conferred on him a larger capacity, bind the persons for whom he acts in a manner that could not be foreseen. What would it avail a joint-stock company to limit the powers of the manager by requiring the assent of a board of direction, or of a general meeting of shareholders, if he is not bound by such a limitation in a contract entered into abroad? The owner or part-owner of a ship who can free himself according to the laws of the place where the shipping company is established by abandoning the ship, might be made liable to pay a balance beyond this by the mere contract of the master in a foreign country (Story, § 286; Judgm. of Ober Appell.-Gericht at Lubeck, 31 March 1846, Seuffert, ii. 324; Fœlix, ii. 31).' The principles laid down by Savigny seem to be in favour of the law of the principal's domicile, the shipmaster contracting at a foreign port being rather comparable to a messenger or a transient representative, or to the principal making a flying visit, in which cases the expectation is raised that the contract will be fulfilled at the headquarters of his business.

More complicated questions involving the doctrine of agency arise in the law of partnership. Corporations are here in the same position as real persons, and never give rise to questions as to the liabilities of the persons composing them, which are always subject to the law of the domicile of the corporation, even if these persons are themselves domiciled in a different country. *Bank of Australasia* v *Harding*, 9 C. B. 661, 19 L. J. C. B. 345; *Ibid.* v *Nias*, 16 Q. B. 717; *supra*, § 354. 'A foreign company has a *locus standi* here, and so, no doubt, has an English company in a foreign country. We make no inquiry into the constitution of a foreign company any more than we should into the generation of an individual suing here.'—Per Erle, C. J., in *Branley* v *S.-E. Ry. Co.*, 12 C. B. N. S. 70. Of course proof is required of the existence of the corporation. *Dutch W. I. Co.* v *Moses*, 1 Str. 611, 2 L. Raym. 1532; *Nat. Bank of St. Charles*, 1 C. and P. 569; Lindley, *On Part.* 80; Kent, *Com.* ii. 284. The question whether a corporation can have two domiciles for jurisdiction was raised in *M'Laren* v *Carron Co.*, 5 H. of L. Ca. 416. See Westlake, §§ 55, 129. The question as to the liabilities of the partners of unincorporated companies and private partnerships is more difficult. It would seem, however, that it should be resolved by the rules above laid down as to agency. The authority of one partner to bind the others must depend on the law of the principal seat of the partnership, unless, perhaps, in the case of a fixed establishment conducted by a partner in a different country. This would seem to subject the whole partners to the law of that country in all transactions entered into there. An agent permanently established abroad would, while his own powers are governed by the *lex loci*, bind the partners in proportions fixed by the contract of copartnery, as construed by, and under conditions imposed by, the law of the partnership domicile. See per Lord Fullerton in *Edin. and Glas. Bank* v *Ewan*, 28 Feb. 1852, 14 D. 557: 'As the pursuers claim against these individual defenders solely through the medium of that English contract, they must be bound by the conditions attached to it by the law of the domicile of the (?) contract. Then, if an English statute be passed, declaring that no partners of a joint-stock company should be personally or individually liable beyond certain limits, or should not be liable at all, it cannot surely be doubted that we should be bound to give effect to those provisions,—not because the statute was anything but an English statute, but that, being an English statute, it regulated or limited the liabilities of the individual partners, and that, consequently, we, in determining the rights of parties, necessarily and exclusively founding on the terms of the English contract of copartnery, as against the individual defenders, would be bound to expound the law of that contract according to the law of the country in which it had its local existence.' This seems to follow from the principles laid down as to agency; for the contract of copartnery is the measure of the authority of one partner to bind another as his principal and guarantor, and is subject to the law of the principal seat of the partnership, with a view to which it is made; unless, by fixing a permanent place of business elsewhere, the partners have given rise to an expectation that they are bound according to the law of the latter place. See Lindley *On Partnership*, Suppl. pp. 26, 27.

Note B. (Bills of Exchange.)

The principle of the English decisions is, that 'when a bill is drawn generally, the liabilities of the drawer, the acceptor, and the indorser respectively must be governed by the laws of the place where the drawing, acceptance, and indorsement respectively took place.'—*Allen* v *Kemble*, 6 Moore P. C. 314; *Potter* v *Brown*, 5 East 124, 1 Smith L. C. 351, 1 Ross L. C. 786; *Burrows* v *Jemimo*, 2 Str. 733; *Trimbey* v *Vignier*, 1 Bing. N. C. 151, 4 M. and S. 695, 6 C. and P. 25, 1 Ross L. C. 804; *Gibbs* v *Fremont*, 9 Exch. 31; *Don* v *Lippmann*, 2 S. and M. 737, 1 Ross L. C. 869 (*Rothschild* v *Currie*, 1 Q. B. 43, 4 P. and D. 737, was wrongly decided in this respect); cf. *White* v *Briggs*, 8 June 1843, 5 D. 1148. The specification of a place of payment relates only to the contract of the acceptor, the obligations of the other parties being governed by the laws of the places where they became bound respectively. *Cases cited; Cooper* v *Waldegrave*, 2 Beav. 282; *Cougan* v *Banks*, Chitty on Bills 683. Against the acceptor the rights of each holder, even under a transference made abroad, are the same as those of the original payee.—Story, §§ 317, 345-347; Westlake, § 241 sqq.; *De la Chaumette* v *Bank of England*, 9 B. and C. 208, 2 B. and Ad. 385, 1 Ross L. C. 792; *Robertson* v

Burdekin, 1843, 6 D. 17, 1 Ross L. C. 812; *Lebel* v *Tucker*, 37 L. J. Q. B. 46;—but he may have different rights in regard to the drawer, acceptor, and indorsers. Thus he may recover higher damages, on dishonour, from one obligant than he could from another, that rate depending on the place of the respective contracts. Story, §§ 307, 314; *Gibbs* v *Fremont*, *Cooper* v *Waldegrave*, *Allen* v *Kemble*, *supra*. Or his right to recover may be conditional upon the observance of rules as to the nature of the demand to be made on the primary debtor (*Williams* v *Wade*, 1 Metc. 82; Story, § 316, *b*); as to the necessity of protest (*Aymar* v *Sheldon*, 12 Wend. 439; Story, §§ 267, 360; Westlake, § 227; Bar, p. 307); or as to notice of dishonour (*Cook* v *Lichfield*, 5 Seld. 279; Story, *Confl.* § 360, *On Bills*, p. 195 sqq.; Westlake, §§ 225, 226; see Byles *On Bills*, p. 372),—differing in each case according to the different places of contract.

While it is quite settled that the acceptor of a bill negotiable by the law of the place of making, is debtor, according to that law, not only of the original payee, but of all subsequent indorsees wherever they may acquire right, a question remains as to the validity of the indorsation of such a bill in a country where it would not have been negotiable, if made there,—*i.e.* where the indorsement of a bill made in that form is invalid. Lord Moncreiff, in *Robertson* v *Burdekin*, *supra*, indicated an opinion that the contract of indorsement, though sufficient to carry a right against the acceptor or original debtor, should be ruled entirely by the *lex loci* of the indorsement with respect to the liability of the indorser. This seems to be agreeable to the general principles applicable to contracts, and to be most consistent with the language used in *Lipmann* v *Don*, *Cooper* v *Waldegrave*, *Allen* v *Kemble*, etc., *supra*. It is supported also by Westlake, § 243; Story, §§ 316, 347 fin.; Pardessus, *Dr. Com.* art. 1499; by *Barney* v *Newcomb*, 9 Cush. 46 (Westl. *l.c.*), and the other American cases above cited; and by the English cases holding the indorsement of a bill not transferable by indorsement, to be good at common law against the indorser himself, though not making the drawer or acceptor liable to the indorsee. *Hill* v *Lewis*, 1 Salk. 132; *Plimley* v *Westley*, 2 Bing. 249, 1 Ross L. C. 50, 51. (The objection to such indorsation under the stamp laws, given effect to in the latter case, might now perhaps be obviated by the use of an adhesive stamp. 17 and 18 Vict. c. 83.) Comp. the judgment in the converse case, *Lodge* v *Phelps*, 1 Johns. 139, 2 Caines 321, Story, § 357; where a note payable to the payee or order, made in a country where notes were not negotiable, was held to be validly indorsed even as against the maker in another country where they were negotiable, the maker being held, by adding the words 'or order,' to have waived all objections founded on its non-negotiability in the former country. The discussion of Bar on this subject, §§ 84-86, is too long to be repeated here.

NOTE C.

A distinction is made between foreign judgments (condemnator) sought to be enforced in a different country, and foreign judgments (absolvitor) pleaded in defence. A third category is added, consisting of foreign judgments condemnator already satisfied. Per Lord Medwyn in *Southgate* v *Montgomerie*, 1837, 15 S. 507, 518; Ersk. iv. 3, 4; Kames, *Pr. of Eq.* iii. 8, 6; Phillimore, iv. 673. As to the first class of decrees, there has been a difference of opinion on the question whether or not they are conclusive or examinable by the court which is asked to enforce them. It is sometimes vaguely said that they are '*prima facie* evidence of the debt,' and that it 'lies on the defendant to impeach the justice thereof, or to show the same to have been irregularly obtained.' *Sinclair* v *Fraser*, 1771, M. 4542, 2 Pat. App. 253. See Taylor, *On Evidence*, § 1551. The true doctrine seems to be, that a foreign decree of either kind, the parties and the subject-matter being the same, will be held conclusive, unless very precise and definite (*Whitehead* v *Thompson*, 1861, 23 D. 772) allegations are made, either that the court which pronounced it had not jurisdiction, that it was obtained by fraud, or that the proceedings involved some manifest violation of the rules of justice, such as condemning a party unheard, and who had no opportunity of being heard. *Don* v *Lipmann*, 5 Cl. and Fin. 20, 2 S. and M'L. 745; per Lord Brougham, *Price* v *Dewhurst*, 8 Sim. 302, 4 Myl. and Cr. 85; *Rose* v *Himely*, 4 Cranch 269, 270; *Henderson* v *Henderson*, 6 Q. B. 298; cases cited in Taylor, *On Evidence*, §§ 1538, 1539, and 2 Smith L. C. 683 sqq.; *Crispin* v *Doglioni*, 32 L. J., P. M. and A. 169, H. of L., 35 L. J., P. and M. 129; *Liverpool Marine Credit Co.* v *Hunter*, 36 L. J. Ch. 567. A foreign judgment is also impeachable for error appearing on the face of it, or established extrinsecus, whether that error consist in a mistaken view or a disregard of international law (*Simpson* v *Fogo*, 1 J. and H. 18, 1 H. and M. 195; *Wolff* v *Oxholm*, 6 M. and S. 92; *Baring* v *Clagett*, 3 B. and P. 215; *Dalgleish* v *Hodgson*, 7 Bingh. 495, 504; *Lothian* v *Henderson*, M. App. Insurance 4, 4 Pat. App. 484, and 3 B. and P. 499; Westlake, § 387; *Castrique* v *Imrie*, 8 C. B. N. S. 1,—in error, *Ibid.* 405, 8 W. R. 344); or in a mistake as to the law of the country it was intended to apply (*Novelli* v *Rossi*, 2 B. and Ad. 757, 9 L. J. K. B. 307); or even for error in the reasons on which it is founded, 'apparent on the face of it, and sufficient to show that such judgment ought not to have been pronounced' (*Reimers* v *Druce*, 23 Beav. 145, 26 L. J. Ch. 196).

In the case of *Southgate* v *Montgomerie*, *supra*, it was decided that 'a foreign decree is not of the same authority as a final decree of the courts of this country, and can only be considered as affording *prima facie* evidence of the truth and justice of the claims of the pursuers;' and it was distinguished from a foreign judgment pleaded in defence, which was said to have been held in the unreported case of *White* v *Haliburton*, in 1820, to be not reviewable on the merits even 'in respect of an allegation of iniquity.' It would seem that the terms of the judgment as to judgments condemnator are scarcely consistent with the doctrine laid down above. *White* v *Haliburton* is quite at variance with the tendency of recent authorities, a foreign judgment pleaded in defence being liable to the same objections as one which is sought to be enforced. Westlake, § 393; *Henderson* v *Henderson*, 3 Hare 115; *Anderson* v *Shand*, 1833, 11 S. 688. See *Boe* v *Anderson*, 1857, 20 D. 11. A much greater effect was at first attributed to decrees of this second class founding the *exceptio rei judicatæ*. *Watson* v *Renton*, Bell's 8vo Ca. 107; *Southgate* v *Montgomerie*, *supra;* Taylor, *On Evid.* 1548; *Ricardo* v *Garcias*, 12 Cl. and Fin. 368. But as more precise rules upon this subject have been laid down, it has become apparent that the decree condemnator and the decree absolvitor are, in all essential respects, to be dealt with and applied by foreign courts in the same way. At the same time, it must be said that some writers (as Taylor, *On Evid.* § 1548 sqq.; Phillimore, iv. 683) appear to go as far as the case of *White* v *Haliburton*, in holding a decree of a foreign court adverse to a party bringing a second suit on the same grounds, to be absolutely conclusive if properly pleaded in defence. But probably this distinction is only apparent, and is occasioned by the fact that questions as to the conclusiveness of foreign sentences have almost always been raised and considered, as is natural, where a court has been asked, by a party who has obtained a foreign judgment, to do something to invert the state of possession, rather than where, from deference to a prior judgment of a competent court, it merely refuses to interfere. In the latter case the law was settled firmly at a very early period; in the former, comity or considerations of expediency have gradually increased the authority allowed to foreign sentences, and narrowed the grounds on which they can be impeached within the same limits which general principles seem to require in regard to the defence of *res judicata.* As to the defence founded on a foreign judgment adverse to the defendant, but satisfied, see *Barber* v *Lamb*, 8 C. B. N. S. 981, 6 Jur. N. S. 95. The English courts make a distinction between foreign judgments *in rem*, which receive unqualified recognition, and foreign judgments *in personam.* The principle is, that the judgment *in rem* (which occurs chiefly in admiralty courts, but also in the Court of Exchequer) is a solemn declaration by a competent court operating directly on the thing whose status is in question, and *ipso facto* making it what it is declared to be. *Castrique* v *Imrie*, *supra; Cammell* v *Sewell*, 29 L. J. Ex. 350, 3 H. and N. 617, 5 H. and N. 728; Phillimore, iv. 691 sq.; Smith's L. Ca. ii. 683 sq.; Best, *Pr. of Evidence*, 731.

Sect. XXXI.—(§ 374.)

III.—LAW OF OBLIGATIONS.—LOCAL LAW. PARTICULAR QUESTIONS.

Hitherto we have spoken of the principles which relate to the local law of the obligation in general. It was acknowledged, however, that this law is not necessarily applicable to all the questions that may arise out of an obligation, and the particular examination of these was reserved (§ 372, p. 177). I now pass to this inquiry.

A. The first of these questions concerns the *personal capacity*, for the particular legal relation, of the creditor or debtor in an obligation.

This first question is not to be decided by the territorial law of the obligation as such, but only by the law which is in force at the domicile of the person. This must be asserted without any qualification, for the distinction often made between general and particular capacity to act is quite untenable (§ 364).

This is especially true in the common law (of Germany) in respect to the personal capacity for bills, which is always to be judged according to the law of the domicile of the party subscribing the bill. But it would be a mistake to confound personal incapacity for bills with the absence of a law of exchange at any place. For at such a place no action on a bill can be brought effectually, even on a bill in itself perfectly regular; on the other hand, the law of such a place has no influence on the validity of a bill there made, so that such a bill can certainly be sued on as a bill at other places where a law of bills exists (§ 364).

B. Another question relates to the *interpretation* of juridical acts, especially contracts, out of which obligations arise (*a*).

This question may be taken, with some writers, in so wide a sense, that it embraces all other questions as to local law; for the application of any local rule to a contract may always

(*a*) Writers on this question: Boullenois, t. ii. *obs.* 46 dixième règle, pp. 489–538; Story, §§ 272 foll., 280 foll.; Wächter, *Archiv für Civil. Praxis*, vol. xix. pp. 114–125.

be conceived as appended to the contract by the probable will of the parties. That may be called suppletory construction, such as lies at the foundation of the dispositive rules of law (*b*). But viewed so generally, the question of interpretation loses its proper meaning. If it is to retain that meaning, we must take it in a narrower sense, referring it to the doubts which arise from the uncertainty of the terms of a contract. This is a question of fact, just as the interpretation of statutes; here as well as there, the object in view is to discover the thought which the oral or written language employed really contains (*c*). This question has nothing to do with the application of any local law, but the local dialect and form of speech may often be useful in helping to discover the meaning of the person from whom the declaration of intention proceeds. If, then, we ask what is the place of which the language is to be considered, the rules as to the local law to be administered cannot guide us to a correct answer; and it is without any reason that many have directed us to the place where the obligation has arisen, or that where it is to be fulfilled, merely because the local law to be administered is in many cases fixed by these places.

Thus in a contract made by correspondence, the language used at the place where the writer of the first letter lives will generally be regarded, not that of the place of the receipt and assent, although the contract is held to be concluded at the latter (p. 168) (*d*); for it must be assumed that the writer will have had in view the language familiar to him.

Further, if a verbal or written contract is concluded at the domicile of both parties, the language of that place is un-

(*b*) *V. supra*, vol. i. § 16.

(*c*) *V. supra*, vol. iii. p. 244. So also the Roman jurists express themselves. L. 34 *de R. J.* (50, 17): 'Id sequimur, quod actum est.' L. 114 *eod.*: 'In obscuris inspici solere, *quod verisimilius est*, aut *quod plerumque fieri solet*.'

(*d*) Wächter *l.c.* p. 117. He illustrates this proposition by the following case:—A Leipsic insurance company had, in its printed conditions, excepted the case of destruction by popular disturbance (Aufruhr). In a conflagration coming from without, the question arose whether the juridical notion of popular disturbance was applicable, seeing that the positive laws of different countries do not define this notion in the same way. Wächter decides correctly that the language of the Saxon law must be looked to, because in its realm the conditions were drawn up, on the basis of which the insurances were proposed and taken up. [See Note A at end of section.]

questionably applicable. On the contrary, this cannot be absolutely asserted, if the contract is entered into at a place which is not the domicile of one or both of the parties. Here we must consider in every case, whether it is probable that the foreigner who became a party to the contract knew that local language or way of speaking, and probably intended to adopt it (*e*).

For the same reasons we cannot unconditionally take as the basis for interpreting a contract the language in use at the stipulated place of fulfilment, although the local law of an obligation is always determined by that place. Here, too, everything depends on the question whether the parties knew the language used at this place, and meant to adopt it. For many parts of the subject-matter of a contract, we shall certainly be able to take as the general basis of our construction the language used at the place of fulfilment. For, if a sum of money is to be paid at a place abroad, if merchandise is to be delivered by measure and weight, or a piece of land is to be transferred according to the definite extent of a superficial measure,—but expressions are used in the contract for the kind of money, the measure, or the weight, which are commonly found in different meanings, with different degrees of extent or value,[1]—then the usage of language at the place of fulfilment must be taken as the rule, not merely because it is to be supposed that the parties have had in view the money, measure, weight there used, but also because at that place there will often be no possibility of adjusting and completing the performance by other weights, etc. (*f*).

(*e*) This assertion might be contradicted from L. 34, *de R. J.* (50, 17): 'Id sequamur, quod in regione *in qua actum est*, frequentatur.' But this certainly gives no arbitrary direction, and must therefore be understood under the natural supposition that the persons contracting are at home at this place; exactly as in L. 6, *de evict.* (21, 2). *V. supra*, § 372, *i.*

[1] The question whether, when a debtor is sued in a different forum from the place of performance, he is to be condemned in the amount of his debt according to the nominal, or according to the real rate of exchange, is decided by Bar, § 70, in conformity with the principle of *Grant* v *Healey*, 2 Chand. *Law Rep.* 113; Story, § 311, *n.* That principle is, that 'the creditor is entitled to receive the full sum necessary to replace the money in the country where it ought to have been repaid, with interest for the delay; for then, and then only, is he fully indemnified for the violation of the contract.' See below, § 374, *dd*, p. 208.

(*f*) Boullenois, pp. 496–498. So, too, it is expressly ordained in the Prussian laws, *A. L. R.* i. 5, §§ 256, 257. [And in Austria, *Allg. G. B.*,

The rules here laid down as to the construction of contracts may appear to stand in opposition to certain rules of the Roman law. For by these the interpretation of an ambiguous contract must always, in a stipulation, prove to the disadvantage of the stipulator (*g*); likewise to the disadvantage of the seller or the lessor, if these other contracts be in question (*h*). The reason for this is said to be, that these persons had it in their power to guard against the doubt by a different form of expression; which is as much as to say that they have occasioned the doubt either by their carelessness, or by dishonest intention. This very reason, however, indicates that quite a different case from that of the question now before us is presupposed. Those passages, moreover, expressly refer to obscure and ambiguous phrases (*i*); whereas, in our present inquiry, the question relates to expressions which are not in themselves either obscure or ambiguous,—they only have a different meaning at different places, which, however, is clear and certain at each of such places.

This question as to the construction of contracts has, from

art. 905; so in the *Allg. Deutsche Handelsgesetzbuch*, § 336. This is a question of fact, determined according to the presumed intention of the parties. *Rossetter* v *Cahlmann*, 8 Exch. 361; *Schuurmans* v *Stephen*, 10 S. 839, 11 S. 779; 1 Bell's *Illustr*. 93; Bell's *Com*. i. 438 (Shaw's ed. p. 90); Addison, *Contr*. 1036; Westlake, p. 173; Bar, pp. 241, 253; Story, § 270, etc. As to local measures within the same territory, see on the question of construction, *Miller* v *Mair*, 22 D. 660. The same principles apply whether the subject-matter of the contract is moveable or immoveable. Thus Molinæus, *Com. ad L.* 1 *Cod. de Sanct. Tr.*, *Op*. t. iii. p. 554 (*Concl. de St. et cons. loc.*), takes the case of a sale of land as illustrating the whole question as to measures: 'Unde stantibus mensuris diversis,' etc.,—a passage which is wrongly quoted as laying down a special rule for immoveables. Where, on the other hand, a sum of money is to be paid for land, or secured on land, the presumption that parties had in view the money of the *locus rei sitæ*, is naturally not nearly so strong as it is in regard to measures, though it will still be one element to be considered in construing the contract. *Stapleton* v *Conway*, 3 Atk. 727; *De Wolf* v *Johnson*, 10 Wheat. 323, 6 Curt. 438, 443. In *Clayton* v *Gregson*, 5 Ad. and E. 302, it was held that the mere existence of a customary use of terms in the district where premises lie, is not sufficient to establish, as a matter of law, that the parties contracting with regard to them used the terms according to that custom, but is only evidence from which a jury might draw that conclusion. Cf. *Smith* v *Wilson*, 3 B. and A. 728.]

(*g*) L. 26, *de reb. dub.* (34, 5); L. 38, § 18; L. 99, *pr. de V. O.* (45, 1).

(*h*) L. 39, *de pactis* (2, 14); L. 21, 33, *de contr. emt.* (18, 1); L. 172, *pr. de R. J.* (50, 17).

(*i*) L. 39, *de pactis* (2, 14); L. 21, 33, *de contr. emt.* (18, 1); L. 26, *de reb. dub.* (34, 5); L. 172, *pr. de R. J.* (50, 17).

an early period, been viewed by the majority of authors in a different way from that which has here been followed, having been referred to the principles of local law. It has, accordingly, been commonly held that the construction must be according to the language of the place of the contract or of fulfilment, if such a place be agreed on (*k*). But several have rightly recognised that the true problem is not to establish a legal rule, but rather to ascertain the true intention of the parties in each case, according to the general principles of interpretation (*l*).

C. The validity of an obligation depends partly on formal, partly on material conditions. The formal conditions will be further considered below, in connection with the forms applicable in other legal relations, when we come to speak of the rule *locus regit actum* (§ 381). We have here to ascertain the local law according to which the material conditions of validity must be judged.

It must be accepted as the rule, that the validity of the obligation depends on the local law to which it is in other respects subject (§ 372); it depends, therefore, according to circumstances, on the law of the place of fulfilment, on that of the place where the obligation has arisen, or on that of the domicile of the debtor. But an exception to this must be maintained in all cases in which it is opposed by a law of a strictly positive and coercitive nature existing at the place where the action is brought.

This rule also is acknowledged by most writers, but, as was to be expected, with the reservation of very many differences in its application, occasioned by their differences in opinion as to the local law of the obligation itself (*m*).

This agreement, however, is confined to the complete antithesis of a perfectly valid or perfectly invalid (null) obligation. Between the two extremes there are many intermediate cases, and opinions are very conflicting as to the local law by which these are to be judged.

Those cases must first be noticed in which merely the legal

(*k*) So Story, §§ 272, 280, and the authors there cited.
(*l*) So Boullenois *l.c.*, especially pp. 494–498, and Wächter *l.c.*
(*m*) Voet, *Pand.* iv. 1, § 29; Hert, § 66; Story, § 332 foll.; Wächter, ii. pp. 397, 403, 404.

remedy by action is denied to an obligation not in itself invalid (*naturalis obligatio*); then the far more numerous cases in which an actionable obligation is deprived of its effect by opposing peremptory exceptions. Many writers have here dealt with actions and exceptions as portions of legal procedure, and have therefore sought to apply to all such cases the law of the place where the action is brought (*n*). This opinion, however, is quite erroneous; all rules of law of this kind only define various degrees and forms of incomplete validity of the obligation (*o*), and therefore belong to the material law just as much as rules of law relating to the perfect validity or invalidity of obligations, and not to the law of procedure (*p*). It is quite illogical to treat the two kinds of rules of law according to different principles. But it is especially hazardous to attempt to apply this treatment to modern legislations, which are often deficient in the clear definitions and technical terms on which alone that distinction could be founded.

This rule, then, is to be applied, in particular, to the *exceptio non numeratæ pecuniæ*; for although in this the question chiefly concerns a rule of evidence, and thus seems to belong to the law of procedure, it is yet founded on the material law of certain kinds of obligations. Of the same class is the *exceptio excussionis*; likewise the exception founded on the *beneficium competentiæ*. On the other hand, this rule does not include the *exceptio Sc. Macedoniani* and *Sc. Vellejani*; for these exceptions do not rest on the defective nature of the obligation in itself, but on the imperfect capacity of the parties; and, consequently, must be judged by the law in force at the domicile of such persons (§ 364).

The same rule applies also to the actions by which an obligation is to be contested and invalidated; they are to be judged

(*n*) Weber, *Natürliche Verbindlichkeit*, §§ 62, 95; Fœlix, p. 146 [ed. Demangeat, i. 218].

(*o*) See above, vol. iv. § 202, 203. Of course the rule here laid down is only applicable to exceptions which have their ground in the material law (and therefore to all peremptory exceptions), not to those which are merely founded on rules of procedure, and which are therefore of a merely dilatory nature. See above, vol. v. § 227, pp. 171–175. The latter are certainly regulated by the law of the place where the action is brought, and perhaps the confusion of the two classes has contributed to confirm the false doctrine.

(*p*) Eichhorn, *Deutsches Recht*, § 36, note *n*; Wächter, ii. pp. 401, 402. [Bar, §§ 68, 69, 116.]

by the law of the place to which the obligation itself is subject (q).

The following are applications of this rule:—The rescission of a sale on the ground of lesion beyond the half; the rescission of a purchase by the redhibitory action or the *actio quanti minoris*. Also every restitution against an obligatory contract (r).

Among the defences by which an obligation may be invalidated, the most general in its application, and therefore the most important, is that of *prescription*. This still demands special consideration, because writers have expressed a great variety of opinions regarding it, yet so that the general conflict of opinions which has already been mentioned as to exceptions in general, here appears somewhat more prominently. In particular, if different periods of prescription exist at the stipulated place of fulfilment, where we assume the seat of the obligation to be, and at the place where the action is actually brought (as at the domicile of the debtor), the question arises, Which period of prescription shall be applied?

Many say that laws as to prescription are laws of procedure, and must therefore be applied to all the actions brought within their territory, without respect to the local law of the obligation (s).

According to the true doctrine, the local law of the obligation must determine as to the term of prescription, not that of the place of the action; and this rule, which has just been laid down in respect to exceptions in general, is further confirmed, in the case of prescription, by the fact that the various grounds on which it rests stand in connection with the substance of the

(q) The local law of the obligation is thus to be applied more generally and unconditionally to the actions in which an obligation is challenged, than the forum of the obligation, for the latter is destined only for the maintenance and execution of the obligation (§ 371).

(r) Even if the restitution is founded on minority; for after its gradual development in Roman law, this can no longer be regarded as a mere consequence of incapacity to act, but as a legal remedy invalidating the obligation as such (§ 365, B. 3).

(s) Huber, § 7; Weber, *Natürliche Verbindlichkeit*, § 95, pp. 413, 419; Story, § 576 foll.; Fœlix, pp. 147–149 [ed. Demangeat, i. 220], (who, however, speaks undecidedly). Weber adds an illogical exception for the case in which the debtor changes his domicile from a place of long prescription to a place where short prescription is in force. Here the course of the short prescription must, he says, begin with the establishment of the new domicile. [See Note B at end of section.]

obligation itself (*t*). Besides, this opinion has always been acknowledged to be correct by not a few writers (*u*).

This doctrine is not only correct in principle, but it is also recommended by a certain equity, since every capricious exercise of free will by one party to the detriment of the opponent, is excluded by the clear settlement of the period of prescription that results from it. Thus the plaintiff cannot select for his action just that one of several concurring jurisdictions under which there is the longest term of prescription. In like manner, the defendant cannot, by changing his domicile to a place where there is a shorter term of prescription, obtain that advantage to himself, seeing that both the local law and the special forum of the obligation are immutably fixed for the debt contracted by him at his former domicile (*v*). There cannot, therefore, be any hardship for the creditor in the fact that, when a place of fulfilment is specified which happens to have a very short term of prescription, the debtor can, if he likes, avoid showing himself at that place during such term, whereby the action is for the time excluded at that place (§ 371, *z*). For the creditor is not prevented from suing at any time at the domicile of the debtor (§ 371, *r*). If, indeed, the jurisdiction at the place of fulfilment were exclusive, the creditor could be aided in such a case only by the means that generally protect against prescription in cases in which it is impossible to bring an action (*w*).

(*t*) See above. vol. v. § 237. [These grounds being, (1) the prevention of uncertainty; (2) the presumption of satisfaction; (3) the punishment of negligence (which, however, is rather a justification of apparent hardship than a ground of the institution); (4) the protection of the debtor, whose disproof is made more difficult by the pursuer's delay; (5) the diminution of lawsuits. It is evident that erroneous views of this subject have generally arisen from exclusive regard being paid to one or two of these bases of all prescriptions.]

(*u*) Hert, § 65; Schäffner, § 87; Wächter, ii. pp. 408-412, where other writers are cited. Of course the agreement here asserted is only in regard to the principle, not to all the applications of it; for the local law of the obligation is not determined in the same way even by these writers. The principle is also recognised in a decree of the Berlin Court of Revision in 1843. Seuffert, *Archiv*, vol. ii. No. 120. In the Prussian law, Koch, i. p. 133, note 23, and Bornemann, i. p. 65, assent to this doctrine.

(*v*) Cf. *supra*, § 370, No. III., § 372, No. III. If it were not so, the debtor would only need to avoid visiting his former domicile during the course of that short prescription in order to be free from the debt (§ 371, *z*). How Weber seeks to provide against this has been noticed above, in note *s*.

(*w*) Namely, by restitution, or by raising action before the Præses-Defensor, etc. See above, vol. vii. § 328.

This rule, according to which the validity of an obligation is to be judged by the law of the place to which the obligation is itself subject (p. 199), must be limited by an important exception. If a law of a strictly positive and obligatory (coercitive) nature is opposed to the validity of the obligation, then not that local law, but rather that of the place where the action is raised, the law of the court that judges in the matter, is to be applied (*x*).

This exception is merely the consequence of the general principle as to the applicability of coercitive statutes (§§ 349, 372 A). It is to be applied positively as well as negatively; that is to say, the judge has to apply the coercitive statute of his own country, even if it does not exist at the seat of the obligation; and also, he must not apply the coercitive statute of any other country (the seat of the obligation), if it is not the law of his own territory.

This exception occurs as well in contracts as delicts.

Among contracts of this kind are those forbidden by usury laws. Thus, a debt bearing interest which is contrary to the law administered by the judge before whom an action is brought to recover it, must be treated as invalid, even if there be no such restrictive usury law at the seat of the obligation; for the meaning of such a law is, that no judge living under it shall employ his official authority to give effect to an undertaking so immoral and so injurious to the community as the usurious contract is considered to be.[2] In the same way, however, in

(*x*) Wächter concurs with this, ii. pp. 389–405.

[2] This view coincides with that of Demangeat on Fœlix, i. 232; and see Bar, p. 257, n. 10. The abolition of all usury laws by 17 and 18 Vict. c. 90, deprives this question of much of its importance as regards this country. The rule in the text was never adopted by British courts, 'for the moderation or exorbitance of interest depends on local circumstances, and the refusal to enforce such contracts would put a stop to all foreign trade.' Blackstone, ii. 464; Stephen, ii. 82. The decisions determine whether a contract is usurious by the law of the place where it is made, or, if a different place of performance is indicated, by the law of that place. *Thomson* v *Powles*, 1 Sim. 211; *Fyffe* v *Ferguson*, 2 Rob. App. 267, 282, 8 Cl. and Fin. 121, 140. 'If the interest allowed by the law of the place of performance is higher than that permitted at the place of the contract, the parties may stipulate for the higher interest without incurring the penalties of usury.' —Per Taney, C. J. (U. S.), in *Andrews* v *Pond*, 13 Pet. 65, 13 Curt. 42. It is more doubtful whether the contract is free from the taint of usury when the interest allowed at the place of performance is less than that allowed at the place of the contract, and the parties stipulate for the latter. In *Depau* v *Humphreys*, 20 Mart. 1, the court of Louisiana held such a

the converse case, in which no prohibition against the interest sued for exists within his territory, the judge must hold the interest as lawful, without respect to the prohibition that may exist elsewhere (at the seat of the obligation). This negative assertion is not only required as a logical consequence of the former positive one, but also for the following reason:—The applicability of a particular local law to an obligation is founded in general on presumed voluntary submission; but such submission cannot be presumed at all if it would point to a law which would directly invalidate the obligation (§ 372, *c*).

What has been said of usurious contracts must also be stated in regard to gaming debts, if they should happen to be held valid according to one law, and invalid by another. The law of the place at which the action is brought can alone determine as to the validity of the obligation.[3]

contract not usurious, and the parties entitled to stipulate for the highest rate of interest allowed by either of these places. This decision is supported by the proposition stated in the text below and at p. 177, and is defended by Parsons, *Contr.* ii. 95, on the same ground. It is accepted by Kent, *Com.* ii. 460, and is understood to have been sustained in subsequent American cases. Although contrary to the tendency of the English cases cited above, it is approved by Westlake, §§ 203, 207, who holds (as does also Bar, pp. 237, 238, 256 sqq.) that the place where money lent is employed by the borrower (usually his domicile), ought to fix the rate of interest paid for the use of it. Perhaps this is the proper application to such a contract of the rule that contracts shall be regulated by the law of the place of performance. The place of performance is not here the place of stipulated repayment, but rather that where the advance or forbearance is made, for which interest is the consideration. A place of payment stipulated for the convenience of a party, may be in no proper sense the place of performance of the contract. For example, in a contract of insurance undertaken by a company in one country on the life of a person domiciled in another, 'the mere payment of the sum due at the termination of the life is not the only element in deciding what country, under this particular contract, is the place of performance. The proper performance of this contract is the continued assurance of the life and undertaking of the risk, as well as the payment of the sum at the close of the life.'—Per Hope, J.C., in *Parken* v *Royal Exchange Assurance Co.*, 1846, 8 D. 372. This view seems to meet the keen contention of Story, §§ 298–305, against the decision in *Depau* v *Humphreys*,—a contention which proceeds on the assumption that that decision implies that the same contract may be subject to the laws of two places as to its substance. That proposition is certainly untenable, but the correctness of the decision in question does not depend on it. See also Burge, iii. 774; Phillimore, iv. 515.

[3] This would be so in Scotland, where both at common law and under statutes the courts of law refuse to take any cognizance of gaming debts (*sponsiones ludicræ*); *Bruce* v *Ross*, M. 9523, 3 Pat.; *O'Connell* v *Russel*, 1864, 3 Macph. 89; *Paterson* v *Macqueen*, 4 Macph. 602; and in England, where a similar result, subject to an exception, is attained by 8 and 9 Vict. c. 109, § 18. See *Savage* v *Madder*, 36 L. J. Ex. 179.

The same is the case with the *Lex Anastasiana*, as to debts purchased below their nominal value. This law proceeds on the ground that such a dealing may be hazardous and oppressive for the debtor, and seeks to prevent it, as immoral and injurious to the community, by the rule that a debt acquired under such conditions can be made effectual only to the amount of the price paid for it (*y*). The applicability of this law depends on the circumstance whether it is in force or not at the place where the action is brought; the law of the place where the claim has arisen, or of the place of the cession, is immaterial (*z*).

Apparently the French law, as to the claims of Jews against Christians, is to be referred to this class; but in reality it belongs rather to the question as to capacity to act, and has already been mentioned under that head (§ 365 A, No. 5). The practical treatment of the case coincides with that here given.

This exception is further to be applied to the obligations arising from delicts, and that universally, since the laws relating to delicts are always to be reckoned among the coercitive, strictly positive statutes.

In them, therefore, we must always have regard to the law of the place of the action, not to that under which the delict was committed (z^2). Here, too, as in contracts, the proposition

(*y*) L. 22, *C. mandati* (4, 35).

(*z*) A different view is taken in a decision of the Supreme Court of Appeal at Munich, in 1845, in which it was held that the law under which the obligation first arose is to be regarded. Seuffert, *Archiv*, vol. i. n. 402. [Bar, § 76 fin., takes a different view from Savigny.]

(z^2) This is, therefore, to be applied to the possessory interdicts, although here in a very limited way. See above, § 368 fin. [Heffter, p. 77, makes the law of the delinquent's domicile alone applicable. Bar, pp. 243, 317 (as to liability for the acts of servants, cattle, see p. 315) adopts the doctrine which, amid some conflict of authority, seems to prevail in England, America, and Scotland,—viz. that the law of the place where the wrong is committed has authority, so far as regards the substance of the matter on which an action of damages is brought. See *Ekins* v *E. I. C.*, 1 P. W. 394, 396; *The Zollverein*, Sw. Adm. 96, 2 Jur. 2d Ser. 429; *The Halley*, 37 L. J. Ad. 1,—revd. 18 L. J. N. S. 879 (P. C.); *Cope* v *Doherty*, 4 Kay and J. 367, 384, 390, 2 De G. and J. 614; *Scott* v *Seymour*, 10 W. R. 739, 11 W. R. 169, 31 L. J. Ex. 457, 32 L. J. Ex. C. 61; *Shaw* v *Robertson*, 13 Dec. 1803, F. C. Mor. App. *Lis alibi*; *Hallam* v *Gye*, 14 S. 199; *Callender* v *Milligan*, 11 D. 1174; Guthrie Smith, *On Reparation*, p. 34; Kent, *Com.* ii. 463; *Consequa* v *Willing*, Pet. Circ. R. 225, 303; *Smith* v *Condry*, 1 How. U. S. Rep. 28, 14 Curt. 48. But by the latest English decision (*The Halley*, *supra*) the injury must be actionable by the *lex fori*. English courts applied the *lex fori* in actions for personal wrongs done abroad in *Rafael* v *Verelst*, W. Bl. 1055; *Mostyn* v *Fabrigas*, Cowp. 174, 1

holds good, both positively and negatively, that is, for and against the application of a law which recognises an obligation arising out of a delict. In reference to no kind of obligations has this question been so much discussed, doubted, disputed, as in regard to the obligations derived from illicit sexual intercourse. It will make the question very plain if I here start from the unqualified rule of the French civil code, which says in Act 340, 'La recherche de la paternité est interdite.' This law rests, apparently, on the conviction that in the interest of morality every claim and lawsuit arising out of illicit intercourse must be prohibited (*aa*); other legislations are grounded on the opposite belief. Both, therefore, are of a coercitive and strictly positive character. If, then, such a claim be made before a court subject to the French law, it is dismissed, even if the alleged intercourse shall have been at a place where the law allows and favours such a claim. But conversely, the claim must be sustained by the court of the latter country, even if the intercourse shall have occurred at a place under French law. What is here laid down as to the extreme cases of rejection or admission of the claim, must be equally maintained if the laws of the different places differ in a less degree, it may be in the conditions or in the extent of the claims. The decisions of courts as to this question are conflicting (*bb*).

Smith's L. C. 656; where the defendants were British governors, and the wrongs were committed, the first in an Indian state, the courts of which could not be expected to give redress, the other in a British dependency. Torts done in respect of immoveable property abroad cannot be sued for in English courts, which go upon the distinction of local and transitory grounds of actions. Stephen's *Com.* iii. 480; Stephen, *On Pleading*, p. 240; Westlake, § 120; 1 Smith's L. C. 656. British seamen are responsible, according to British law, for crimes done out of the British dominions. 17 and 18 Vict. c. 104, § 267; *Reg.* v *Lesley*, Bell Cr. C. 220; 8 Cox Cr. C. 269; 27 L. J. M. C. 97.]

(*aa*) This view of the French law is unequivocally announced in the absolute prohibition of all procedure, addressed to the judges.

(*bb*) For the place of the action (which will generally coincide with the domicile of the defendant), Obertribunal at Stuttgart. Seuffert, *Archiv für Entscheidungen der Obersten Gerichte in den deutschen Staaten*, vol. ii. N. 4. For the place of intercourse, Supreme Court at Munich, and two decisions at Jena. Seuffert, vol. i. N. 153, vol. ii. N. 118. [The law of Scotland does not rank the obligation to aliment (maintain) a natural child among the obligations arising *ex delicto*. It places it on the same line with them, with restitution of fruits, recompense, etc., under the head of natural or *obediential* obligations. Stair, i. 3, 3, 4; Ersk. *Inst.* iii. 1, 9, i. 6, 56; Monypenny (Lord Pitmilly), *Remarks on the Poor Laws*, pp. 331–352 (2d ed. 1836). Cf. Lord Gillies in *Pott* v *Pott*, 12 S. 183; Lord Ivory

This whole question is nearly akin to that of penal law, whether a crime committed abroad is punishable by our courts, and with what penalty. Yet the two questions must not be identified, because in penal law, as a part of the public law, considerations are to be kept in view of which no account is taken in obligations arising from delicts.

It certainly results from the principles just laid down in regard to coercitive laws, that in such cases a very important power is frequently placed in the hands of the plaintiff; for he has often a choice between several courts, and can thus determine which of several local laws shall be applied. But this is the inevitable result of the particular nature of this class of laws. Besides, the danger to the defendant is diminished by the very great restrictions to which the special forum of the obligation is always subject (§ 371, *z*).

in *Thomson* v *Westwood*, 4 D. 839; L. J. C. Inglis in *Crichton* v *Robb*, 22 D. 728; *Clarkson* v *Fleming*, 20 D. 1224. In England the support of illegitimate children is looked upon as a matter of natural obligation (Stephen's *Com.* ii. 309); and is provided for by statutes 7 and 8 Vict. c. 101, and 8 and 9 Vict. c. 10, repealing previous Acts. In Ireland there was no action on obligations of this kind till 25 and 26 Vict. c. 83 § 10; amended by 26 and 27 Vict. c. 21. These English statutes appear to contemplate only the case of children born in England, and will not confer a claim on a foreign (?) mother whose child is the fruit of intercourse had in England, but is born abroad. *Reg.* v *Blane*, 13 Q. B. 769; 18 L. J. N. S. Mag. Ca. 216. Neither can a summons in bastardy under these Acts be served on one in Scotland, so as to found the jurisdiction of an English court (justices of peace). *Reg.* v *Lightfoot*, 6 E. and B. 822, 25 L. J. N. S. Mag. Ca. 115. It does not appear to have been decided in either country, whether in an action of this kind the courts will apply the law of the bastard's and his mother's domicile, or that of the defendant's domicile, which will also be the *lex fori*. It would seem that, although Savigny's opinion that the obligation arises *ex delicto* is not admitted, yet it is founded on considerations of morality and public policy, which require the judge to apply only the *lex fori*. At the same time it might be argued (and it is to some extent countenanced by *R.* v *Blane*, *supra*), that the right being a personal quality of the child, must be governed by the law of his domicile (cf. *in re Wright's Trusts*, 2 K. and J. 595). This is so in regard to the personal status, the mere affiliation; and it is clear that the mere right to sue an action of affiliation must be governed by the law of the bastard's domicile. *R.* v *Blane*, *supra*. Bar, p. 362 sq., makes the rights of the child depend on the law of the mother's domicile, limited apparently by that of the place where the intercourse took place. The Prussian courts apply the law of the mother's domicile, regarding the claim against the putative father as a quality attaching to the child by its birth. Cases in Bar *l.c.* n. 8. See further as to the law of France, Fœlix, i. 79; Bar, 110, 364, n. 13. The view of Savigny is also adopted by Mittermaier, *Gem. Deutsches Privatr.* § 30, and Schäffner, § 98, and in the New Saxon code. As to the decisions in note *bb*, see Bar, p. 365, n. 14.

D. The effect of an obligation, and in particular the extent of its effect, is always determined by the law of the place which is regarded as the seat of the obligation in general; indeed, herein lies the chief significance of the local law of the obligation. Precisely for this reason has this particular question given the least occasion for doubt and controversy. A few examples will suffice to illustrate it.

By many local laws a seller has the right of resiling until delivery is completed,—a proposition which is unknown to the common law. Here the point on which the question turns is, whether such a law subsists at the place where the immoveable subject is situated, irrespective of the place where the contract was concluded, or the place of the action; for the sale of an immoveable always implies a determinate place of fulfilment, which is also the seat of the obligation, and fixes its local law (§§ 370, 372). It is the same with a local law which establishes the tacit relocation of farms for a space of three years. This law, too, will be applied to all immoveables lying within its territory, for the reasons assigned in the previous case (*cc*).

The amount of moratory interest depends by common law on the rate of interest from time to time, and therefore on actual usage. But if a legal rate is fixed for moratory interest, and if that be different at many places, then the law of the place which is its seat will be applied to every obligation, and therefore, where there is a stipulated place of payment, the law of that place (*dd*).

The obligation may be connected with a tacit right of pledge (lien), (general or special). Whether such a tacit contract is to be presumed, depends on the local law to which the obligation is subject. Whether the effect of right of pledge is to be

(*cc*) Both cases are specified by Boullenois, t. 2, p. 452 foll. He decides the first case as has been done here, but finds the second unnecessarily doubtful.

(*dd*) Voet, *Pand.* xxii. 1, § 11. In L. 1, *pr. de usur.* (22, 1), it is said: 'Ex more regionis, *ubi contractum est.*' The ordinary case is contemplated, in which two inhabitants of the same town there make a contract; there is no mention of a contract away from the domicile, or of a place of payment otherwise fixed. [See above, § 356, p. 74; § 374, p. 197, n. 1; Phillimore, iv. 513, 519; Bar, § 71; Kent, *Com.* ii. 460; *Cash* v *Kennion*, 11 Ves. 314; *Ferguson* v *Fyffe*, 6 S. 1038, 2 Rob. Ap. 267; *Pyronon* v *Morison*, 1677, M. 4529, 3 Br. Sup. 205; *Cooper* v *Waldegrave*, 2 Beav. 282, Chitty on Bills 439.]

ascribed to it, can, on the other hand, be determined only by the law of the place where the thing is situated (§ 368).[4]

E. The position of obligations in bankruptcy (Concurs) requires special consideration, because the greatest diversities in this respect are found in different legislations. It is necessary, above all, clearly to understand the peculiar nature of bankruptcy.

Bankruptcy presupposes a debtor unable to pay, and on the other hand several creditors,—a case, therefore, in which a complete execution of all judgments of debt pronounced, or that may yet be pronounced, is impossible, so that the object in view can only be to operate execution partially, as far as that is possible. This is done by collecting together the means and estate of the debtor in existence at the present moment, converting them by sale into cash, and then dividing them according to some rule among the creditors. Thus bankruptcy appears to be in substance a mere process in execution as to a determinate mass of property, the function of the judge consisting in adjusting the claims of the individual creditors to this mass. The bankruptcy has no influence on the ultimate fate of the claims; so that every creditor who wholly or partially fails in it can still make his right effectual against the debtor, if the latter afterwards acquires new means.[5]

As the bankruptcy has in view an adjustment of the claims of a number of creditors, it is possible only at one place, namely, at the domicile of the debtor, so that the special forum of the obligation is here displaced by the general personal forum.

The functions of the judge in bankruptcy (Concurs) consist of two distinct portions,—preparatory acts, and the division of the estate (competition, Concurs).

Among the preparatory acts are the determination of the claims themselves (liquidation), then the formation and determination of the estate in bankruptcy (common fund, Concursmasse) by elimination of all portions not belonging to the estate of the debtor (Vindicanten, Separatisten),[6] by collection of all portions really belonging to the estate, and by converting them

[4] See Story, § 322; Westlake, §§ 220, 272.

[5] *I.e.* in the common Roman law, founded on L. 1 *C. qui bonis cedere possunt* (7, 71).

[6] See *Dig.* l. 42, tit. 6.

into cash by sale. In respect of the local law to be administered, the general principles already laid down as to real rights and obligations are here entirely applicable. As to what especially concerns the first point, the determination of claims, it is not left altogether to accident what creditors shall choose to appear, but all are called by public advertisement, with notification of a particular term for claiming. He who does not observe this term is foreclosed by decree, and thereby loses, not indeed his debt, but the claim to have it satisfied in this bankruptcy out of this common fund. The intimation binds even creditors who have already brought actions on their debts elsewhere, but have not yet brought them to an end; so that the process of bankruptcy absorbs the actions for debts elsewhere depending (*ee*).

The bankruptcy or process of competition (Concurs) itself has for its object the determination of the claims (classification, marshalling, ranking) of the individual creditors to existing assets (die vorhandene Activmasse). As this adjustment belongs to the process in execution, which is merely a part of the law of procedure, no other local law can be applied to it than that in force at the place of the court of bankruptcy; indirectly, therefore, the local law of the domicile of the debtor (*ff*).

The whole question might be settled with this simple rule, were it not that many claims, and those generally the most important, are of a mixed nature, compounded of an obligation and a real right—the right of hypothec.

The matter will become clearer by being applied to the common law of bankruptcy founded on the rules of the latest Roman law, as it has been developed in the theory and practice of modern times.

The whole creditors are arranged in five classes: 1. absolutely privileged; 2. privileged hypothecs; 3. common hypothecs; 4. personally privileged; 5. all others (*gg*). Among these five classes, the first, fourth, and fifth contain pure obligations, and are subject to the law in force at the place of the court of bankruptcy exclusively, without respect to the possibly different law of the place where the obligation has arisen or

(*ee*) Wernher, *Obss.* t. ii. p. 10, obs. 297; Leyser, *Sp.* 478, med. 8.

(*ff*) Leyser, 478, 10.

(*gg*) The more minute exposition of this classification is beyond the present purpose; cf. Mühlenbruch, i. § 173; Göschen, *Vorlesungen*, ii. 2, § 424. [Matthæus, *de Auctionibus*, l. 1, cc. 19, 20.]

the place of its fulfilment. There remain, therefore, for closer examination only the second and third classes, comprising the creditors holding hypothecs.

Every such creditor has in fact a composite right, of which the two constituents are quite different in their nature; he is a true creditor, but he has at the same time a real right in security of his obligation. To make it clear how these dissimilar rights can be adjusted to the unity of the bankruptcy, it is necessary first to supplement this sketch by a glance at the formation (realization) of the bankrupt estate, leaving out of sight for the present the creditors holding hypothecs.

The formation of the common fund by collection and sale of the various parts of the estate presents no difficulty, if the latter are all situated within the jurisdiction of the court of bankruptcy. On the other hand, the treatment of this matter is very much disputed when parts of the estate lie in other jurisdictions, or in a foreign country. I will examine first this last case, as the extreme one. Many make the following assertion: The foreign sovereign and his judge are not obliged to observe the orders of our court of bankruptcy; nay, we find by experience that they commonly avoid doing so (*hh*). Therefore, according to that opinion, there remains no other remedy than for our judge in bankruptcy to refuse to include in his judgment the property situated abroad, while the creditors can still sue the debtor in that foreign country; so that, besides the first bankruptcy, a second, and even, where the property is very much scattered, a third or a fourth may be occasioned.

I cannot accept as satisfactory the proposed remedy, nor even acknowledge the alleged difficulty in which it originates. As to the remedy, it assumes that an action on every debt can be brought wherever a debtor has property; or, in other words, it assumes a universal *forum rei sitæ* for personal actions. This is just what must be decidedly denied; and therefore a plurality of bankruptcies in different countries is not admissible. How far something similar to this may take place in consequence of the existence of real securities, will be noticed immediately.

(*hh*) It is admitted that this difficulty is much less in regard to things in another jurisdiction of the same country, since help may here be afforded partly by mere requisition, as between co-equal courts, or where there is a common superior tribunal, by an order to the other court, obtained from it by the court of the bankruptcy.

But the difficulty itself is less than is commonly supposed. When the curator of the estate, appointed by a court (*ii*), sells the goods of the debtor under the superintendence of the judge in bankruptcy, he only performs one of the acts pertaining to the execution of a judgment, whether that judgment be already pronounced, or impending and still expected. Now it is a result of the community of law between different states which has long been progressing, that they mutually extend to each other equal legal remedies (§ 348). Among these is the execution of a judgment pronounced in one state within every other state (§ 373, B), and consequently the assistance of the curator in the measures necessary for the sale of the effects situated abroad, and the realization of the common fund to be distributed. If this aid were denied to him, it would imply a complete refusal of justice, since it has just been remarked that in this foreign land no jurisdiction at all has been established against the debtor for personal actions.

This view has long since been accepted as the correct one by many writers (*kk*). Others assert the opposite, not in consequence of a juridical principle, but only because foreign sovereigns refuse their co-operation (*ll*). In English courts moveable things situated abroad are included in the bankruptcy at the domicile, while immoveables are not; in most American courts neither the moveables nor the immoveables (*mm*).

There is certainly a peculiar complication and difficulty when the things situated abroad are subject to a right of pledge, and the consideration of this very common case has undoubtedly had an influence in producing the adverse opinion of many writers and courts, although the two questions are evidently quite different, and a separate treatment of them is more conducive to the success of the inquiry.

(*ii*) Tit. D. *de curatore bonis dando* (42, 7), esp. in L. 2, tit. cit.

(*kk*) J. Voet, § 17, and *Comm. ad Pand.* xx. 4, § 12 (where he derives this rule just from the aforesaid *comitas*); Pufendorf, t. i. obs. 217 (with a limitation in the case of hypothecs, of which we shall speak directly); Dabelow, *Lehre vom Concurse*, pp. 746–765 (who only weakens his correct exposition by remarking at the close, that the practice is contrary to it, and that, therefore, a plurality of bankruptcies is necessary).

(*ll*) Struben, *Bedenken*, i. 118, v. 27.

(*mm*) Story, § 403 foll. He himself prefers the English practice to the American. That he means to speak only of moveable things, appears from his treating of this whole question in ch. ix. 'Personal Property' (bewegliches Vermögen).

This last case is distinguished from the preceding, in which the things situated abroad are supposed to be unhypothecated, chiefly by the fact that the creditor in right of the hypothec can bring his action in the *forum rei sitæ.* If, then, the *actio hypothecaria* is brought against another hypothecary creditor who possesses the thing, or simultaneously by two such creditors against a third possessor, the judge has to determine as to their priority by the same principles as in bankruptcy (*nn*); and this rule is applicable whether the things hypothecated are in the same country or not. Yet it would be quite wrong to regard this proceeding as a separate bankruptcy, for the forms of bankruptcy do not occur in it at all. There is, however, nothing to hinder the foreign effects hypothecated from being included in the bankruptcy at the domicile of the debtor, if only care be taken that every one who has a right of pledge over such a thing situated abroad, shall receive the same preference over the price of this thing which belongs to him by the law of the place where the thing is at the time of the sale; for the *lex rei sitæ* determines as to this preference (§ 368).

It may sometimes be difficult to attain this end: it is not impossible; and it will especially conduce to make it easier, if a special fund be made of the price of the various things situated abroad. When this is done by the same judge, the adjustment of the claims is more certainly attained than it could be by constituting several bankruptcies in different courts (*oo*).

The possibility of this method is most clearly evident, from the circumstance that it has been actually established by a considerable number of public treaties entered into by the Prussian government with neighbouring states. The Prussian law of bankruptcy is the basis of these treaties. By this law there is always only one bankruptcy, and that at the domicile of the common debtor. The judge in bankruptcy procures, by requisition, the co-operation of the Prussian courts, in whose terri

(*nn*) *L.* 12 *pr.* § 7, *qui pot.* (20, 4); cf. P. Voet, § 10, *C. un.* § 5. The latest Prussian legislation permits every creditor holding a pledge or hypothec, even where no relation to a foreign country is in question, to sue directly for his satisfaction out of the thing, without involving himself in the bankruptcy. *Gesetzsammlung*, 1842, p. 4.

(*oo*) Pufendorf (note *kk*) considers the establishment of priority in a foreign court so difficult that he prefers to open a special bankruptcy at the place where the thing is situated, as soon as the creditors having hypothecs demand this.

tory parts of the estate are situated. If parts of the estate are abroad, then the judge has to inquire whether there are public treaties. If there are none, he must propose to the foreign judge to co-operate in the bankruptcy in Prussia, in the same way as has already been indicated in regard to Prussian courts. If this fails, the curator has to watch the interest of the creditors in this country in the special bankruptcy abroad (*pp*). All treaties concluded subsequently to this law rest on the principle that only one bankruptcy is to take place, and that as a rule at the domicile of the debtor. The goods of the common debtor situated in the other state must be sold, and the proceeds handed over to the court of bankruptcy. In this all the creditors must appear. The marshalling (ranking) of the creditors is determined, for the purely personal claims, according to the law of the forum; for all real rights, according *to the laws of the place where the thing is situated* (*qq*). There is a difference only in this respect, that by the modern treaties (since 1839), real rights in things situated out of the country of the bankruptcy can be insisted in also at the place where the thing is situated, before its surrender to the judge of the bankruptcy. If this is done by hypothecary creditors, the things hypothecated are to be sold there, the money paid to the creditors, and only the surplus, if any, is to be paid in to the court of bankruptcy.

What is here settled by treaties must not be regarded as a new and arbitrary invention; it is merely the expression of the community of law that is ever increasing in our time (§ 348). Hence there is no doubt that the same principle might be established elsewhere also in public treaties, and might even be made effective without such treaties, by the concurrence of the courts of different states, with the express or tacit sanction of their governments.

The contents of these treaties are not only directly of importance for the relation between Prussia and the states that are parties to them, but also indirectly as the basis of a kindly intercourse with other foreign states, as was just remarked.

(*pp*) *Allg. Germ. Ordnung*, i. 50, §§ 25–32, 647–671.

(*qq*) Treaty with Weimar, 1824, arts. 18–22; then to the same effect with Altenburg, Koburg-Gotha, Reuss. Gera; afterwards with the kingdom of Saxony, 1839, arts. 19–21; and in similar terms with Rudolstadt, Bernburg, Brunswick. (See above, § 348, p. 30.)

Rather these treaties, as they indicate the spirit of our legislation, supply an answer to a question of law as to the internal relation of the various parts of our country. If a bankruptcy takes place in Berlin, but the estate of the debtor includes lands and moveables which are situated in Western Pomerania (Neuvorpommern), where the Roman law prevails, and are there hypothecated by simple contract, the question arises how the value of these things stands with respect to that bankruptcy. If the judges of that district were under the Prussian judiciary system, they must deliver up to the Berlin judge in bankruptcy the value of these things (or the moveable things themselves) (*rr*); and he would distribute the proceeds according to the Prussian classification. Thus those creditors would sustain a serious loss, since their obligations have no claim to be either in the second or the third class of the Prussian system of marshalling. But these judges are not bound by the laws referred to, and the debts and hypothecs are to be dealt with just as if they belonged to a foreign country, and to one whose authorities are ready to give mutual support to ours on equitable principles. This leads to the application of the principles of the treaties above cited. According to these, the courts of Western Pomerania would have to sell the parts of the bankrupt estate lying within their territory, and hand over the price to the judge in bankruptcy at Berlin. The creditors, however, who had hypothecs over those things, would be able to obtain in the court at Berlin, so far as the price goes, the same priority that would have been awarded to them if the bankruptcy had taken place in Pomerania.[7]

NOTE A, p. 196. (CONTRACTS OF INSURANCE.)

It was held that a contract of insurance on the life of a domiciled Scotchman with an English company was an English contract, in re-

(*rr*) *Allg. Ger. Ordnung*, i. 50, § 648; Law of 28 Dec. 1840, § 2 (*Gesetzsammlung*, 1841, p. 4).

[7] The concursus or bankruptcy spoken of in the foregoing pages differs so materially from the more fully developed bankruptcy of Great Britain and America, that the principles laid down are, with some exceptions, applicable only by a distant analogy. No attempt has been made to show the bearing of them on our law, to do which would carry us far beyond the bounds of our undertaking. See Bar, §§ 78, 128; Story, §§ 323 sqq., 338 sqq., 403 sqq., 423, 433; Westlake, §§ 253 sqq., 277 sqq.; Bell's *Com.* ii. 680 sqq. (p. 1294 ed. Shaw); 24 and 25 Vict. c. 134; 31 and 32 Vict. c. 104; 19 and 20 Vict. c. 79; 23 and 24 Vict. c. 33, etc.

spect that, though it was made through the company's agents at Edinburgh, the agents had no power to bind the company, the proposals for insurance and the policy in the English form being merely transmitted through them, and the insurance or continued undertaking of the risk being in England. The interpretation of the contract and liability of the insurers (especially as to interest) are therefore governed by the law of England. *Parken* v *Royal Exchange Assurance Co.*, 13 Jan. 1846, 8 D. 365. Where the agents had authority to bind the company by entering into contracts without reference to the head-office, the contract was held to be made at the place where the agency was established. *Brebner* v *St. Patrick As. Co.*, 14 Nov. 1829, 8 S. 51; *Mills* v *Albion Ins. Co.*, 5 S. 930, 6 S. 409, 3 W. and S. 218, 1 Dow and Cl. 342. (Cf. as to jurisdiction, *Douglas Heron and Co.* v *Palmer*, 1777, 5 B. S. 449, Hailes 748; *Haldane* v *York Bgs. Co.*, 1724, M. 4818; *Bishop* v *Mersey and Clyde Co.*, 19 Feb. 1830, 8 S. 558.) Cases occur as to the insurer's liability to make good contributions of the insured, under a law of general average differing from that of the country where the insurance was effected. The law is thus stated by Lord Ellenborough in the leading case of *Power* v *Whitmore*, 1 M. and S. 141, 150: 'This contract must be governed, in point of construction, by the law of England where it was framed, couched as it is in the terms of an instrument in general and familiar use, and of known meaning in England; unless the parties are to be understood as having contracted on the footing of some other known general usage amongst merchants relative to the same subject, and shown to have obtained in the country where, by the terms of the contract, the adventure is made to determine.' This has been understood by Westlake, § 209, as overruling previous cases in which the law of the place of destination was held to govern. But the following sentences clearly show that the application of the English law in this case was rested on the fact, that there was no allegation or sufficient evidence of 'a known and invariable usage amongst merchants at Lisbon, the port of discharge.' Hence 'the underwriters have a right to insist that the general average to which their claim is confined is general average as it is understood in England, no other distinct and different sense and use of that term being proved in evidence to obtain, in point of fact,' at the port of discharge. See per L. Tenterden, C. J., in *Simmonds and Loder* v *White*, 2 B. and C. 805, 810; Shee's Abbott *On Shipping*, pp. 554-556; Shee's Marshall *On Insurance*, 435; Voigt, *cit. ap.* Bar, p. 260, n. 5; American cases cited by Westlake, p. 196. For another case of conflict in regard to contracts of insurance, see Story, § 327, *b.*—'Si des etrangers ont contracté entré eux dans les pays etrangers des assurances payable en France, on se dirigera pour la decision du fonds par les loix du lieu du contrat. Deux Anglois plaidant en France, . . . il fut jugé par le Parlement de Paris, que l'ordonnance n'avait point lieu d'autant qu' elle va *ad litis decisionem.*

Si en pays etrangers un Français contracte des assurances avec d'autres *Français*, sans qu' aucun etranger y soit intéressé, on le jugera en France suivant l'ordonnance de la marine; car la loi de leur prince les suit partont. Si en pays etranger un Français contracte des assurances avec un etranger les juges de France connaitront de la matiere, a moins que quelque traité ne s'y oppose. Je crois que dans ce cas, on doit suivre les loix du lieu du contrat, afin que l'etranger qui ignore nos usages ne soit pas trompé. Il en seroit de même du cas où un Français feroit faire pour son compte des assurances dans l'etranger.'—Emerigon, *Tr. d. Assur.* i. 4, 8, § 2. On this, Bar, p. 260, n. 5, observes: 'But these rules will not apply universally. When one carries on the business of insuring at a particular place, as is generally the case, the *lex loci contractus* will apply without respect to the domicile of the insured. When, on the contrary, two subjects of the same country casually enter into a contract of insurance abroad, the first of Emerigon's rules will apply.' In *Cook* v *Greenock Ins. Co.*, 18 July 1843, 5 D. 1379, the verdict of a jury, in an action against Scotch insurers at the instance of foreign owners, was set aside on the ground that the jury had given weight to the usage or understanding as to seaworthiness at the domicile of the owners, which was different from that at the place of the insurers' business. But it does not appear that in that case the doctrine above stated was fully adopted, some of the judges seeming to construe the contract by the general usage of trade, and others by the usage of the place of contract. Lord Mackenzie's remarks are worthy of attention: 'I am not satisfied that the custom and understanding, either of the place of the contract of insurance, or of the building and usual resort of the ship, or residence of the owners, can be exclusively and absolutely and decisively looked to. Put this case: An insurance is effected in Glasgow by the owners, who write from Nova Scotia to that effect, on a ship built and belonging to a port in Nova Scotia, and on a voyage from that port to Glasgow. I think it would be a strong thing indeed to hold, that the understanding of seaworthiness in Nova Scotia was, in such a case, to be disregarded, and that in Glasgow to be taken as conclusive. On the other hand, if a Nova Scotia owner builds a ship there, and sends her to Glasgow to trade between that port and Liverpool, and insures her by her agent in Glasgow on a voyage between these places and back, I think it would be strange to look solely to the nature of seaworthiness in Nova Scotia. I do not see that either can be taken absolutely, or generally and absolutely conclusive. And such being my view, I think, in this case, the mutual custom and understanding was that of Greenock and Britain, not Nova Scotia. The ship was put into the Glasgow trade with the Havannah, and insured by a branch agent in Greenock; so, without notice of any kind that she was a Nova Scotia ship, or that the case differed at all from ordinary insurances on ships in that trade, I think it was natural and reasonable in the underwriters to conceive that she was to be seaworthy like other ships in that trade, and that these underwriters were not bound to look at all to Nova Scotia, but the understanding of Greenock and of Britain.'

NOTE B, p. 201. (LAWS OF PRESCRIPTION.)

Some find an additional reason for applying the *lex loci* in the alleged coercitive nature of laws of limitation, which are enacted *ut sit finis litium*, or rather *minuendarum litium causa*. See Oppenheim, *Syst. des Völkerr*, p. 378 (Frankf. 1845). Bar, p. 283, cites two judgments at Celle proceeding on this view. Compare Blackst. iii. 307: 'The use of these statutes of limitation is to preserve the peace of the kingdom.' The laws of England, Scotland, and America agree in regarding statutes of limitation of actions (that is, statutes which operate on obligations by limiting the action or the mode of proof, but which do not profess to extinguish the obligation) as belonging to the rules of procedure, as relating to the remedy. *Lipmann* v *Don*, 14 S. 241,—revd. in H. of L., 2 S. and M. 682, 5 Cl. and Fin. 1; 1 Ross L. C. Com. 847, where the cases are reviewed. *Bank of U. S.* v *Donally*, 8 Pet. 361, 11 Curt. 127; *M'Elmoyle* v *Cohen*, 1839, 13 Pet. 312, 13 Curt. 169; Story, §§ 558, 582, *a; Townsend* v *Jenison*, 1849, 9 How. 407, 18 Curt. 200. Mr. Westlake, § 250-252, adopts the view of the text, holding that *Lipmann* v *Don*, as being a Scotch case, does not fix the law of England; and that the cases of *British Linen Co.* v *Drummond*, 10 B. and C. 903, 1 Ross L. C. Com. 841, and *Huber* v *Steiner*, 2 Scott 304, 2 Bingh. N. C. 202, were decided on partial and erroneous views of the authorities. He says that Lord Brougham's reasoning in *Lipmann* v *Don* 'rests on two fallacies. *First*, "the argument that the limitation is of the nature of the contract supposes that the parties look only to the breach of the agreement. Nothing is more contrary to good faith than such a supposition." But this is to confound the interpretation of the contract with the operation on it of the *lex loci contractus* . . .' '*Secondly*, "it is said that, by the law of Scotland," the *lex fori*, which it was proposed to apply as governing the remedy, "not the remedy alone is taken away, but the debt itself is extinguished . . . I do not read the statute in that manner . . . . The debt is still supposed to be existing and owing." There is, however, little or no meaning in saying that a debt subsists which cannot be recovered . . . . A right is only a faculty of putting the law in force. There is nothing, therefore, at bottom in any statute of limitation but an essential modification of the rights created by the jurisprudence in which it exists, and which is, therefore, incapable of a just application to rights created by the jurisprudence of another country.'

Bar, p. 283, argues against the application of the *lex fori* to that which is not a right merely incident to a process (ein nur processualisches Recht): 'The effect of that is limited to a particular process, and its existence depends on the raising of the action (cf. *supra*, note *o*). As a natural obligation from its origin gives birth to no action, but is an imperfect obligation, for reasons entirely unconnected with procedure, neither is it for such reasons that an obligation, at first perfectly valid, is reduced to a merely natural one by the lapse of time.' This author rejects the principle of the text, and makes the law of the debtor's domicile regulate the prescription, because the end of statutes of limitation is the protection of the debtor against doubtful or groundless claims. He is supported by the authority of Merlin, *Repert. Prescr.* i. 3, 7; Pardessus, No. 1495; J. Voet, *ad Pand.* 44, 3, 12; P. Voet, 10, § 2; Boullenois, i. 365; Pöhl, *Wechselrecht*, p. 655; Thöl. *Deutsches Privatr.* § 85; besides judgments at Berlin and Paris, which he cites (p. 288, n. 12). He also claims the English and American writers as supporting his view, because, the domicile of the debtor being the place where by the common law the action is brought, their rule of the *lex fori* really is the same in the result. This, however, is not so, as in the case where a foreigner transiently in Scotland, or against whom jurisdiction is founded in Scotland by the possession of property there, is sued in that country. Since the rule of the *lex fori* was established in *Don* v *Lipmann*, the decision here would be the same as if the defender were a domiciled Scotchman. Before that decision the Scotch courts repeatedly admitted the foreign prescription in such cases; *e.g. Delvalle* v *Crs. of York Buildings Co.*, M. 4525, Hailes 926; Ivory's Ersk. p. 788, 3 Pat. App. 98; *Cheswell* v *York Buildings Co.*, Bell's 8vo Ca. 364, M. 4528; *Fraser's Trs.* v *Fraser*, 9 S. 174; *Richardson* v *Lady Haddington*, 20 F. C. 302, 2 S. Ap. 406, etc. The Scottish courts, since the middle of last century, decidedly preferred the prescription of the debtor's domicile, although before that they had not based their decisions on any clear principles, following sometimes the limitation of the *lex loci contractus*, and sometimes that of the forum. But they looked, not to the debtor's domicile at the time of the action, but rather to his domicile during the whole currency of the term of limitation. They regarded the limitation as a penalty, or at least, a result of the creditor's negligence, which can be established only by his failing to sue in the debtor's domicile, which is his principal forum (for 'the forum arising from the situation of his effects is merely accidental.'—Per Lord J. C. Macqueen in *Cheswell*, *supra*). In this way they made the endurance of the obligation depend on the laws of the place where there was a *valentia agendi* against the debtor. Unless the debtor resided long enough in one place for the limitation of that country to operate on his debt, the Scotch courts seemed to hold that no prescription was applicable. See *Cheswell*, *supra*; *Boog* v *Watt's Crs.*, M. App. Prescr. 5; *M'Dowall* v *M'Lurg*, M. App.

Prescr. 6; *Anderson and Child* v *Wood*, Hume 467, etc.; *Watson* v *Renton*, *infra*. There was thus, indeed, always regard to the *forum*, not to that in which the action was accidentally brought, but to the debtor's natural and permanent forum. On this principle, and not on the ground that prescription pertains to the remedy, the cases were decided, in which the Scotch courts sustained the Scotch limitations, or refused effect to that of the *locus contractus; e.g. Renton* v *Baillie*, 1755, M. 4516, 11,124; *Macneil* v *Macneil*, M. 4518; *Randal* v *Innes*, 1771, M. 4520, 5 B. S. 541, Hailes 225; *Thomson* v *Duncan*, 1808, Hume 466; *Ross and Ogilvy* v *Ross' Trs.*, 1811, Hume 473; *Campbell* v *Stein*, 23 Nov. 1813, 17 F. C. 456, aff. 6 Dow 116; *Banner* v *Gibson*, 9 S. 61; *Gibson* v *Stewart*, 9 S. 525. The fullest and best view of the former Scotch law on this subject is in Tait *On Evidence*, 3d ed. pp. 460-465. The case of *Lipmann* v *Don*, however, although it proceeded on an inaccurate view of the cases (only two out of many previous cases being *clear* applications of the *lex fori: Hay* v *E. Linlithgow*, 1708, M. 4504; *Robertson* v *M. Annandale*, 1740, 1 Pat. 293), rendered it imperative to apply the *lex fori* without respect to the domicile of the debtor, except in so far as this may fix the place where the action is brought. (Opin. in *Farrar* v *Leith Banking Co.*, 1839, 1 D. 936, in which, though subsequent to *Don* v *Lipmann*, a strong bias was visible in favour of the real Scottish rule of the *lex domicilii debitoris*, and indeed a doubt whether, notwithstanding the strong views expressed by Lord Brougham in the latter case, it really decided more than that the domicile of the debtor during the course of the prescription should rule. Opin. in *Robertson* v *Burdekin*, 1843, 6 D. 25, 26, 37, 38; 1 Ross L. C. 812. Opin. in *Mackenzie* v *Hall*, 1854, 17 D. 164; Dickson *On Evid.* § 528.) It has been accepted as an authority in England, and, notwithstanding Mr. Westlake's objections, must be taken, along with previous cases, as fixing the law of that country. *British Linen Co.* v *Drummond*, and *Huber* v *Steiner*, *supra; Ruckmaboye* v *Mottichund*, 8 Moore P. C. 4, 5 Moore I. A. C. 234.

It has been said, though not expressly decided, that where the effect of a statute of limitation is not to bar the remedy, but by the lapse of a certain time to extinguish the obligation, and make it absolutely void, then, 'if the parties are resident within the jurisdiction (of the *lex loci contractus*) during all that period, so that it has actually operated upon the case,' this prescription will be ranked among the *decisoria litis*, and have effect given to it by a foreign court. *Huber* v *Steiner*, *supra; Don* v *Lipmann*, 2 S. and M. 699, 5 Cl. and F. 16, 17; Story, § 583; Burge, iii. 883; Kent, *Com.* ii. 462. The words quoted affix a condition which seems 'not quite reasonable,' as is well argued by Mr. Smith, *Leading Cases*, i. 642. The law of the *locus contractus* imports into the contract, *ex hypothesi*, a stipulation, that it shall be void if not enforced within a certain time; and (unless indeed the law makes that a condition of the avoidance of the contract) it is difficult to see how the residence of the parties in one country or the other should affect this more than any other question relating to the nature of the contract. Cf. Westlake, § 252; and Phillimore, iv. 573. Besides, the qualification implies that, without this residence, limitations which avoid the right would be differently treated; so that it would depend on a subsequent event whether they go *ad decisionem* or *ad ordinationem litis*. Why, then, should not limitations which merely take away the action not have such effect where the same residence has taken place? Is a debt, which is no longer actionable in the place of the contract where the parties have lived during the time of the prescription there existing, to revive, if the debtor removes to a place of longer prescription, or if he acquires property in such a country? Parsons (*Contr.* ii. 102) holds that it does, because 'the whole question of limitation or prescription is one of process and remedy, not of right and obligation.' A better doctrine is thus stated by L. Pres. Campbell in *Watson* v *Renton*, Bell's 8vo Ca. 108: 'As to the case of prescription, it comes more closely to the present question; but it is to be determined by distinctions. If the parties are both Englishmen, and have continued resident in England during the term of the English statutory limitations, they will in vain sue one another in Scotland after that term. The court may say they are not bound by the act of prescription in England; but if they should decide against it, they would do injustice, and this not so much *vi statuti*, from the mere force of an English statute, as from the implied agreement and conduct of parties; for having once submitted to an extinction of the debt by the law of their own country, the claim cannot justly be revived elsewhere. But if the debtor takes up his abode in this country before the term of the English limitations, the Scots law of prescription will thenceforward attach upon him, and not the English law.'—M. 4582. The truth is, that the doctrine of the English lawyers is founded on mere verbal distinctions occurring in their own statutes, and nearly parallel with the celebrated contrast of Bartolus between 'bona decedentis veniant in primogenitum' (real statute) and 'primogenitus succedat' (personal statute).

It seems to be a further over-refinement to distinguish, as one able writer does, between prescriptions 'which extinguish the obligation by an *ex post facto* operation,' to which alone he holds the doctrine last mentioned to apply; and 'those which enter into the obligation at its outset as implied conditions limiting its endurance.' —Dickson, *Evid.* §§ 525, 532–537. The Scotch case which he cites as an instance of the latter, appears to be decided upon grounds which equally apply to the former class, namely, that the limitation in question (that of cautionary obligations) 'affecting the contract itself with regard to endurance, which is one of its essentials,' was inapplicable to a foreign bond. *Alexander* v *Badenach*, 1843, 6 D. 823. It was decided in *Richardson* v *Lady Haddington*, 2 S. Ap. 406, that residence in a country which is not the *locus contractus* for the whole term of a prescription of that country extinguishing the debt, will not make the debt null or bar action in the *locus contractus* (which was here the original domicile of the debtor).

Another instance of the difficulties into which the advocates of the *lex fori* are led, is afforded by Weber's 'illogical exception,' mentioned in the author's note, and which is adopted by Ersk. iii. 7, 48. Schäffner (p. 111, n. 1) remarks that this leads to the following dilemma: 'Either a prescription begins not at all, or it begins *a tempore actionis natæ*. But this last moment is quite independent of the change of domicile or the possibility of another jurisdiction.' See *Bulger* v *Roche*, 11 Pick. 36; Story, § 582. But the exception must be admitted in some form wherever the *lex fori* or the law of the debtor's present domicile is held to govern. Bar (p. 290), who adopts the latter as the true theory, says that, if half of the term fixed in the former domicile has elapsed, the same proportion of the shorter prescription of the new domicile should be held to have passed.

Sect. XXXII.—(§ 375.)

IV. SUCCESSION.

We have now to inquire, in regard to rights of succession, as has already been done for other legal institutions, to what local law they naturally belong, and therefore where they have their proper seat (§ 360). In order to ascertain this, we must revert to the nature of succession as before indicated (vol. i. § 57). It consists in the passing of an estate, at the death of its owner, to other persons. This implies an artificial extension of a man's power, and therefore of his will, beyond the limits of his life, which continuing will may either be an expressed intention (in the testament), or a tacit one (in intestate succession) (*a*). This relation is entirely and immediately connected with the person of the deceased, just in the same way as was before observed of capacity for rights (§ 362), and as will hereafter be shown in regard to the family. If this

(*a*) This second kind of continuing will stands also in connection with the continuation of the individuality of the man by relationship. See above, vol. i. § 53.

view of the matter be correct, it must be asserted that succession in general is regulated by the law of the domicile which the deceased had at the time of his death (*b*). In order to connect this assertion with the technical terms before explained, we must say that laws as to succession are *personal statutes*, since they have for their object *principaliter* the person, and only indirectly things (§ 361).

The correctness of this view is further confirmed by the following considerations. If we did not regard the domicile of the deceased as fixing the local law, there would be no other place with which we could connect the right of succession, except the place where the property left, the inheritance or succession, is situated; so that then the *lex rei sitæ* must determine. Where, then, is this place? The estate as a whole is an ideal object of perfectly indefinite contents (*c*), possibly consisting of property and other rights in particular things, of obligations and debts, which last constituents at least have a quite invisible existence. This estate, therefore, is everywhere and nowhere, so that a *locus rei sitæ* cannot be discovered for it at all. It would be a very arbitrary expedient to adopt the place where the greater part of the succession is situated, both because this notion is fluctuating and uncertain, and because the lesser part has just as much claim to be considered as the greater. But if we give this up, it only remains to fix the place of succession wherever any single thing belonging to the estate is to be found. This, however, would lead, where the estate is extensive and widely scattered, to the assumption of many independent successions, subject possibly to quite different laws; and which after all would include only one portion of the succession (real rights), leaving the other part (obligations) altogether untouched. It is plain that this course would be entirely arbitrary and without principle, nay, would end in an empty show without any truth. Yet it has found many followers, of whom we shall have to speak immediately.

The foundation of the Roman law of succession is the

(*b*) See above, § 359. By the Roman law, the law of the *origo* was decisive in the first instance (§ 357). On the death of a vagabond, who had no domicile, the law of his origin determines; and if this too cannot be ascertained, the law of his last residence, *i.e.* of the place where he died (§ 359).

(*c*) See above, vol. i. § 56.

successio per universitatem, which must be assumed in every succession, and beside which all other legal relations take up a secondary position. This, however, is merely the juridical form into which the substance of succession, as above explained, is brought; and from this point of view we must still maintain that, according to the Roman law, the doctrine here asserted as to the seat of the succession appears to be subject to no doubt. But the view of many modern writers is altogether to be rejected, according to which universal succession is alleged to be a legal institution peculiar to the Romans, in contrast to other (Germanic) legislations, which, it is said, know nothing of it. The truth rather is, that in the positive law of many states the law of succession has remained at a lower degree of development, while it received among the Romans from a very early period, in consequence of a happy tact, the treatment alone suited to its peculiar nature, towards which, moreover, every positive law which differs from the Roman is incessantly striving (*d*). It would also be incorrect to view this difference as a merely theoretical one, as to the value or worthlessness of which we may think in one way or another. On the contrary, the practical wants of modern times find their full satisfaction only in the perfected universal succession; since obligations are obtaining an ever increasing importance in the enormous multiplication of patrimonial relations.

Sect. XXXIII.—(§ 376.)

IV. SUCCESSION.

(CONTINUATION.)

I now proceed to state the most important varieties of opinion as to the laws applicable to succession, as they have been gradually developed among writers, and consequently in the practice of different countries and times. These opinions may be referred to three principal classes.

(*d*) See above, vol. i. § 57, pp. 382, 383. [Bar, § 107, criticises this section.]

One is that above described, according to which the succession generally is governed by the law of the place at which the deceased had his domicile at the time of his death. It holds positive laws as to succession to be *personal statutes*.

Another, which has already been indicated, is just the opposite of the foregoing, and is to this effect, that succession is regulated according to the place where the things belonging to the inheritance are situated. This opinion involves the possibility that the different parts of the succession may be dealt with according to different laws. It also leaves the obligations and debts that may be included in the estate in an extremely indefinite condition, with the natural reservation, that the practical necessity of each particular case may be met by any convenient device.

The last opinion stands between the two above mentioned. It adopts the *lex rei sitæ* as to immoveable property, and for all other effects (moveable property and obligations) the law of the domicile of the deceased. This opinion is partly free from the practical weakness of the preceding one, since it enables us to know definitely who shall obtain the obligations; but only partly, because the debts in every case must attach to the whole estate, even to immoveables in foreign countries, so that the debts are perhaps to be borne by very different persons (*a*). In accordance with the technical language above explained, this opinion may be briefly described as holding the laws regarding succession to be *real statutes* (§ 361) (*b*).

I shall now discuss these three opinions separately in the order of their origin and prevalence.

A. The oldest opinion is that according to which succession to all things, moveable and immoveable, is subject entirely to the law of the country in which they are situated (*c*). This opinion is a particular application of the strict law of territoriality (§ 348).

(*a*) This serious difficulty in carrying out the principle is not overlooked by writers, and plans are proposed to remedy it, which for the most part seem arbitrary and insufficient. Comp. Hert, § 29. This, however, is but a proof of the essential falsehood of the whole system. The same objection applies to the previous opinion also, but in a far higher degree.

(*b*) This term would suit the previous opinion in a still higher degree, if it were not usual to limit the expression, real statutes, to immoveables.

(*c*) Writers in favour of this opinion are cited in great numbers by Wächter, i. 275, 276; ii. 192.

By the oldest and rudest form of it, no part of a succession (moveable or immoveable) situated in the country, ever fell to foreign heirs, but devolved in their stead to the sovereign (or immediate feudal lord—Vogteiherr) (*d*). The milder form merely subjects these parts of the succession unconditionally to the laws of the country, without respect to the domicile of the deceased, but also without distinguishing between national and foreign heirs.

The reasons against this doctrine have already been mentioned. I will now add the following practical observation:— If this principle were universally admitted and carried out, every provident head of a family who has any property abroad, must seek for some protection against unwished-for heirs, as well as against inevitable confusion in respect to debts and obligations. He could find security against the oppression of this principle only by the timely alienation of all his outlying property, or by bringing his moveables into the country of his domicile. In this natural desire and endeavour, we find an unmistakeable evidence of the gratuitous hardship arising out of the principle.

B. The intermediate opinion is closely connected with the preceding, only restricting it to the immoveable property belonging to the inheritance; it leaves the moveable property under the law of the domicile of the deceased, even if it should happen to be abroad. All the reasons urged against the previous opinion are valid against this, only in a less measure, because it differs from the correct one in a less extensive sphere.

This opinion has prevailed chiefly since the sixteenth century (*e*). In Germany it has been more and more displaced since the eighteenth century. On the contrary, it has survived till our own time in England and America (*f*), as well as in France (*g*). It stands in connection with the general distinction, which is firmly maintained in the practice of these countries, between moveable and immoveable estate (§ 360, No. 3).

(*d*) 'Droit d'aubaine.' Comp. Eichhorn, *Deutsches Recht*, § 75.

(*e*) A great number of writers are cited in Wächter, ii. pp. 188–192; Fœlix, pp. 72–85 [ed. Demangeat, i. 111, 128].

(*f*) Story, chaps. xi. xii.

(*g*) Fœlix (note *e*). Vinnius, *Sel. Quæst.* ii. 19, says the same as Holland, as was natural in his time.

C. The opinion which I maintain, namely that the domicile universally determines, has, since the eighteenth century, gained constantly increasing recognition, especially in Germany, after it was first adopted by preference for intestate succession (*h*). It is defended not only by Romanists (as one might perhaps expect in reference to universal succession), but also, with a just feeling of what is practically expedient and necessary, by Germanists (*i*); the practice, also, of the superior courts has decided in favour of it (*k*). The fundamental reason of this opinion lies in the general character of succession as before explained, and this reason is applicable just as much to testaments as to intestate succession. In intestate succession, however, the following consideration also comes into view :—It rests chiefly on the presumptive, and therefore tacit, intention of the deceased; not that such an intention can be asserted as a certain fact for this particular person with regard to his individual relations, but that every positive law establishes a general presumption in accordance with what appears to be the nature of the family relations. It is quite natural that such a presumption should take different shapes in different legislations. On the other hand, it would be quite unnatural, in a single given case of succession, to suppose that the deceased has had a different intention for the different parts of his estate, and thus to assume that he wishes one person to be heir to his house, and another to his landed estate or his money, if he has not expressly declared himself on the subject (by testament).

With regard to the intermediate opinion explained under B, which distinguishes between moveable and immoveable estate, two views have been suggested, of which the more

(*h*) A great number of writers are cited by Wächter, ii. 192-198, and Schäffner, § 130. The following deserve to be mentioned :—Pufendorf, i. Obs. 28; Glück, *Intestaterbfolge*, § 42; Martin, *Rechtsgutachten der Heidelberger Fakultät*, vol. i. pp. 175-186. Wächter, who avows himself of this opinion, defends it (ii. 198, 199, 363) quite correctly, in the following way :—The state, in its laws as to succession, does not seek to regulate the destiny of the objects (die Güter, *bona*), but that of the subjects, the persons. Hence it establishes such laws with a view to those who belong to the state (the inhabitants); and the succession to the estates of deceased foreigners is a matter of indifference to it. That is only another expression of the proposition that laws as to succession are to be regarded as personal, not as real, statutes.

(*i*) Eichhorn, *Deutsches Recht*, § 35; Mittermaier, *Deutsches Recht*, § 32.

(*k*) *O. A. Gericht zu Cassel*, 1840; Seuffert, *Archiv*, vol. i. No. 92.

minute examination may lead perhaps to an approximation of opinions.

A late writer finds fault because others have always expressed themselves in favour of the one or the other opinion exclusively, whereas each of them is correct under certain suppositions (*l*). In the countries which treat succession (according to the Roman principle) as universal succession, the domicile, he says, is decisive for the whole estate. In those countries, on the other hand, which do not recognise the theory of universal succession (such as England and America), the succession to immoveables must be judged by the *lex rei sitæ*. This view originates in the mistaken notion that the adoption or rejection of universal succession is something absolute and independent, from which a further inference can be drawn to the seat of the right of succession, and the local law that governs it. But in fact the two are identical, and universal succession is only the juridical form and the technical expression for that view of rights of succession which places their seat universally at the domicile, without distinguishing between the different portions of the estate. So apprehended, therefore, that distinction must be expressed as follows: From the standpoint of the countries and the writers that deal with succession with reference to the estate as a whole, the *lex domicilii* is decisive, even for immoveables: from any other standpoint it is not. In this sense, however, the distinction is not disputed in any quarter.

Much more important is the following reason, which is not unfrequently brought forward in support of the intermediate opinion (B). There are, it is said, certain kinds of immoveables as to which every one admits that in their case the succession is to be judged by the *lex rei sitæ*: to these belong in particular *feuda* (Lehen) and *fideicommissa* (entails, substitutions). What, then, is universally admitted as to these, must in consistency be maintained in regard to all other lands. Let us look a little more closely at this argument.

Feuda and *fideicommissa* are similar in their position to the Roman usufruct; they do not pertain to the patrimonial estate (Vermögen, *patrimonium*), and therefore not to the inheritance. The usufructuary has the right to enjoy the fruits during his life. This alone is in his estate; it vanishes with his

(*l*) Schäffner, §§ 57–59, 126–152.

death, and hence no further trace of it is found in his succession. Just so is it with the *fideicommissum* and the *feudum*. The possessor of the *fideicommissum* has the right to enjoy the fruits during his life; it vanishes with his death, and the estate returns to the proprietors, the family entitled under the *fideicommissum;* only, not as in the usufruct, in full property, with absolute power of disposal by dividing or selling it, but so that the member of the family indicated by the deed constituting the *fideicommissum* enters for the term of his life into the enjoyment of the fruits that have become vacant by the death of his predecessor. Since, then, the *feudum* and the *fideicommissum* cannot, by their very nature, belong to an inheritance, neither are they at all affected by the laws of succession, whether of the country in which the deceased possessor lived, or of the country in which they are situated. They are special legal institutions applying to particular immoveables, such as can only be governed by the *lex rei sitæ* (§§ 366, 368, No. 5). We may also express this proposition so: The laws as to the order of succession in *feuda* and *fideicommissa* are real statutes. Or in other words: Every legislator, as to *feuda* and *fideicommissa*, intends to determine something as to the lands of that kind lying in his own country; not as to the foreign lands whose present possessors only reside in this country.

The position of many other classes of immoveables is somewhat different, and yet the result is the same. If a law attempts to promote the preservation of a well-to-do order of peasantry by so fixing the order of succession in peasant properties, but without any limitation of property, and in particular of the right to alienate, that the oldest (or even the youngest) son shall always succeed as sole heir, such a law is of the following nature. It excludes testamentary succession, the partition of the property, the succession of daughters so long as sons exist. It is thus, indeed, a law of succession; but it has a political purpose that lies beyond the domain of pure law, and it is therefore a statute of a coercitive and strictly positive character (§ 349). Such a law is a real statute, and embraces all the peasant properties in the country, without respect to the domicile of the present proprietor. But it does not at all extend to the peasant lands which an inhabitant of the country may possess abroad. It does not, therefore, like ordinary laws of succession, propose to assign to the estate of deceased inhabitants the most appropriate destiny; but it seeks to advance certain political ends by the way in which it disposes of a certain kind of immoveables. Similar rules, and with an entirely similar result, occur in the case of property belonging to nobles, for the purpose of preserving wealthy families of the nobility. Such a law was the 'Erblandesvereinigung' (union of hereditary lands) of 1590, in the duchy of Westphalia, which deprived the daughters of the possessor of the right to succeed to the lands of nobles. A remarkable lawsuit as to the application of this law arose in 1838, and it was rightly decided by the court at Münster, as well as by the supreme tribunal at Berlin, that the law was a real statute, applicable to the lands of nobles lying in the duchy, without respect to the domicile of the persons concerned (*m*).

All the cases here adduced, however different they may be in themselves, agree in this, that the laws as to the order of succession do not aim at devolving the estate of a deceased person in an appropriate direction, but are rather intended to regulate the destiny of certain special immoveables, or classes of immoveables. Hence they must be regarded as real statutes, not as personal statutes (*n*). The doctrine laid down does not therefore conflict with the rule before given as to the treatment of pure laws of succession, and it cannot therefore be used for the purpose of raising doubts as to that rule.

In the particular legal relations hitherto treated of, we have constantly alluded to the intimate connection between the special forum and the local law to be administered (§ 360, No. 1). Such a connection might be looked for in the law of succession also; yet it must here be decidedly denied, for this reason, that no other locality whatever can be discovered for rights of succession than the universal one which is established at the domicile of the deceased (§ 375).

In the Roman law (*o*) there was for a long time no other

(*m*) Graf Bocholtz c. Freifrau von Benningen, in Ulrich and Sommer, *neues Archiv*, vol. vi. p. 476–512. The most decisive passages of the judgment are at pp. 481, 507, 508.

(*n*) Wächter, ii. p. 364, expresses himself entirely in the same sense.

(*o*) Comp. Bethmann-Hollweg, *Versuche*, pp. 61–69; Arndt's *Beiträge*, No. 2.

forum for the *hæreditatis petitio*, than that of the domicile of the defendant (*p*). After the legislation of Justinian, it could also be brought in the *forum rei sitæ* (*q*). That, however, only means that every one who violates the rights of the heir by possessing, *pro herede* or *pro possessore*, anything belonging to the inheritance, may be sued where the thing is situated; that is, where the wrongful possession which constitutes the violation of right is exercised (*r*). But it is evident that the local law of the succession cannot also be determined by this place, since it is possible that the things belonging to the inheritance lie dispersed at many places, and are possessed by persons without any right. But the inheritance as a whole, or even the greater part of it, cannot with certainty be referred to any particular place (§ 375), and in no passage of the Roman law is such a place said to be the foundation of a special jurisdiction. The Roman law has certainly appointed a special forum for the *fideicommissa* where the greater part of the inheritance is situated (*s*); but of course this arbitrary and exceptional direction, in regard to a solitary legal institution, cannot create a rule for the local law of succession in general.

Many modern writers have fixed as the forum of the inheritance the place where the succession opens (*t*); which is equivalent to saying, the last domicile of the deceased (*u*).

(*p*) *L. un C. ubi de hæred.* (3, 20). The words 'vel si ibi ubi res hæreditariæ sitæ sunt, degit,' are to be thus rendered: 'the *hæreditatis petitio* belongs exclusively to the *forum domicilii* of the defendant, and this rule is to be applied *even* (*vel* si ibi, etc.) although the defendant resides (si ibi *degit*) for some time at the place where the things belonging to the inheritance are situated.'—Arndt's *Beiträge*, pp. 122–124.

(*q*) *Nov.* 69, *C.* 1, which is of a very comprehensive nature. The L. 3, *C. ubi in rem* (3, 19), refers, according to the true construction, only to the vindication, not to other actions *in rem*, and therefore not to the *hæreditatis petitio*.

(*r*) The *Nov.* 69, *C.* 1, always refers the forum to the place of violation of rights. So also says L. 3, *C. ubi in rem* (if this is applied at all to the *hæreditatis petitio*): 'in locis, in quibus res . . . constitutæ sunt, *adversus possidentem* moveri.'

(*s*) See above, § 370, notes *bb* to *ee*.

(*t*) *Code de Procedure*, art. 59: 'le tribunal du lieu ou la succession est ouverte.'

(*u*) *Preussische Allg. Gerichtsordnung*, i. 2, § 121–125.

SECT. XXXIV.—(§ 377.)

IV. SUCCESSION.—PARTICULAR QUESTIONS.

As has already been done for obligations (§ 374), so now in regard to succession we have to consider particular questions which may occur as to the local law. These need a special discussion only where the general rule, that the domicile at the time of death determines, is insufficient (*a*).

1. The personal capacity of the testator in respect to his *legal relations*, as it is required at two different times (*b*), so also in the case where he has altered his domicile, is necessary at two different places. If, then, this capacity be wanting according to the law of the domicile where he makes the testament, the testament is and remains invalid even after the change of domicile. It is likewise invalid when that capacity is wanting according to the law which exists at his last domicile at the time of his death.[1] The reason is, that the last will is to be regarded as expressed at two different times, and possibly also at two different places; in fact, at the time of executing the deed, and at the place where the domicile of the testator is at this time; in law, at the time of death, and at the place which is the domicile at this time (§ 393).

2. The personal capacity of the testator in reference to his *physical qualities* (*e.g.* age), is ruled by the law of his domicile at the time of executing the testament, without respect to subsequent changes of domicile.[2]

3. The substance of the testament, and in particular its legal validity or invalidity, is governed by the law of the last domicile of the testator.[3] So, in particular, the rules as to dis-

(*a*) The rules that are laid down below as to the collision in time of the laws of succession (§§ 393, 395) should here be compared. The more minute discussion of the nature of the testament there given applies also to this place.

(*b*) At the time of making the testament, and at the time of his death (§ 393).

[1] By 24 and 25 Vict. c. 107, § 3, 'No will or other testamentary instrument shall be held to be revoked or to have become invalid, nor shall the construction thereof be altered, by reason of any subsequent change of domicile of the person making the same.'

[2] See Bar, § 108, p. 393, n.; Burge, iv. 576.

[3] *Boe* v *Anderson*, 1862, 24 D. 1362; *Ommanney* v *Bingham*, 1796, 3 Pat.

inheriting, præterition, and the legal portion (*legitima portio*, legitim). The same must be asserted of legacies and *fideicommissa*. These, indeed, relate to particular and limited objects, and it might therefore be supposed that the *lex rei sitæ* should be applicable to them; but, in fact, these legal institutions are but subordinate modifications of the whole inheritance, and they can be rightly judged only from its general standpoint. Any separate treatment might lead to the greatest contradictions.

Exceptions may be created by opposite coercitive laws. If, then, a testament establishes a family entail (*fideicommissum*) for an estate situated in a foreign country, whose positive law does not recognise *fideicommissa*, the law of the judge's country determines, and it here leads to the invalidity of the direction.

The interpretation of the testament is subject to rules similar to those applicable to the construction of contracts (§ 374, B). These will here mostly refer us to the last domicile of the testator (*c*).

4. The personal capacity of those called to the whole succession, or to parts of it (heirs or legatees), is in general to be judged according to *their* domicile, not according to that of the deceased; and that according to the domicile which they have at the time of the death of the deceased, at which time the right of succession devolves on them.

Exceptions may take place where there are laws of a coercitive nature. If, *e.g.*, the instituted heir is incapacitated for succeeding, according to the law of his domicile, by civil death or by heresy,—hindrances which are not recognised elsewhere,—or if a restrictive law as to acquisition in mortmain[4] stands in the way, then not the law of the domicile of the heir, but that of the place of the tribunal, is applicable; and the latter will very often coincide with the domicile of the deceased (§§ 349, 365).

448, 3 Hag. Ec. 414, n.; *Hog* v *Lashley*, M. 8193, 3 Pat. 247, 4 Pat. 581; *M. of Breadalbane* v *M. of Chandos*, 2 S. and M'L. 377, 402; *Sommerville* v *Sommerville*, 5 Ves. 749, etc.

(*c*) Fœlix, p. 171 [ed. Demangeat, i. 239. See *Yates* v *Thomson*, 1 S. and M'L. 835, 3 Cl. and Fin. 544; *Ommanney* v *Bingham*, *supra;* Story, §§ 479 sqq., 490. The latest and fullest summary of the British cases on the interpretation of wills will be found in Mr. M'Laren's *Law of Wills and Succession*, i. 30-40, Edinr. 1868].

[4] *Mackintosh* v *Townsend*, 16 Ves. 330; *Att.-Gen.* v *Mill*, 2 Russ. C. C. 328, 5 Bligh 593; *Macara* v *Coll. of Aberdeen*, M. 15,946, Hailes 975.

5. As to the form of the testament, we shall speak below, in connection with the rule, *locus regit actum* (§ 381).

6. If the positive law of the place where the testator has his domicile at the date of the will does not recognise testaments at all, the testament there made is and remains invalid. The testament is likewise invalid when the law of the last domicile does not recognise testaments. In this respect, therefore, the same rules are observed which have been laid down above (No. 1) as to the juridical capacity of the person of the testator.

7. Intestate succession is regulated by the law which exists at the last domicile of the deceased at the time of the opening of the succession (*d*). This is true in particular with regard to the legal order of the heirs called *ab intestato*. But it is equally true of the conditions of relationship in general, and therefore of the existence of relationship arising from marriage as well as of legitimation (*e*).

8. Contracts as to successions are alien to the Roman law. Where they occur, they are subject to the same rules as testaments.

The unilateral contract of succession is to be judged according to the law of the domicile of the deceased. So also are bilateral (mutual) contracts of succession; but which of the two parties is to be regarded as testator depends on the accidental circumstance, which of them dies first. This rule follows from the analogy of testaments. But it appears not less correct in principle to regard the local law of the contracts as regulating; because, in regard to the estate as a whole, only the domicile of the deceased can be considered as the place of fulfilment for the contract.

If the laws as to contracts relating to succession at this

(*d*) As to the more exact determination of this time, comp. below, § 395.

(*e*) Wächter, ii. p. 364. [On the contrary, legitimacy and legitimation are ruled by the law of the domicile of the person whose *status* is in question—*Munro* v *Munro*, 1840, 1 Rob. Ap. 492; *C. Dalhousie* v *M'Douall*, 16 S. 6, 1 Rob. Ap. 475—except where the law of the situs of immoveable property holds legitimation *per subsequens matrimonium*, or any law or institution on which legitimacy depends, to be contrary to good morals or the fundamental institutions of the country. *Birtwhistle* v *Vardell*, *Fenton* v *Livingstone*, *etc.*, *supra*, pp. 41, 106–108, 137; *In re Wright's Trusts*, 2 K. and J. 595; Fraser, *Parent and Child*, ch. iii.; Fraser, *Conflict of Laws in Divorce Cases*, Edinr. 1860.]

place are altered, the law in force at the time when the contract is concluded alone determines (§ 395).

9. Caduciary rights (rights to *bona vacantia*) are always to be regarded as a surrogate of the right of succession, and are therefore, in like manner, regulated by the law of the domicile of the deceased, without respect to the situation of the effects, even of the foreign immoveable estate. In particular, by the Roman law the right of the *fiscus* to succeed is not indeed to be called *hereditas*, yet is to be dealt with entirely in accordance with the same principles; so that the *fiscus* itself may come into quite the same position towards legatees and *fideicommissarii* as a real heir (d^2). Independent of the question as to the local law applicable to *bona vacantia*, which alone belongs to this place, is the inquiry, to *what fiscus* such a claim is competent,—to the *fiscus* of the domicile, or to that of the place where the thing is situated? For this question may arise between two countries, both of which recognise the Roman law. It must be determined in favour of the *fiscus* of the domicile, for the same reason which determines the local law, namely, that this right of the *fiscus* has the juridical nature of a succession, and wants only its name (e^2).

SECT. XXXV.—(§ 378.)

IV. SUCCESSION.—PRUSSIAN LAW.

Writers.

BORNEMANN, *Preussisches Recht*, 2d ed. vol. i. pp. 54–62.
RINTELEN, *Abhandlung* in Kamptz's *Jahrbüchern*, vol. xxx. p. 89 foll.
KOCH, *Preussisches Recht*, vol. i. § 40, No. II.
Ergänzungen, etc., by GRAEFF, etc. (*Fünfmännerbuch*), 2d ed. vol. i. pp. 116–121.

A keen controversy has lately been raised on the question, what local law is made the basis of succession by the Prussian

(d^2) Glück, *Intestaterbfolge*, §§ 147, 150; Puchta, *Pandekten*, § 564.
(e^2) Glück, *Intestaterbfolge*, § 149.

legislation; whether in general the law of the domicile of the deceased (as the two last cited writers maintain), or rather, in the case of immoveables, the law of the place where the thing is situated (according to the two first cited)?

If we look at the matter merely from the standpoint of general principles, we must unquestionably take the domicile as the universal basis, in accordance with the Roman law. For this follows strictly and necessarily from the Roman notion of universal succession (§ 375). This notion, however, is not by any means smuggled by us into the Prussian legislation, but it undoubtedly lies at the foundation of the whole Prussian law of succession. If, therefore, it were otherwise, according to special Prussian laws, we could only regard that as an inconsistency.

The whole controversy turns, in fact, on the interpretation of the following passage of the Allgemeine Landrecht (Introd. § 32):—

'In respect to immoveable estate, the laws of the jurisdiction under which it is itself situated, shall govern without respect to the person of the owner.'

If we give to this very abstractedly expressed direction the utmost extent of which the words are susceptible, the sense attributed by our opponents can certainly be given to it. But the question is, what sense is to be found in it according to the sound construction? It must first be admitted that this rule has no reference at all to succession *mortis causa*, but only to intercourse among the living (*a*). This is shown by the following terms of the corresponding passage in the previous printed draught (Introd. § 30):—

'What the provincial positive laws and statutes direct in respect of immoveables is to be applied to all those lying in the province or under the ordinary magistrate of the place, without respect to the place where the possessor lives, or where the contract relative to them has been concluded.'

Here it is plain that acts *inter vivos* are alone thought of. It might indeed be maintained that the altered expression in the Landrecht indicates an intention of further extending the object of the rule. But if this had been intended, it would

(*a*) This is also the opinion of Koch, *Preussisches Recht*, § 40, note 12, where, by a misprint, § 23 stands instead of § 32.

certainly have been more distinctly indicated. Without doubt, the change of expression arises only from the effort, everywhere apparent in the Landrecht, to manifest what was supposed to be a purer taste, by a phraseology as abstract as possible.

But even if, in construing the passage, we give up this limitation to acts *inter vivos*, and agree to include under it the law of succession to persons deceased, there still remains another important restriction, that lies in its very words. It speaks apparently only of 'statutes *in respect of* immoveable estates,' of laws which are to govern '*in respect of* immoveable estate.' What laws are pointed out by this expression? Clearly the true *Real Statutes*, which relate *principaliter* to immoveable things,—a notion which, as even our present opponents admit, is well known and familiar to the Landrecht (§ 361, *t*). But we cannot possibly ascribe this quality to a law as to the ordinary intestate succession merely because, among other things and accidentally, a man's estate may include landed estates which that law had not in view at all. On the contrary, this quality certainly exists in the case of certain laws relating to succession *mortis causa*, those, namely, as to the order of succession in *feuda, fideicommissa, etc.* (§ 376). The laws as to this are in fact real statutes; and if we apply the passage above cited to them, we do so in conformity with its true sense, whether the authors thought of this particular object or not. And our chief opponent declares that he formerly gave the passage this limitation, and only at a later period extended it further (a^2). It would, however, be quite a mistake to assume in this limitation any third intermediate opinion. It rather constitutes part of our whole complete opinion; for no one thinks of excluding succession in *feuda, fideicommissa, etc.*, from the *lex rei sitæ*. The only controversy is, whether, in regard to ordinary, pure succession *ab intestato*, the *lex rei sitæ* shall be applied (as our opponents hold), or not (as we maintain), to the immoveable parts of the estate. But a very important reason for accepting our construction, not merely as expedient and desirable in its consequences, but also as true, lies in the great practical difficulty that would arise from the adoption of the opposite interpretation. An example will make this difficulty evident. An inhabitant of Berlin dies without a testament, and leaves a widow and several

(a^2) Bornemann, p. 61.

near relations of different classes. The estate consists of a landed property near Berlin, one in Silesia, a house at Ehrenbreitstein, a house at Coblentz; besides, he has many personal debts, which of course affect all parts of the estate. According to the opinion of the opposite party, not fewer than four positive laws, which may designate quite different heirs, must come into application in the succession to these real estates;—in the Mark Brandenburg, the Joachimica of 1527 (*b*), with the claim of the widow to the half of the conjoined estate of both spouses; in Silesia, the Allgemeine Landrecht (*c*); at Ehrenbreitstein, the Roman law; at Coblentz, the French law; so that in fact four different inheritances would be formed. To the creditors it is of no consequence who is heir, provided that they are satisfied; but that is not possible until the value of each real property, and its relation to the whole estate, are fixed by judicial valuation. Our opponent thinks, indeed, that these difficulties ought not to alarm us (*d*). That might well be said, if the question were how to spare the judge trouble and doubt; but the difficulties and disadvantages touch the parties, especially the creditors; and why should these be burdened with them? Not, in the present case, in order to maintain a sure and certain legal principle, but to preserve the literal interpretation of a paragraph of the Landrecht, of which our opponents must at least admit that it allows of another construction. Just in this fact do I find the strongest argument for the correctness of our construction, since the legislator cannot certainly have intended to establish a principle that would involve the parties, especially the creditors, in quite useless embarrassment. This purely practical argument appears to me far more important than the one urged by our opponents, viz., that, at the time when the Landrecht was compiled, the opposite doctrine was predominant in practice, and that an adherence to this practice in the Landrecht must be assumed where a deviation from it is not distinctly expressed (*e*).

(*b*) *Corpus Constitut. Marchicarum*, by Mylius, Th. 2, Abth. 1, p. 19.

(*c*) Since the law of 11th July 1845, which abrogated all the provincial laws of Silesia as to succession.

(*d*) Bornemann, p. 62.

(*e*) It must be particularly observed, that shortly before the compilation of the Landrecht, Pufendorf, who was also a practical lawyer, very thoroughly exposed the perversity of that system (§ 376, *h*).

The following passages of our legislation also require consideration :—

1. It is laid down as a general rule that, in intestate succession between spouses, the law of the domicile of the deceased shall be administered (*f*); and a subsequent addition to this passage runs thus :—

> Appendix, § 78 : 'Even the immoveable estate of married persons forms no exception to this rule, although it is situated under another jurisdiction.'

Nothing is simpler and more natural than to regard this law as a particular application of our principle, and therefore a confirmation of it. Our opponents see in it an intentional exception to the rule adopted by them, but try in vain to deduce this intention from the history of the origin of the passage (*g*).

2. According to the opinion of our opponents, several successions to the same person must often be assumed to exist; in the example above given, four successions. It would thus be logically consistent to set up for each of them a special forum where each real estate is situated. But the Prussian law acknowledges throughout but one forum of succession, at the last domicile of the deceased (*h*), without excepting the case of real estates abroad. It thus acknowledges that there can be in all cases but one succession.

3. If any one institutes an heir, and substitutes to him without further condition several persons who would be the heirs *ab intestato* of the institute, the substitution must be so construed that it shall take effect according to the rules of intestate succession, and this intestate succession shall be judged by the law of the domicile of the instituted heir (*i*). Here it is evidently assumed that the domicile exclusively determines

(*f*) *A. L. R.* ii. 1, § 495.

(*g*) Bornemann, pp. 58-60. The 78th section of the appendix is derived from a decision of the Gesetz Commission of 1794. This, again, was occasioned by an inquiry of the government at Cleves, in which the erroneous doctrine was incidentally laid down as true for other cases. The Gesetz Commission gave their decision without entering on the discussion of the reasons for it, and thereby is supposed to have tacitly affirmed the false opinion of the government of Cleves, and to have recognised the decision itself as a mere exception. The judicial documents are printed in Klein's *Annalen*, vol. xiii. pp. 3-6.

(*h*) *Allg. Gerichtsordnung*, i. 2, § 121.

(*i*) *A. L. R.* i. 12, §§ 536, 537.

the succession *ab intestato*, without any exception of landed estates that may be situated abroad (*k*).

It must be observed, finally, that most writers (*l*), as well as the greater number of courts (*m*), accept the doctrine here vindicated.

SECT. XXXVI.—(§ 379.)

V. LAW OF THE FAMILY.—A. MARRIAGE.

Rights arising from the family relations are most nearly akin to personal status (capacity to have rights and capacity to act, § 362), and are essentially distinct from the patrimonial relations by which a person is brought into connection with external and arbitrarily chosen objects (*a*). On the other side, considerations, partly moral and religious and partly political, have great influence upon it, for which reason statutes of a coercitive and strictly positive nature most frequently occur in this department.

A. MARRIAGE.—There is no doubt as to the true seat of the marriage relation; it must be presumed to be at the domicile of the husband, who, according to the laws of all nations and of all times, must be recognised as the head of the family (*b*). For this reason, too, the territorial law of every marriage must be fixed according to it; and the place away from the domicile where the marriage may be celebrated, is quite immaterial (*c*).

(*k*) Bornemann, p. 60, attempts to weaken this argument by imputing to the testator, quite arbitrarily, the intention to admit only a single substitute.

(*l*) This fact is admitted by Bornemann, p. 54.

(*m*) Admitted by Bornemann, p. 62. Among these is a very exhaustive judgment at Glogau in 1828 (*Fünfmännerbuch*, pp. 118, 119). Quite in harmony with this doctrine is the judgment above cited, § 376, *m*, although in that case much that is incorrect is mixed up with the grounds of the judgment.

(*a*) See vol. i. § 53.

(*b*) L. 5, *de ritu nupt.* (23, 2): '. . . . deductione enim opus esse in mariti, non in uxoris domum, *quasi in domicilium matrimonii.*' In this there is neither a peculiarly Roman provision, nor a positive rule of any kind, but only the incidental recognition of the relation which necessarily springs from the general nature of marriage.

(*c*) Huber, § 10; Story, §§ 191–199. ['The marriage contract is emphatically one which parties make with an immediate view to the usual place of their residence. . . . The parties to a contract like this must be held

Many doubt this last proposition, because they regard marriage as an obligatory contract, but are accustomed in such contracts to regard the place where they are made as determining the local law. The first of these two views is false, because marriage has nothing in common with the obligatory contracts. If, however, it were true, it would not lead us to the place where the marriage originated as the criterion of the local law, but rather to the place of performance (§ 372). But assuredly it is only the domicile of the husband that can be the place of the performance of the duties arising from marriage.

From this standpoint a number of legal questions in regard to marriage are to be examined.

1. The conditions of the possibility of marriage, or (viewed from the other side) the impediments to marriage, are founded partly on the personal qualities of each of the two spouses separately, partly on their relation to one another. According to general principles, it may be supposed that the personal capacity of the wife is to be judged according to the law of her home (§ 362). But the laws that here come into operation rest on moral considerations, and have a strictly positive nature; and therefore the hindrances to marriage which are recognised in the domicile of the husband are absolutely binding, without respect to the differences which may exist at the home of the wife, or at the place where the marriage is celebrated. This rule holds, in particular, in regard to the forbidden degrees, and the obstacles founded on religious vows (*d*).

2. The formalities necessary for the conclusion of marriage are necessarily regulated by the place of celebration. Of this we shall speak afterwards (§ 381).

3. Especially difficult and controverted is the question, By what law are rights of property as between spouses to be judged? for this is a point as to which positive laws very widely differ. In every particular case the decision mainly lies between

emphatically to enter into it with a reference to their own domicile and its laws.'—Lord Brougham in *Warrender* v *Warrender*, 2 S. and M'L. 154, 204, 205; 2 C. and F. 532.]

(*d*) Wächter, ii. pp. 185, 187; Schäffner, §§ 102, 103. The practice of some countries is very various as to this point. Story, § 79 foll. [See Note A at end of section.]

the (Roman) Dotal Régime and the (German) Communion of Goods. The first, however, is found sometimes in its purely Roman form, sometimes with modifications, which are very widely spread in Germany. The Communion of Goods also occurs in the most different degrees.

The principle is not disputed on any side, that the property of the spouses is to be regulated according to the domicile of the husband (*e*), not according to the place where the marriage was contracted. But within this principle there are found two great differences of opinion.

First, many assert that this principle does not apply to land estates abroad, which must rather be judged by the *lex rei sitæ* (*f*). According to the more correct opinion, the *lex domicilii* is to be applied to foreign real property also (*g*). Since the decision is here the same as above in the case of succession, it might occur to us to seek for a similar foundation by referring it to a universal succession (§ 376). But such a basis can be admitted for none of the legal institutions with which we are here concerned, and, in particular, not for the *dos*, which comprehends the whole estate of the wife. The true reason is, that the choice of the local law must be referred to voluntary submission (§ 360, No. 2); while it certainly cannot be assumed with probability that the spouses intended to make the arrangements of their property depend on the accidental circumstance, whether or not a part of the estate consists of immoveables situated abroad. The difference that might thus arise as to the law governing different portions of the estate might lead to the greatest perplexities and uncertainties; and that certainly cannot be regarded as the probable purpose of the parties.[1]

(*e*) P. Voet, sect. 9, c. 2, §§ 5, 6; Wächter, ii. p. 47; Fœlix, p. 127 [ed. Demangeat, i. 88].

(*f*) P. Voet, sect. 4, c. 3, § 9; J. Voet, *in Pand.* xxiii. 2, § 60; Hommel, *Rhaps.* obs. 175 409, n. 15; Story, §§ 186, 454.

(*g*) Hert, § 46; Wächter, ii. p. 48; Fœlix, pp. 127-129 [ed. Demangeat, i. 188-194]; Schäffner, §§ 106, 107. The Prussian *Allg. Landrecht*, ii. 1, §§ 365-369, agrees with this.

1 'The legal assignment of a marriage operates without regard to territory all the world over.'—Per Lord Meadowbank in *Royal Bank of Scotland* v *Stein*, Jan. 20, 1813, 17 F. C. 72; 1 Rose B. R. 462; Buchanan's Ca. 358. But this applies only to moveables. Story, §§ 159, 186; Burge, i. 618. See *M'Cormick* v *Garnett*, 5 De G. M. and G. 278; *Duchess of Buckingham* v *Winterbottom*, 1851, 13 D. 1129.

A second controversy relates to the case in which the domicile of the husband is changed during the marriage (g^2).

Here one opinion is, that the local law of the earliest domicile remains decisive at all periods, and cannot therefore be changed by the election of a new domicile. The reason is generally stated to be, that in the inception of the marriage there is included a tacit contract, that the conjugal rights of property shall be immutably settled according to the law of the present domicile (*h*). This opinion I hold to be correct. The reason assigned for it will be further examined.

A second opinion refuses to assume a tacit contract, and makes the matrimonial rights of property depend solely on the law of the domicile. Hence it is concluded, that in the case where a new domicile is chosen, its law must decide, and that therefore every change may have as its consequence a different law as to the matrimonial rights of property (*i*).

Finally, a third and intermediate opinion rejects, like the second, the theory of a tacit contract, and likewise allows only the law of the existing domicile to decide, but with the reservation, that the estate acquired at the time of the marriage remains unchanged (*jus quæsitum*), and that only future acquisitions shall be governed by the law of the new domicile (*k*).

Let us examine the arguments for these opinions a little more closely. Our unprejudiced sense of right certainly speaks in favour of the first. When the marriage was about to be contracted, it was entirely in the wife's option, either to abstain from it altogether, or to add certain conditions touching patrimonial rights. She has made no such contract, but has accepted the conjugal rights as fixed by the law of the domicile, and naturally has reckoned on its perpetual continu-

(g^2) The discussion of this important controversy partly satisfies the reservation above made in § 344, *e*.

(*h*) P. Voet, sect. 9, c. 2, § 7; J. Voet, *in Pand.* xxiii. 2, § 87; Hert, §§ 48, 49; Pufendorf, ii. obs. 121; Wächter, ii. pp. 49–55; Schäffner, §§ 109-114; Fœlix, pp. 130–132 [ed. Demangeat, i. 195]; Bülow and Hagemann, *Erörterungen*, vol. vi. No. 24; Pfeiffer, *Praktische Ausführungen*, vol. ii. No. 6; Judgments of the Courts of Celle (1836) and Munich (1845), in Seuffert, *Archiv*, vol. i. n. 152.

(*i*) Eichhorn, *Deutsches Recht*, § 35, *g*, § 307, *d*, § 310, *e*, *f*; Story, § 187. Other writers are cited by Wächter, ii. p. 49.

(*k*) Kierulff, pp. 78, 79 (at the end of the whole note); Puchta, *Pandekten*, § 113, and *Vorlesungen*, § 113. Comp. as to this Wächter, ii. p. 50 (note 264), and p. 54: he declares himself of the first opinion (note *h*).

ance. The husband now changes the domicile by his own mere will, as he is undoubtedly entitled to do, and quite a different distribution of the conjugal estate is thus introduced for this marriage. If the wife is satisfied with it, our whole controversy is less important, since an alteration of her rights could have been effected by contract. The question, however, is important, if the change is detrimental to the wife, and she is not content with it. Precisely in order to exclude this unjustifiable one-sided power of the husband over the rights of the wife, was the existence of a tacit contract presumed by the defenders of the first opinion. The opposite party have recoiled from this, and not altogether without reason. The same end, however, may be attained, even if we renounce the tacit contract. By a contract, tacit as well as express, we understand a declaration of intention to the same effect, which is not conceivable without the distinct consciousness of both parties (*l*). If we ask, then, whether in the inception of a marriage there has always been a distinct understanding of both parties, especially of the wife, as to the distribution of the property of the spouses, we must certainly deny this; and hence the general assumption of a tacit contract is unfounded. But we must always admit of a voluntary submission as the foundation of the local law; and this is conceivable even in a negative fashion, as mere absence of contradiction (§ 360, No. 2). Now this does not exist at all as to the law of the new domicile in the supposed case of a disagreement between the spouses. We must therefore deny in this case any *alteration of the conjugal rights of property*, for presuming which there is no sufficient reason, even from the standpoint of the opposite party, who regard the positive law, and not the contract, as the criterion of the local law. Thus we arrive in a different way at the same result to which the assumption of a tacit contract would conduct us (*m*).

(*l*) See above, vol. iii. § 140.

(*m*) This basis for the first opinion, which perhaps would have removed the opposition of many opponents, is found in Schäffner, § 114. Perhaps the difference of the two views, and the reconciliation of them here suggested, might be thus described: that the rights established at the original domicile are supposed to have not so much the nature of a *tacit* as of a *feigned* contract, like the *pignus tacite contractum;* in which case nothing depends on a distinct consciousness of the parties. This is only a difference of expression. The essence of the thing consists in the definite right of each party, independently of the will of the other.

It has hitherto been assumed that the alteration of the law as to the conjugal estate by change of domicile tends to the injury of the wife, and is therefore contrary to her will. But this case, in which the unjust consequence of the opposite opinion is certainly most prominent, is by no means the only one. When an official is removed to a part of the country in which another rule prevails as to the property of the spouses, the change of domicile is involuntary for him too, and perhaps the change of the law as to their property is not wished for by either of the spouses. But they might be able to prevent this change, perhaps not at all, perhaps only by burdensome and expensive contracts, according to the terms of the rules of the local law.

The following consideration will make the argument still clearer:—When a law fixes the patrimonial rights of the spouses, the first question is,—for what persons was it intended to make rules? Certainly the legislator has in view all the marriages that are contracted in his realm, and means to prescribe in respect to them what he deems to be most salutary, or what he finds to be consistent with the previous customs of the country. But does he intend to obtrude this rule on marriages contracted elsewhere, the parties to which have immigrated into his country? There is no sufficient ground for supposing this, especially in opposition to the objection which has just been considered. But if the law, in accordance with its probable intention, is not to be applied to immigrant marriages, the argument of our opponents has lost all force in regard to these.

If the arguments here advanced are held to be just, the second and third opinions are completely refuted by them. The second, moreover, appears specially harsh and inequitable in relation to the estate already acquired. If, at a place where the law establishes as the rule universal communion of goods of the most extensive description, a marriage is contracted by a rich man with a poor woman, the estate becomes common by the completion of the marriage. If the man afterwards changes the domicile to a place where the dotal régime prevails, the wife must, according to the second opinion, lose in a moment, and against her will, the share of the estate to which she had already acquired right. The third intermediate theory has been proposed just in order to prevent this alarming result.

But apart from the fact that it is equally confuted by the foregoing arguments, it is subject to the usual defects of half measures. If the rights in the conjugal property be regulated by the old domicile in respect to the existing estate, and by the new domicile in respect to that afterwards acquired, perplexities and contradictions may arise which cannot be at all foreseen, and which might conduce as little to the advantage as to the wishes of the spouses.

The second opinion must indeed be adopted, if a law as to conjugal property of a strictly positive exclusive nature should exist at the new domicile. This would be presumed if a law were there enacted prohibiting any marriage whatever to be contracted, or if constituted elsewhere, to be continued, otherwise than under the dotal régime, or otherwise than with the communion of goods (m^2). Whether such laws exist at all may remain undecided.

The Prussian law recognises, as a general rule, the opinion here maintained, according to which the local law of the domicile subsisting at the beginning of the marriage is decisive for its whole future endurance; but with two subordinate modifications for the case, when a marriage, begun under the dotal régime, is removed to a new domicile in which community of goods prevails (n).

4. Those laws require special consideration by which the liberality of one spouse towards the other is restricted, among which there is, in particular, the prohibition in Roman law of all donations beween spouses.

(m^2) Wächter, ii. pp. 55, 362.

(n) *Allg. Landrecht*, ii. 1, §§ 350–355. [It cannot be said that there is any distinct decision of British courts on the one side or the other of the question discussed in the text, although there is at least one judicial opinion, that 'when the domicile is changed, the implied contract changes along with it' (*sic*). *Kennedy* v *Bell*, 1864, 2 Macph. 587; cf. *Hall's Trs.* v *Hall*, 1854, 16 D. 1057. The cases in which it has been conclusively settled, that under the old Scotch law (altered by 18 and 19 Vict. c. 23) the right of the representatives of a predeceasing wife to her share of the goods in communion at her death depends on the law of the domicile at the dissolution, not at the constitution of the marriage, may be held to involve an adhesion to the second opinion, rejected by Savigny; although, perhaps, they truly rest on the distinction pointed out below, p. 247. See *Hog* v *Lashley*, M. 8193, 3 Pat. 247, 4 Pat. 581; *Newlands* v *Chalmers' Trs.*, 1832, 11 S. 65; *Maxwell* v *M'Clure*, 20 D. 307 (aff. 3 Macq. 852); *Kennedy* v *Bell*, 2 Macph. 587; revd. on another point, 1 L. R. Sc. Ap. 307. Cf. *Sommerville* v *Sommerville*, 5 Ves. 749; *Munroe* v *Douglas*, 5 Madd. 394.]

In this respect the law of the domicile decides; here, however, not that of the original domicile, but that of the domicile at the time when the act is performed. The reason of this variation from the foregoing rule is, that laws of this kind are directed to the preservation of the moral purity of marriage, and are therefore of a strictly positive character (§ 349). If we compare this with the case before discussed (under No. 3), it cannot be maintained that the marriage entered into at a place under the Roman law, and afterwards transferred to another place, was constituted under the tacit contract that an effectual donation between the spouses could never take place at any time. The prohibition of gifts is rather a mere restriction of freedom to which the spouses must accommodate themselves, not a legal institution imported into the marriage by voluntary submission.

On the other hand, it cannot be admitted that such laws should be applied to all immoveable property lying within their territory, even when the marriage subsists in a country that knows no such restriction of freedom (*o*). For the purpose of these laws is not to ward off a danger from the things, as if they could suffer injury from a gift *inter conjuges*, but rather, as already stated, the preservation of purity of morals in the marriage. The legislator addresses himself, therefore, to married persons living within his territory, without respect to the situation of their estate.

5. Intestate succession between spouses is regulated, as between strangers, by the last domicile of the deceased. In many cases, however, it may be doubtful whether the claim to the inheritance is to be deduced from the rules of proper intestate succession, or from the mere continuance of the relations as to conjugal property which subsisted during the marriage (*communio bonorum*). In the first case the last domicile determines; in the second case, the domicile at which the marriage began, as has been shown before (No. 3).

Such a question may be conceived, for instance, in the case of the Joachimica, above mentioned as prevailing in the Mark Brandenburg (§ 378, *b*). Yet the claim of the survivor, under

(*o*) This is the opinion of Rodenburg, tit. 2, c. 5, § 1; J. Voet, *in Pand.* xxiv. 1, § 19; Meier, p. 44. [See Demangeat on Fœlix, i. 109, 228; Bar, § 97; *Nisbett* v *Nisbett's Trs.*, 1835, 13 S. 517.]

this law, to the half of the united estate of the two spouses, is to be regarded in fact as pure intestate succession, not as the result of a kind of *communio bonorum*, and therefore is to be judged according to the last domicile. This follows from the connection established by law between this claim and the rest of the intestate succession. That claim is therefore of a similar nature to the institutions of Roman law,—the *Bonorum possessio unde vir et uxor*, and the succession of the indigent spouse.[2]

6. Divorce is distinguished from the legal institutions relative to property, by the circumstance that the láws relating to it depend on the moral nature of marriage, and therefore have in themselves a strictly positive character. Hence the judge, in a case of divorce, must follow only the law of his own country, without respect to the other relations of the spouses (*p*). This principle, however, will generally lead us back to the law of the domicile of the husband, because it is only there that a true jurisdiction for divorce is established.

Thus it is not, as in patrimonial questions, the domicile at the time of the marriage which is to be regarded, but rather the present domicile. For the law subsisting at the former domicile cannot have given to either of the spouses a right, or even a well-founded expectation, of being at some future period divorced according to the same law, because, as we have just seen, the character of laws of divorce leads to a different result. Upon this subject, however, the opinions of writers, as well as the decisions of courts, present an extraordinary diversity (*q*).

NOTE A, p. 241.

Bar objects that, in the case in question, the matter in dispute is a condition precedent of the man's right to fix the woman's domicile, and that the argument from the general principle above laid down, which he admits, therefore fails. While adopting the view of Wheaton and Wächter, that the capacity of each spouse must be ruled by the law of his or her domicile, he allows this modification: 'Where there is an impediment to the marriage by the law of the woman's domicile, but not by that of the man, the woman acquires the same domicile as the man, not by virtue of the marriage, but because, in fact, she

[2] *Ante*, p. 246, note *n*; Westlake, § 373.

(*p*) See above, § 349. On the whole, Schäffner, § 124, and Wächter, ii. pp. 184–188, are of the same opinion.

(*q*) Schäffner, §§ 118-125; Story, chap. vii.

follows the man to his domicile. If she thus acquires a new domicile, the laws of that place determine her capacity. An exception occurs only where the woman is incapable of changing her domicile without the consent of third parties, *e.g.* of a guardian.'—Bar, § 90 fin. English cases tend, as Story shows, to make the *lex loci contractus* decisive. See, *e.g.*, at least in regard to incapacity arising from defect of age, *Scrimshire* v *Scrimshire*, 2 Hag. Con. 418. In regard to prohibited degrees, the law of the forum, which will generally, though not always, be the law of the husband's domicile, would seem to prevail. See *Fenton* v *Livingstone*, 3 Macq. 497, 534; *Sussex Peerage Case*, 11 Cl. and F. 85; *Brook* v *Brook*, 3 Sm. and G. 481, 9 H. L. Ca. 193. The question most keenly discussed in this country refers to the effect upon the capacity to marry of a foreign decree of divorce, —a question which is sometimes treated as belonging rather to the subject of foreign judgments or of jurisdiction. The leading cases are: *R.* v *Lolly*, Russ. and Ry. 237; *M'Carthy* v *Decaix*, 2 Russ. and My. 614; *Warrender* v *Warrender*, *supra; Dolphin* v *Robins*, 3 Macq. 563; *Shaw* v *Gould* (*in re Wilson's Trusts*), 35 L. J. Ch. 243 (aff. in H. of L., 18 L. T. N. S. 833, 37 L. J. Ch. 433); *Beattie* v *Beattie*, 1866, 5 Macph. 181. The ablest discussion of questions arising on foreign decrees of divorce is in Fraser's *Conflict of Laws in Cases of Divorce*, Edin. 1860. The law is thus stated by the Royal Commissioners on the Laws of Marriage, 1868, *Report*, p. 26:—

'It is a settled point in the law of Scotland, that a sentence of dissolution of marriage (on proof of facts constituting sufficient ground for dissolution of marriage according to that law, which admits of more latitude in this respect than the law of England) may competently be pronounced by a Scottish court between persons having their legal and matrimonial domicile and ordinary residence in England or in any other country, who have only resided in Scotland for a very short space of time, who have resorted thither (perhaps by mutual arrangement) for the express purpose of obtaining such a sentence, and who have no intention of remaining there after their divorce has been obtained.

'The English courts, on the other hand (with which, as we apprehend, the Irish courts agree), refuse, under such circumstances, to acknowledge the validity of such a Scottish sentence: they treat a marriage subsequently contracted in England by either of the parties so divorced as bigamous, and the issue of such subsequent marriage as illegitimate.

'If indeed the suit were *bona fide*, and the legal domicile of the husband Scotch at the time of the divorce, although the marriage might have been originally English, the English courts, according to the most recent authorities, might regard the marriage as effectually dissolved by a Scotch sentence; but it may perhaps be considered still an unsettled point whether they would recognise a *bona fide* temporary residence of both parties in Scotland, unconnected with any purpose of obtaining a divorce (but without a legal domicile in that country), as sufficient to enable English persons, when divorced by a Scottish sentence, to marry again in each other's lifetime.'

SECT. XXXVII.—(§ 380.)

V. FAMILY LAW.—B. PATERNAL POWER.—C. GUARDIANSHIP.

B. PATERNAL POWER.—The origin of paternal power in birth in wedlock, as well as the grounds on which it may be controverted, are to be judged of by the law of the place where the father had his domicile at the child's birth.

On the other hand, the patrimonial relations between a father and his children are to be judged by the law of the father's domicile at the time when the question arises, so that a change of domicile may bring with it a change of these relations (§ 396, II.).

Legitimation by subsequent marriage is regulated according to the father's domicile at the time of the marriage, and in this respect the time of the birth of the child is immaterial. It has indeed been asserted that this latter point of time must be regarded, because by his birth the child has already established a certain legal relation, which only obtains fuller effect by the subsequent marriage of the parents; and it is added that the father could arbitrarily elect before the marriage a domicile disadvantageous to the child (*a*). But we cannot speak at all of a right of such children or of a violation of it, since it depends on the free will of the father not only whether he marries the mother at all, but even, if he contracts such a marriage, whether he will recognise the child. In both these cases the child obtains no right of legitimacy, for a true proof of filiation out of wedlock is impossible; and, accordingly, voluntary recognition, along with marriage and independently of it, can alone confer on the child the rights of legitimacy (*b*).

(*a*) Schäffner, § 37.

(*b*) This is so in common law. In the Roman law this proposition was less prominent, since legitimation applied only to the children of concubines (*naturales*), in whose case the paternity was just as certain as in the case of those born in marriage. We have no *naturales*, but only *spurii*;

Wherever English law prevails, on the contrary, it is assumed that the operation of paternal power and legitimation on foreign immoveables must be determined, not according to the *lex domicilii*, but by the *lex rei sitæ* (*c*).

C. Guardianship.—There is an essential distinction between guardianship and the legal institutions hitherto discussed. Only in the most ancient Roman law could it be regarded as an institution of purely private law. It has since gradually assumed the character which it presents in the modern common law of Germany, as well as in other legislations. Guardianship in the present day is the exercise of the protection which the state is entitled and bound to give to the most numerous and most important class of those who need such care, pupils and minors. So viewed, guardianship belongs essentially to the public law, and only some special consequences fall within the province of private law. In conformity with this view, however, guardianship is not only subject to different rules in different countries, but even in one and the same country is susceptible of a less rigid treatment, on the part of the public authorities, than legal relations belonging to the strictly private law. These differences appear not merely in the rules of law themselves, but even in the selection of the local law by which these rules are fixed.

I now turn to the most important legal questions relating to this subject.

1. *Constitution of Guardianship.*—It is correctly laid down as the rule, that the law of the ward's domicile, which generally coincides with the last domicile of the deceased father, is decisive with regard to the establishment of a guardianship, and that such guardianship then includes also the estate of the ward situated elsewhere (*d*). Here, however, the following deviations from the strict principle are to be kept in view :—

and in regard to these, everything depends on the voluntary recognition of the father. The Prussian law indeed regards mere proof of carnal intercourse within a certain time before the birth as itself proof of paternity (*A. L. R.* ii. 1, § 1077); yet in legitimation by marriage, it makes the rights of legitimacy begin from the nuptial ceremony (*A. L. R.* ii. 2, § 598). Hence, according to the sense of the Landrecht, legitimation has no place if the father, before the marriage, transfers his domicile into a country where the common law prevails, and then refuses to recognise the child.

(*c*) Story, §§ 87, 456. Schäffner rightly declares against this, § 39.

(*d*) P. Voet, sect. 9, c. 2, § 17 ; J. Voet, *in Pand.* xxvi. 5, § 5 ; Schäffner, § 41.

First, if immoveable estate of the ward lies within a different jurisdiction, or, it may be, in a foreign country. It may happen, in this case, that a special guardianship is constituted for such parts of the estate, so that the same ward may have several tutors in territories locally distinct (*e*). Such an arrangement occurs in Roman law. Neither the testamentary nor the legal tutors were affected by these local varieties. If, on the contrary, the magistrate had to appoint tutors over a widely scattered estate, these were specially appointed for each sovereign jurisdiction,—some for the *res Italicæ*, others for the *res provinales* (*f*). By the Prussian code there is constituted, as a rule, one guardianship for the whole estate, and that according to the law of the domicile of the father: a subsequent change of domicile is allowed to have influence only exceptionally. Special curatories may be constituted for parts of the estate situated abroad, and these have to place themselves in connection with the proper guardianship (*g*). It is provided by treaties between the Prussian Government and neighbouring states, that the guardianship shall be constituted according to the domicile of the ward: if, however, he possesses immoveables in the other country, its court shall have the choice of subjecting these to the general guardianship, or of constituting a special guardianship for them (*h*). The practice in the countries subject to English law is extremely uncertain, because in these, partial and special guardianships are constituted not merely for the immoveable, but also for the moveable estate situated abroad (*i*).

But, secondly, even irrespective of the situation of the estate, the necessity of the individual case may justify a complete deviation from the principle, especially if, according to the family relations, no influence on the future condition of the ward is to be ascribed to the last domicile of the father. A case taken from real life will illustrate this: The father of a family died at his domicile at Bonn, where also was the seat of his estate, especially of several immoveable properties. The

(*e*) Comp. the writers cited in note *d*.
(*f*) *L.* 39, § 8, *de adm.* (26, 7); *L.* 27, *pr. de tutor. et cur.* (26, 5).
(*g*) *A. L. R.* ii. 18, §§ 56, 81–86.
(*h*) Treaty with the kingdom of Saxony, 1839, art. 15, and in the same terms with other states. (See above, § 348.)
(*i*) Schäffner, § 41; Story, § 492 foll.

children, in accordance with the provisions of their father's testament, immediately changed their domicile to the residence of a distant relation out of the Prussian state. At the same time the testament had, from personal confidence, committed the guardianship to an inhabitant of Berlin, with very ample powers. According to the principle above stated, the guardianship must have been constituted at Bonn, under French law, and must have continued there. But the Ministry of Justice, as the supreme superintendent of guardianships throughout the whole state, transferred the guardianship to Berlin, whereby the supreme control over it passed to the Kurmärkische Pupillen-collegium (Board for the Supervision of Wards) in Berlin, and at the same time the Prussian code became applicable.

2. *Administration of Guardianship.*—It cannot be doubted that, as a rule, the administration of guardians is regulated by the law of the court under which their office has been established and is carried on. Here, again, a question arises as to the case in which foreign immoveables belong to the estate, and are administered, not by a special guardianship (as may be done according to No. 1), but by the general guardianship.

It is asserted by many that, according to a universal practice in regard to such immoveables, and especially in respect to their alienation, the *lex rei sitæ* must be observed, so that then the management of the same guardian would have to be judged according to different laws (*k*). It is evidently assumed that the law as to the alienation of pupils' property is a real statute. I can admit this assertion neither in principle, nor with respect to the alleged general practice.

In the first place, I cannot admit it in principle. If a law ordains that the property of pupils shall be alienated only under certain restrictions (such as by auction, judicial decree, etc.), that is a measure of precaution—not for the security of the transmission of such property, nor for the increase of its produce (which would show the law to be a real statute), but for the person of the ward as standing in need of protection. For his security certain forms of alienation are required; and only when these are observed is the act of the alienating guardian allowed

(*k*) Schäffner, § 41. Somewhat more careful is the expression of P. Voet, sect. 9, c. 2, § 17. He holds it to be advisable that in alienation the guardian should secure himself by a decree of both courts.

to have the same effect as the alienation of a proprietor of full age. Hence the purpose of such a law is the completion of the guardian's acts; it is a personal, not a real statute. In other words, the legislator makes provision with respect to the minors placed under his care, not with respect to property situated in his country.

But even the general practice is more easily asserted than proved, as is usual with general statements of this kind. I will cite a very instructive case relating to this matter (*l*):—A minor of noble family lived in Bavaria, and had guardians there. He had land estates in the Rhenish provinces of Prussia, over which no special guardianship was there established. The Bavarian guardians sold the lands at their own hand, and without exposing them to public auction. After he had reached majority, the former proprietor challenged the sale as null, because the French laws as to the alienation of the property of pupils were not observed (*m*). In all the instances this plea was repelled, because these statutory restrictions form an inseparable whole, and several parts of them (Family Council and the *subrogé tuteur*) are entirely inapplicable to foreign guardianships. It was held, therefore, that these laws were to be applied only to guardianships subsisting in the territory of the French legislation, not to all immoveables situated there.

The treaties of the Prussian Government with neighbouring states (Note *h*) give the following direction to the personal guardian who administers immoveable properties in a foreign country: 'The latter, however, has to observe, in the affairs relating to the immoveables, the statutory rules in force at the place where they are situated.' If we take this passage in the widest extent of which the words are susceptible, they must be referred also to the restrictions on alienations by guardians, and then they would be in opposition to the judicial sentence just quoted and approved. I would be inclined, however, to suppose in the passage a somewhat inaccurate phraseology, and not to refer it at all to statutory rules as to *guardianship*, but

(*l*) Judgment of the Court of Cassation at Berlin, 1847, in the case of *Bassenheim* contra *Raffauf*; see Seuffert, *Archiv*, vol. ii. n. 2.

(*m*) *Code Civil*, arts. 457–460. There is required, (1) resolution of a family council in concurrence with the court of first instance; (2) public sale in presence of the *subrogé tuteur* (chosen by family council, art. 420), and with concurrence of the court or of a notary.

only to the rules touching the ordinary commerce in immoveable property, such as the constitution of mortgages, judicial confirmation, publication, etc.

3. Lastly, the personal legal relations of the guardian are still to be noticed.

Only the positive law of the domicile of the guardian can determine as to the obligation to undertake the guardianship, and the allowable expenses.

The principles before laid down as to the forum and the local law as connected therewith (§ 370, No. 2, § 372), are to be applicable also to the obligations which the guardian contracts by his management.

It has recently been maintained, on grounds of expediency, that the court superintending the guardianship must always be regarded as competent, although it is not the court to which the guardian is personally subject, nor that which would be held to be the special *forum gestæ administrationis* (*n*). So general an assertion is to be doubted, if it were only because the judicial system of each country must be considered. But it must also be rejected as impossible at many places, viz. wherever the magistrates that control the affairs of minors have no ordinary civil jurisdiction.[1]

NOTE A. (LEGITIMATION PER SUBSEQUENS MATRIMONIUM.)

The following are the passages of Schäffner, Bar, and Heffter on this disputed subject.

SCHAEFFNER.

In considering the application of the rule of international practice, which refers questions regarding a person's status and his capacity for rights to the law of his domicile, Schäffner says (*Entwickelung des internationalen Privatrecht*, Frankfurt-am-Main 1841, p. 49 sqq. :—

'§ 37. Positive laws as to legitimation by subsequent marriage[2] are very various. The laws of most of the states on the continent of Europe admit this legitimation *generally*, though with distinctions in

(*n*) Mühlenbruch, *Archiv*, vol. xix. pp. 362–365.

[1] On the law relating to guardianship, see, in general, Fraser, *On Parent and Child*, p. 588 sqq. ; M'Laren, *On Wills and Succession*, vol. i. pp. 43 sq., 48 sq. ; Bar, § 106 ; *Stuart* v *Moore*, 23 D. 51, 446, 595, 902, 4 Macq. 1, 9 H. L. Ca. 440 ; *Enohin* v *Wylie*, 10 H. L. Ca. 1, 31 L. J. Ch. 402 ; *Nugent* v *Vetsera*, 35 L. J. Ch. 777.

[2] Alef, *de Stat. concursu* (in Diebus Academicis iv.), § 40 ; Burge, *Com.* i. 101.

respect of *certain* illegitimate children, or in respect of the form of the acknowledgment by the parents.[3] It is also the law in the law of the Isle of Man,[4] Guernsey and Jersey, in Lower Canada, St. Lucia, Trinidad, Demerara, Berbice, at the Cape of Good Hope, Ceylon, Mauritius,—as well as, in North America, in the States of Vermont, Maryland, Virginia, Georgia, Alabama, Mississippi, Louisiana, Kentucky, Missouri, Indiana, and Ohio,[5]—also in Scotland.[6] In Ireland, England,[7] and those of its dependencies in the West Indies and North America which have not been named, as well as in the other States of North America,[8] legitimation by subsequent marriage is not admitted at all.

'The question thus arises, what law ought to determine whether an individual is or is not legitimized by a subsequent marriage? Is the decision to be according to the law of the place where the marriage is entered into, or according to the law of the place where the parents have their domicile at the date of the marriage, or according to the law of the place where the child to be legitimized was born, or according to the law of the *situs* of immoveable property, which the child claims as heir *ab intestato* of his parents?

'As to the law of the place where the marriage is entered into, there will be no difficulty in rejecting it; for this reason, that the opposite course would place it in the power of the parents, by contracting marriage abroad, to impress the character of illegitimacy, even in respect of their own country, on a child who, by the law of that country, was capable of legitimation. It has therefore been decided that persons who had procreated an illegitimate child in England, do not legitimize it, so far as regards England, by their subsequent marriage in Scotland. Conversely, persons who had had an illegitimate child in France, would legitimize it by their marriage in England.[9] Just as little can the question be determined by the law of the place where the parents have their domicile[10] at the time when the mar-

[3] Comp. *e.g.* Febrero, *Noviss.* tom. i. tit. 3, c. 2, p. 118; D'Aguesseau, *Œuvres*, vii. 381, 470.

[4] *Lex Scripta of the Isle of Man*, pp. 70, 75.

[5] Burge, i. 101.

[6] Ersk. *Inst.* i. 6, 52; Bankton, i. 5, 54.

[7] Co. Litt. 245 (*a*) note.

[8] Griffith's *Law Register*, *passim*.

[9] Story, § 87; Burge, i. p. 102.

[10] Tittmann (*de compet. legg. extern. et domest. in defin. juribus conjugum*, Halle 1822), § 17, seems to be of a different opinion:—'Si quis *Anglus*, juncto post natum filium *in Anglia* matrimonio, vel ipse *in Saxonia* sedem figit, vel filius, hic *in foro Saxonico legitimis* accensendus esse videtur liberis. Ea enim est apud *nos* matrimonii vis. Fac vero, Saxonem cum liberis per subsequens matrimonium legitimatis in Angliam domicilium transferre, legitimi et in Anglia, opinor, habebuntur liberi, quoniam id jus acquisiverunt in Saxonia. Nec, si Angli illius filius, qui vi matrimonii inter parentes initi et domicilii in Saxonia fixi legitimatus est, in Angliam redit, jus in Saxonia acquisitum amittere videtur.'

riage is entered into; for otherwise, it would be in their power, by the capricious choice of a domicile, to destroy the status of a child capable of legitimation. It may indeed be objected to this reasoning, that the parents may omit the marriage altogether. But the argument *a majori ad minus* cannot well be applied here, because, from the moment of the child's birth, a certain legal relation must always have subsisted between him and his parents, from which either the possibility or the impossibility of legitimation by a subsequent marriage must result. But this possibility or impossibility is in turn conditioned by the existence of the child; and in this, as in every legal relation, we must look to its commencement; *i.e.* in the case before us, to the birth of the child. The laws of the place where the birth of a child actually takes place, exclusively determine, therefore, whether he can be legitimated by subsequent marriage.[11]

'This process of reasoning leads to the same result to which many jurists have come by a different way.[12]

'§ 38. Some examples will further illustrate this theory. In F. J. de la Goestiere[13] a case occurs, in which a certain Jeanne Peronne Dumay, from Flanders, had borne an illegitimate child to a certain Conty de Quesnoy, of Picardy, in France. The parents afterwards went to England, and were there married. The question arose, whether the natural child was to be held as legitimated by the French law, and capable of succeeding to property left by his father in France? It was decided that the child had lost nothing of his original capability of being legitimated by the subsequent marriage of his parents; and the place of entering into marriage could be regarded only in so far as concerned the solemnities there required.

'The converse of this is found in a case decided by the courts of Scotland.[14] Alexander Ross, a Scotchman by birth, had begotten in England, where he was domiciled, a natural son by an Englishwoman. The parents afterwards travelled to Scotland, and there contracted marriage with each other. The natural son claimed in the Court of Session, as having been legitimated, certain immoveable property of his father, situated in Scotland; but the action was dismissed in the Court of Appeal, on the ground that the status of illegitimacy, and consequently an incapacity to be legitimized, had been impressed upon him by the English law as the *lex originis;* and this incapacity could in no way be removed by the accidental celebration of a marriage in Scotland.[15]

[11] Alef, § 40, seems to be of the same opinion.

[12] Comp. Bouhier, *Cout. de Bourg.* c. 22, §§ 4–10; Boullenois, i. 62, ii. 10; Merlin, tit. *Légitimité*, sect. 2, § 11, p. 865; Sœfve, *Nouveau Recueil de plusieurs Questions Notables*, tom. 2, c. 4, c. 20.

[13] *Journal des Principales Audiences du Parlement*, tom. 3, L. 2, c. 17.

[14] Fac. Coll. 15 May 1827; 4 W. and S. 289; Burge, i. 108.

[15] Burge, i. 108, cites other similar decisions. 4 W. and S. 289; *Shedden* v *Patrick*, Dict. *voce* Foreign, Append. 6, 1 July 1803. [See *Munro* v

'§ 39. If the theory above stated is admitted as correct, it cannot be contended that the operation of legitimation *per subsequens matrimonium* is to be restricted in regard to such immoveables as are situated in a country which does not recognise legitimation by subsequent marriage. Some have been led into this error by the doctrine of real statutes.

'It is not at all the province of the so-called real statute to declare *who* is legitimate, and who is not; if so, it might expatiate over the whole subject of personal status, which would be quite inconsistent with the nature of the real statute.

'The adherents of this opinion arrive also at singular results. For while they make the real statute decide the matter of legitimacy in reference to immoveables, they apply the personal statute in respect to moveables situated in the same state. Must it not happen in this way, that the same person in the same state is to be regarded as at the same time illegitimate and legitimate?

'The case is somewhat different when the real statute is *expressly* opposed to the legitimation in a prohibitive form. Thus, in England, *e.g.*, it is the common law that no one can succeed to land in England, who has not been born in lawful wedlock.[16]

'§ 40. It has been doubted whether a subject legitimized by the rescript of his sovereign is to be held as legitimate in foreign countries. The question, it seems to me, must be unconditionally answered in the affirmative. If the legitimation is effectual according to the laws of the country where the person legitimated has his domicile, why should it not exert the same virtue everywhere, since it rests on no other foundation than an application of the law of the domicile as to status, in conformity with that law?[17]

'The arguments urged against this appear to be untenable. Some say, to admit the validity of such a legitimation abroad, would be to confer on the governor of the country where it is granted, the right of disposing of immoveable property situated in foreign states; because the person so legitimated might acquire, as legitimate, rights in immoveables, which previously, as illegitimate, he would not have had.[18] Those who thus argue, evidently make an entirely perverted application of the real statute; they entertain a view of it which has never been recognised in practice. The *lex rei sitæ*, in principle, does not affect in any degree the status of foreigners.[19] In the circum-

Munro, 1 Rob. App. 492. In these cases, the domicile of the parents at the time of the marriage was regarded as the criterion.]

[16] *Mirror*, fo. 16; Bracton, 63; Glanville, by Beames, p. 180; 2 Inst. 96; Burge, i. 110; Story, § 87.

[17] Anton. de Rosellis, *tract. de Legit.* (in Oceano Juris), l. 2, n. 24.

[18] Cf. Alef, § 39; Voet, *de Statut.* sect. 4, c. 3, § 15, p. 138; Le Bret, *Quest. Notables*, liv. 3, decis. 7; Boullenois, i. 64.

[19] Maurenbrecher's *Lehrbuch der heutigen gemeinen Deutschen Rechts*, § 126

stance that effect is given, in reference to immoveables situated abroad, to the due and effectual legitimation of a foreigner by rescript, according to his own domestic law, it is not implied that the governor of that country is invested with any power of disposal as to these immoveables. His act operates only upon the status (Er disponirt lediglich über den Status).

'Nor can any weight be given to the argument that, *e.g.*, it would thus be allowed to the foreign prince to confer on his subjects the character of legitimacy *in necem* of the subjects of this country. This proposition may more fairly be inverted, and expressed thus: Why, then, is the foreigner held illegitimate in this country? The native-born subject will say: Because the law of his domicile declares him so. To which it may be replied: Good; if this law prevails to make him illegitimate, it must then prevail also for the contradictory of this, so as to make him legitimate. This is also the view taken in practice.[20]'

BAR.

'RELATION BETWEEN PARENTS AND CHILDREN.

§ 101.

'The purely personal relation between parents and legitimate children is, like the personal relation of the spouses, and under the same limitation that no one can make effectual in any country rights which are there regarded as contrary to morality, or public decency and order,[21] to be judged according to the law of the domicile of the parties concerned.[22]

'PATERNAL POWER—ITS CONSTITUTION BY BIRTH—LEGITIMATION.

§ 102.

'The question whether a child is born in wedlock, and is thus subject to the paternal power, must be judged by the laws of the place

[20] Wening-Ingenheim, *Lehrbuch des gemeinen Civilrechts*, § 22; Mühlenbruch, *D. P.* § 72.

[21] *E.g.* the right of parents to chastise. Wächter, ii. p. 188.

[22] Argentræus, No. 7; Phillips, *D. Privatrecht* (Berlin 1846), § 24, p. 189. The actual domicile, not the domicile at the birth of the child, determines as to the religious education of the children; yet, in case of doubt, a permanent determination obtained according to the laws of the earlier domicile, must be maintained also at a new domicile, although contracts as to the religion in which the children are to be brought up may be null, according to the laws of the new domicile. This is unquestionable in Hanover, according to the analogy of the transitory provisions in the ordinance of 31st July 1826 (*G. S. I.* p. 174). As to the laws of different states on this subject, see Fœlix, ii. p. 497; Unger, *Œsterr. Privatrecht*, p. 195. Cf. Savigny, *supra*, p. 250. The relation of servant and master follows the rules of the law of obligations.

at which the father had his domicile at the time of his child's birth;[23] for the place of the marriage is here of no importance.

'The effect of the various presumptions which exist as to paternity, is to be determined according to the same laws; they are not rules for the persuasion of the judge, which are subject to the *lex fori*,[24] but actual rights of the child.[25] The reasons for this view can be assigned only in treating of the law of procedure; here we can only suggest how hazardous it would be if the child could not rely for the evidence of his legitimacy on the presumptions which were decisive at the time of his birth, or if different judgments should be pronounced in different countries as to legitimacy.

'If a particular form is required for the acknowledgment of a natural child, the rule *locus regit actum* takes effect, so far as the intention to recognise the child comes into consideration, which may certainly in some circumstances be questionable in regard to an act essentially belonging to the law of the domicile of the person making the recognition.[26]

'The legitimation of natural children, whether by subsequent marriage or by an act of the sovereign power (*rescriptum principis*), is nothing but the legal equalization of certain illegitimate children with the lawful children. That positive law, therefore, which determines as to the rights of the lawful children, must be the rule also for the legitimation of natural children; and as the former are subject to the laws of their father's actual domicile, so this is to be judged by the laws of that domicile[27] which the father has at the time of the event constituting the legitimation.[28]

'Some writers have adopted the view that the time of birth alone determines the question, because birth itself confers on the child,

[23] Bouhier, ch. 24, No. 122; Günther, p. 732; Walter, § 46; Gand, No. 430 ff.; Savigny, p. 338; Unger, *Œsterr. Pr. R.* p. 195; Burge, i. 89; Fœlix, i. No. 33, p. 79.

[24] Burge, i. 88, is of a different opinion.

[25] See Bar, *infra*, § 123. Bouhier and Fœlix adopt this view. Even Burge admits that the so-called *præsumptiones juris et de jure*, such as that of the *Code Civil*, art. 314, to rebut which no proof, however strong, is admissible, are not mere rules for determining the force of the evidence on the mind of the judge.

[26] Gand, No. 436. A child begotten and born of foreigners in France may avail himself, in proving his legitimacy, of an *Acte de Naissance* executed in France, and also of the kind of evidence competent in his own country. Fœlix, *l.c.* and No. 73, Demangeat.

[27] The place where the subsequent marriage of the parents is entered into is of no importance. See Wheaton, i. 111, and the authors cited below.

[28] If the child has acquired a special domicile or a nationality of his own, legitimation cannot take place against his will (or that of his guardians), unless it must necessarily be submitted to by the laws of his special domicile. Gand, No. 446. It is otherwise in regard to the rights of the mother. Here, as a proof of the birth is possible, the will of the child is immaterial as to the leading of this proof. Gand, No. 458.

finally and conclusively, the quality or capacity of being legitimated in a particular way, or of not being legitimated at all (die Eigenschaft ob und wie es gültig legitimirt werden könne),[29] or, as it has been said, because the birth of the child itself founds a certain legal relation between him and the father, which must be judged only according to the positive laws under which it has originated.[30] But although the birth of the natural child may impose certain obligations on the man who has had carnal connection with the mother before the birth,—and to this extent the birth of the child originates a legal relation between him and the reputed father,—yet that is precisely the meaning of illegitimate birth, and the matter with which alone we have here to do; that is, the existence of a *family relation* to the father is denied. From the purely arbitrary expression, 'capacity or incapacity of the child to be legitimated,' nothing can be inferred. One might with equal justice assert that, if the law, at the place of birth, forbids marriage between first cousins, and the child is thus declared incapable of such a marriage, he cannot, in consequence of his original incapacity, even after the acquisition of another domicile the laws of which contain no such prohibition, contract such a union with a person domiciled there. Neither can it be argued that, according to the view we have taken, the father may choose, before entering into the marriage with the mother of the child, a domicile disadvantageous to the latter. For on the one side the legitimation depends on the voluntary recognition of the father;[31] and on the other side, *if* a recognition of the child, made at a previous domicile, has actually given a right conditional on the subsequent celebration of a marriage, this right is not lost, according to our view of the law, by the transference of the domicile;[32] for

29 Merlin, *Quest. de Dr.* art. Légitimation, § 1; Story, § 93. Cf. Burge, i. 102, 106, 107. It appears, however, that the English decisions there referred to depend, not on this principle, but on the circumstance to be illustrated below, note 35. The decision of the Court of Caen, Nov. 18, 1852, given by Demangeat (Fœlix, i. 97, n. 6), that the child of an Englishman and a Frenchwoman born in England is not legitimized by a subsequent marriage of its parents, is not, as it is there stated, at variance with the view here adopted; it would only be so if the Englishman had afterwards got himself naturalized in France.

30 Schäffner, pp. 50, 51, *ante*, p. 257.

31 Savigny, *ante*, p. 250.

32 It is not quite exact to say that the domicile of the father at the time of the marriage shall decide (Savigny, *ante*, p. 250; Walter, § 45; Unger, i. p. 197). The decision given in Schäffner, pp. 51, 52, may be reconciled with the view here adopted, but not with that which takes the domicile at the time of the marriage as the criterion. According to the view of the text, the child may avail himself of the laws of that one among several successive domiciles of the father which are most favourable to him. But the fact of birth *per se* constitutes no *family rights* in the child against the father. Savigny (*supra*, p. 250, *c*) observes as to the Allgem. Preuss. Landrecht: 'The Prussian law certainly regards the proof of mere concubitus

although the laws of the new domicile do not assign the same effect to a recognition made within their territory, yet they will by no means refuse to a declaration emitted under the authority of other laws the efficacy which originally belonged to it.

'The effect of legitimation when it has taken place by the law of the domicile, must extend also to the succession to immoveables situated abroad,[33] so far as this depends only on the question whether the child is to be regarded as legitimate.[34] The decisions of the English courts[35] differ from this doctrine; and notwithstanding that they adopt the view, that a child who is not legitimate by the law of the domicile is excluded, irrespective of the laws of the *locus rei sitæ*, from claiming, as a legitimate child, the succession to immoveables, they yet require for such successions that the child shall be held legitimate also according to the *lex loci rei sitæ*.[36] These decisions are explained in the following manner: The English law gives no action against the father for recognition or acknowledgment even to the legitimate child: the illegitimate child recognised by the father has against him the same rights as a legitimate child,[37] and the legitimacy of the child who has been acknowledged by his father comes under consideration only as a prejudicial point in questions of succession. The exclusion of acknowledged children born out of wedlock does not therefore rest (as *e.g.* in the modern common Roman law) upon the legal uncertainty, only removeable by legitimation, whether the children are really the offspring of the alleged father, but on the imperfect capacity for rights which exists in the

within a certain time before the birth as evidence of paternity (*A. L. R.* ii. 1, p. 1077). Yet in the case of legitimation it makes the rights of legitimacy begin with the solemnization of the marriage (*A. L. R.* ii. 2, p. 598). Hence, according to the spirit of the Landrecht, legitimation cannot be admitted if the father changes his domicile before the solemnization of the marriage, into a country where the common law prevails, and then refuses to acknowledge the child.

[33] Schäffner, p. 53; Bouhier, chap. 24, No. 123; Günther, p. 732; Hommel, *Rhaps. Quæst.* ii. obs. 409, No. 3; Hert, iv. 14; Boullenois, i. pp. 62, 63, 130, 131.

[34] Story is in favour of this opinion, §§ 87 *a*, 105; and Lord Brougham (in Story, § 93, No. 93). Cf. judgment of the Supreme Court of Appeal at Oldenburg, 5 March 1853, Seuffert, vi. 433, 434: 'What children are to be held as legitimate, and what as validly legitimated, is determined by the laws as to legitimation existing at the time of birth. But the laws of the domicile of the deceased decide as to succession of legitimated children, as well as that of children born in wedlock.'

[35] Burge, i. 109, adopts the principle of these decisions. 'The personal quality or status of the person, if it constitutes his title to succeed to real property, must be that which the *lex loci vel rei sitæ* has prescribed.'

[36] Story, 87, *a*.

[37] Burge, i. 90; Blackstone, i, 451; Stephen, ii. 269. In respect of the succession to moveables also, the bastard is held as *filius nullius*; but the Crown can make a special disposition. Stephen, ii. 187.

case of illegitimate children [38] in the older German law, and in many *Lehnrechte*. Just as one in his native country, if such a *Lehnrecht* prevails there, cannot claim the succession to a fief (Lehn) in virtue of the legitimation conferred on him by his own sovereign, which is complete and conclusive for all other relations; so the foreigner, who has no greater capacity for rights than the native Englishman, is not entitled to acquire landed property in England, since principles of feudal law have there absolute authority in regard to land.[39] That one whom the *lex domicilii* declares incapable cannot, irrespective of the English law, succeed *ab intestato* to landed property in England, is explained by the fact, that in such a case the *lex domicilii* denies the relationship between the ancestor and the descendant; and relationship must be judged according to the *lex domicilii*, and is the ground and condition of succession to immoveables in England.

'The imperfect capacity for rights which in the middle ages, and afterwards even in modern times, often attached to those born illegitimate, illustrates also the opinion of the older writers, which confined the effect of the legitimation bestowed *per rescriptum principis* to the territory of the granter,[40] especially as the legitimation, even within the dominions of the prince who conferred it, had only the effect that the succession of the *legitimatus* was not confiscated by that prince, and passed to the relatives, by dispensing with the older German rules of law, which permitted bastards neither to inherit nor (within a certain limit) to leave an inheritance.[41] In most territorial

[38] The exception which the English law makes in the case of a *Bastard puis né* is only referable to principles of equity.

[39] Cf. above, § 27, for the principles as to the capacity for rights. The reasons assigned in England for this decision are not conclusive, as indeed Lord Brougham has shown. In particular the words of the *Statute of Merton*, which is appealed to on this point, and which requires birth 'in lawful wedlock,' only lay down generally the requisite of legitimacy. And in like manner, it cannot be argued that we are here dealing with a prohibitive law, because confessedly there are even prohibitive laws which are without cavil enumerated among the personal statutes. A similar decision to that given in England is found in Molinæus, *ad Consuet. Paris.* § 8, gl. 1, Nos. 36, 46; and Bouhier, ch. 24, No. 123 ff., for the case in which a statute calls to the succession only children 'nés en loyal mariage.'

[40] Alb. Brun. *De Statut.* art. xiii. § 51 ff.: 'Et ideo differt (legitimatus) a legitimo tanquam imago ab eo, cuius imaginem repræsentat. Et propterea, Salycetus dixit, quod legitimatio non facit esse essentialiter legitimum.' Bald. Ubald. in *L.* 1, *C. de S. Trin.* No. 75; Chassenæus *in consuet. Burgund. Rubr.* ix. *in tit. des mains mortes, verb. va demeurer*, Nos. 17, 18; P. Voet, iv. 3, § 15; Argentræus, No. 20; J. Voet, *de Stat.* § 7; Bartol. *ad L.* 1, *C. de S. Trin.*; Alef, No. 59; Cocceji, *de Fund.* v. § 7, 8; Boullenois, *I. S.* 64. Cf. Bouhier, ch. 24, No. 129.

[41] Chassenæus, *l.c. Rubr.* viii. *in tit. des Successions de Bastards, verb. ab intestat.* Nos. 32, 41, 250; Mynsinger, *Observ. Cent.* iii. obs. 26, Nos. 7, 8, 11; Gerber, *D. Pr. R.* § 39.

laws in modern times[42] illegitimate birth no longer creates a diminution of the capacity for rights, and lawful birth only bestows the concrete rights depending on relationship. Even, therefore, if we extend the efficacy of a legitimation granted by rescript to the succession to foreign immoveables, it would be erroneous to speak of legitimation in this manner, as if the sovereign disposed of landed property not situated in his own dominions;[43] and as a foreigner is illegitimate among us when he is so by the law of his domicile, he must also be held to be legitimate when the law of his domicile declares him to be legitimate.[44] On the other hand, legitimation so conferred in a state of which the father is not a subject, can constitute no rights of relationship as against him.[45] If the child has a different domicile from the father, then, in order to establish the rights of the latter as against the child, legitimation must be admissible also according to the law to which the child is subject.[46] But this condition flies off when the child (of course under the sanction of guardians) removes to the domicile of the father.'

Heffter.

Heffter, like most other writers on public international law (*Das Europäische Völkerrecht der Gegenwart*, 4th ed. Berlin 1861), treats only cursorily of the conflict of laws. In his chapter on Municipal Law (§ 37, p. 73) he lays down the principle, that 'every legal relation which has sprung up under the sanction of a competent state is an accomplished fact for every one; only no state is thereby obliged to allow to that fact the same effects as the other state allows or determines.' Each may fix, by positive law, the consequences of particular legal relations within its own territory at its own discretion. If, however, it does not lay down such a positive rule, it is to be assumed that it intends a legal relation originating abroad to have its original force and effect. 'But never can a legal relation be forced

[42] Except in regard to *Lehnrechte*. Cf. Gerber, § 110.

[43] Several of the writers quoted in note 40 adduce this argument.

[44] Schäffner, p. 55; Wening-Ingenheim, § 22; Mühlenbruch, § 72; Günther, p. 732; Hommel, *Rhaps. Qu.* ii. obs. 409, No. 3; Supr. Court of Appeal at Kiel, 2 Feb. 1853 (Seuffert, 7, 399). 'The legal efficacy of a legitimation granted by a foreign sovereign extends also to the foreign estate of the deceased.' One who is legitimated at his domicile *per rescriptum principis* must therefore be held as legitimated in France also, although the *Code Civil* does not recognise a legitimation *per rescriptum*. (Cf. *Code Civil*, art. 331–333; Zachariä, *Civilrecht*, iii. § 370.)

[45] Judgment of the Cour d'Appel de Paris, 11 Feb. 1808 (Sirey, 8. 2, p. 86). Such a legitimation certainly confers a complete capacity for rights as to all legal relations pertaining to the territory of the sovereign who grants it, if the bastard enjoys there only an imperfect capacity for rights.

[46] Cf. above, note 29.

upon another state which that state reprobates;[47] never can a legal relation be made to operate to effects which are repugnant to the legal system of the country,[48] or to effects which are only permitted to its own domestic relations; *never is the mere legal fiction of one state obligatory for another which does not possess such a fiction*,[49] although indeed further legal relations, which have already originated abroad on the basis of such a fiction, cannot be denied effect so far as they actually exist.[50] But it can by no means be maintained that the very existence and conditions of a legal relation which has sprung up in a foreign independent state, are to be judged entirely according to its own law by every other state where the consequences of it come into question. A state would thus give to its own law an ultra-territorial, and even a retroactive force.'

See further on this subject, Thibaut, *Versuche*, i. No. 10; Jordæus, *Diss. duæ de legit.* in Fellenberg, *Jur. Ant.* ii. No. 17; *Shaw* v *Gould* (*in re Wilson's Trusts*), 35 L. J. 243, H. of L. 37 L. J. Ch. 433; *Goodman* v *Goodman*, 2 K. and J. 595; *In re Wright's Trusts*, 2 K. and J. 597; *In re Don's Estate*, 27. L. J. Ch. 7. 98, 4 Dr. 194.

SECT. XXXVIII.—(§ 381.)

VI. FORMS OF JURIDICAL ACTS—(*LOCUS REGIT ACTUM*).

After the foregoing examination of the several legal relations with respect to the local law applicable to them, the exposition of a special rule of law still remains. This rule must be spoken of separately and at the close of the whole inquiry, because it is applicable to the most numerous and most important of the legal relations which have been discussed.

[47] Thus no Mussulman can appeal in a Christian state to the law of polygamy in his own country as warranting him in entering into a polygamous connection. No foreigner divorced *quoad vinculum* in his domicile, can contract another valid marriage in a state which repudiates this kind of divorce.

[48] Thus *e.g.* the paternal power of a foreigner over his children must be modified according to the laws of his residence.

[49] *E.g.* no judicial declaration of death (Todeserklärung) can supply the place of actual proof of death for other states, which have not this institution at all, or have it in another form; *no legitimation of a natural child can come in place of the proof of legitimacy requisite in another state.* [Are these not questions of evidence, as here stated, and *therefore* in this country governed by the *lex fori?*]

[50] *E.g.* a succession, which has already taken effect, to the rights of one judicially declared dead (eines Todterklärten).

It relates to the positive forms of expressing intention that are often prescribed for juridical acts (*a*). In this matter, collisions between different local laws occur very frequently and in many ways. One law may prescribe a positive form as necessary, another may require no such form; or forms may be required by both laws, but different forms. In all such cases the question arises: What local law is applicable to the particular legal act in respect of its form? From this alone, in many instances, is the validity or invalidity of the act to be discovered.

If we consider this question from the general point of view, from which the whole foregoing inquiry has been conducted, we can hardly hesitate as to the answer. We must, as it seems, judge of the requisite form according to that local law to which the juridical act is itself subject according to the rules already laid down. Thus, in this view, contracts must be made according to the statutory forms of the stipulated place of fulfilment; testaments according to the forms which prevail at the domicile of the testator; marriages contracted according to the forms required at the domicile of the husband. The observance of this rule is subject neither to doubt nor to difficulty, if the juridical act is performed at one of these places. But it very often happens that the preparatory arrangements for the act take place at another and, it may be, a very distant place; and this circumstance may result in the greatest difficulties.

At the place where the juridical act is to be completed, it will often be very difficult to discover with certainty the legal forms of that other place which properly regulates, or, if they are known, to apply them practically; indeed, this will often be quite impossible, as must be apparent in the following example:—If a Prussian becomes ill in France, and wishes to make a will, he must, according to the rule provisionally laid down, obtain the co-operation of a court of law, because the Prussian law recognises none but judicial testaments. But in France no court has authority to take part in making a testament, since such matters are only competent to notaries (*b*). Hence every Prussian would be obliged altogether to abstain from making a will, perhaps to the great disadvantage of his family.

(*a*) As to the nature of these forms, see above, vol. iii. §§ 130, 131.
(*b*) *Code Civil*, arts. 971–979.

The great hardship of these circumstances is obvious. Juridical acts sometimes become impossible, and still oftener incur the risk of invalidity from imperfect execution; and all in consequence of forms imposed by positive law, certainly not for the purpose of hampering and hindering the ordinary course of civil affairs. This consideration has, since the sixteenth century, introduced with ever increasing consent[1] a universal consuetudinary law, which takes the place of the provisional rule above stated, and removes the difficulties that attend it. This new rule is thus expressed: *Locus regit actum;* and it means that the form of a juridical act shall be considered satisfactory, if it be in accordance with the law of the place where the act is done, even if another form is prescribed by the law of the place where the legal relation itself has its seat. This rule is unanimously acknowledged by the writers of various periods and nations (*c*).

We have now to consider more minutely the application of this important rule to the various kinds of legal relations. From the general form of expression employed, it might readily be supposed that it is applicable to all relations, and that it is in all of equally important and frequent use. More accurate consideration, however, will in some measure restrict this notion.

I. Hardly any application of the rule will take place where the status of the person is concerned; for the mere expression of will, to the legal form of which alone the rule refers, has here little influence. Thus it would be quite a mistake to suppose that a minor could attain majority, or an infamous person be rehabilitated in a foreign country by a declaration of the supreme authority in that country, according to the rule *locus regit actum*. For these changes of status are not wrought by any expression of will by the party interested, for the form of which only it is necessary to provide. They can arise only from a voluntary resolution of the supreme power in the

[1] Bar, § 34, shows that the customary reception of this rule was considerably earlier than the sixteenth century. He also traces its origin to the custom of authenticating contracts and other legal acts in a judicial manner, and the maxim, 'Acta facta coram uno judice fidem faciunt apud alium.'

(*c*) P. Voet, sect. 9, c. 2, § 9; J. Voet, §§ 13-15; Hert, §§ 10, 23; Eichhorn, *Deutsches Recht*, § 37; Story, §§ 260, 261; Fœlix, p. 97 foll. [ed. Demangeat, i. 149]; Schäffner, §§ 73-85; Wächter, ii. pp. 368-380, and p. 405 foll.; [Bar, § 35 n. 2, where many other authors are cited.]

state, and of that power to which the party interested is subject.

II. Neither can this rule have any important influence on juridical acts relating to the law of things, and that for the following reason:—It will be remembered that a very thorough-going distinction in the acts of men was noticed above for a different purpose (p. 155). There are acts which are everywhere equally possible, so that it depends only on accidental circumstances whether they are done in one place or in another. Among these are obligatory contracts, the execution of a will, etc. There are, however, other acts which, by their very nature, can be done only at one place. Among these are the most numerous and important acts belonging to the law of things. In that department the *lex rei sitæ* always governs (§ 366), and the acts, so rich in consequences, that fall within it are generally so intimately connected with the thing itself on which they operate, that they can only be conceived as taking place where it is situated. Of these acts the chief is tradition (delivery); and there are also a variety of merely formal acts—such as judicial cession, recording in the registers of hypothecs, etc.—which can only be done before a public officer fixed at a particular place. The rule *locus regit actum* applies, by its very nature, only to acts of the first kind, because only in these can the place where the act is done chance to be different from the true seat of the legal relation, and thereby require such an artificial expedient. But for the same reason it is not applicable to the most numerous and important acts concerning the law of things. Nor is this remark confined to immoveable things, but it is true as to moveables also, in which tradition is likewise impossible except at the place where they are. But in the case of moveable things this circumstance is less important and less prominent, because the possessor can at any time change their place at his own pleasure, so that they are at once subjected to a new *lex rei sitæ*.

The reason why the rule does not apply to real rights is therefore essentially the same with that which operates in regard to the status of the person. It is that in real rights it is not the will in itself that determines, but everything depends on the relation in which the person stands to the thing as the object of the real right. This relation then may, according to the terms of many positive laws, consist in a mere declaration of intention; but that circumstance is in itself accidental, and alien to the essence of the real right.

III. There is nothing to prevent the most extensive application of our rule to obligations, and particularly to obligatory contracts (*d*), although this kind of application is less frequently spoken of. Some examples will illustrate this.

In many positive laws special forms are required for obligatory contracts as to immoveables (which contracts are quite distinct from the transference of property), while the Roman law knows nothing of such forms. According to our rule, then, there is no doubt that the validity of such an act must depend on the law of the place where the contract is made, without respect to the *lex rei sitæ*.[2] I notice this case specially, in order to observe that the Prussian law expressly requires the contrary (*e*). Here, therefore, there is a decided exception to the rule *locus regit actum*, purposely and knowingly enacted.

The authority of merchants' books as evidence is to be judged according to the law of the place where the books are kept (*f*). Their probativeness, indeed, appears to belong to the law of process, and hence to be properly subject to the *lex fori*. But here it is inseparably connected with the form and effect of the juridical act itself, which must here be regarded as the preponderating element. The foreigner who deals with a merchant belonging to a place where mercantile books are probative, subjects himself to its local law.

(*d*) Wächter, ii. p. 405.

[2] *Govan* v *Boyd*, 1790, Bell's Ca. 223. For a full discussion of the rule, see *Earl of Hopetoun* v *Scots Mining Co.*, 1856, 18 D. 739.

(*e*) *Allg. Landrecht*, i. 5, § 115: 'In all cases in which immoveable things —their property, possession, or use—are the object of a contract, the laws of the place where the thing is situated must be observed in respect of the form;' but the Prussian law requires writing in all contracts as to land, which is not indeed said expressly, but follows undoubtedly from i. 5, § 135, i. 10, §§ 15-17, i. 21, § 233, and also from the fact that the object of such contracts will almost always be worth more than fifty thalers (i. 5, § 131). On the other hand, the maxim *locus regit actum* is the rule for contracts in general (i. 5, § 111); and this rule is recognised in regard to contracts as to moveables entered into out of the country, even if the action is before Prussian courts: i. 5, § 148.

(*f*) Judgment of Ober-Apellationsgericht at Cassel, 1826; Seuffert, *Archiv*, vol. i. No. 132. [See *contra*, *Leroux* v *Brown*, 12 C. B. 801; Phillimore, iv. 440 sqq.; Westlake, § 171 sqq.; Kent's *Com.* ii. 459; Sugden, *Law of Vendors and Purchasers*, 128, 139 (14th ed.).]

The formal validity of every signature on a bill is judged by the law of the place where that signature is affixed (*g*).

IV. The most important, and from an early period the most generally discussed, application of our rule, is that which relates to the making of a will, when the testator happens to be away from his domicile. On this question, as far as concerns the rule itself, there has long been a general concurrence (*h*).

There are, however, two deviations from this application of the rule. In the countries subject to English law, the rule is indeed held to govern, but yet the testament is not effectual as to immoveables situated abroad (*i*). The distinction between moveable and immoveable estate appears, however, to have still less meaning and reason in regard to the application of this rule than in other respects. A modern writer adds the following limitation: The will shall be valid if the testator dies abroad; but if he returns home, it loses its validity, at least in the case in which this kind of testament is unknown in the law of his own country (*k*). I do not think that this restriction can be justified on principle, and it seems to have met with no approbation from other writers. Yet a prudent father of a family would certainly do well to make a new will on his return home, in order to be quite secure against every possible future objection on this ground.

V. It is generally admitted that our rule applies to the constitution of marriage (*l*). Yet the matter seems to me not free from doubt. If the inhabitants of a country, the law of which requires merely juridical (civil) forms for the constitution of a marriage, enter into a marriage abroad, the matter is subject to no doubt. But it is different with the inhabitants of a country the law of which connects marriage with the eccle-

(*g*) Judgment of Revisionshof at Berlin, 1844; Seuffert, *Archiv*, vol. ii. No. 121.

(*h*) Rodenburg, tit. 2, c. 3, §§ 1-3; Vinnius, *Selectæ Quæst.* ii. 19; Hert, § 23; Wächter, ii. pp. 368-380. In the time of Durantis the question was still much controverted. *Speculum*, ii., *tit. de instrum. edit.* § 12, *Num.* 16.

(*i*) Story, §§ 474, 478. [See M'Laren, *Law of Wills and Succession*, vol. i. pp. 26-28; 31 and 32 Vict. c. 101, § 20 sqq.; Jarman, *On Wills*, p. 1; Burge, iv. 218 sqq.; *Bremer* v *Freeman*, 10 Moo. P. C. 312; *Purvis' Trs.* v *Purvis' Exrs.*, 23 D. 812; 24 and 25 Vict. c. 114.]

(*k*) Eichhorn, *Deutsches Recht*, § 37.

(*l*) Hert, § 10; Schäffner, §§ 100, 101; Story, § 121 foll. It is remarkable that the theory and practice of the English law seems to be singularly correct on this point.

siastical ceremony. For such a law has a basis in religion and morality, and is therefore of a coercitive nature (§ 349). For this reason I would hold the repetition of the ceremony in the country to which the parties belong to be necessary,—not, however, because it must be presumed that the spouses had concluded their marriage abroad *in fraudem legis*, which purpose may not have existed at all, or at least may not be susceptible of proof. If, however, the marriage ceremony is repeated, then, even according to the principles of the common law, the marriage must be regarded as valid and effectual during the intermediate period. This stricter principle, however, can in no case be applied to the subsisting marriage of persons who immigrate into such a country. For a law to such an effect, with its coercitive nature, affects only the constitution of marriages, not the continuance of those already subsisting.

In conclusion, some general observations are still to be added.

Many have maintained that our rule does not hold if a transaction is effected abroad in order to evade domestic laws (*in fraudem legis*),—for instance, to avoid greater expense connected with the juridical act, the use of stamped paper, etc. (*m*). Others have rightly rejected this restriction (*n*). Such evasions can be guarded against by other means; in particular, by fines. There is no sufficient reason for making the validity of legal acts depend on such a question, and, at all events, it would require a positive law to produce this result.

A very important question concerns the proper position of this rule: Is the observance of the form in use at the place of the act unconditionally necessary, or is it merely facultative, so that the person doing it has the choice either to observe this form, or that of the place to which the juridical act properly belongs (*o*)? If we look to the reason for introducing our

(*m*) J. Voet, § 14; Fœlix, p. 105 [ed. Demangeat, i. 161].

(*n*) Schäffner, § 85. [On this subject, see Lord Meadowbank in *Utterton* v *Tewsh*, Ferg. *Con. Rep.* 63 sqq.; Westlake, § 343; and especially the raciest and ablest of controversial law tracts, Fraser's *Conflict of Laws in Divorce Cases*, p. 43 sq. (Edin. 1860); *Geils* v *Geils*, 1 Macq. 275; *Warrender* v *Warrender*, 2 S. and M'L. 154, 219; *Shaw* v *Gould*, H. of L., 37 L. J. Ch. 433, 3 L. R. Ap. 55.]

(*o*) Thus only can the question be stated so as to avoid the supposition of an entirely arbitrary choice between the *lex domicilii*, *rei sitæ*, etc. So, however, J. Voet, § 15, seems to view it.

special rule as a mere measure of favour and assistance, we cannot hesitate to hold it as merely facultative, and therefore to allow an election. This also is generally acknowledged (*p*).

If, therefore, the inhabitant of a country subject to the Roman law desires to make a will at Paris, he can use one of the various forms of the French law; but he can also make the testament before seven witnesses. In this last case also the testament is valid in his own country, on the supposition, of course, that evidence of the observance of the proper form is not wanting. If inhabitants of a country where the ecclesiastical ceremony is required enter into a marriage in a country that prescribes a juridical form, and not a religious ceremony, and if they there get themselves married in the religious form without observing the juridical form of the country, the marriage is valid, because they have used the form of their own country, the natural and permanent seat of the marriage (*q*).

SECT. XXXIX.—(§ 382.)

VI. FORMS OF JURIDICAL ACTS—(*LOCUS REGIT ACTUM*).

(CONTINUATION.)

Hitherto the special rule of law as to the form of legal acts has been considered from the standpoint of a universal customary law, which has sprung from an acknowledged want, and has been further developed by jurists. The question is still to be answered: What position does positive legislation occupy towards that rule? First, that which is the foundation of the common law (Roman and canon law), and then some modern legislations.

Some writers have attempted to derive the rule from the

(*p*) Rodenburg, tit. 2, c. 3, §§ 2, 3; Hert, §§ 10, 23 (somewhat undecided); Fœlix, p. 107 foll. [ed. Demangeat, i. 163 sq.]; Schäffner, § 83 (undecided); Wächter, ii. pp. 377-380. [Bar, § 36; Heffter, p. 76, note; *Purves' Trs.* v *Purves' Exrs.*, 1861, 23 D. 812; Westlake, § 323 sqq.]

(*q*) Recognised in a judgment of the Ober-Apellationsgericht at Dresden, 1845. Seuffert, *Archiv*, vol. ii. No. 5.

sources of the written common law; others have rightly remarked that this attempt has failed (*a*). A review of the passages cited for the rule will confirm this opinion, without in any degree detracting from the truth and certainty of the rule itself.

1. *L.* 9, *C. de testamentis* (6, 23).—This is the most specious of the passages, and yet it does not establish the rule.

It was the case of a testament made without observing the well-known rule of the Roman law, by which the witnesses must be in the immediate presence of the testator (*b*). To a question of Patroclia (probably the instituted heiress) the emperor answers in a rescript, that the testament was null, 'si non speciali privilegio (*c*) *patriæ tuæ* juris observatio relaxata est.' An apparent argument for referring this passage to the rule of law now being considered is found in the words 'patriæ tuæ,' which seem to indicate a collision between different local laws. But this semblance disappears when we reflect that the *patria* of the heiress could not possibly be decisive: it is not said where the testament was made. Probably the deceased had tested at his domicile, which was also the home of the heiress. Thus the application of the rule is not at all in question, but the passage simply contains the unquestionable proposition, that in collision the particular prevails over the common law.

2. *L.* 2, *C. quemadm. test. aper.* (6, 23).—A father, who was absent from his domicile, had before his death delivered a testament to his son, with the injunction to carry it to the domicile. The emperors decide in a rescript, that with respect to the opening of the testament before the municipal *curia*, the laws and customs of that place must be observed. Here there is no question of a collision of territorial laws, but only the undoubted proposition is expressed, that in a judicial act the law of its place shall be observed.

3. *L.* 1, *C. de emanc.* (8, 49).—A man had emancipated his

(*a*) Wächter, i. p. 246.

(*b*) *L.* 9, *cit.* 'in conspectu testatoris;' *L.* 30, *Cod. eod.* 'sub præsentia ipsius testatoris;' *L.* 3, *C. Th. de test.* (4, 4), 'præsentes videant subscriptores.' Comp. Glück, vol. xxxiv. p. 292.

(*c*) *Privilegium* is here a municipal constitution (Stadtrecht), or part of a municipal constitution, bestowed by an imperial *constitution* on the town here in question.

son before the *duumviri* of a town to which he did not belong, and the validity of this act was questioned. The doubt arose from the fact that, as a rule, the municipal magistrates had no *legis actio*, but could only obtain it exceptionally by *privilegium* (*d*). The emperors reply in a rescript, that the validity of the act depends on the rules of the municipal law. If this gives the *legis actio* to the *duumviri*, and that to such an extent that they can exercise it even as to strangers, the act is valid. There is here no trace of a collision of local laws.

4. *C.* 1, *X. de spons.* (4, 1). A Saxon had married a Frenchwoman, and in so doing had observed, not the Saxon, but the French usage. After he had lived with her many years, and had children by her, he availed himself of the flaw in the constitution of the marriage, repudiated the woman, and married another. An ecclesiastical assembly declared this conduct culpable, the attempted second marriage null, and ordained the restitution of the former marriage. Here, again, there is no mention of a collision of local laws, and in particular the place where the marriage was entered into is not mentioned at all. The decision is founded on this reason, that by the doctrine of the canon law the first marriage was valid and indissoluble, and that in regard to it the observance of this or that custom of the civil law must be considered quite immaterial.

In the draught of the French code there was the following proposition: 'La forme des actes est reglée par les loix du lieu dans lequel ils sont faits ou passés.' This passage was omitted in the code itself, not because it was held to be false or questionable, but just for the opposite reason, that it seemed so certain and well known that its mention was superfluous (*e*). In the following applications our rule of law is presupposed.

1. If a Frenchman or a stranger performs an *acte de l'état civil* in a foreign country according to the forms in use there, that *acte* must be regarded as valid in France also (*f*).

2. Natives of France can contract a valid marriage abroad according to the usual forms of the place where they happen

(*d*) Savigny, *Geschichte des R. R. im Mittelalter*, vol. i. § 27.
(*e*) Fœlix, p. 111 [ed. Demangeat, i. 168].
(*f*) *Code Civil*, art. 47.

to be (*g*). The laws as to the preceding proclamation of banns, and as to the conditions of a valid marriage, are not affected by this provision.

3. A Frenchman who desires to make a will in a foreign country can do this in either of two ways: either by holograph writing and signature (as in France), or by *acte authentique*, according to the forms in use at the place where the testament is made (*h*).

The Prussian law contains no general recognition of the rule *locus regit actum*. The Allgemeine Landrecht (Intr. § 33) has a merely apparent deviation from the rule. This passage does not mean that foreigners may not observe the forms introduced by a particular statute, or that an act so done would not be valid; but that only subjects, not foreigners, are bound to observe the statute (*i*).

In regard to contracts, it recognises this rule, and it gives it universal force in respect of moveable things. As to immoveables, however, it makes an exception, and requires the exclusive observance of the form directed by the *lex rei sitæ* (§ 381, *e*).

The Landrecht has no direction at all as to the forms of testaments made abroad. Hence a recent writer concludes that the general rule which requires the judicial testament must be held the sole standard, and that the rule *locus regit actum* cannot here apply (*k*); which is as much as to say, that a Prussian, in many foreign countries, *e.g.* in France, can make no will at all. I must utterly deny this assertion, for the following reasons: When the Allgemeine Landrecht was composed, the rule *locus regit actum* was one of the best known and most certain propositions among the German jurists, especially in reference to testaments. But it is very unlikely that there should have been any intention to set aside a rule of such a character by mere silence.

In the year 1823 a new form of testaments was introduced

(*g*) *Code Civil*, art. 170.

(*h*) *Code Civil*, art. 999; cf. art. 1317.

(*i*) The ambiguity is in the words, 'are established only for acts,' etc.; that is, are established as obligatory only for such acts. For they are admissible and effectual in their application for foreigners also.

(*k*) Koch, *Preussisches Recht*, § 40, note 18.

for the convenience of persons attached to Prussian embassies in foreign countries (*l*). This provision proclaims itself by its substance and expression, as well as by the preamble of the law, to be a quite new positive rule. The following introductory passage, however, precedes it:

§ 1. (The testamentary appointments of our ambassadors . . . . . shall be valid in their external form, *in future as in the past* (auch ferner wie bisher), if they conform to the laws of the place where they are made).

I ask, then, What mean the words, *in future as in the past ?* The Landrecht contains nothing at all as to the form of testaments made abroad. On the other hand, the rule we are now discussing was part of the common law of Germany from an early period, and that not specially for ambassadors, but for all subjects of the country who wished to make wills abroad. The meaning of the whole passage is therefore as follows: Ambassadors, like all other inhabitants, can test abroad according to the forms of the place where they reside. This right, then, which they already share with all other subjects, they are to be allowed to exercise *in future as in the past* (§ 1). For their convenience, however, a new form of testaments is introduced, and left to their free choice, along with the older form (§ 2).

In the year 1824 a treaty was concluded with Weimar as to the mutual legal relations of the subjects of the two states; and a great number of treaties, in the same or very similar terms, with other neighbouring states followed upon it (§ 374, *qq*). In art. 34 of this treaty (*m*) it is said: 'All juridical acts, *inter vivos* and *in prospect of death*, shall be judged, as to their validity in point of form, according to the laws of the place where they are entered into.' This provision is evidently no mere courtesy, no concession to the neighbouring states; indeed, it is to be reciprocal. Neither was it supposed to be a new contrivance, but the expression of a universal legal principle, which follows also from the frequent repetition of the same terms. This legal principle, however, could be no other than the immemorial rule that had long prevailed all over Germany—*locus regit actum;* which therefore here receives the most unquestionable recognition on the part of our legislation.

(*l*) Law of 3d April 1823, § 2, *Gesetzsamml.* 1823, p. 40.
(*m*) *Gesetzsamml.* 1824, p. 154.

CHAPTER II.

LIMITS IN TIME OF THE AUTHORITY OF RULES OF LAW OVER LEGAL RELATIONS.

SECT. XL.—(§ 383.)

INTRODUCTION.

Writers.

CHABOT DE L'ALLIER, *Questions Transitoires sur le Code Napoleon.* Paris 1809, 2 vols. 4to.

WEBER, *über die Rückanwirkung positiver Gesetze.* Hanover 1811.

MEYER, *Principes sur les Questions Transitoires.* Amsterdam 1813.

BERGMANN, *das Verbot der Rückwirkenden kraft neuer Gesetze in Privatrecht.* Hanover 1818.

STRUVE, *über das positive Rechtsgesetz rücksichtlich seiner Ausdehnung in der Zeit.* Göttingen 1831 (*a*).

THE object of the Third Book of this system of law is to fix the territory within which the rules of law shall govern legal relations, and the limits of this territory (§ 344). Such a determination of boundaries may be necessary in two respects, according as different rules of law are contemplated as prevailing simultaneously, or in succession. Of the former case, the determination of the local limits, we have hitherto treated (Chap. I.). It still remains to ascertain the second kind of limits in time.

Let it be supposed that at the same place, at two different times, different rules of law prevail, as to which a given legal relation, or a particular question of law, stands in such a position that it is doubtful which of those two rules of law ought

(*a*) Many others are enumerated by Bergmann, pp. xxi.-xxiv.

to govern the decision of the question. Such a conflict for mastery, therefore, between two rules of law always implies the occurrence of a change. But this change, so far as it belongs to the following inquiry, must be further defined to be a change in the rules of law themselves (the objective right), not a mere change in the facts which determine the legal relation (the subjective right); for changes of the latter kind have already been discussed in connection with the local limits of the authority of the rules of law (*b*). We presuppose, therefore, in the course of the following inquiry, a legal relation, which has remained in itself unchanged, and two rules of law, different in time, which contend for authority over it.

But a change in the rules of law, as the cause and condition of all questions of collision in time, may occur in the following various forms:—

1. Promulgation of a single new law having for its object the legal relation in question.
2. Compilation of a new code, and therefore of a body of laws in which new rules are laid down for the legal relation in question (*c*).
3. Adoption of a whole foreign code instead of the previously existing law (*d*).
4. Separation of the place which is the seat of a legal relation from its former political connection, its reception into another state, and subjection to the whole law of this other state; in which case this newly adopted law may consist of a whole code, or (perhaps along with the code) of particular laws, or even of particular rules of customary law (*e*).

However different these cases may be in extent and importance, they stand in principle in the same relation to the question of collision now before us. In all of them it is possible to decide this question beforehand by special statutory rules, and

(*b*) See above, § 344 fin.

(*c*) This case occurred at Constantinople from 529 to 534, in Prussia in 1794, in France in 1804, in Austria in 1812.

(*d*) As took place with the Code Napoleon in several countries in Germany and elsewhere, under the influence of the French power.

(*e*) Important instances of this kind occurred in the cession of many countries to France; afterwards when Prussia recovered her old provinces and acquired new; but not in the cession of the left bank of the Rhine to the German States, because the French law was then retained.

in the three last cases there is special cause for doing so. Such laws are called *transitory*, because they have for their object the transition from one rule of law to another.

When Justinian promulgated the Institutions and the Digests, he gave them retroactive force (*f*). In this, however, there was no expression of a permanent principle as to retroaction, nor the establishment of a true exception, since these law-books were not intended to make new laws, but to ascertain and purify the existing law. There might be discovered in it a sort of authentic interpretation of the existing law as a whole,—an interpretation which was necessarily retroactive (§ 397).

In no legislation has so much care been bestowed on this question of collision as in the Prussian (*g*); and I will here give a view of the Prussian transitory laws, in order to be able in the sequel more easily to refer to them. The oldest of them is the patent of publication of the Allgemeine Landrecht of 5th February 1794 (*h*), which contains in §§ 8 to 18 very full transitory rules. There are, besides, the following laws by which the Prussian legislation was introduced into newly acquired provinces, or re-established in recovered provinces.

1803. Principality of Hildesheim and city of Goslar (Stengel's *Beiträge*, vol. xvii. p. 194).

1803. Paderborn and Münster (Stengel, vol. xvii. p. 235).

1803. Eichsfeld, Erfurt, Mühlhausen, Nordhausen (Stengel, vol. xvii. p. 253).

1814. Former Prussian provinces beyond the Elbe (*Ges. Samml.* 1814, p. 89).

1816. West Prussia (*Ges. Samml.* 1816, p. 217).

1816. Posen (*Ges. Samml.* 1816, p. 225).

1816. Duchy of Saxony (*Ges. Samml.* 1816, p. 233).

1818. Enklaven (*Ges. Samml.* 1818, p. 45).

1825. Duchy of Westphalia (*Ges. Samml.* 1825, p. 153).

(*f*) *L.* 2, § 23; *L.* 3, § 23, *C. de vet. j. enucl.* (1, 17). The *Const. Summa*, § 3, as to the code, is in somewhat different terms. Comp. Bergmann, § 14.

(*g*) The law introducing the Austrian code contains only a few provisions as to this matter. In the French code there are transitory rules in some particular articles (*e.g.* art. 2281); but several separate transitory laws were also promulgated at the same time as the code, especially as to adoption, divorce, natural children.

(*h*) Printed before all the editions of the Landrecht.

It is to be observed that the patents of introduction of 1803 are little more than abridged copies of the patent of 1794, while those issued since 1814 contain many peculiar and different provisions.

Sect. XLI.—(§ 384.)

TWO KINDS OF RULES OF LAW.

A principle is commonly laid down as the starting-point in this doctrine, for which universal authority is claimed, and which, though it appears in different authors under different aspects, may be reduced to the two following formulas :—

No retroactive effect is to be attributed to new laws.

New laws leave acquired rights unaffected.

Neither the truth nor the importance of this principle can be disputed. Yet the way in which it is generally understood and expounded cannot be considered satisfactory, because it is usually treated as universally authoritative; whereas it is true only for one kind of rules of law, for another entirely false. At first sight we might be disposed to attribute to this difference of opinions greater importance than it really deserves, since the treatment of the matter which is here censured might be supposed often to lead to the erroneous decision of practical questions. But it is not so. When the logical application of the alleged general principle leads to a result so important and so dangerous as to be evidently inadmissible, recourse is commonly had to exceptions from it. But it is just this expedient of mere exceptions that must be entirely rejected, as will afterwards be fully shown (§ 398). I must therefore persist in denying the universal authority commonly ascribed to the principle, although this error has less dangerous practical consequences than might be supposed.

In order to fix more accurately the limits within which the principle is really to be admitted, I must examine into the different contents of the rules of law, with the possible alterations of which we are now to be engaged (§ 383).

The first kind of rules relates to the *acquisition of rights*, that is to say, to the connection of a right with an individual person, or to the transformation of an (abstract) legal institution into a (personal) legal relation (*a*). The nature of these rules of law, and of their possible changes, may be illustrated by the following examples:—When property in any country could previously be alienated and acquired by simple contract, and a new law requires tradition for its transference, the change of the rule of law relates only to the question, under what conditions can the individual acquire property in a thing, and thus establish *his* right to it. So it is also when all obligatory contracts were competently concluded to all effects verbally, and a new law prescribes that only a written contract shall ground an action in regard to things worth more than fifty dollars.

A second kind of rules of law concerns the *existence of rights*, that is, the recognition of a legal institution in general, which must always be presupposed before there can be any question of its application to an individual person, or of the transformation of a legal institution into a legal relation. The rules of this class consist, again, of two subdivisions, which are of different extent, but of the same essential nature, and which therefore stand on the same line with regard to our present inquiry.

Some of these rules refer to the *existence* or *non-existence* (das Seyn oder Nichtseyn) of a legal institution. The following are examples:—When the Roman slavery, or German villenage, or the right of tithe, existed in a state, and a new law abolishes one of these legal institutes, declares it impossible, and thus deprives it of the protection of the law.

Another class of these rules of law does not relate to the existence or non-existence, but to the *mode of existence* (das So oder Andersseyn) of a legal institution, and thus to a profound and material change in it, while, as a whole, it is preserved. Among these are the following cases:—Instead of property with strict vindication (according to the Roman law), a new statute ordains that property shall no longer be protected by vindication, but only by possessory actions and obligations. Instead of an irredeemable tithe, a new law ordains that each party may demand the redemption of the right of tithe. To the same class belongs Justinian's well-known law as to the right of

(*a*) See above, vol. i. §§ 4, 5.

property. For centuries there had been two kinds of property, *ex jure quiritium* and *in bonis*. Justinian abolished these two kinds by a new law, so that in future only one kind of property should exist, to all effects complete; and in connection with this, the previous distinction of *res mancipi* and of the *fundus Italicus* ceased.

But it must be repeated, that the two kinds of rules last mentioned relate to the existence of rights, that they are therefore identical in character, and that we have therefore no occasion to distinguish them in the course of the present inquiry. Their natural distinction was only mentioned in order to show the extent and variety of the rules of law relating to the existence of rights, and in order to guard against every possible doubt as to this extent.

The following remarks must still be added as to this distinction of two kinds of rules of law,—those relating to the acquisition and to the existence of rights (*b*).

First, as to the designation of these two kinds of rules, I have chosen that which seemed to me the most intelligible. They might also be distinguished by saying that the one class refers to right in the subjective sense, and the other to right in the objective sense (*c*). Or, again, that the one class relates to the permanent nature of the legal relations, the other to their changeable element.

The boundary between the two classes of rules is not always free from doubt, since it may often appear uncertain whether many belong to the one or to the other class. These doubts can be removed only by close examination of the meaning and intention of new laws (§ 398).

The first kind of rules of law concerns the acquisition of rights, but it also includes the loss of them, the dissolution of the legal relations (or their separation from the person of the previous owner); and this is not expressed only for the sake of

(*b*) In order that this classification of rules of law, on which the whole succeeding inquiry depends, may not be thought incomplete and insufficient, I here observe, at starting, that the inquiry is confined to the material private law, and therefore does not include the public law (particularly penal law) and the law of procedure. This limitation is the same as that fixed above in regard to the local limits (§ 361, *a*), as well as for this whole system of law (vol. i. § 1).

(*c*) See vol. i. §§ 4, 5.

brevity (*d*). In the most numerous and most important applications, the two things coincide: thus in alienation, usucapion, prescription, the extinction of an obligation, the one party always gains exactly what the other party loses. But also, in the rarer and less important cases in which there is only the loss of a right, as in dereliction, there is no doubt that the collision of laws in time is to be judged just as in the case of acquisition.

By their nature, many rights are of an indefinite duration, such as property which is transmitted by means of succession, slavery which is transmitted by birth; so that a complete cessation of these rights can occur only by accidental circumstances, in contradistinction to other rights which, by their very nature, are destined for a transient existence, such as nearly all obligations, usufruct, the family relations. In both cases, questions of collision are to be decided in the same way. But it must be remembered that the rules concerning the existence of rights, and consequently the principles applicable to their collision, are of infinitely greater importance for rights of indefinite duration than for transient ones.

If the question be raised, which of those two kinds of rules is the more important in itself, and consequently also in respect of possible collisions? the answer differs according to the point of view that may be chosen. On the one hand, new laws as to the existence of rights are more important, because they have a more profound effect on the general state of the law, and modify subsisting rules. On the other hand, however, new laws as to the acquisition of rights appear more important, because they are more frequently spoken of and felt. For they form the foundation of juridical acts (*e*), and therefore of the whole of human intercourse. Thus this question of collision is in their case more important and more intricate; for which reason, especially, I have given this kind of rules the first place in the following inquiry.

(*d*) This class might therefore have been called, *Rules for juridical facts* (vol. iii. § 104). I have avoided this expression as being too abstract.

(*e*) By far the most numerous and important juridical facts consist of voluntary acts; certainly not all, for they embrace also accidental events, which, however, as to collisions are subject to the very same rules as voluntary acts. Among these are, *e.g.*, as bases of the acquisition of property, the different forms of accession; and, as founding a right of succession *ab intestato*, the death of a determinate person.

From the preceding considerations, the following order appears to be the more natural and convenient for the solution of our problem :—

The question is, to determine the limits in time of the empire of two kinds of rules of law.

A. First, of the rules of law which have for their object the acquisition of rights.

Here the fundamental principle is first to be laid down in its true signification, and at the same time we have to show the position of ancient and modern legislation, as well as of the opinions of writers, with regard to this principle.

The principle is further to be applied to particular legal relations and questions of law.

Finally, the nature of the numerous exceptions to this principle is to be expounded.

B. Secondly, of the rules of law which have for their object the existence of rights. The order of the particular questions is similar to that assigned for the first class, only that these questions are here of a simpler character.

Sect. XLII.—(§ 385.)

A. ACQUISITION OF RIGHTS.—PRINCIPLE.

We have now to determine the principle of collision in time with regard to those rules of law which have for their object the acquisition of rights. For this class we must admit the truth of the principle, of which we had before (§ 384) to deny the general authority. I will try to establish it in the two formulas before given, and thus the intimate relation between these will also become evident.

The first formula runs thus : No retroactive force is to be attributed to new laws.

First of all, the true meaning of the retroaction which this formula negatives must be ascertained.

It is evident that it is not to be taken in a literal, material sense. This would mean that what has happened should be undone,—the past annihilated. But as this is impossible, no rule of law is needed to prevent it. The retroaction must therefore be taken in a juridical or formal sense; and it thus means that the retroactive law would draw under its dominion the *consequences* of past juridical facts, and therefore influence these consequences. But such a retroaction upon the consequences of past facts may be conceived in the following degrees:—

A. Upon these consequences alone which take place after the date of the new law.

B. On such consequences, and also upon those which fall within the interval between the juridical fact and the new law.

Two examples will illustrate this retroaction: If, in a country which does not limit the rate of interest, a loan of money is given at ten per cent., and after three years the Roman law is introduced, which prohibits higher interest than six per cent., the retroaction of the former and lower degree would have this effect: that from the time of the new law the excess of four per cent. could no longer be demanded, but that what had become due in the previous three years would remain good, and might still be sued for. The second and more extensive degree of retroaction would have this effect: that the excess of four per cent. could be demanded neither for the past three years, nor for the future. Again, in a country which allows the alienation of property by simple contract, if a rural estate is sold in this way, and after five years a new law requires tradition in alienating, the retroaction of the first degree would have this effect: that during the past five years the purchaser was the proprietor, and obtained the fruits in this character, while he must henceforward cease to be proprietor. According to the second degree, he would not have been proprietor in the past years, and would have obtained the fruits unlawfully.

Now the formula given above (the principle of non-retroactivity) absolutely denies the influence of the new law on the consequences of past facts, and that in every conceivable degree. It therefore maintains the rate of interest at ten per cent. as well for the future as for the past three years (*a*). It

(*a*) This will generally be unimportant, because the debtor may repay the loan, and, in consequence of the new law, will easily find money to borrow at lower interest. It is important, in the less frequent cases in

allows the property acquired by simple contract to continue in its effects, not only for the past five years, but also for all the future.[1]

I pass now to the second formula, which is thus expressed:

New laws leave vested (acquired) rights unaffected.

This means that rights already acquired should be respected, or, to speak more exactly, that legal relations should be preserved in their original nature and efficacy.

Many have regarded this second formula as if it contained a new and independent principle, different from that expressed in the first (*b*). But, in fact, there is in both formulas only one and the same principle contemplated and described from different sides. The application of this to the examples already used for the first formula will make it evident. By his stipulation for interest at ten per cent. the creditor has acquired the right to demand interest to this amount so long as the loan subsists (*c*); and this vested right ought to be maintained, although a new law limits the rate of interest to a lower sum. By the simple contract the purchaser of the estate has acquired the right of property, and this vested right ought to be pre-

which it is stipulated that the debt shall not be paid for a stated time. [In *Lord Colvil* v *Andrew*, 9 Feb. 1628, 1 Br. Sup. 53, 150, the Court of Session found that the Act of 1597, restricting annualrent (interest) to ten per cent., 'struck only contracts and writs astricting parties to pay more than ten for the said hundred since the date of the Act. But the Lords declared, that if the debtor redeemed the annualrent by paying principal and by-past interest at the stipulated rate, he should be free henceforth of all greater annualrent which might be sought from him for that term thereafter.']

[1] In considering a case arising under the clause in the constitution of New Hampshire, prohibiting retrospective laws, Story, J., says: 'What is a retrospective law, within the true intent and meaning of this article? Is it confined to statutes which are enacted to take effect from a time anterior to their passage? Or does it embrace all statutes which, though operating only from their passage, affect vested rights and past transactions? It would be a construction utterly subversive of all the objects of the provision to adhere to the former definition. It would enable the legislature to accomplish that indirectly which it could not do directly. Upon principle, every statute which takes away or impairs vested rights acquired under existing laws, or creates a new obligation, imposes a new duty, or attaches a new disability, in respect to transactions or considerations already past, must be deemed retrospective.'—*Society for Propagation of the Gospel* v *Wheeler*, 2 Gallis. *U. S. R.* 139.

(*b*) Bergmann, p. 92; Puchta, *Vorlesungen*, p. 223.

(*c*) It would be a mistake to give the name of vested right only to interest already due. The right to future interest is also an acquired right, only differing from the former in the fact that its exercise depends on the arrival of a point of time which is still future.

served to him, although a new law makes delivery a necessary condition of alienation.

The formula concerning the maintenance of vested rights needs more accurate definition on two sides, in order to guard against very hazardous mistakes.

First, by vested rights, which ought to be maintained according to this formula, we are to understand only the legal relations of a determinate person, and therefore the constituent parts of a sphere within which the individual will has independent sway (*d*), not the abstract faculties or qualities of all men, or of whole classes of men (*e*). Some examples will illustrate this distinction, and the practical limitation of the formula which arises from it. When duelling is subjected to punishment in a state where it was not formerly penal, all the present inhabitants are thus deprived of the faculty which they before enjoyed—of fighting duels with impunity. But the immediate efficacy of this new law is not excluded by our formula, because the previous abstract faculty of all men to fight duels without punishment has not the nature of an acquired right. It is the same also if the Roman law, and with it the *Sc. Vellejanum*, is introduced into a state which before allowed full effect to the suretyships of women, so that all women lose their previous faculty of validly becoming sureties. And we must say exactly the same if the Roman law fixing majority at twenty-five years is introduced where majority has hitherto commenced at twenty-one. All who have not yet completed twenty-one years at the date of this new law (*f*), thereby lose the faculty of becoming major at this age, and are kept four years longer in minority.

In the second place, vested rights are not to be confounded with mere *expectations*, which were founded by the former law, and are destroyed by the new law. This result is by no means excluded by the principle which maintains acquired rights. Thus an existing law of succession may have led certain persons in a family to expect to be heirs *ab intestato* of another member of the family, and they may have fixed their course of

(*d*) See vol. i. §§ 52, 53.

(*e*) Bergmann, § 20.

(*f*) It is otherwise for those who at the date of the new law have already attained twenty-one years of age, since majority had already become an acquired personal right for each one of these; *v. infra*, § 389.

life in accordance with that expectation. If a new law as to succession disappoints the expectation, the change may be very vexatious to them; but our principle does not prevent this result, since it protects only acquired rights, not mere expectations. It is the same when any one receives from a rich and childless man a promise that he will make him his sole heir, even if the testament is actually made and shown to him. This mere expectation may be disappointed by a new law prohibiting testaments, enacted during the life of the testator, just as much as by a change in the testator's intentions (*g*). On the contrary, it would be wrong to rank among mere expectations rights which cannot yet be *exercised*, because they are coupled with a condition or a term. These are really rights, since even in the case of a condition the fulfilment is drawn back. The difference is, that in a mere expectation the result depends *entirely on the freewill* of a stranger, which is not the case with the *conditio* and the *dies* (*h*).

The principle here laid down, flowing from these two formulas, has two different significations, of which each is true and important: the one has reference to the lawgiver, the other to the judge.

For the lawgiver, the principle means that he ought not to enact new laws having retroactive force, or endangering acquired rights (*i*).

For the judge, the principle means that he is to interpret and apply every new law, even if its terms are indistinct as to this point, so that no retroactive force is ascribed to it, no acquired rights disturbed.

If, therefore, in a state which previously allowed alienation by simple contract, tradition is prescribed as a condition, the new law will satisfy the requirements of this principle if it be thus conceived: 'In future he who desires to alienate shall make use of tradition for that purpose.' In this spirit ought

(*g*) Meyer, pp. 32, 33.

(*h*) See vol. iii. §§ 116, 117, 121; Chabot, t. i. p. 128; Meyer, pp. 30, 32, 172.

(*i*) To this effect is *L.* 65, *C. de decur.* (10, 31): '*Cum conveniat* leges futuris regulas imponere, non præteritis calumnias excitare.' Most other texts rather convey instructions to the judge. So, among others, is the passage from which the *L.* 65, *cit.* is almost literally borrowed. *L.* 3, *C. Th. de const.* (1, 1): 'Omnia constituta non præteritis calumniam faciunt, sed futuris regulam imponunt.'

the legislator to understand the new provision (although he may not so express it), and so ought the judge to apply it.

I have hitherto attempted clearly to exhibit the principle in its true meaning and its various applications, as well as to confine it within its proper limits. But the main question has not yet been touched, whether we are to hold it in general as true, and on what grounds.

We might be tempted to make the following objection to it: A new law is always enacted in the persuasion that it is better than the former one. Its efficacy, therefore, must be extended as far as possible, in order to communicate the expected improvement in the widest sphere. This view has some similarity to the theory above noticed relative to the territorial law (§ 348), according to which, in every collision of local laws, the law of our own country ought always to be adhered to. But as we had to oppose to this plausible principle the true one, according to which every legal relation is to be judged according to the law of the country to which it naturally belongs, so here it will be our task to fix, for the operation of every new law in point of time, that extent of authority which naturally pertains to it. Now, the natural limits of this authority of a new law are indicated by the principle of non-retroactivity and the maintenance of acquired rights. The truth of this assertion is shown by the following considerations:—

First, an immoveable confidence in the authority of the existing laws is extremely important and desirable. I do not mean confidence in their permanent endurance, because, according to circumstances, the expectation and the desire of amelioration may be well founded and salutary. But I mean the confidence that their authority and efficacy will be unassailable as long as they subsist. Every one therefore ought to be able to reckon upon the continued efficacy in the future of the juridical acts which he has performed for the acquisition of rights, according to the existing laws.

Secondly, the preservation of the state of rights and property existing at each period is equally important and desirable. And this, so far as legislation can have any effect on it, is promoted by the principle in question, and is endangered by the opposite one.

Thirdly, the opposite principle must be rejected, if it were only because it is impossible to carry it out to its logical results, so that it would operate only accidentally and inconsistently (and therefore unjustly) on particular kinds of juridical acts, while all others would remain unaffected by it. If it were desired to carry out that opposite principle rigorously, a new law, requiring tradition for the alienation of property where simple contract previously sufficed, must have this result, that all past alienations would become ineffectual, or must be confirmed by subsequent tradition. The complete impracticability of such a state of the law is so evident,[2] that certainly no one has thought of adopting these consequences along with the assumption of a retroactive force, which is regarded by many as correct according to the nature of things, and only rejected by positive laws. Imagining that they were stating, in a general manner, the question as to retroactivity, our adversaries thought in reality only of juridical acts initiated but not yet executed, in particular of obligatory contracts formerly concluded, of which the fulfilment is first required after the promulgation of the new law (*k*). In this restricted application it is certainly conceivable that retroactivity might be carried out; but even this accidental and arbitrary limitation proves that the adoption of retroactivity as a general principle is altogether inadmissible, and that it is unjust in the accidentally restricted application in which it might be possible.

SECT. XLIII.—(§ 386.)

ACQUISITION OF RIGHTS.—PRINCIPLE.

(CONTINUATION.)

The principle governing the rules concerning the acquisition of rights has hitherto been considered only from the general

[2] See an instance in *Urquhart* v *Urquhart*, 13 D. 742, 1 Macq. 658.

(*k*) This is the view, in particular, of Weber, p. 108, who makes rights of property, acquired by simple contract under a previous law, remain effectual even when a new law requires tradition in alienation. In this, however, he is not faithful to his principle, since, without observing it, he illogically and arbitrarily limits its application.

standpoint of the nature and purpose of laws. I now turn to the legislative provisions as to this important question.

Here we first encounter a law promulgated for the East by the Emperor Theodosius in the year 440 (*a*), which has had the most decided influence on all subsequent ages, as well in legislation as in practice and the doctrine of writers. It is as follows:—

> 'Leges et constitutiones futuris certum dare est formam negotiis, non ad facta præterita revocari, nisi nominatim et de præterito tempore et adhuc pendentibus negotiis cautum sit.'

The important contents of this law fully confirm the doctrine above laid down, and may be reduced to the following leading propositions:—

It does not distinguish between past and future *effects* of juridical facts, but between past and future *facts* themselves. New laws, it says, are to be applied to all juridical acts afterwards undertaken (futuris . . . *negotiis*), not to be applied to past juridical acts (non ad facta præterita revocari), even if their effects should still be in the future (adhuc *pendentibus* negotiis) (*b*).

It makes the reservation, however, that a future law may exceptionally attribute to itself a retroactive force, which must be recognised. Hence it is evident that this law is intended as an instruction to the judges (a rule of interpretation), and not for the legislator, for whom complete independence in every particular case is expressly reserved. But even if this reservation had not been added, it would follow of course, because the

(*a*) *L.* 7, *C. de legibus* (1, 14). The passage is repeated word for word in a decretal of Gregory IX., *C.* 13, *X. de constit.* (1, 2). It agrees in substance with *C.* 2, *X. eod.*

(*b*) The *pendentia negotia* are mentioned only in the exception, and therefore fall under the prohibition which applies to the ordinary cases. *Pendens negotium* is a contract which is concluded at the time of the new law, but is still wholly or partially unperformed, so that its effects are in the future. The term *negotium* is used in the text *à potiori*, since the greater number of juridical facts (though not all) are true juridical acts (§ 384, *e*). The word *negotium* also occurs elsewhere for a fact, which is certainly no juridical act,—namely, the opening of a succession *ab intestato*. *L.* 12, *in f. C. de suis* (6, 55). Among *pendentia negotia* are also, unquestionably, those as to which a litigation is already begun, but not yet decided; yet I do not think that the term here used specially denotes this case. It is otherwise with the '*causis* . . . quæ *in judiciis* adhuc pendent' in the *const. Tanta*, § 23.

rule could in future have been abolished, whether as a whole, or in its application to each particular case.

The point of view from which this law is enacted is also important. It is not conceived as a rule arising from something newly discovered, previous to which an opposite principle prevailed. It only claims to express what necessarily follows, as a rule, from the nature and purpose of legislation (*certum est*), and therefore to give an instruction for the avoidance by judges of possible errors as to this question. And we cannot doubt that that rule had been recognised at all times by the Roman jurists, and that it is purely accidental that no statements of it are preserved from earlier times (b^2).

Finally, it has been above remarked that new laws may occur in two ways,—as solitary and special rules (§ 383, No. 1), or in the connection of a whole code, or system of rules of law invested with statutory force (§ 383, Nos. 2, 3, 4). In this constitution only the first case seems to be thought of; but it applies equally to the second.

The same principle, which the text above cited expresses in a general form, is recognised in a series of constitutions which were enacted as new laws with regard to particular questions, with the proviso that they should only take effect for the future, and should not be retrospective: this proviso has here the nature of a transitory law (§ 383). Some of these constitutions are remarkable, because they distinctly express the character which has just been assigned to this principle,—namely, that it is intended to maintain the *future consequences of past facts* (c). Others correctly state the *reason* of the rule, by saying that he who orders his juridical acts in reliance on the subsisting law merits no blame, because he could not foresee and observe the future law (d).

(b^2) The rule is very distinctly recognised in Cicero, *in Verrem*, i. 42, as something that had always been regarded as unquestionable.

(c) *L. un.* § 16, *C. de rei ux. act.* (5, 13): 'Instrumenta enim jam confecta viribus carere non patimur, *sed suum expectare eventum.*' *L. un.* § 13, *C. de latina libert. toll.* (7, 6): 'Sed si quidem liberti jam mortui sunt et bona eorum quasi Latinorum his, quorum intererat, aggregata sunt, *vel adhuc vivunt*, nihil ex hac lege innovetur, *sed maneant apud eos jure antiquo firmiter detenta et vindicanda.*'

(d) *L.* 29, *C. de test.* (6, 23): ['Quid enim antiquitas peccavit, quæ præsentis legis inscia, pristinam secuta est observantiam?'] *Nov.* 22, *C.* 1: ['Qui enim illis (*i.e.* prioribus legibus) crediderunt, atque ita contraxerunt, eos nemo culpabit quod et futurum nesciverint,' etc.] Other constitutions

We have next to inquire what significance these statements of the Roman law have for us, from the standpoint of the common law. This discussion may also be extended to the exceptions which occur in Roman law, allowing a retroactive force, and falling under the general reservation already mentioned; while the enumeration of the particular cases will find its place at a later stage. Our writers are agreed, that all these decisions of the Romans, whether they regard the rule or the exception, have the effect of true laws wherever the Roman law itself is received. I cannot persuade myself of the truth of this assertion.

First, I must reject it on principle. Whether we regard those decisions as directions to the lawgiver or to the judge, both of which opinions are in themselves correct (§ 385), they have not for us the force of binding laws, even where Roman law is received (*e*).

which recognise the same principle are: *L.* 65, *C. de decur.* (10, 31); *L.* 18, *C. de testibus* (4, 20); *Nov.* 66, c. i. §§ 4, 5. [See *Hughes* v *Lumley*, 4 Ell. and Bl. 358. Baron Parke there observed, that 'in *Mayor of Berwick* v *Oswald*, all the judges in this court agreed that, *primâ facie*, the parties must be taken to contract with reference to the existing law only, though the majority thought that in that particular case there was enough to show that the parties contracted with reference to possible alterations in the law.' Lord Chief Baron Pollock, in the case referred to (3 Ell. and Bl. 678), said: 'I think every contract (which does not expressly provide to the contrary) must be considered as made with reference to the existing state of the law; and if, by the intervention of the legislature, a change is made in the law which in any degree affects the contract, such contract, made without some clear and distinct reference to the prospect or possibility of a change, does not hold with reference to the state of things as altered by the new law. I am not aware there is any authority which expressly decides this, but also I am not aware there is any authority to the contrary; and I think the intervention of the legislature in altering the situation of contracting parties, in principle is analogous to a convulsion of nature, against which parties may provide, but if they have not provided, it would generally be considered as excepted out of the contract.' The question in this case was, whether the Act 6 and 7 Vict. c. 89, § 6, making the election of the treasurer of a burgh during pleasure instead of annual, so altered the responsibility of his sureties as to liberate them from their contract. The judgment of the Queen's Bench and Exchequer Chamber was affirmed in the House of Lords (5 Clark, *H. of L. Ca.* 856), but the principle stated by Baron Parke was assumed to be correct. Lord Cranworth, C., said: 'By the law as it then stood, there could be no election but an annual election; but the parties chose to enter into a contract, binding themselves as sureties for David Murray, as treasurer, under any election, whether "annual or other." There could be no other election than an annual one, except by virtue of an alteration in the law. The law has been altered.' See *Pybus* v *Gibb*, 6 Ell. and Bl. 902.]

(*e*) See vol. i. §§ 27, 49.

Secondly, I must reject that assertion on account of the special character of the decisions which are here in question. The general statement which denies retroactivity, as well as the various repetitions of it (Notes *a*, *c*, *d*), were not intended to make new laws, and are in fact mere instructions, in which the correct treatment of new laws is naturally recognised. In the case of these statements, therefore, the question is an entirely idle one. It is different with the particular exceptions to the principle, which certainly have a quite positive character. And yet here, too, a more minute examination leads to the same result. To make this clear, I will examine Justinian's laws as to interest. In the year 528 he had decreed that, instead of twelve per cent., which had been allowed for centuries, only six per cent. might in future be stipulated (*f*). As doubts soon arose as to interest stipulated for before 528, he promulgated in 529 a transitory law (*g*), providing that the interest due before 528 should be judged by the old law,—that which had fallen due subsequently, and the future interest, according to the new law (*h*). Now, every one will grant that there can now be no question as to the literal contents of the law, since it is quite certain that no judge will be required to decide as to a contract for interest concluded before 528. Neither can there be any question of an application of the law in countries where the Roman law has prevailed for centuries, because there can be no facts to give any occasion for such an application. The only case of a possible application would be, if a country that had previously known no prohibition of usury were incorporated with a state which observes the Roman law with its prohibition of higher interest than six per cent. Here it might be thought possible to apply the foresaid transitory law to the contracts for interest formerly concluded in that country. But this application also I would be obliged to reject as improper, being in accordance with the literal meaning, but quite opposed to the spirit of the law. For every transitory law, as far as it exceeds the limits of a mere instruction, and, like this of Justinian's, introduces a retroaction, is of a strictly positive character, and

(*f*) *L.* 26, *C. de usuris* (4, 32).
(*g*) *L.* 27, *C. de usuris* (4, 32).
(*h*) The last provision relates to retroactive force, and therefore contains an exception to our principle (§ 385).

therefore altogether dependent on the circumstances and wants of the time. It is not the expression of a rule of law authoritative for all times and circumstances. Justinian therefore may have decreed this retroactivity, because (rightly or wrongly) he supposed it to be necessary or useful in the circumstances of his time. But if we sought to apply it now, we should go beyond its spirit, since without any reason we should be forced to assume that he intended the rule to have force for all future times, the wants of which he could not possibly foresee.

Although, then, we must, for these reasons, refuse to such decisions of the Roman law the force of obligatory laws, even within the domain of our common law, yet we must not be understood to hold them as indifferent or unimportant. They have, on the contrary, been of the highest importance, because, as a weighty authority, they have influenced for centuries legislation, judicial practice, and the doctrine of writers; so that, notwithstanding many varieties in details, there has been, in the main, such a unanimity as certainly could not have been expected without this common foundation.

SECT. XLIV.—(§ 387.)

A. ACQUISITION OF RIGHTS.—PRINCIPLE.

(CONTINUATION.)

The principle of the Roman law as to non-retroactivity (§ 386) has been transferred into the chief modern codes.

I. PRUSSIAN LEGISLATION. — The introduction to the Allgemeine Landrecht contains this principle in the following terms:

§ 14. New laws cannot be applied to acts and events that have previously occurred.

This rule is apparently intended as an instruction for the conduct of judges, so that the word *cannot* properly means *ought not* or *shall not*.

As regards the legislator, there was a passage in the draught which was intended to reserve exceptions in the same way as the Roman law (*a*). This reservation has been omitted in the code, and in its place comes the general exception, that new penal laws, if they are milder than the former laws, shall be applied to crimes committed before their date (*b*). This omission, however, is quite unimportant, for it is already evident that in every future case the lawgiver is entitled to attribute to a new law, by way of exception, a retrospective force.

This rule also agrees with the Roman law in expressly withdrawing the *juridical facts* of the past ('acts and events') from the operation of the new law; and thus it sustains both the past and the future consequences of these previous facts unaffected by that law.

Along with this general rule, which fixes for all present and future laws the limits in time of their efficacy, there are to be noticed a number of transitory rules occasioned by the introduction of the present Prussian code into the whole country or into particular provinces (§ 383). In these the same principle is recognised, and in some particulars applied.

II. French Code.—Our principle is here recognised for the private law in the following words (*c*):

> La loi ne dispose que pour l'avenir; elle n'a point d'effet rétroactif.

The brevity of this text, and the employment of the usual technical term (*effet rétroactif*), leave no doubt that simply the doctrine derived from the Roman law, and long ago more fully developed by the scientific law of all countries, was here intended to be fully recognised; and it has been so understood in the French practice.

The rule in penal law is expressed quite in the same spirit (*d*). The retrospective force of new penal laws, when they are milder than the former laws, is not, as in Prussia, declared by the law, but is acknowledged in practice.

III. Austrian Code.—Here, again, there is only the following short provision (*e*):

(*a*) *Entwurf eines Gesetzbuch*, *Einleit.* § 20: 'The sovereign alone, on the strongest grounds of public interest, can make a new law reach back to previous cases.'

(*b*) *Einleitung zum A. L. R.* §§ 18–20. Another exception relating to the form of juridical acts (§§ 16, 17) is mentioned below (§ 388, *c*).

(*c*) *Code Civil*, art. 2.

(*d*) *Code Penal*, art. 4.

(*e*) *Gesetzbuch*, § 5.

Laws have no retroactive effect; they have therefore no influence on previous acts or acquired rights.

The same remark applies here which was made as to the French law. Nay, from the terms used, it is even less doubtful that the legislator meant to adopt the whole theory recognised in the common law.

The operation of legislation on this doctrine having been so slight, an influence proportionably greater has fallen to scientific law, and hence it seems necessary to offer some preliminary remarks on the position of legal writers towards this doctrine. On the whole there is a greater accordance of opinion than might have been expected, partly from the great authority which the decisions of the Roman law have for ages exercised (§ 386), partly from the intrinsic force of the things themselves, which in many cases cannot be ignored. The differences of opinion, which do nevertheless exist, are of two kinds. Some arise from the more or less correct apprehension of the various legal relations with reference to the question before us; and these we can only consider below in speaking of the legal relations themselves. Others have been occasioned by the various attempts to express, as general principles, conceptions more or less clear. These differences are principally of a theoretical character. A very minute comparison and criticism of these attempts would not bear any reasonable proportion to the fruits to be expected from it. It will be sufficient, in reviewing some writers who have bestowed more pains than others on the statement of such general principles, to indicate what is peculiar to each of them.

Weber lays special weight on the following distinction (*f*): It may be attempted, in the first place, to deal with a new law as if it had already existed at an earlier time, so that it could be brought to bear even on the past effects of previous juridical acts. There would here be a retroaction, and this would be objectionable. But, in the second place, it may only be proposed to judge the future consequences of previous legal acts according to the new law, and this would be correct. He believes that he has derived this distinction, which he holds to be the foundation of the whole theory, from the nature of the

(*f*) Weber, § 21, *a*, to § 27.

thing; but in reality he is subject to the influence of *L.* 27, *C. de usuris* (§ 386, *g*), and he has unconsciously transformed its peculiar and arbitrary rule into a general principle. We have already seen how he is unconsciously driven in this way to an illogical application of his principle, in order to avoid utter impracticability (*g*).

Bergmann adopts as his basis a more general distinction (*h*). One rule is conformable to the nature of the thing, another to the positive rules of the Roman law. According to the nature of things, that, he says, is true, which Weber declares to be the doctrine of the Roman law. The new law simply ought not to be antedated that is applied to past consequences; its application to the future effects of previous juridical acts should be allowed. The positive rule of the Roman law differs from this, according to Bergmann, in two ways: first, because it protects also the future consequences of past juridical acts; second, because it protects not only legal consequences (vested rights), but even mere expectations.

The last writer must be specially censured for putting the contents of the Roman law in fundamental opposition to the principles derived from the nature of the thing. This is directly contrary to the design of the leading text of Theodosius II., inserted by Justinian in the code (§ 386, *a*), and can therefore be justified only by the assumption that the Roman legislators were completely in error as to the nature of the thing, and not by the supposition that they deliberately intended to prescribe a new positive law. In other respects Bergmann follows essentially the same course as Weber. The latter, we have seen, is under the influence of the *L.* 27, *C. de usuris*, without being himself aware of it; so Bergmann is under the influence of two Novels of Justinian (*N.* 66 and *N.* 22, *C.* 1). With a false appearance of historical criticism, he creates from some general expressions in these Novels, and from their very arbitrary directions, a general theory of permitted and unpermitted retroactivity of laws, making the very uncritical tacit assumption, that Justinian meant to lay down such a theory in these Novels, and that they furnish, therefore, a universal standard for the application of all new laws.

(*g*) See above, § 385, *k*.
(*h*) Bergmann, §§ 4, 22, 30.

Struve, finally, is not distinguished for any special views as to retroactivity in general, for in this respect he differs from others more in expression than in reality. On the other hand, he stands quite alone in asserting that rules as to the application of new laws to the past and the future must be sought exclusively in the judge's apprehension of the nature of the thing, and never from positive laws. He holds that every attempt to regulate this matter by positive law is entirely null, and should not be regarded at all by the judge; for which reason he utterly rejects all transitory legislation (*i*). In this view we have chiefly to admire the modesty with which the writer confines his doctrine of the judge's relation to the law within the narrow circle of the questions concerning retroactivity. On unprejudiced consideration, we shall be convinced that the same principle, if it is true at all, must be extended to legal questions of every kind.

Sect. XLV.—(§ 388.)

A. ACQUISITION OF RIGHTS.—APPLICATIONS OF THE PRINCIPLE.

I am now to pass to the practical application of the principle which has been laid down; but I must first advert to a distinction in the nature of juridical facts which has much importance for our investigation. Most of these facts are simple events belonging to a single point of time, such as contracts, whose essence consists in a declaration of will to the same effect,—therefore in a momentary act,—in which the long preparation that may have preceded is not taken into account. Here it is always easy to determine whether a new law has been promulgated before or after such a fact.

On the other hand, there are many facts which extend over a period of time, either because they suppose the continuance of the same state of things (as usucapion and prescription), or because they consist of several events distinct in time (such as testaments). In these the determination of their relation in

(*i*) Struve, pp. 6, 30-34, 153-154.

time to a new law is difficult and complicated, so that it can only be successful if the particular circumstances are carefully examined and distinguished; for the new law is often enacted at a time between the beginning and completion of such a fact.

In juridical facts of the first and simpler kind (momentary events), two points deserve special attention, as to which a preliminary observation common to both will here be in its proper place,—the capacity of the parties for acting, and the juridical form of the acts.

The capacity to act must be judged exclusively as at the time of the juridical fact, in regard both to the facts and to the subsisting law. If, therefore, a minor without a guardian concludes a contract, that contract is and remains invalid, even after he has attained full age; and in like manner, if a subsequent law shifts the period of majority to an earlier age than before. The same is true in the converse case. If, therefore, a person aged twenty-one enters into a contract under the French law, the contract is and remains valid, even if the place soon after comes under the empire of the Roman law, which fixes majority at twenty-five. So far as I know, a doubt has never been suggested as to this point. The same must be said if a woman becomes a surety during the prevalence of the Roman law, including the *Sc. Vellejanum*, which law is afterwards abolished, or *vice versa*. In the first case, the suretyship is and remains invalid; in the second, it is and remains good after the change of the law (*a*).

So also the juridical form of an act must be judged exclusively according to the law subsisting when the act is executed, so that a subsequent law has no influence on its validity, whether it makes the previous form easier or more difficult. This proposition may be thus stated: *Tempus regit actum;* corresponding with the rule as to the local law: *locus regit actum* (§ 381). Indeed it has a still higher degree of truth and necessity than that rule, which is regarded merely as a favour to juridical acts resting on a general custom. For as to this rule of the local law, it is often (though not always) possible for the parties to observe another form; and therefore it

(*a*) We shall find, under the head of Contracts, an adverse opinion of Meyer as to the *Sc. Vellejanum;* *v.* § 392.

is equitably allowed to them to choose which law they will observe in point of form,—the law of the place of the act, or the law of the place to which the juridical act belongs in other respects, *e.g.* the law of the domicile. Such a possibility, and the right of election arising from it, do not exist with respect to the rule *Tempus regit actum;* for no one can foresee that a future law will alter the form, or wherein the change will consist. Hence also this rule has been admitted by writers without any contradiction (*b*).

Only in one respect might it be possible to raise a doubt as to the general authority of the rule, namely, when the new law does not make the form more difficult, but facilitates it. Here it might be supposed that, from an apparent liberality and forbearance, from an unrestrained effort to uphold the validity of juridical acts, the act would be valid if the form used and formerly insufficient should by accident satisfy the requirements of the new law. The Prussian code has in fact adopted this view (*c*). But I hold the rule to be a mistake, and believe that where such a law does not exist, the opposite rule must be adopted on general principles.

The rule referred to seems to have for its basis the notion that the positive forms of juridical acts are restrictions of individual freedom for the public benefit, somewhat in the same way as taxes, which the state, without any violation of right, can not only lower for the whole community, but gratuitously remit to individuals. This view can only be admitted for the stamp duties attached to many juridical acts, and even there only in so far as the use of stamped paper is required as the condition of the validity of a deed. For all other forms the theory is incorrect, as will be apparent from the following example:—

At the present time, if a holograph testament is privately executed at Berlin, it is an ineffectual act, from which no rights accrue at the death of the testator. But if before his death the French form of testament is introduced, according to which the privately made holograph will is valid, then, by the rule of the

(*b*) Weber, p. 90 and foll.; Meyer, pp. 19, 29, 43, 61, 89.

(*c*) *Allg. L. R. Einleit.* § 17. 'Acts which were null according to former laws in consequence of a defect in form, are valid only so far as the forms required by the subsequent law shall have been executed at the time when the litigation is raised.'

code (Note *c*), that testament would become valid, and regulate the future succession. This seems to involve a humane indulgence towards the testator, the propriety of which must, however, be gravely doubted. A law which, like the present Prussian code, absolutely requires the juridical execution of the testament, is unquestionably produced by several co-operating and kindred motives, which are all founded on the special importance of testaments in comparison with other juridical acts. By the necessary co-operation of the judge, the substitution of a forged testament is prevented; also the imprudent haste that may be caused by momentary liking or aversion towards particular persons; finally, the interested influence of many persons, from which a solitary and unadvised testator may be too feeble to withdraw himself. All these motives depend on private, not on public interests; and even if the new law no longer attributes to them the same importance, it is yet a difficult question whether the real interest of the testator—namely, the maintenance of his true, serious, deliberate will—is promoted by the retrospective rehabilitation, in defiance of legal principle, of a testament hitherto ineffectual. This becomes very clear if we try to ascertain why the testator has not observed the legal form required when he executed the testament. This may happen from mere ignorance of law, while a serious and deliberate will really exists. Doubtless the provision in the Landrecht, which is conceived as a mere favour, rests on this assumption. But it may also have happened in the full knowledge of the existing law, the holograph private will being merely preparatory to a juridical act, the performance of which the testator delayed for more mature consideration. Then we confirm, in consequence of this law, a testament as to which the true final resolve perhaps never existed. On the other hand, it may be said that the testator, by preserving the private testament after the promulgation of the new law, is to be regarded as if he had then written it anew, which he was certainly entitled to do. But just in regard to testaments, nothing is more common than indefinite delay, and therefore nothing is so unreliable as any inference which can be drawn from this as to the true and final intention. This is to entangle ourselves in the consideration of accidental, barely possible circumstances; and on impartial reflection, it will be admitted that there is no satisfactory reason whatever for abandoning the simple juridical rule, *Tempus regit actum;* and that by doing so, we run the risk, by a questionable indulgence, of admitting a result which may be directly contrary to the actual intention of the testator.

In applying the principle to the particular legal relations, the same order will now be followed which was adopted in the first chapter (*d*).

I. Status of the Person.
II. Law of Things.
III. Law of Obligations.
IV. Succession.
V. Law of the Family (Domestic Relations).

There is no need for a special section for the forms of juridical acts, as this question has already been disposed of in these introductory paragraphs.

Sect. XLVI.—(§ 389.)

A. ACQUISITION OF RIGHTS.—APPLICATIONS.

I. STATUS OF THE PERSON.

New laws, which have for their object the status of the person, especially the capacity to act, are here to be considered in two different aspects. First, in respect of the possible influence of the new law on juridical acts of the person interested, which have been executed before its promulgation; secondly, in reference to the personal status itself, which is to be governed by the new law. The first question has already been answered (§ 388), and only the second remains: How does a new law, touching personal status, operate on legal relations of this kind subsisting at its date? and, in particular, does the principle excluding retroaction come into application here?

(*d*) Of course the same restriction to private law and to the material private law is here to be observed as above, in treating of the limits of local laws (§§ 361, *a*, 384, *b*).

This principle has but little application to the status of the person, since most qualities constituting such status are of so abstract a character that they cannot be regarded as vested rights; still, under special circumstances, and exceptionally, we have to acknowledge the existence of acquired rights even here (§ 385, *d*, *e*, *f*). Only in these special cases, therefore, is the operation of the new law on previous status to be limited by our principle; in all others it immediately receives full and unrestricted effect. This must now be shown in its application to the most important cases of personal status.

1. The following rules are to be observed as to *age*:—If minority is prolonged or shortened by a new law, that law is immediately applicable to all minors, so that none of them can maintain that he has a vested right by the old law to become of age at the precise time appointed by it.

It is otherwise with those who had already attained majority under the old law, although they would still be minors according to the new law. Majority, with the independence which attaches to it, is for them a vested right, established by the arrival of the appointed period under the authority of the old law. To make them once more minors, and subject them to guardians, would involve a retroaction contradictory to our principle,—a retroaction which could be effected, even by an express statutory provision, only as an (unjustifiable) exception to the principle (*a*).

The correctness of this assertion is confirmed by comparing it with the following case:—If a minor is declared to be of full age, whether by the sovereign (as in Roman law), or by a court having jurisdiction over guardianships (as in Prussian law), none will doubt that, for him, majority with its results has the character of an acquired right. Suppose, then, that soon after, and before this person has attained the legal age, the law as to concessions of majority (*venia ætatis*) should be altogether abolished in that country, he must still continue to be regarded as major. But that which, in this case, is bestowed by the declaration of the sovereign or the tribunal, cannot be refused to him who has attained, under an old law, the age which it prescribed.

(*a*) The same rule, therefore, is to be applied to this case of the new law, which was above laid down in the case of a change of domicile (§ 365, *p*, *q*).

This view has often been recognised in the Prussian legislation.

The patent introducing the *A. L. R.* into the provinces beyond the Elbe (9th Sept. 1814) contains the following words, § 14 (*b*):

'Majority arrives only at the completion of the twenty-fourth year, in the case of all persons *who have not attained majority according to the former laws before January* 1*st*, 1815' (*c*).

A similar provision occurs in the other transitory laws of the following years (§ 383), and likewise in a special ordinance as to majority, issued for Erfurt and Wandersleben in 1817 (*d*).

A writer on French law holds a different opinion as to this question,—maintaining that in such a case he who has already become of age must again, in consequence of the new law, be regarded as a minor; and in support of this assertion, he cites judgments of the courts of Nismes and Turin to this effect (*e*).

2. Similar questions may arise in respect to *sex*, with this difference, that the case of a right personally acquired cannot there occur, as in minority.

If in a country which did not before recognise the tutory of women, that kind of guardianship, in one of its many gradations (*f*), is introduced by a new law, all women living at the time are immediately subject to it. So is it, conversely, if the previously existing tutory of women is abolished by a new law (*g*).

If the *Sc. Vellejanum* is introduced in a country where women, as well as men, can validly become sureties, this new restriction immediately takes effect on all women living at the time, if they afterwards desire to become sureties. Just the same is to be said if the *Sc. Vellejanum* already existing is abolished by a new law (*h*).

In all these cases, therefore, there could be no reason for ascribing to women living at the time a vested right in the more

(*b*) *Gesetzsammlung*, 1814, p. 93.

(*c*) The 1st of January 1815 was the day on which the Landrecht was to receive the force of law.

(*d*) *Gesetzsammlung*, 1817, p. 201.

(*e*) Meyer, pp. 97, 98.

(*f*) Eichhorn, *Deutsches Recht*, §§ 324-326.

(*g*) Chabot, t. i. pp. 29–36.

(*h*) Chabot, t. ii. pp. 350-353.

extensive capacity to act which they previously possessed, and limiting the efficacy of the new restrictive law to the future female generation.

3. The question here discussed has been raised in regard also to *infamy* (*i*).

The most numerous and important cases of infamy do not fall within the limits of our inquiry, which is confined to private law, and excludes penal law; I mean all the cases in which infamy appears as a criminal punishment, whether alone or in combination with other punishments, or, it may be, as the result of other punishments.

The question might here arise in reference to many cases of what is called *infamia immediata*, under which the Roman law includes several kinds of disreputable callings (*k*). If a new law introduces infamy for these cases, there is no doubt that it must be applied to all who are henceforth found in such a position, and that they can claim no vested right to prosecute such a way of life free from infamy.

4. Finally, our question may also occur in regard to *prodigality* judicially declared, and the disabilities connected with it, especially interdiction from administering one's own property.

What is prescribed in this respect by a new law, whether it be more severe or more lenient than the previous law, must be immediately applicable, and the continuance of the previous state of things as an alleged vested right cannot be claimed (*l*).

(*i*) I have attempted to show above (vol. ii. § 83) that infamy has no longer any significance for our modern common law. The present mention of it therefore refers, partly to the contrary opinion held by many as to that point, partly to modern legislations in which infamy is recognised.

(*k*) See above, vol. ii. p. 183. [*Infamia immediata* is opposed to *infamia mediata* in the language of civilians. The latter, which is the result of a judicial sentence, is the only kind of *infamia juris* now known. Where such infamy has been introduced by statute, it has been applied only to future cases. See as to fraudulent bankrupts, Act 1696, c. 5; Hume's *Com.* ii. 527. Where the principal disability arising from it (inadmissibility as a witness) has been removed, both past and future cases have been included. Acts 1 Will. IV. c. 37, § 9; 15 and 16 Vict. c. 27, § 1.]

(*l*) Meyer, pp. 99-111, who adduces, in confirmation, a judgment of the Court of Cassation at Paris. Chabot, t. ii. pp. 174-179, is here of a different opinion.

Sect. XLVII.—(§ 390.)

A. ACQUISITION OF RIGHTS.—APPLICATIONS.

II. LAW OF THINGS.

In the law of things, the principle of non-retroactivity generally receives simple and complete application.

1. Property.—If this right is alienated by simple contract under a law which recognises such alienation as valid, the right of property thus acquired remains, even if a subsequent law requires delivery in alienation (*a*).

So, under a law which requires tradition, no property is passed by a simple contract of sale without tradition; and if a subsequent law declares the simple contract to be sufficient, the transmission of the property is not effected even by it. For this purpose there must be either a new contract, or subsequent tradition (*b*).

2. Servitude.—Here the same rules apply as in the case of property: if, for example, one of two consecutive laws requires the simple contract, while the other requires tradition, or some other positive form for the constitution of servitudes (*c*).

It is different with what are called legal servitudes. When these have not before existed, but are introduced by a new law, our principle is not applicable to them. But such restrictions of property exist immediately after the enactment of the law wherever the conditions of fact are found (*d*). The true reason, however, is, that such a law has for its object, not so much the acquisition of a right, as the existence (the state and condition) of property, and thus the conditions and limits which attach to the recognition of property in general. But the principle which prohibits the retrospective force of laws has no reference to this whole class of rules (§§ 384, 399).

3. Right of Pledge.—If a new law introduces into a country where the Roman law of pledge exists a new species

(*a*) This is also recognised by Weber, p. 108, but inconsistently. See above, §§ 385, *k*, 387, *i*.
(*b*) Weber, pp. 108, 109.
(*c*) Chabot, t. ii. p. 361.
(*d*) Chabot, t. ii. p. 361; Struve, p. 267.

of tacit hypothec for the protection of any juridical act, the new law is to be applied to all juridical acts of this kind afterwards entered into, not to former acts. This proposition was recognised by Justinian when he introduced a tacit hypothec for the protection of dotal rights; for he added, at the end of his new and comprehensive dotal law, that all its provisions (and therefore those relating to the tacit hypothec) should be applied only to future dotal contracts (*e*).

If a new law assigns to a right of pledge a certain rank in the series of privileged hypothecs, only those hypothecs of such a kind can claim the privilege which have their commencement after the new law (*f*). But they possess it even against all hypothecs which originated before the new law. The holders of these, therefore, have to take measures, on the appearance of the new law, to protect themselves against the risk of such subsequent privileged hypothecs (*g*).

In the older Roman law it was permitted to pledge a thing, with the stipulation that the creditor should acquire the property of it in satisfaction of the debt, if the debt should not be paid (*h*). This contract was afterwards forbidden (*i*). In consequence of our principle, this prohibition could be applied only to subsequent contracts of this kind; but the Emperor Constantine, its author, gave it a retroactive force, making it applicable to anterior contracts. In accordance with the arguments which were before urged with respect to a similar law about usury (§ 386), this transitory provision has no practical importance for us, even where the Roman law is recognised.

The rules here laid down for new laws as to the right of pledge, are, however, altogether inapplicable, if these laws have for their object, not the adoption or abolition of particular kinds of pledge or privileges (as we have hitherto assumed), but rather a new system of the law on this matter. This occurs when, in place of the Roman law of pledge, a new law introduces the

(*e*) *L. un.* § 16, *C. de rei ux. act.* (5, 13); Bergmann, p. 126.

(*f*) *L.* 12, § 3, *C. qui pot.* (8, 18) (privilege of the *dos*). *L.* 27, *in f. C. de pign.* (8, 14) (privilege of *militia*).

(*g*) They can at once enforce their right of pledge; therefore at a time when the future possible competition does not exist.

(*h*) *Vatic. Fragm.* § 9 (Papinian). Such a contract is called *lex commissoria.*

(*i*) *L.* 3, *C. de pact. pign.* (8, 35), *i.e. L. un. C. Th. de commiss. resc.* (3, 2); Weber, pp. 6, 51; Meyer, p. 17, who is wrong as to the historical connection.

system of registers of hypothecs, or *vice versa*. In such a case the new law no longer relates to the acquisition of rights by determinate persons, but to the existence of such rights generally (of the legal institution). But then the principle which excludes retroaction is not at all applicable (§§ 384, 385); the two legal systems cannot exist together in their particular applications, and the new law must have immediate and exclusive efficacy. How the transition from the old to the new state of things is here to be managed, in order to guard against injustice, will be shown at a more suitable place (§ 400).

4. Other Jura in Re.—Besides property, the Roman law recognises only a small and rigidly defined number of real rights; it does not allow, therefore, the creation of new real rights at pleasure.

The Prussian legislation has here adopted quite a novel course. It allows every merely personal right of using or profiting by a thing belonging to another to be transformed into a real right, as soon as the possession of the thing has been conceded to the person having the right (*k*). Under this condition, therefore, all hirers and tenants have a real right in Prussian law, although by Roman law they can have no more than a personal right to use.

If, then, the Prussian law is introduced at any place instead of the Roman, all existing hirers and tenants retain the personal right which they hitherto had, and only new contracts of this kind give a real right. So, in the converse case, the hirer retains the real right that has been constituted under the empire of the Prussian law, but new hirers are regarded in accordance with the Roman law as having merely a personal right. Here too, therefore, the time when each legal relation has its commencement decides unconditionally as to the law to be administered, and there can be no question as to a retroactive force of the new law.

We might be led by an imaginary analogy to treat this case in the same way as the immediately preceding case of the Roman and Prussian system of hypothecs. The introduction of the real right of hirers and tenants would then be regarded as a new law as to the existence of rights (the legal institution); the principle which excludes retroactivity would no longer be

(*k*) Koch, *Preussisches Recht*, vol. i. §§ 223, 317.

in question, but the new law would at once embrace all existing legal relations.

But in reality the two cases are entirely different in their character. The two systems of hypothecs cannot subsist together at the same time, just because the most frequent and most difficult case in the law of hypothecs is that in which several persons have rights at the same time in the same thing; in which, therefore, their priority can only be determined by the one or the other system exclusively. On the other hand, there is not the least doubt that the rights of several hirers at the same place are judged by different rules, if their contracts have been concluded at different times, and under the authority of different laws. Hence the question as to the real right of hirers belongs entirely to the class of rules relating to the acquisition of rights, and therefore to that department in which the principle prohibiting retroaction is applicable.

Sect. XLVIII.—(§ 391.)

A. ACQUISITION OF RIGHTS.—APPLICATIONS.

II. LAW OF THINGS.—*Continuation.*

In considering the legal institutions belonging to the law of things, some of these were purposely passed over, because they present peculiar difficulties and complications, and therefore need to be treated in a larger connection.

Such are the acquisition of property and of servitudes by usucapion and *longi temporis possessio* (both embraced under the name of prescription, *Ersitzung*), as well as the extinction of servitudes by *non-usus* and *libertatis usucapio*, equivalent to acquiring freedom from the servitude on the part of the proprietor (§ 388). All these cases of acquisition have the following common peculiarity: They are not completed by a simple momentary act, but by a continuing state, which must remain the same for a whole period of time. This state may consist in a continuous activity (possession, *quasi*-possession), or in a continuous inaction.

In these qualities, however, many legal institutions beyond

the limits of the law of things entirely coincide with those here enumerated; in particular the limitation of actions, which equally depends on continuous inaction for a certain period, and which leads, just as much as these institutions, to the acquisition of a right—namely, the right to an exception by which the right of action previously belonging to another person is completely repelled.

The recognition of this intimate connection has therefore led from an early time to the ranking of all legal institutions of this kind under one class, and designating them by the common name of prescription (*Verjährung*). Although this procedure is much to be censured, and has led to confusion of ideas (*a*), the intimate connection of all these legal institutions cannot be denied; and it is extremely distinct and prominent in this subject of retroactive force. All these institutions must therefore be now grouped together; and usucapion and the limitation of actions may serve as their two most important representatives.

Where, therefore, a new statute modifies in any respect the law of usucapion or of the limitation of actions, the two following cases are possible:—

The new law may appear before the commencement of the usucapion. Then there is no doubt that it must govern this usucapion, so that the old law can no longer come into question. It may also appear after a usucapion has been completed. Then, again, there is no doubt that the new law cannot be applied to it at all. The completed acquisition of a right under the old law must be fully maintained. But, finally, the new law may appear during the period in which the usucapion is still current—after its beginning, before its end. These are the doubtful cases for which we have now to ascertain the rules.

During this period no right is acquired; only an acquisition is prepared for. Hence the new law must immediately act on this incomplete state of things. It is true that even during this period the expectation of an acquisition was raised, and this expectation might be more or less near; but mere expectations are not protected by the principle which excludes retroaction (*b*). Let us now consider the various possible cases of such new laws.

(*a*) See vol. iv. § 177; vol. v. § 237.

(*b*) See above, § 385. On the whole, Weber agrees with this view,

1. Usucapion or prescription of actions, before permitted, is abolished, either altogether or for certain specified cases. This law comprehends all cases of current usucapion, so that all acquisition by this means becomes impossible.

2. Conversely, usucapion or prescription of actions, being before unknown, is introduced. The new institution is immediately to be applied to all legal relations in suspense at the time, yet so that the term is to be reckoned from the date of the new law. He who possessed a thing belonging to another under the conditions prescribed by the new law, immediately commences the usucapion of it, just as if his possession had begun at the time when the new law was enacted: the time of his previous possession is not reckoned. All rights of action which have accrued before the passing of the new law immediately become subject to the prescription of actions, but in the same way as if they had now first begun: the time of the previous delay or negligence is not reckoned.

We find in Roman law a remarkable example of this last kind. For a long time the most numerous and important kinds of actions were not subject to limitation,—they were *perpetuæ actiones* in the strictest sense of the word. The Emperor Theodosius II. introduced for all these actions a prescription, which, as a rule, was to endure for thirty years. According to the principle just laid down, rights of action then existing could be extinguished only after thirty years. But the emperor gave to his law partial retroactivity, so that the past time was to be included in the calculation; yet the person in right of the action was in no case to have less than ten years from the date of the law, within which he might effectually bring his action (*c*). When Justinian inserted this law in the code, he naturally

pp. 147-158; likewise Bergmann, pp. 34-36, in regard to the nature of the thing, while at p. 163 he adopts for Roman law the opposite view, namely, the continued operation of the old law, since, in his opinion, mere expectations are protected by the Roman law (see above, § 387, *h*). In reality, the same principle is here encountered which was above applied to the collision of different local laws as to usucapion (§ 367, *k*).

(*c*) *L. un.* § 5, *C. Th. de act. certo temp.* (4, 14). A pressing necessity could not be asserted for this deviation from the principle. It is some justification for it, that among the reasons for the prescription there is the presumption of payment (see vol. v. § 237). This presumption has a real bearing even for the time that has elapsed before the promulgation of the law as to prescription, during which the action has not been brought.

dropped this transitory provision (*d*), which had of itself lost all efficacy for about a hundred years.

3. If a kind of interruption which was previously admissible is abolished, or, conversely, a new kind of interruption is introduced, the one or the other provision is immediately to be applied to the current usucapion.

4. A new law extending the term is immediately applicable to the current usucapion or prescription of actions (*e*).

5. More difficult, and also more important, is the question as to a new law which shortens the term. Here we must, in accordance with principle, leave the acquirer free to elect whether he will avail himself of the old law or of the new; in the latter case he must reckon the time from the enactment of the new law, so that he cannot include the time that has already elapsed. He is entitled to the first choice, because it certainly was not the purpose of the new law to give his opponent a more favourable position than he occupied under the old law; he is entitled to have the second option, because he can have no less right than one who begins his usucapion or prescription of actions at the same moment. On the other hand, it would be an undue retroactivity if he were allowed to take advantage of the new term, including in it the term already elapsed; because there his opponent would be allowed for bringing his action neither the space accorded by the old law, nor that allowed by the new. It might even happen, contrary to all reason, that the prescription of the action was completed at the very moment when the new law appears (*f*).

The principles here expounded have been fully recognised

(*d*) *L.* 3, *C. de præscr.* xxx. (7, 39).

(*e*) In 528 Justinian granted to churches the privilege that their actions should not prescribe for a hundred years. *L.* 23, *C. de SS. eccl.* (1, 2); see vol. v. p. 355. At the end of this law there are the following rather obscure words: 'Hæc autem omnia observari sancimus in iis casibus, qui vel postea fuerint nati, vel jam in judicium deducti sunt.' Literally, the last words apply also to the actions whose previous prescription (of thirty years) had already elapsed before the action was brought. This retroaction is justified by no reason. Comp. Weber, p. 7.

(*f*) Thus, *e.g.*, if a right of action, subject to the limitation of thirty years, subsists for ten years unexercised, and a new law is then promulgated, appointing for legal relations of this kind a prescription of three years. Bergmann, p. 36, proposes a proportional calculation as conformable to the nature of the thing. According to this view, where a third of the old period of prescription has elapsed, a third of the newly introduced term of three years must likewise be held to have elapsed, so that two years still remain. This complicated treatment can neither be maintained as

reject the assertion which is often made, that new prohibitive laws can change the nature of previously concluded contracts (*b*).

The rule here laid down has found very general recognition in the transitory laws promulgated at different epochs in Prussia (*c*). It is likewise recognised with great distinctness, and with full and consistent detail, by one of the most eminent writers on French law (*d*).

This rule is a necessary logical consequence of our general principle. But also from a purely practical point of view it appears true and important, because it alone suffices to maintain that confidence in the undisturbed efficacy of contracts which is indispensable for the security of civil transactions. Its influence is most extensive and important in its application to many contracts connected with real rights which are intended to be effective for many generations (*e*).

We have now to mention some contradictions of this rule, which are found in certain laws and in many writers.

Such a contradiction is found in the law of Justinian already mentioned as to forbidden rates of interest (§ 386, *f*, *g*); according to which the prohibition was held to refer to stipulations of interest previously made, although only for the interest afterwards falling due. A modern writer has attempted to erect this provision into a general rule (§ 387, *f*), while others have rightly seen in it only an exception from our rule —a solitary deviation from it (*f*). It is very remarkable that the transitory laws of Prussia since 1814 have adopted a similar provision (*g*), without its being perceived that they thus

(*b*) With this Bergmann agrees, § 30.

(*c*) *Einführungspatent des A. L. R.* § xi.: 'In particular, all contracts which have been concluded before the 1st July 1794 are to be judged, as well in respect of their form and matter as of their juridical consequences, only according to the laws subsisting at the time of the conclusion of the contract; although an action for its fulfilment or extinction, or for the prestation of interest and damages, should not be brought on such a contract till a later period.' Exactly similar provisions are contained in the transitory laws of 1803, § 5, 1814, § 5, and in later transitory laws (§ 383).

(*d*) Chabot, t. i. pp. 128–139.

(*e*) The peculiarity of this case has been well indicated by Götze, *Altmärkisches Provinzialrecht*, vol. i. pp. 11-13. We shall return to this kind of legal relations from another side, when we treat of those rules of law which have for their object the existence of rights (§ 399).

(*f*) Bergmann, § 30.

(*g*) *Law for the Provinces beyond the Elbe*, 1814, § 13; and likewise in the subsequent transitory laws (§ 383).

directly contradict the principle which subjects the consequences of contracts to the law in force at the time when they were made (Note *c*). Least of all in the stipulation for interest was there need of such a deviation from the correct principle expressly recognised in the laws referred to, because just in this matter the application to past contracts is generally of very slight importance (§ 385, *a*).

But two modern writers have brought against the generality of the rule here laid down a much more important and very extensive controversy. It relates, not to the rule itself, but only to its application to the challenging of contracts, in so far as this is founded, not upon the circumstances attending the conclusion of the contract itself, but on subsequent facts, *e.g.* on the future resolution of one party to raise an action of nullity (reduction) (*h*). Weber has not laid down this as a general principle, but he has applied it in a number of important cases (*i*). But soon after him Meyer reduced it to an abstract principle, and attempted to carry it out in the following way (*k*).

We must (he says) distinguish two kinds of consequences of a contract,—necessary, or immediate, on which the laws cannot be retroactive; and accidental, or remote, in which the retroaction of a new law upon previous contracts is admissible. To the first class belong those consequences of which the parties thought or *could* think, which therefore they tacitly included in the contract (*l*). To the second class belong the consequences which are first occasioned by future facts: among these are the actions of nullity (reduction) founded on *læsio enormis*, fraud, force, error, minority, and also the recall of a donation for ingratitude, or on account of the subsequent birth of children (*m*). This whole distinction is absolutely untenable, if it were only because there is certainly not one of the cases of the second class which the parties *could* not think of as a

(*h*) The laws of Prussia have expressly recognised the application of our rule to such cases (note *c*).

(*i*) These cases are mentioned below in treating of the particular applications.

(*k*) Meyer, pp. 36–40, 153–155, 174–210. He does not indeed cite Weber as an authority, but as he is acquainted with his work (Preface, p. xi.), it can hardly be doubted that he has here followed him.

(*l*) Meyer, pp. 38-39, 180, 187-191.

(*m*) Meyer, pp. 175–178.

will be further confirmed in this disposition by recollecting the law which authorizes the recall of the gift. The supposition, therefore, that the donor thought of that law, or may have thought of it, is certainly quite consistent with the circumstances.

4. Restitution against a contract. The time of the contract is decisive, not the time when restitution is demanded (*w*). The opposite is asserted because the contract is in itself valid, and is first annulled by the judicial act (*x*). The same idea is further developed by others, and carried further from the truth by the doctrine that restitution is granted as a matter of favour by the sovereign (*y*). These assertions are conclusively refuted by the circumstance that, according to the nature of restitution as presented to us in the law of Justinian, he who claims it has a true vested right to it, differing but little in form from the right to an action or an exception (*z*).

5. *Exceptio doli* or *metus* is judged according to the time of the contract, without regard to the fact that here the contract is invalid, not *ipso jure*, but *per exceptionem* (*aa*).

6. *Exceptio Sc. Vellejani.* According to the time when the suretyship was entered into (*bb*).

7. *Exceptio Sc. Macedoniani.* The same (*cc*).

8. *Exceptio non muneratæ pecuniæ.* The same.

9. By a law of the Emperor Frederick the First (Auth. *Sacramenta puberum*), which he incorporated in the collection of Justinian, the greater number of the defects of a contract are completely removed by the debtor's confirming the contract by oath (*dd*). The applicability of this law is to be judged according to the time when the oath is made. Weber wrongly

(*w*) Struve, p. 266.

(*x*) Weber, pp. 113, 114.

(*y*) Meyer, p. 184. As to this, comp. above, vol. vii. § 317.

(*z*) See above, vol. vii. pp. 112, 113, 117.

(*aa*) In the case of *dolus* it is very doubtful whether Meyer means to rank the challenge of the contract and its invalidity on this ground among the necessary or the accidental consequences (pp. 154, 179, 183). In regard to restitution on the ground of *dolus*, see vol. vii. § 332.

(*bb*) Chabot, t. i. p. 352. See above, § 388. Here Meyer, pp. 196–198, attempts to defend the contrary opinion by quite different and partly self-destructive arguments.

(*cc*) Here Meier, p. 194, agrees, because such a contract is opposed to good morals, and because the renunciation of the debtor has no effect. By the way, he confounds the *filiusfamilias* with the *minor*.

(*dd*) Savigny, *Geschichte des R. R. im Mittelalter*, vol. iv. p. 162.

disputes this on the ground that such a contract is in itself null, and is only afterwards protected by an act of the judge (*officio judicis*); that therefore the time of this judicial sentence is decisive (*ee*). But it is evident that the rights of the parties are previously unalterably fixed, just as in any other legal relation; and that the judge, in this as in other cases, is only called upon to recognise and to protect these rights.

Some other questions remain which lie beyond the sphere of the great diversities of opinion with which we have been engaged.

Among these are the obligations arising from *delicts*. It is generally admitted that these are to be judged according to the law in force at the time when the delict is committed (*ff*). The rights arising from illicit intercourse might be drawn into this category, but these will be better dealt with elsewhere (§ 399).

Further, the laws concerning bankruptcy belong to this place. As to these, I can abridge by referring to the discussion of them in relation to the local law (§ 374). Bankruptcy concerns, as was there shown, not the rights themselves, but execution against a determinate estate existing at a particular time; for the purposes of this execution the priorities of the individual creditors have to be determined. What law is to be applied to these priorities? Here creditors who have hypothecs are to be distinguished from the other creditors.

Hypothecary creditors are to be judged according to the law which existed at the time of the constitution of their real right (§ 390); the other creditors according to the law existing at the time when the bankruptcy opens (*gg*). This rule is confirmed by the following propositions of the Roman law: The creditors of the fifth class are satisfied *pro rata*, without respect to the time when their debts originated, for they all have hypothecs originating in the *missio in possessionem*, which is connected with the opening of the bankruptcy. In like manner the creditors of the fourth class have privileged hypothecs; but their right of hypothec, as well as the order of

(*ee*) Weber, pp. 109–113.

(*ff*) Recognised in the Prussian *Allg. Landrecht*, Introd. § 19.

(*gg*) Recognised in the Prussian transitory laws (§ 383): thus in the law of 1814 for the provinces beyond the Elbe (§ 15), and in similar terms in the rest. Weber, pp. 167–178, is of the same opinion.

their privileges, first arises at the time of the *missio in possessionem*, and through it. Previously, therefore, they had a mere expectation of this kind of execution in their favour (as an act of procedure), but no right to it.

Sect. L.—(§ 393.)

A. ACQUISITION OF RIGHTS.—APPLICATIONS.

IV. SUCCESSION.

We now come in our inquiry to the rules relating to *testamentary* and *intestate* succession, and *contracts* about successions.

I. Testaments.—This case is the most difficult and most controverted in the whole scope of the present inquiry.

We must first seek to obtain a firm standpoint for the juridical nature of the testament.

The destiny of an inheritance is to be determined by the last will of the deceased (*suprema, ultima voluntas*), which must be expressed in an appropriate manner. By this is meant the intention existing at the moment of death, because every former purpose may have been changed in the interval. But it is in itself impossible to make a testament at the exact moment of death; nay, more, on account of the entire uncertainty of the time of death, it will often be necessary or expedient to declare the will that is to stand as the last will, at a much earlier and often very distant period. Hence, every testator is to be regarded as acting at two different points of time,—at the time when he makes the testament, and at the moment of death, when he leaves unchanged the testament previously executed. The former may be described as his action in point of fact, the latter as his juridical activity. Only the product of the second can, and ought to have effect; that of the first remains during the whole interval generally quite unknown, always ineffectual, and always subject to the unchecked and arbitrary power of the testator. These considerations lead us to judge the testator's activity in point of fact (and therefore the form of the testament) according to the law subsisting at the time of execution; the juridical activity (and therefore its substance and contents) according to the law at the date of the death (*a*). And even at this stage we may put aside two different opinions. The one proposes to judge the substance as well as the form as at the time when the testament is made, because the testator is only entitled to have the contents held valid if his will is in conformity with the known (existing) law. In this view prohibitive laws are specially contemplated. A second opinion goes still further, and declares the testament invalid, if it be inconsistent either with the law at the date of the testament, or with the law at the date of the death. To both opinions it may be objected, that it is the substance of the testament of a deceased person only, and one, therefore, which may be operative, that has any importance for the legislator; whereas, what may be written in the testament of a living man is altogether immaterial. How these two opinions have originated in a misapprehension of the rules of the Roman law, can be shown only in the sequel.

From the foregoing considerations, it results that this question as to testaments is analogous to, though not quite identical with, that before discussed relative to usucapion and the prescription of actions (§ 391). Usucapion rested on a continuing state of things, extending without variation over a space of time. The testament consists of two separate activities belonging to different points of time. The two agree in this, therefore, that the fact on which the acquisition of a right depends is *not* of a simple and *transient* nature, such as most juridical facts (contract, tradition, etc.). Hence the following distinction is applicable and important in both cases: A new law, the effect of which is to be determined, may be enacted, first, before the beginning of a usucapion, or before the execution of a testament; secondly, after the expiry of a term of usucapion, or after the death of the testator; thirdly, in the interval between the beginning and the end of the usucapion, between the making of the testament and the testator's death. In the first case the operation and authority of the new law must certainly be affirmed; in the second, as certainly denied. The

(*a*) The personal capacity, as well of the testator as of the heirs and legatees, remains for the present undecided, but will be treated of hereafter.

third case, therefore, is the only object of our present inquiry, just as we have already seen with regard to usucapion (§ 391).

In seeking for the rules applicable to this case of a new law enacted after the execution of a testament, but before the death of the testator, we must keep in view a twofold connection of these rules. First, with the rules above laid down as to collisions of the local law (§ 377); second—and this is more important and more difficult—with the rules as to alterations which take place in the interval between the making of the testament and the testator's death, not in the law, but in the relations of fact. Only alterations of the first kind belong immediately to our subject. Yet, for various reasons, we must not only keep in view changes of the second kind, but we must not shrink from subjecting them to minute and accurate examination. We must do this, first of all, on account of this intimate connection, because the two kinds of changes are in great measure to be judged by similar rules. But it is made still more necessary by the procedure of most modern writers, whose mistakes have generally been occasioned, partly by their mixing up indiscriminately the two kinds of changes referred to, and partly by their erroneous apprehension of the rules of the Roman law as to changes in matter of fact.

I now leave for a time the proper object of the present inquiry, which is confined to the applicability of new laws, in order to answer a different question: What are the rules of Roman law, when, in the interval between the making of a testament and the death of the testator, a change takes place in those relations of fact which may have an influence on the validity of the testament? I repeat that this question is analogous to, but not identical with, the question as to the effect of new laws, and that therefore an application to the one question of the rules regulating the other must be attempted only with great caution.

The objects of such a possible change are the following: personal capacity of the testator in respect to his legal relations, as well as his physical qualities; contents of the testament; personal capacity of the heir or legatee.

1. Personal capacity of the testator in respect of his *legal relations*. This has two distinct conditions, which, however, are subject to the same rules.

A. The testator must have *testamentifactio*. This expression is used in different meanings even by the Roman jurists,—sometimes quite literally, for the making of a testament; elsewhere for the capacity to test irrespective of its conditions, so that in this sense *testamentifactio* is denied to the child and the insane person. But where the expression is used accurately and technically, as, in particular, in Ulpian, it signifies the possession of the *class qualification* in the Roman state, which makes capable of mancipation as the fundamental form of Roman testaments. Thus *testamentifactio* is equivalent to *commercium:* all *cives* and *Latini* have it, all *peregrini* want it (*b*).

B. The testator must be capable of having and leaving estate; he must not therefore, in relation to a future succession, be juridically and necessarily without any estate. In this respect the *filiusfamilias* is incapable, although he has *testamentifactio* and can therefore be a witness to a testament (*c*). In like manner, the *Latinus Junianus* is incapacitated, who also has *testamentifactio*, and can be a witness to a testament. But the *lex Junia* has forbidden him to make a testament for himself, for it ordains that his estate shall, at the moment of his death, fall to his patron, not as an inheritance, but as if he had remained all his life a slave, and therefore incapable of holding property (*d*).

These two conditions of the capacity for testing agree in this, that they are equally necessary at both points of time,—that of making the testament, and that of death,—which is as much as to say that they must apply as well to the actual as to the juridical activity in the testament. He, therefore, who is juridically incapable can *make* no testament, and just as little can he *leave* a testament. But a change of capacity begun and ended within the interval does not affect the testament, for in this case the prætor will support it (*e*).

Two examples will make these rules clear. The testament

(*b*) Ulpian, xx. § 2, compared with xix. §§ 4, 5.
(*c*) Ulpian, xx. §§ 2, 4, 5, 6, 10.
(*d*) Ulpian, xx. §§ 8, 14.
(*e*) Gaius, ii. § 147; Ulpian, xxiii. § 6; *L.* 1, § 8, *de B. P. sec. tab.* (37, 11); *L.* 6, § 12, *de injusto* (28, 3).

is invalid if the testator has not *civitas* at the time of the testament, *or* of his death; not invalid, if he has lost the *civitas* only temporarily in the intermediate period. It is invalid if the testator was a *filiusfamilias* at the time of the testament, *or* at the time of the death; valid, if he was arrogated in the interval, and afterwards emancipated.

It follows, from this treatment of the matter in the Roman law, that the Romans rightly acknowledged and maintained the capacity of the testator at two points of time as a necessity arising from the nature of the thing; that, on the contrary, they regarded the continuance of this condition in the whole intervening period as a mere deduction from strict theory, not demanded by any practical need, and therefore did not require it.

2. Personal capacity of the testator in respect of his *physical qualities*.

This is of quite a different nature from the first kind of capacity. It relates exclusively to matters of fact, and is therefore necessary at the time when the testament is made. But every subsequent change is quite immaterial, and will neither make the testament valid if the capacity for it were wanting at the time of making it, nor invalid if the capacity then existed.

Among these causes of invalidity are minority, insanity; by the older Roman law, also deafness and dumbness. If, then, a minor or an insane person makes a testament, it is and remains invalid even when majority arrives, or the insanity disappears. So the testament of a man of sound mind is and continues valid when he afterwards becomes insane, and even if he dies in this condition (*f*).

3. The contents of the testament belong exclusively to its juridical aspect. Hence no regard is paid to the circumstances which existed only at the time when the testament was made, although the testator had these immediately before his eyes, but only to the circumstances at the time of his death.

This was unquestionable in those relations of fact which had an altogether material nature. The integrity or violation of the *legitima portio* often depends on the amount of the

(*f*) § 1, *J. quib. non est perm.* (2, 12); *L.* 2; *L.* 6, § 1; *L.* 20, § 4, *qui test.* (28, 1); *L.* 8, § 3, *de j. cod.* (29, 7); *L.* 1, §§ 8, 9, *de B. P. sec. tab.* (37, 11).

estate. This is judged as at the time of the death, never as at the time of making the testament, although that was then before the eyes of the testator (*g*). So the lesion of the instituted heir in respect to legacies, which various laws (*Lex Furia*, *Voconia*, *Falcidia*) were intended to prevent, is judged according to the amount of the estate at the time of death, so that its former condition is immaterial (*h*).

In many other cases the invalidity of the contents was of a more rigorously juridical nature: thus the nullity of the testament in which a *Suus* or a *Posthumus* was passed over. Yet the principle above laid down, according to which the contents of the testament were to be judged exclusively as at the time of death, was here also held so just and so conformable to the practical necessity of the case, that it was helped and supplemented by artificial means. If, therefore, the *Suus* or *Posthumus* who was passed over died before the testator, still the testament was and remained null; but it received effect by the prætor granting a *Bonorum Possessio secundum tabulas* (*i*). The same thing took place if the testator erred by passing over an emancipated son, or by unjustly disinheriting a near relation entitled to succeed *ab intestato*, only with this difference, that here the result followed of itself, not by an intervention of the prætor. For the emancipated person who was passed over had no more than a claim by *B. P. contra tabulas*, which was an entirely personal remedy offered to a *præteritus* alive at the opening of the succession. Hence, the preterition of an emancipated son who died before the testator had no effect, because to him no such *B. P. c. t.* could be granted. It was just the same with the *Querela inofficiosi* of a relative unjustly excluded from intestate succession. For this, too, is a purely personal legal remedy, which cannot come into question if the person so excluded dies before the testator. Comp. vol. ii. § 73, G.

(*g*) *L.* 8, § 9, *de inoff.* (5, 2).

(*h*) § 2, *J. de L. Falc.* (2, 22); *L.* 73, *pr. ad. L. Falc.* (35, 2).

(*i*) Ulpian, xxiii. § 6, *L.* 12, *pr. de injusto* (28, 3). This treatment of the matter may be thus expressed: The nullity caused by preterition was an absolute one by the *jus civile*. The prætor changed it into a relative one, so that it could be appealed to only by the living *præteritus* himself, and not by a third party, for whose benefit it was not introduced. According to the strict civil law, the preterition of the *Suus* or *Posthumus* was a nullity in form, but the prætor treated it as a mere portion of the contents of the testament.

4. Personal capacity of the *person favoured* (the heir or legatee).—This case is the most difficult of all, and it has created the most numerous misunderstandings in this doctrine.

In itself this point pertains to the contents of the testament, so that, on general principles, we should only have had to consider the relations of fact at the time of the death, without regard to previous circumstances. Yet the Romans have treated it quite differently, and we must attempt to elucidate the grounds of this treatment.

The Roman theory is as follows: The juridical capacity of the heir and the legatee depends on the same *testamentifactio* as that of the testator (Note *b*), so that all *cives* and *Latini* have it, all *peregrini* have it not (*k*). This class capacity must exist at three points of time (*tria tempora*),—at the date of the testament, at death (*l*), at the time of acquisition. Properly continuing capacity in the interval would also be necessary; yet this requirement is overlooked, so that a temporary incapacity in the intervening period does not disqualify (*media tempora non nocent*) (*m*).

What, then, is the reason for deviating in this special case from the treatment that we should expect in accordance with general principles? We may here disregard the third point of time (acquisition of the inheritance), which is implied as a matter of course, and is generally unimportant. Thus there remains to be explained and accounted for the remarkable rule, that the capacity of the person favoured is required *not only* at the time of the testator's death (as might be expected), but also at the time of making the testament, so that incapacity existing at this time (*e.g. peregrinitas*) makes the testament invalid for

(*k*) Ulpian, xxii. §§ 1, 2, 3. Here neither the *filiusfamilias* nor the *Latinus Junianus* is excluded, because he who is without means can indeed leave nothing, yet can acquire what is bequeathed to him. Neither is the child and the insane person, because it is not necessary to will or to act in order to be instituted.

(*l*) In conditional institutions the time of the fulfilment of the condition takes the place of this point of time, and therefore does not constitute a fourth point.

(*m*) The chief texts for this doctrine are the following: § 4, *J. de her. qual.* (2, 19); *L.* 6, § 2; *L.* 49, § 1; *L.* 59, § 4, *de her. inst.* (28, 5). The interval here mentioned is, however, to be referred only to the first period, between the testament and the death; incapacity in the second, between the death and acquisition, certainly disqualifies, because by it the succession instantaneously devolves on some other person, whether the substitute or the heir *ab intestato*.

ever, even if the instituted heir afterwards acquires the Roman citizenship.

The explanation of this striking phenomenon is neither difficult nor doubtful. It is found in the fundamental form of the Roman testament as a mancipation of the existing patrimony (*n*), as of an ideal whole (without respect to its separate constituents or to possible increase or diminution), whereby the whole operation assumed the form of a fictitious contract as to the succession, and thus of a juridical act *inter vivos*, all the persons interested in the testament (represented by the *familiæ emtor*) being regarded as the active and co-operating parties to it. Hence they were all required to have personal capacity at the date of this imaginary contract.

That this rule was in fact purely theoretical, adopted for the sake of the juridical form, and therefore was not founded on the recognition of any practical want, appears from the following circumstance. Somewhat later, restrictions of the personal capacity to acquire were introduced by positive legislation, in which it was supposed to be possible to escape from the observance of those ancient forms: this case occurred in regard to the unmarried, the childless, and the *Latini Juniani*. In this newly invented incapacity the status at the time of making the testament was not at all regarded; nay, the change went a step farther on the other side; for not even the time of death was regarded, but only the time of acquisition. This last rule, however, had the practical end, that the offered succession should be a motive to the unmarried immediately to enter into wedlock; to the *Latinus Junianus*, to make himself rapidly worthy of the *jus quiritium* (*o*).

This, and not, as many believe, the *regula Catoniana* (*p*), is the true reason of the remarkable rule of the *tria tempora*. The error of this view of its origin results from the following considerations: The *tria tempora* are nowhere referred to this isolated and comparatively late rule, and must therefore have had a more general and more ancient basis. Moreover, the rule of Cato applies only to legacies (Note *p*), and, in particular,

(*n*) Gaius, ii. § 103.

(*o*) Ulpian, xxii. § 3, compared with xvii. § 1, and iii. §§ 1-6.

(*p*) *L.* 1, *pr. de Reg. Cat.* (34, 7): 'Quod, si testamenti facti tempore decessit testator, inutile foret; id legatum, quandocunque decesserit, non valere.'

not to successions (*q*). Thus it does not in general affect the personal capacity of the party favoured, which alone is here in question, but other conditions of the invalidity of a legacy; in particular, the case in which the testator bequeaths a thing *per vindicationem*, without having Roman property in it at the date of the testament. This legacy is invalid, even if he afterwards acquires the Roman property of the thing (*r*).

Summarizing the foregoing discussion, we may say that the whole doctrine of the *tria tempora* was not founded at all on the nature of the thing, on the essential nature of the testament, but had a merely accidental historical occasion. Nay, we must add that it would have been logically consistent to give up this doctrine altogether in the law of Justinian, seeing that the notion of mancipation as the basis of the testament had then altogether vanished.

The preceding inquiry did not concern the question as to the collision of laws in time, and it was therefore a digression, but an indispensable one. For in now applying myself to the investigation of the changes which take place, not in the facts, but in the laws, I must constantly recur to the analogy of the rules just laid down. Still we must make use of them with caution and discrimination, especially distinguishing whether the rules are deduced from the nature of the thing, or from special grounds. I shall adhere to the same order of the cases as has been followed in treating of alterations in matter of fact.

1. Personal capacity of the testator with reference to his *legal relations*.

This must exist at *two* periods,—at the time of making the testament, and at the time of death; if it is wanting at either of them, the testament is and continues null (p. 325). But it may fail just because the status of the testator is not such as is required by the law in force at one of these periods (*s*).

(*q*) *L.* 3, *eod.*: 'Catoniana regula non pertinet ad hereditates.' Cujacius, *Obs.* iv. 4, it is true, proposes to read 'libertates,' but this emendation is quite arbitrary, and supported neither by manuscripts nor by any real necessity. Comp. Voorda, *Interpret.* ii. 22.

(*r*) Ulpian, xxiv. § 7.

(*s*) Chabot, t. ii. pp. 438, 439. On the other hand, Meyer, pp. 121-131, thinks that incapacity at the time of making the testament does not affect it, and attempts to defend this groundless assertion against irrelevant objections founded on the *regula Catoniana*.

The following examples will illustrate the matter: According to the Roman law, all *cives*, all independent *Latini* (*t*), but not the *peregrini*, could test (p. 325). Suppose, then, such a *Latinus* had made a testament, and during his life *testamentifactio* had been withdrawn from all Latini by an imperial constitution, the testament would have become null on account of his incapacity at death. Suppose a *peregrinus* had made a testament, and during his life an imperial constitution bestowed *testamentifactio* on all *peregrini*, the testament would have remained invalid on account of his incapacity at the time of executing it.

2. Personal capacity of the testator with reference to his *physical qualities*.

This must exist only at the time of the execution of the testament, and therefore the law then in force exclusively decides. A testament validly made according to that law cannot become invalid through a later law, and so also *vice versa*.

Thus, in the older Roman law, dumb persons were incapable of testing; Justinian gave them this capacity (*u*). If, then, a dumb man had tested shortly before this law was enacted, the testament did not become valid in consequence of the new law; but he could execute a new testament. The Roman law fixes at twelve years of age the ability of females to test (*v*), the Prussian law at fourteen (*w*). If, then, a girl of thirteen makes a will under the authority of the Roman law, it remains valid even if the Prussian law is soon after introduced, and death ensues before the completion of the fourteenth year. If the testament is executed under the Prussian law at the age of thirteen, it remains invalid even if the Roman law is introduced immediately after.

3. The *contents* of the testament are regulated entirely according to the time of death, so that the law then in force exclusively determines as to the validity of the contents, irre-

(*t*) Among these were formerly the *Latini colonarii* (Ulpian, xix. § 4), and, after these had ceased to exist, all descendants of a *Latinus Junianus*, for the prohibition of the *Lex Junia* affected only himself, not his descendants, who were *Latini ingenui*.

(*u*) *L.* 10, *C. qui test.* (6, 22).

(*v*) *L.* 5, *qui test.* (28, 1).

(*w*) *A. L. R.* i. 12, § 16.

spective of the rules of the former law, even of that under which the testament was made (*x*).

The following are applications of this rule, which is of greater practical importance than all the others.

Legitim and preterition are to be judged according to the law in force at the time of death (*y*). Likewise the *fideicommissa* (*substitutions*) prohibited in the French code (*z*). Likewise the vulgar substitution which was forbidden in France in 1790, but again permitted by the code (*aa*).

4. Personal capacity of the *person favoured* (heir or legatee).

In the cases and questions hitherto discussed, exactly the same rules have necessarily been applied to changes in law which were before recognised by Roman law in respect to changes in the relations of fact (pp. 325–327), for this recognition was founded on the general nature of the testament itself, and therefore on the actual necessities of the case. It is quite different with the question as to the personal capacity of the person favoured, as to whom changes of fact are judged in Roman law according to the rule of the *tria tempora*. For this rule was founded on no internal, but only on historical reasons,—reasons which had already disappeared at the time of Justinian, and certainly can no longer have any significance for us. Here, therefore, we must altogether abandon the analogy of that rule of the Roman law, and confine ourselves to the real nature of the testament. But this leads us to regard the personal capacity of the person favoured as a component part of the contents of the testament, and therefore to judge it exclusively according to the law in force at the time of death, with-

(*x*) Chabot, t. ii. pp. 367–370, 382, 445–454, who takes the most correct view of this point, though with an intermixture of many errors as to the Roman law. Weber, pp. 96–98, makes the testament become invalid, if its contents are at variance *either* with the law at the time of the testament, *or* that at the time of death; he therefore treats this point in the same way as the juridical capacity of the testator (No. 1). Bergmann, §§ 16, 19, 51, assumes that by Roman law the substance is to be judged only according to the law at the date of the testament, and that to pay regard to the time of death is an erroneous view of the French jurists, but one that has penetrated into their legislation.

(*y*) Chabot, t. ii. pp. 225, 464–475.

(*z*) Chabot, t. ii. p. 382. Comp. Meyer, pp. 132–148.

(*aa*) Chabot, t. ii. pp. 367–370.

out respect to the law which may have existed previously, as at the date of making the testament (*bb*).

It was shown above, that the *regula Catoniana* need not lead us astray in this matter, and that we have therefore no occasion to attempt, by technical reasoning, to dispute the applicability of this rule in our time, as many have sought to do. In particular, that rule cannot for a moment be applied with any plausibility to the capacity of an instituted heir (Notes *p*, *q*).

5. The law as to the form of the testament has still to be considered; of which there was no occasion to speak in regard to changes in the state of facts.

The form of the testament is entirely a matter of fact. The testament, therefore, must be held valid or invalid, according as its form corresponds to the law in force at its date, or not, so that in this respect a subsequent law can make no change whatever either to the advantage or the disadvantage of the testament (*cc*). This proposition also is entirely in accordance with the more general rules before laid down (§ 388).

Under this rule, therefore, a holograph testament made under the French law remains valid, although before the death of the testator the Prussian law is introduced, which does not recognise private testaments. Conversely, a holograph private testament executed under Prussian law remains null, even if the French law, which allows this form of testament, is introduced during the life of the testator (*dd*).

6. Finally, we have still to mention the case in which a law entirely *abolishes* testamentary succession, and consequently declares legal succession to be alone valid; not that this case can be of practical importance, but because the consideration of it may serve better to establish the theory as to the whole subject.

If, then, a testament is made under a law which prohibits testaments altogether, it is and remains null, even if, before the death of the testator, a new law should permit them to be made. This must be admitted, if it were only because no suitable form

(*bb*) Chabot, t. ii. pp. 462–464, quite agrees with this decision, without going into the justification of it here attempted.

(*cc*) Chabot, t. ii. pp. 394–399; Weber, p. 90.

(*dd*) A somewhat different rule of the Prussian law has already been mentioned (§ 388, *o*), and will again be discussed in § 394.

can be employed for such a will according to the existing law; but that would be requisite according to the rule above laid down (No. 5).

The testament is also invalid, if testamentary succession was allowed at the time of making it, but forbidden at the time of death by a new law. In fact the new law was intended to deprive of effect the whole contents of the testament; but the validity of the contents is to be judged according to the law in force at the time of death (No. 3). But a second and still more decisive reason leads to the same result. Such a new law properly concerns, not the acquisition of a right (namely, of the succession by means of a testament), but the existence of a whole legal institution (testamentary succession), and in laws of this kind there is no question whatever as to their retroactive force (§ 384).

The most doubtful case seems to be that in which testaments are recognised by law at the time of execution, and at the time of death, but a temporary law had prohibited them in the interval. I would be inclined to apply to this case the analogy of the Roman rule, *media tempora non nocent* (Note *m*), and to admit the validity of the testament.

SECT. LI.—(§ 394.)

A. ACQUISITION OF RIGHTS.—APPLICATIONS.

IV. SUCCESSION.—*Continuation.*

The limits in time of the authority of new laws in reference to testaments has hitherto been examined only from general points of view, with regard to the general nature of the testaments, irrespective of the direct provisions of positive laws. The Roman law was discussed in relation to a different question, —that as to alterations in the circumstances which exert an influence on the validity of testaments. An application, merely by way of analogy, of its rules as to this other question was attempted for the solution of the problem before us. I will now inquire what decisions of positive legislations can be used to aid us in the solution of this question; that is to say, to determine what influence on the validity of testaments must be ascribed to new laws.

First, the Roman law is to be discussed. In it we find no general rule as to this question. The general principle which prohibits the retroactivity of laws (§ 386) is not sufficient for testaments, because these do not, like contracts and alienations, belong to a single point of time, but to several (§ 393); so that it may be dubious in what respects the testament may be ranked among *futura negotia*, or rather among *facta præterita* (*pendentia negotia*).

On the other hand, we find in many Roman laws very distinct transitory provisions upon the question to what testaments these new laws shall, or shall not, be applied. It was very natural to suppose that such transitory dispositions contained also the expression of the general and permanent principle relating to this question, and many modern writers have constructed their theories under the influence of this idea. But the supposition is very questionable, and in many cases demonstrably false. For the transitory provision may, in the particular case, have originated, not so much from the conviction that it ought to be so according to general principles and because it was in accordance with the nature of testaments, as from considerate regard for existing facts; but if so, the transitory provision is not the enunciation of a rule recognised as true, but rather of an indulgent exception from that rule. This purpose of the legislator is not only always possible, but in this very subject it is in several cases quite apparent. We shall therefore compare the various transitory provisions of the Roman law as to the law of testaments, which are now to be stated in their order, with the general principles before established (§ 393), in order to see as to each of these provisions whether it should be regarded as recognising and stating the rule, or rather as creating an exception.

1. Such a transitory disposition occurs in the *Lex Falcidia*, which has these words in its first chapter (*a*):—

(*a*) *L.* 1, *pr. ad leg. Falc.* (35, 2). A similar transitory provision of the *Lex Voconia* (qui heredem fecerit) is mentioned by Cicero (*in Verrem*, i. 41, 42),—a law to which the unjust edict of Verres had given retroactive force by the words, '*fecit fecerit.*'

[illegible]

[illegible]

[illegible] from the neglect of this precaution. [illegible] because [illegible] it might be very immaterial to the lawgiver whether [illegible] application some years sooner or later.

It must, however, be specially observed, that it was not the *purpose and consequence* of this law to limit a liberty of testators in reference to legacies till then unrestrained, but rather to substitute new and more appropriate regulations for the quite different, and in many cases more rigorous, restrictions of the *Lex Furia* and the *Lex Voconia* (b). The intention, therefore, was to apply to the pending testaments of living persons the *Lex Furia* and *Lex Voconia*; to future wills only the *Lex Falcidia*.

2. In 531, Justinian ordained that the institution of an heir should be valid only when the testator wrote the name of the heir with his own hand, or declared it aloud before the witnesses. But this rule was applicable only to future testaments, not to those already made (c). In this transitory provision there was a simple application of the principles above established, for the new law related entirely to the form of the testament (§ 393, No. 5). But three years after (534), that law was adopted into the last code, along with the transitory addition. This involved a provision that the testaments made

(b) Gaius, II. §§ 224–227.

(c) L. 29, C. de test. (6, 23). All this law has only a historical interest, as it was abrogated a few years afterwards. Nov. 119, C. 9 (A.D. 544).

in the three years that had elapsed (between 531 and 534), to which the law had already become applicable, should be exempt from it; and thus in some sort it was an amnesty to breaches of the law committed in these testaments. This remarkable repetition of the transitory rule might perhaps have been held as a mere oversight; but Justinian himself in a later law declared it to be intentional, and founded on the observation that the new law was not at first sufficiently known, a defect which its insertion in the new code was to repair (*d*).

3. The *legitima portio*, according to the old law, was a fourth of the heir's intestate portion. Justinian increased it, according to circumstances, to a third or a half (*e*). As this law concerned the contents of the testament, it would necessarily have been applied to testaments already made. But Justinian ordained that it should be applied only to future testaments, thus making again a favourable exception (*f*).

4. By imperial constitutions, the power of a father to provide by last will for his children by a concubine, was restricted in many varying ways (*g*). One of these restrictive laws enacts that such children, if there were no lawful issue, might obtain the half of the estate. But it was added that this should apply only to testaments afterwards to be made (*h*). Here there was another exception; for the law related to the contents of the testament, and would therefore have been properly applicable to pending testaments.

5. By the *Lex Julia* and the *L. Papia Poppæa* under Augustus, a very intricate caducity of successions and legacies had been introduced. This legal institution, which was modified by many subsequent laws, was altogether abolished by Justinian in 534, yet with the provision that the new law should be applied only to testaments afterwards made (*i*). Here, again, was an exception to the rules, as the new law had for its object the contents of the will.

The Prussian law has only a few permanent rules, made

(*d*) *Nov.* 66, *C.* 1, § 1.
(*e*) *Nov.* 18 (A.D. 536).
(*f*) *Nov.* 66, *C.* 1, §§ 2–5 (A.D. 538).
(*g*) Göschen, *Vorlesungen*, iii. 2, § 793.
(*h*) *L.* 8, *C. de natur. lib.* (5, 27). Justinian (A.D. 528).
(*i*) *L. un.* § 15, *C. de cad. toll.* (6, 51).

for all times, as to our question; and these do not answer the question directly, but can be made use of only inferentially. It will be more convenient to notice these at the close of this inquiry.

On the other hand, our legislation is rich in transitory provisions as to testaments which enunciate no universal and permanent principle, but which, in introducing new laws, regulate the treatment of testaments, and in doing so, at the utmost, but not always, allow us to catch a glimpse of a general principle.

These transitory rules are the following (§ 383):—

The patent introducing the Allgemeine Landrecht in 1794 enacts, in § 12, that all testaments then made 'shall be judged *entirely* by the rules of the old laws, although the decease of the testator should happen afterwards.' *Entirely*, therefore in respect both of form and matter. The first is a simple application of the principles above stated; the second is a favourable exception to these principles (§ 393, No. 3), similar to the many exceptions already cited from the Roman laws.

The three patents of 1803 agree with this in the very words of their 6th section.

A novelty in two respects occurs in the patent of 1814 for the provinces beyond the Elbe (*k*).

The first new provision stands in connection with the previous rules just cited, and modifies them.

§ 6. All testaments and last wills which have been executed before 1st January 1815 must, *in respect of their form*, be judged entirely by the rules of the older laws, although the death of the testator should have occurred afterwards.

The addition, 'in respect of their form,' which is altogether wanting in the earlier patents, evidently expresses the opposite of 'in respect of their matter,' and therefore indicates that the matter should be judged rather according to the new law (the law at the time of death). This involves the recognition of the rules before stated as to the laws applicable to the form and the contents of testaments (*l*).

(*k*) *Gesetzsammlung*, 1814, pp. 89–96.

(*l*) Bergmann wrongly supposes (p. 565) that there is here no deviation from the older patents.

The second innovation will be stated below.

The new rule just cited was more minutely and more accurately expressed in the patent of 1816 for West Prussia (§ 383).

§ 8. All testaments . . . . in respect of their *form*, are to be judged entirely according to the former laws. *The contents of testaments are also valid in so far as they are not contrary to prohibitive laws at the time when the succession opens. In this latter respect particularly, the instituted heir's capacity to inherit, and the legitima portio, are to be judged according to the laws prevailing when the succession opens.*

The transitory laws since promulgated adopt the terms of this.

A distinction is here unquestionably drawn between form and matter with reference to the application of different laws. In laws as to the form, the time of executing the testament; in laws as to the matter, the time of death—is to be regarded; and the laws as to the capacity of the person favoured are quite rightly placed in this second class. Thus the whole series of rules above established is recognised as correct, with the single exception of the laws as to the personal capacity of the testator, about which nothing is said.

Among the regained provinces, however, there were three in which, until this time, French law had prevailed, and in which; therefore, there were necessarily testaments of living persons accredited partly by the holograph of the testator, partly by notarial attestation. This was held too hazardous; and hence, along with that general law, and partly deviating from it, the special direction was given for these provinces, that *such* pending testaments should continue effectual for one year only. Within this year the testator might make a new testament according to the judicial form required by the Landrecht. If the testator should die after the expiry of this year without having executed a new testament, the earlier one was declared ineffectual, unless it could be proved that he had been continuously disabled from making a new testament (*m*). In this very special rule there is evidently no expression of a general

(*m*) *Provinces beyond the Elbe* (1814), § 7; *West Prussia* (1816), § 9; *Posen* (1816), § 9. See above, § 383.

and permanent principle, but only an expedient for a single case. And in the other transitory laws there is no similar regulation.

Independently, however, of these transitory laws, the Landrecht itself contains the following permanent provisions, which may be used in determining the present question as to testaments (pp. 337–8):—

A. If a juridical act satisfies, in the forms employed in its execution, not the law under which it was done, but a later law, it shall by way of exception be maintained (*n*).

This rule does not apply specially to testaments, but to juridical acts in general, and therefore to testaments; and it derogates in regard to them from the rules above laid down. It is, however, quite unimportant for the new introduction of the rules of the Landrecht in regard to testaments; for a stricter form for testaments than that imposed by the Landrecht can hardly be imagined as existing in any country, so that nowhere could a testament be maintained by the supervening form of the Landrecht being less strict than that previously in use. The provision would be of practical importance only if at some future time an easier form of testament, such as that of the French law, should be introduced in the Prussian state.

B. The personal capacity of the testator is to be judged as at the time of making the testament (*o*). This maxim relates, however, as the following sentences show, to changes in the fact, not in the law, and can therefore be applied only by analogy to changes of the latter kind. Particular applications of it have been made in the following way:—

a. Natural incapacity at the time of the testament makes it invalid, even if the defect then existing should afterwards be removed, *e.g.* by the attainment of maturer age (*p*). This principle is in harmony with our rules.

b. Incapacity at the time of the testament resting on legal grounds loses its influence if the defect is afterwards removed (*q*). Here there is a deviation from our rules (§ 393, No. 1).

(*n*) *A. L. R. Einl.* § 17. See above, § 388, *c*. The very questionable contents of this law are there discussed.
(*o*) *A. L. R.* i. 12, § 11.
(*p*) *A. L. R.* i. 12, § 12.
(*q*) *A. L. R.* i. 12, § 13.

c. If, on the other hand, the testator had capacity at the time of making the testament, but afterwards loses it as a penalty for an unlawful act, the testament becomes invalid (*r*). This is in accordance with our rules.

C. 'In judging of the capacity of an heir or legatee, the time of the opening of the succession must be looked to' (*s*). This disposition, like the foregoing, is certainly intended to refer only to changes of fact relating to the person, but may unquestionably be applied by analogy to changes in the legislation also; and in this application it perfectly agrees with our rules.

The Austrian code contains no special transitory disposition as to testaments, but it has the general rule that the new code *shall have no effect on* past acts, even if these acts consist of declarations of intention which could still be altered by the sole power of their authors, and could be repeated according to the rules contained in the present code (*t*). Here testaments are evidently intended, and the words contain just the same rule which has been cited from the Prussian patent of 1794, and compared with our rules.

The opinions of the most authoritative writers have already been stated in treating of the particular questions. Weber errs chiefly in making the juridical validity of the matter of the testament depend on its conformity to the laws of both points of time, while Bergmann wrongly regards the time of making the testament alone. Chabot here takes more correct views than the other two writers (§ 393, *x*). But all have fallen into many errors in consequence of the following mistakes.

They have not sufficiently distinguished between the changes which may occur in relations of fact, and those which may take place in consequence of new laws; nor between natural defects and the legislative rules by which the personal capacity of the testator may be restricted. In the Roman law they have mistaken the true principles of many rules (especially of the *tria tempora*), and have wrongly suggested other inadmissible prin-

(*r*) *A. L. R.* i. 12, § 14.
(*s*) These are the words of the *A. L. R.* i. 12, § 43.
(*t*) The words of the patent of 1811, pp. 5, 6.

ciples, among which especially the *regula Catoniana.* But above all they have generalized the particular transitory rules of the Roman law, and have discovered in these the expression of general and permanent principles as to the relation of old and new laws about testaments, quite contrary to the intention of the authors of these rules.

SECT. LII.—(§ 395.)

A. ACQUISITION OF RIGHTS.—APPLICATIONS.

IV. SUCCESSION.—*Continuation.*

II. *Intestate Succession* has much simpler relations than testamentary, because here we have not to consider two often very distant facts,—the execution of the testament, and the opening of the succession. The two cases, however, are alike in this, that in intestate succession also, relations of fact with their alterations, as well as new laws, are to be regarded; and that the Roman law has laid down minute rules as to the former, the analogy of which is to be used in the case of new laws.

The personal capacity of the deceased to leave succession *ab intestato* is to be judged as at the time of death. The Roman law requires *civitas*, in the sense that the rules of Roman intestate succession could be applied only at the death of a Roman citizen, while the succession of foreigners dying in the Roman state was regulated by the law of their own country. A Roman who had undergone a *magna capitis deminutio* (a *deportatus* or a *servus pœnæ*) could leave no succession; what he had, or seemed to have, belonged to the fiscus.

The personal capacity to be called to any intestate succession depended on the same condition of *civitas;* the *magna capitis deminutio* caused incapacity, while the *minima* was not an absolute hindrance, but only removed certain claims to intestate succession founded on agnation (*a*). It was certainly necessary that this capacity should exist at the opening of the succession, and also at the time of the acquisition, nay, even in

(*a*) *L.* 1, §§ 4, 8, *ad Sc. Tert.* (38, 17).

the whole intermediate period, since every incapacity of an heir called *ab intestato* occurring within this period at once devolves his share of the succession on some other person, called along with him or after him (§ 393, *m*). These rules operate alike, whether the change which causes the incapacity to succeed is produced by new relations of fact or by a new law.

But the personal relation of the heir *ab intestato* to the testator, which chiefly consists in kindred, is the most important as well as the most difficult question. This relation regulates both the claim of each individual to the quality of heir, and the definite position which he is to hold in the series of all the conceivable heirs to the succession. This personal relation must be judged as at the time of *the opening of the succession*, which generally, but not always, coincides with the time of the *death*.

We have here to consider the two kinds of possible changes.

A. Changes in the *relations of fact*.

Circumstances and changes before the death of the testator have here no influence. It is true that very definite and reasonable expectations may have arisen. Near relations may have reckoned with great certainty on the intestate succession of a rich childless man of advanced age, and this expectation may have been disappointed by a late marriage, with children. But mere expectations are never protected by rules of law, and those relations were bound to keep in view the possibility of such a change, as well as of a will.

But in order to determine more exactly the decisive period, two preliminary, and in some sort negative, rules have to be stated.

1. No one can be considered as heir *ab intestato* who is conceived after the death of the ancestor. The fundamental condition is, therefore, that an heir *ab intestato* was born, or at least begotten, during the life of the deceased (*b*).

2. If one who is called to a succession declines it, or dies before having acquired it, it seems natural that, in consequence of this change of circumstances, he who is called after him should come in his place; and this is called a *successio* (*ordinum, graduum*). This *successio*, however, was not admitted in the old civil law, when the letter of the Twelve Tables was anxiously

(*b*) § 8, *I. de her. quæ ab int.* (3, 1); *L.* 6, 7, 8, *pr. de suis* (38, 16). As to the assimilation of the *nasciturus* to the *natus*, comp. vol. ii. § 62.

adhered to. The prætor allowed it in the new classes of succession which he introduced (*c*); but Justinian made it universal (*d*).

Having stated these two preliminary rules, we have now to determine more exactly the point of time at which the existing relations of fact regulate the succession *ab intestato*. Generally, we can state this to be the time of *the opening of the succession*, which may, however, according to circumstances, occur at two different times.

In this respect we have to distinguish two cases.

The first is when a testament exists, and the intestate succession only opens by its invalidation. Then the time of this invalidation is to be regarded as the time when the succession opens. This occurs if an heir called by the testament refuses to accept, if he dies before acceptance, if the institution is subject to a condition which is not fulfilled. In all these cases it is assumed that there are no other testamentary heirs by whom the testament may be supported. The opening of the succession takes place in these cases when the testamentary heir refuses or dies, or the condition fails. It may be said of each of these facts, that it makes it certain that no testamentary succession will take place, and that it thus opens the succession *ab intestato*.

The second case is when no testament exists. Then the opening of the succession is to be placed unconditionally at the time of the death, at no other conceivable point either sooner or later.

This important question is thus decided in the following passage of the *Institutes* (*e*):—

> Proximus autem, siquidem nullo testamento facto quisquam decesserit, per hoc tempus requiritur, *quo mortuus est is, cujus de hereditate quæritur*. Quod si facto testamento quisquam decesserit, per hoc tempus requiritur, *quo certum esse cœperit, nullum ex testamento heredem exstituturum;* tunc enim proprie quisque intestato decessisse intelligitur.

(*c*) Gaius, iii. §§ 12, 22, 28; Ulpian, xxvi. § 5.
(*d*) § 7, *I. de legit. agnat. succ.* (3, 2).
(*e*) § 6, *I. de legit. agnat. succ.* (3, 2). For the first case, that in which the testament is invalidated, there are many authorities. Gaius, iii. § 13; *L.* 1, § 8; *L.* 2, § 5; *L.* 5, *de suis* (38, 16).

We are now to consider the second case, in which there is no testament. By the foregoing rule we are directed to fix the heirs, called and not called *ab intestato*, entirely according to the personal relations which existed at the time of death. It may be said perhaps that this is no positive direction, that it is a matter of course, because no later time could be even imagined. But this view would be quite erroneous. The greater number of the cases which have just been mentioned in respect of testamentary heirs, may also occur with those called *ab intestato*. Several of these may refuse, or may die before acceptance; what shall then become of the shares which fell to them?

Two courses are here possible. First, we may adhere to the distribution fixed as at the time of death, and apply the vacant share according to it as far as possible. This share will then fall to the co-heirs by the *jus accrescendi*, and the *successio ordinum* or *graduum* will come in only if there are no such co-heirs, and therefore as a secondary expedient. But, secondly, we can take the opposite course, adopt the present time when the share becomes vacant as the time of the opening of the succession, and regulate the whole succession anew. Then the *successio ordinum* or *graduum* will be preferred, and the *jus accrescendi* may perhaps be applied as a secondary expedient.

In accordance with the principle formerly laid down, we must unquestionably prefer the first method, which treats the time of the death as the fixed period for the opening of the succession, even if a subsequent change of circumstances should render necessary a supplementary distribution. Or, in other words, in the collision of the *jus accrescendi* with the *successio ordinum*, the *jus accrescendi* should have the preference (*f*).

B. Changes in Legislation.

We have here, as in regard to testaments (§ 393), to follow

(*f*) This question is the object of an old and famous controversy. The opinion which I have adopted is defended by Göschen, *Vorlesungen*, iii. 2, § 929, and Baumeister, *Anwachsungsrecht unter Miterben*, §§ 5-7. A plausible objection is founded on *L.* 1, §§ 10, 11, *L.* 2, *ad Sc. Tert.* (38, 17), which certainly regulate the matter according to the later period, at which the person first called refuses. But according to the plain meaning of these passages, they involve no application of a general principle, but a special rule for the relation of the new civil succession between mother and children to the *jus antiquum* of agnates. The purpose was to prevent the agnates, among whom there was no *successio graduum*, from being totally deprived of the succession by the refusal to accept of the mother or child, quite contrary to the intention of the Senatusconsultum.

the analogy of the rules laid down as to alterations of fact; and we can here do so without hesitation, since these rules are to be considered as the expression of general and permanent principles, on which no merely accidental historical motives have operated, as in the case of testaments.

Following this analogy, we shall be led to the following rules as to the effect of new laws on intestate succession.

1. A new law enacted *before the opening of the succession* must alway take effect on the particular case of intestate succession.

2. We must regard as the time when the succession opens—

a. If there is no testament, the time of death;

b. If there is a testament, the time when it becomes certain that no testamentary succession will take place.

3. A law enacted *after the succession has opened* has no effect, even if it appears in the interval between the opening of the succession and the acquisition of the inheritance. This last proposition is recognised by most jurists (*g*), but disputed by many (*h*).

The opposition to it is based chiefly on the following confusion. It is said that the principle of non-retroactivity has for its object only the preservation of acquired rights. But by the opening of the succession (*delatio*) the heir called has not yet acquired any right; such an acquisition takes place only by the acceptance of the inheritance, and therefore before this a new law may alter the order of succession, without violating the principle of non-retroactivity. The two points (opening and acquisition) coincide only exceptionally in the case of the *suus hæres*, who acquires the inheritance *ipso jure*.

But the heir called does in fact acquire an actual right by the mere opening of the succession, and that without any act of his, even without his knowledge—namely, the exclusive right to enter upon the inheritance, and thereby to make it part of his estate, or, if he so please, to refuse it. This is a true vested right, just as much protected as any other by the principle of non-retroactivity against the undue effect of new laws, and

(*g*) Weber, p. 96. Chabot, t. i. p. 379 ('au moment de l'ouverture de la succession').

(*h*) Heise and Cropp, *Juristische Abhandlungen*, vol. ii. pp. 123, 124, 130–132.

therefore quite different from a mere expectation. Yet it is a right of quite a different kind, and of less extent, than that which afterwards arises through the acceptance of the succession, and by which an estate, formerly belonging to another, is immediately incorporated with the estate of the heir.

This rule is confirmed by the following transitory provisions:—

A law of the Emperor Valentinian II. had given to descendants who were only cognates a succession *ab intestato* to three-fourths of the estates of their ascendants, so that competing agnates could take only a fourth (*i*). Justinian declared the descendants in this concourse to be the exclusive heirs, and therefore exempt from the necessity of giving a fourth to the agnates (*k*). But he added the following words:

> Quod tantum in futuris, *non etiam præteritis negotiis*, servari decernimus.

These words are certainly most simply understood of the future opening of a succession, so that this, and not the *aditio* of the inheritance, is indicated as *futurum negotium*. But that this was really the meaning of the legislator follows incontestably from the words that immediately precede, 'Sed descendentes soli ad mortui successionem *vocentur*,' from which it is clear that the *calling* to the succession, the *delatio*, is the thing which the legislator has in view, in so far as this was not one of the *præterita negotia* upon which the law is to have no effect.

The Prussian transitory law of 1794 says, still more distinctly (in introducing the *A. L. R.*), § 13:

'The legal succession . . ., if the opening of the succession takes place *before* the 1st June 1794, is to be judged according to the previous laws, but afterwards . . . according to the rules of the new Landrecht.'

All the subsequent transitory laws of Prussia are in accordance with this (§ 383).

III. *Irrevocable Contracts as to Successions.*—These are of the same nature as other contracts, and must therefore be judged according to the law in force when they are entered into (*l*). It has been objected that a contract as to a succession

(*i*) *L.* 4, *C. Th. de leg. hered.* (5, 1); § 16, *I. de her. quæ ab intest.* (3, 1).
(*k*) *L.* 12, *C. de suis* (6, 55).
(*l*) Chabot, t. i. p. 133; Struve, pp. 247–249. Comp. above, § 392.

gives no absolutely vested right, because it is always uncertain which of the two parties shall survive the other (*m*). This objection, however, is of no importance, because conditional rights, as well as unconditional, are genuine rights, and are protected by the principle of non-retroactivity against the undue influence of new laws (§ 385, *h*).

SECT. LIII.—(§ 396.)

A. ACQUISITION OF RIGHTS.—APPLICATIONS.

V. LAW OF THE FAMILY.

Among French writers there is often an erroneous confusion of the laws as to the domestic relations with those as to personal status. As, then, in the latter there is generally no question as to the preservation of vested rights (§ 389), so that every new law can have unrestrained influence, they transfer this relation to the laws as to the family, without suspecting that these have always to deal with veritable vested rights, and have to respect them, just as much as the laws relative to things and obligations. The cause of this confusion is found in the excessive use which they make of the division of statutes into *statuts personnels* and *réels*, (§ 361, No. 1), as well as the division of rights under the same names (*a*), by which the pure law of the family, like the status of the person, is ranked with the *droits personnels*, and only the applied law of the family with the *droits réels* (*b*). Although this view is in principle untenable, it has yet been less injurious in its application than could have been expected, because many of the most important questions which these writers include under the law of the family, truly relate to the capacity to act (*c*); and, on the other

(*m*) Weber, pp. 98, 99.

(*a*) *Droits personnels* are those *qui sont attachés aux personnes; droits réels* are the *droits attachés aux biens.*

(*b*) Chabot, i. pp. 23, 29–31, 34, 377, 378. Bergmann, § 50, rightly blames, but without sufficiently marking, this confusion.

(*c*) Among these is, in particular, the *autorisation maritale*, which belongs properly, not to the law of marriage, but to the tutory of women. See above, § 389, No. 2.

hand, many important laws as to the family relations, especially marriage, are not subject to the principle of non-retroactivity, because they relate, not to the acquisition, but to the existence of rights.

I. Marriage (*d*).—As marriage is a veritable contract (*e*), we might expect that the laws in force when it is entered into should necessarily and exclusively decide as to every question connected with it. Yet this rule, in itself correct, has in the pure law of marriage (*i.e.* irrespective of the influence of marriage on the patrimonial estate) (*f*), only a very limited application.

The question as to the validity of a marriage must certainly be judged exclusively according to the law in force at the time (*g*).

The personal power of the husband over the wife is always but slightly affected by the operation of the positive law and the judicial office. But the most important practical application of this power, in a legal point of view—namely, the marital guardianship—does not pertain to the law of marriage at all, but to that of personal status (Note *c*).

Divorce would be more important than any other matter, if it were to be judged according to the law in force at the time of contracting the marriage. But it will afterwards be shown, that neither this time, nor that of the fact which is alleged as the ground of divorce, ought to regulate, but only the time when the action is brought (*h*).

On the contrary, the law of matrimonial property (applied marriage law) is a very important object in the application of our principles. Here we must assert that the law in force at the time when the marriage is contracted must, as a rule, be applied, even if subsequent laws alter the patrimonial rights of the spouses (*i*). This question is similar to that as to the local

(*d*) The rules as to the local limits of laws should be compared; *v.* § 379.

(*e*) See vol. iii. § 141.

(*f*) As to the notion of the pure and applied law of the family, see vol. i. §§ 54–58.

(*g*) For the same reasons as were before adduced in regard to the local law (§ 379); comp. *Code Civil*, art. 170. Reinhardt, *on Glück*, vol. i. p. 10, is of the same opinion. Bergmann, p. 30, somewhat differs.

(*h*) See below, § 399. Comp. § 379, No. 6.

(*i*) The greater number of writers are of this opinion. Chabot, vol. i. pp. 79–81; Meyer, p. 167; Pfeiffer, *praktische Ausführungen*, vol. ii. pp. 271–276; Mittermaier, *deutsches Recht*, § 400, No. V.

law applicable, and most of the reasons (*k*) that were urged in discussing that question (§ 379) in favour of applying the law in force at the domicile of the husband at the time when the marriage was contracted, without respect to a subsequent change of domicile, are also arguments against the influence of subsequent changes in the laws.

The following are applications of this important principle:—

The relation of the *dotal régime* to the communion of goods: whether one of these institutions shall govern exclusively, or both together, and in what position towards each other.

The nature of the *dos; dos profectitia;* transmission to heirs of the right of repetition; immediate return of the property to heirs. It must be remarked, however, that where the *dos* is constituted (not *ipso jure*, but) according to the pure Roman principle only by the voluntary act of the person who appoints it, the law applicable must be determined, not as at the time when the marriage is contracted, but at the time when the *dos* is constituted. This point is expressly recognised in a transitory law of Justinian (*l*). Just in the same way, however, the community of goods must be judged by the law of some subsequent period, if it is founded in any particular case, not by the law subsisting when the marriage is concluded, but by a contract between the spouses afterwards made (*m*).

The consequences of a second marriage in regard to the estate. This also is recognised by a transitory rule of Justinian (*n*).

The restrictions on the liberality of spouses to one another will be treated of below (§ 399).

The so-called succession between spouses is of a twofold nature. It is often the mere development and effect of a state of matrimonial rights already subsisting during their lives, especially of the communion of goods in some one of its numerous forms. It is then regulated by the law of the time when

(*k*) I say, the most of the reasons, not all. For here we cannot apply the argument, that the sole will of the husband, on which the choice of the domicile depends, ought not to change the subsisting law of marriage property. A change of the positive law certainly does not depend on the mere will of the husband.

(*l*) *L. un. in fin. C. de rei ux. act.* (5, 13).

(*m*) This involves a reasonable exception to the rule above recognised (note *i*).

(*n*) *Nov.* 22, *C.* 1.

this legal relation arises, which will generally be the time when the marriage is concluded; sometimes that of a contract afterwards made (Notes *i* and *m*). But in other cases, the succession of the spouses is a true and simple succession *ab intestato;* and this is always to be judged according to the law in force when the succession opens. Among such cases is the edict *unde vir et uxor*, and the succession of the indigent spouse in Roman law. Also, according to the provincial law of Brandenburg, the *Joachimica* (*o*).

The same distinctions and rules are applicable to the succession of children, in so far as that stands in connection with the matrimonial rights of property subsisting between their parents.

All these rules will naturally be applied only when the new law as to matrimonial property is not accompanied by special transitory provisions; and this is to be expected in the case before us more frequently than elsewhere. If a legislator, in place of the *régime dotal* hitherto exclusively observed in his country, desired to introduce universal communion of goods, or *vice versa*, he would hardly fail to think of the numerous existing marriages, and to define the relation of the new law towards them.

I will conclude this subject by a review of some transitory provisions actually promulgated as to new laws touching marriage.

Two laws of Justinian, in which the principles here asserted are admitted and applied, have already been cited (Notes *l* and *n*).

In the Prussian law there are the following transitory provisions (*p*):—

The patent which introduced the Allg. Landrecht in 1794, ordains (§ 14) that the matrimonial rights of property, including the separation occasioned by a divorce, shall be judged according to the law in force at the time of the marriage; quite in accordance with the principle here asserted. In the case of an intestate succession founded on the common law

(*o*) As to this distinction, comp. § 379, No. 5; and as to the rule applicable in real intestate succession, § 395, *b*.

(*p*) The provisions as to the reasons of divorce will be mentioned afterwards, § 399, *e*.

(not on a provincial law), the surviving spouse is allowed to elect whether he will succeed according to the law in force when the marriage is contracted, or according to the Landrecht. This is a new positive rule, which can be rested on no legal principle. Yet there is no hardship or injustice in it; for a married person can always prevent this result by making a will. If, therefore, the deceased has neglected to do this, it may be presumed that he concurred in this statutory favour to the survivor.

The transitory laws of 1814 and 1816 agree in essentials with these rules (*q*).

II. Paternal Power.—Its origin is to be judged by the law of the time of the facts in which it originates. Thus Justinian introduced the new rule, that the adoption of a child subject to the paternal power of another should not, in most cases, create a new paternal power, nor extinguish the former (*r*). This law was certainly applicable to all adoptions afterwards made; but previous adoptions were not relieved from the more stringent operation of the former law. So legitimation by subsequent marriage is regulated entirely by the law which exists when the marriage is contracted, irrespective of a subsequent law, or of the law at the birth of the child (§ 380).

The personal rights of the father over the child do not belong to this place; the laws which regulate them relate to the existence, not the acquisition of rights, and therefore affect already existing legal relations (§ 398).

In regard to patrimonial rights, it naturally suggests itself to apply to the paternal power the same rules which have just been laid down for marriage. The result would be immutably to fix patrimonial rights by the law under which the paternal power originated, that is, by the law existing at the birth of the child, so that a new law would be applicable only to children

(*q*) (See above, § 383.) *Provinces beyond the Elbe*, § 9; *West Prussia*, §§ 11, 12; *Posen*, § 11; *Saxony*, § 11. The different provisions which are found here and there in other passages relate to the provincial law, not to this question. The law of 1825 for the Duchy of Westphalia says nothing at all as to these matters, because in the fourth section it excludes from its adoption of the Prussian code the first three titles of the second Part, which alone treat of marriage and intestate succession.

(*r*) *L.* 10, *C. de adopt.* (8, 48); § 2, *J. de adopt.* (1, 11). But with an exception in the case in which the adoptive father is also a natural ascendant of the child.

afterwards born. But on closer inspection this analogy appears to be a mere illusion, and we are forced to conclude that the new law immediately alters the patrimonial relations, even for children already born. I will proceed to illustrate this proposition by an example, before I undertake its demonstration.

According to the older Roman law, a child under paternal power could have no estate, for everything acquired by its acts was immediately acquired by the father. This rule was in course of time restricted in regard to many kinds of acquisition, especially in the *castrense peculium*, the *bona materna*, etc.; but as a general rule, it still subsisted. Justinian entirely abolished it, enacting that every acquisition of the child, including those arising from his own industry and business transactions, should belong to his own estate, not to that of the father (*s*). If we ask, then, to what cases this new law was applicable, the false analogy above referred to would lead us to apply it only to children born after the law. But according to the view here adopted, it must be said, that from the promulgation of the law, every new acquisition of children was to be held as their own; only that which they had already acquired remained the property of the father. Thus, the destiny of new acquisitions, the capacity to acquire, was instantaneously altered by the new law; that which was already acquired was not affected by it.

The correctness of this view is proved by the fact, that the rules which govern the child's acquisition are to be regarded as consequences of his more or less restricted *capacity for rights* (*t*); but as such they relate to the status of the person, in regard to which the principle of non-retroactivity has no application (§ 389). Just in this point there is a complete difference between paternal power and marriage, because the patrimonial relations of the spouses (dotal *régime* or communion of goods) have no connection whatever with the capacity for rights. This is the juridical expression of the radical difference between the two legal relations. But we are led to the same result if we look at the matter from another standpoint. Marriage is a legal relation between two independent persons, constituted by their free will, by contract. The paternal power, on

(*s*) *L.* 6, *C. de bona quæ lib.* (6, 61); § 1, *I. per quas pers.* (2, 9).
(*t*) See vol. ii. § 67.

the contrary, originates by the birth of the child, and therefore by a mere natural event, in the most involuntary manner. There can thus be no question of a continuing will, of a settlement of legal relations by means of contract.

What has here been said of new laws which create the strongest contrasts must also be applied to minor legislative changes; for laws of this and of that description differ only in the degree of their efficacy, being alike in their nature. If, therefore, a new law introduces or abolishes the father's usufruct of the estate of his children, or prescribes for it a longer or shorter period, it must be immediately applicable, even to the existing estate of living children (*u*).

These rules are not only recognised by writers, but also in the recent transitory laws of Prussia in regard to parental usufruct (*v*).

The dissolution of the paternal power, particularly by emancipation, is subject to the law of the time when the act causing the dissolution takes place. The consequences of the dissolution are also subject to it, including the *præmium emancipationis* (Note *u*).

We shall afterwards speak of the legal relations of illegitimate children (§ 399).

III. *Guardianship.*—In modern law this presents itself as the exercise of a right of protection pertaining to the state, and therefore as a branch of the public law (§ 380, *c*). There is therefore no doubt that it may always be modified by new laws. If such new laws relate to the way in which it originates in particular cases, the necessity of altering guardianships already constituted in conformity to them will not readily be admitted, although the right to make such alterations could not be doubted. If the law says nothing about it, it is to be referred only to guardianships thereafter constituted.

The obligations arising from a guardianship (*actio tutelæ*

(*u*) Weber, p. 86; Reinhardt, *on Glück*, vol. i. p. 11. It might be supposed that in Roman law this is at variance with the nature of the usufruct, which, once acquired, continues till the death of the usufructuary. But this usufruct arising from the family relation is of a different nature, even in Roman law, which gives the emancipating father, as a special *recompense* for emancipation, the perpetual usufruct of the *half* of the estate. *L.* 6, § 3 *C. de bon. quæ lib.* (6, 61).

(*v*) *Provinces beyond the Elbe* (1814), § 10; *West Prussia* (1816), § 13; *Posen* (1816), § 3. (See above, § 383.)

directa, contraria) are to be judged by the rules regulating obligations (§ 392).

IV. *Freedmen.*—An ancient law touching the manumission of slaves is here mentioned, because it contains a transitory direction which modern writers commonly misapprehend.

The *lex Junia* had ordered that in many cases of imperfect manumission the person manumitted should become free and a *Latinus*, and should also be capable of acquiring property, but that at his death the estate he had acquired should fall to his patron, not as succession, but in virtue of the fiction that the freedman had died a slave (*w*). This incomplete manumission was changed by Justinian into a perfect manumission, so that the estate of the freedman no longer fell to the patron in this way. But he added that this new rule should apply only to future manumissions; to those bygone the old law was to be applied, whether the freedman was already dead or still alive (*x*). This was not a new law as to succession (as modern writers generally suppose), but as to manumission, and the restriction of the estate therewith connected. The transitory rule was quite in harmony with the nature of the legal relation.

SECT. LIV.—(§ 397.)

A. ACQUISITION OF RIGHTS.—EXCEPTIONS.

By the foregoing inquiry a normal limitation has been assigned to the action, in point of time, of new laws on the various classes of legal relations. Exceptions from the rules laid down are possible in two directions: they may either extend or limit the efficacy of the new law in comparison with these rules.

An *extension* of the effects of a new law, that is, an exceptional retroactivity, will generally mean that the lawgiver, persuaded of the importance of a new measure, attempts to secure for it authority as far as his power extends. An example has been cited above in a Roman usury law (§ 386, *f*, *g*). An exception of this kind can hardly be justified, for the advantage

(*w*) Gaius, iii. § 56.
(*x*) *L. un.* § 13. *C. de Lat. libert. toll.* (76).

so to be gained is always counterbalanced by the unfavourable impression which generally attends so arbitrary an interference, even when done with good intentions. But there are cases in which such exceptions arise from other motives, especially from the desire to favour individuals without injuring others. This is the intention of the Prussian provision, that a new penal law in milder terms shall be applied to crimes committed under the old law (*a*). A like benevolent spirit accounts for another Prussian law, by which a defect in the form of a juridical act is rendered innocuous, if a new law prescribes an easier form which the act, though previously executed, fully satisfies. The objectionable character of this provision has already been noted (§ 388 *c*).

An exceptional *limitation* of the effects of a new law is less objectionable. Its purpose is to favour mere expectations, which are certainly not protected by the principle laid down above (§ 385); and it always arises from the belief that the directions of a new law, although in themselves salutary, are not of such paramount importance as to demand an immediate and absolute application, by which individual interests may perhaps be endangered.

It has already been observed that the same law of the Roman emperor which denies in general the retroactivity of laws, expressly adds a reservation of particular exceptions (§ 386, *a*),—a reservation which was unnecessary, being implied as a matter of course. In the course of this inquiry, many examples of such exceptions have been given, partly from the Roman law, partly from modern legislations. These exceptions were of both kinds,—extensive (*b*) and restrictive (*c*); and it is worthy of mention, that cases of the second kind are more numerous than those of the first. It was also observed that the particular exceptions found in the Roman law are of no practical importance for us, even if the Roman law should be newly introduced into any country as its common law (§ 386).

In future we have to recognise such exceptions only where they are distinctly expressed; for the legislator, when he resolves on such an exception, is clearly conscious of the contrast

(*a*) See above, § 387, *b*. This provision is justified by the prerogative of grace which pertains to the legislator for each case.

(*b*) Such cases are found in §§ 386, 388, 390, 391, 394.

(*c*) So in §§ 391 and 394.

between the exception and the rule, and certainly has the opportunity of giving an express and unambiguous statement of it. It is also remarkable that the Roman constitution which has at all times been the basis of this doctrine, states the reservation of exceptions thus: 'Nisi *nominatim* et de præterito tempore . . . . cautum sit' (§ 386, *a*).

Entirely rejecting this precaution, recognised and required by the Roman law itself, a modern writer attempts to discover and mark by many different indications the retroactive force concealed in new laws (*d*). For this purpose, distinctions wholly foreign to this subject are introduced, such as that between nullity and the refusal of action, *ipso jure* and *per exceptionem*, etc. In this way he is led, not only to admit exceptions with undue facility, but also imperceptibly to confound the notions of rule and exception, and obliterate the limits between them. Such a method is particularly dangerous in regard to modern legislations, in which no such firmly settled system of legal ideas and technical terms as that of Roman law can be expected, and to which, therefore, we do violence by an interpretation which tacitly rests on this supposition (*e*).

It is very remarkable that the Roman law, in the case of the extensive exceptions, adds a limitation, which must be regarded as the exception to an exception. The exceptional retroactivity is not to take place if the legal relation to which it could be applied has already been the object of a judicial decision or compromise (*judicatum vel transactum*). This restriction is nowhere expressed as a permanent and universal principle, but it is repeated in similar terms in so many passages of the Roman law, that it must undoubtedly be regarded as a rule universally recognised by the Romans (*f*). It is founded on this sufficient reason, that both the judgment and the transaction transform the original legal relation, so that, in place of the legal relation to which the new law related, there is substituted one essentially different.

(*d*) Weber, pp. 78, 106-109, 137, foll. Bergmann, §§ 26, 29, lays down more sober opinions, yet not without having participated somewhat in §§ 4 and 5 in the mistake of Weber.

(*e*) A similar censure has been passed in treating of the local limits of laws (§ 374, *c*).

(*f*) Bergmann, pp. 138, 146, where there is a summary view of these passages.

But by the judgment we are not here to understand only a final one capable of execution (rechtskräftiges), but also, in a pending lawsuit, one in the first instance, if the new law appears during the dependence of the appeal (g). The reason is, that the first judge could pronounce only according to the law in force at the time of his judgment, and the Court of Appeal can only alter a judgment in itself erroneous and unlawful.

Moreover, by transaction we are here to understand, not only a transaction in the strict legal sense of the word (*transactio*), but every conventional settlement of a lawsuit, which may be effected by voluntary concession on one side or the other, by release, renunciation, acknowledgment, satisfaction of a claim, whether the concession be partial or total, if only it effect the definitive settlement of the dispute (*h*).

Among the exceptions here enumerated, is commonly placed the case of an authentic interpretation of a law (*i*); so that such a law is held to have retrospective effect on previous legal relations. Certainly nothing can be objected against the retroactivity of a purely interpretative law (*k*), only it should not be regarded as an exceptional case; a difference of opinion which is therefore more theoretical than practical in its nature. If a declaratory law is enacted, its substance, that is to say, the meaning it establishes for the earlier law, is for the judge true and certain, whether his personal conviction agree with it or not. If, therefore, he judges in conformity with the declaratory law, he applies in reality the law interpreted, not that which interprets it (and which only reveals to him the sense of the earlier one); and here, therefore, there is no retroaction.

That there is here no exception, is evident from the circumstance that this kind of application is recognised so generally, and not merely in the case of particular explanatory laws. If it were an exception, it would necessarily be different in particular instances, which, however, would be quite unnatural, and inconsistent with the relation of the lawgiver to the judge.

It might be supposed that this difference of opinion is in

(*g*) *Nov.* 115, *pr.*, and *C.* 1.
(*h*) Bergmann, § 25. Comp. vol. vii. § 302.
(*i*) See vol. i. § 32.
(*k*) It is expressly confirmed in *Nov.* 143, *pr.*, at the end of the text.

one aspect of practical importance, because, according to the view maintained by me, the restrictions above referred to (judgment and transaction) would not apply. But in fact these do apply, though for a somewhat different reason. If we learn by the declaratory law that the anterior judgment or transaction proceeded on an erroneous interpretation, yet they never lose their efficacy (*l*). Here, therefore, the circumstance that the judgment and compromise transform the legal relation is still decisive.

This rule as to well-grounded retroaction refers not only to the proper interpretation of an obscure law, but also to the recognition and confirmation of an earlier positive law, or of a customary law, if its existence or its obligatory force was hitherto doubtful. But it does not apply to the restoration of a more ancient law that has fallen into disuse.

Many wrongly distinguish between laws which interpret correctly and falsely, because the latter really make new law. By such an assumption the judge would in fact set himself above the legislator, and would therefore entirely mistake his true position. All depends on the question whether the legislator has intended and declared the law to be explanatory, not whether it contains a correct interpretation in the opinion of the judge (*m*).

The retroactivity of explanatory laws has obtained recognition in the Prussian law, and correctly as a permanent rule applicable to all times (*n*). But besides this, there is a different purely transitory rule relative to the introduction of the Allgemeine Landrecht. It is to this effect, that in judging of former legal relations, if the laws then in force were obscure and doubtful, so that there have hitherto been differences of opinion in the tribunals, that opinion shall in future be preferred which agrees with the contents of the Landrecht, or approaches nearest to them (*o*).

(*l*) The judgment is not null, for it was certainly not pronounced contrary to a distinct law. Weber, pp. 212–214. (Only if the explanatory law appears during the dependence of the appeal, the higher court might have something to alter in conformity with it.) The transaction cannot even be attacked on the ground of an error in fact. *L.* 65, § 1, *de cond. indeb.* (12, 6); *L.* 23, *C. de transact.* (2, 4). Comp. also vol. vii. p. 42.

(*m*) As to the retrospectivity of explanatory laws, see, in general, Weber, pp. 54–61, 194–208; Bergmann, §§ 10–12, 31–33.

(*n*) *Allg. Landrecht*, *Einleitung*, § 15.

(*o*) *Publicationspatent*, 1794, § 9.

SECT. LV.—(§ 398.)

B. EXISTENCE OF RIGHTS.—FUNDAMENTAL PRINCIPLE.

The basis of the present inquiry was laid in the distinction of two kinds of rules of law (§ 384). One class of these had for its object the acquisition of rights; and in regard to it, the principle of non-retroactivity, or of the maintenance of vested rights, was recognised. The second class of rules of law, which is still to be considered, has for its object the existence of rights; and to it that principle has no application.

We understand by rules as to the existence of rights, first, those concerning the existence or non-existence of a legal institution, and therefore laws by which a previously existing legal institution is entirely abolished; also those which essentially alter the nature of a legal institution without abolishing it, and therefore distinguish two modes of the existence of a legal institution. With regard to all these laws, then, it is asserted that the preservation of vested rights (non-retroactivity) cannot possibly be conceived as a ruling principle for them as it is for the rules of law as to the acquisition of rights; because, if we were to give them such a sense, the most important laws of this kind would have no meaning at all.

To make this evident, I shall take three laws which have been passed in modern times at different places, and apply to them, by way of experiment, the principle of non-retroactivity. A law abolishes villenage; another abolishes tithes without compensation, as was done for example at the beginning of the French Revolution; a third law changes tithes, before irredeemable, into redeemable rights, by permitting the debtor (perhaps also the creditor) to commute them at his own pleasure into a prestation of another kind of the same money value. If these three laws are subjected to the principle of non-retroactivity, they will have the following signification: Every future constitution of the relation of villenage (or of a right of tithe) is forbidden, invalid, ineffectual. Every future constitution of a right of tithe shall include the faculty of commutation at the pleasure of one of the parties. But in this sense these laws would be utterly vain and superfluous, for no one has dreamed for generations of constituting a new right of villenage or of tithe. Hence it follows that the lawgiver certainly had not this meaning, and that therefore his intention was in direct contrast to the intention of the laws touching the acquisition of rights; because these do not operate retrospectively, but only on future juridical acts, and therefore they maintain acquired rights; certainly with exceptions, which, however, are of very slight importance, and almost vanish away in comparison with the rule which is actually observed.

The question may be asked, whether all laws of this kind are not thoroughly unjust and objectionable, simply because they destroy or transform acquired rights. I will not by any means evade this question, but rather subject it to a special examination; only it will be advantageous for our inquiry to reserve in the meantime this totally distinct question, and first to ascertain what is the spirit and meaning of the laws with which we are engaged. The justice and equity of such laws will be specially examined at the close (§ 400).

The spirit and meaning of laws of this class may be expressed by the following formulas, which present a marked contrast to the principle above laid down for the first class of laws (§§ 384, 385):

To new laws of this class retroactive force is to be ascribed.

New laws of this class do not leave vested rights unaffected.

The following consideration will serve to confirm this view of the spirit and meaning of such laws from a different side. The most numerous and most important of these laws have the strictly positive and coercitive nature described on another occasion, for they have their roots beyond the region of pure law, and are connected with moral, political, and economical motives and purposes (§ 349). But it belongs to the nature of such laws to extend their power and efficacy farther than other laws, as I have already shown in discussing local collisions.

I have still to state what is the position of our writers towards the doctrine here adopted. The distinction of two classes of rules of law which are subject to different, indeed contrary, principles, is nowhere made; but the principle of non-retroactivity is regarded as universally applicable to all laws. It might therefore be expected that writers would in fact give to the laws of which we here speak the perfectly unpractical sense above explained, and thus would treat the abolition of villenage as a mere prohibition to constitute it in future. But they are very far from doing so. They rather class such laws among the *exceptions* from non-retroactivity (§ 397) reserved as early as the Roman law, and from this standpoint they admit their application to acquired rights (*a*).

Although, then, the immediate difficulty is evaded by this view of the matter, the expedient must be entirely condemned. Exceptions to the principle of non-retroactivity are of an accidental nature, are in themselves not indispensable, and would be better wanting. All this is not so with the laws which are here in question. If we contemplate these without prejudice, we must at once be convinced that, in regard to them, that expedient is forced, and thrusts on the laws a sense which is entirely strange to them. The law abolishing villenage would be placed by it on the same line with Justinian's law forbidding usury, and its whole contents so apprehended would be thus logically stated: It is hereby forbidden to create in future any relation of personal bondage, and this rule shall have as an exception retroactive force, so that even existing relations of that kind shall be abolished. Thus a totally useless provision, of which nobody ever thought, would take rank as the leading idea, and the thing which alone the lawgiver had in his mind would be added as an incidental exception. But in most laws of this kind there is assuredly no trace of anything which points to the notion of an exceptional retroaction.

But to these reasons there is added one purely practical, which makes such a treatment of the matter entirely inadmissible. If in these laws we had to do with an exceptional retroaction, we should be obliged to place it under certain limitations (§ 397, *f*); it would necessarily cease whenever a legal relation had been the object of a judgment, or of a transaction. But that would lead to this absurd result, that the abolition of tithes would be applicable to all rights of tithe that had never been made the subject of litigation, but not to tithes as to which a suit had once been decided or compromised. The writers referred to do not in fact admit this absurd result, and, according to them, such an abolition is general in its effects (*b*). But it is evident

(*a*) Weber, pp. 51, 52, 188, 189; Bergmann, pp. 156, 177, 257.
(*b*) Weber, pp. 213–215; Bergmann, p. 259.

that they can arrive at this result, only by evading that restriction (which is itself an exception to an exception) by means of a new exception, and thus admitting, as it were, an exception of the third power. Thus it becomes still more evident how unnatural is a doctrine which necessitates such expedients.

The very different way in which another author attempts to solve this difficulty, is extremely characteristic (*c*). He admits of no exceptional retroaction, nor even any influence whatever of the legislator upon the collision of laws in time (§ 387, *i*). He gets over the difficulty which we are now considering, by merely fixing his eyes on the institutions which he specially disapproves, such as slavery, and exemption of the nobility from taxation. These he calls atrocities, moral turpitudes, iniquities, which have in themselves no legitimate existence. When a law abolishes them, it can have no need of the appendage of retroactive force. Rather, each of the three political powers (legislative, judicial, executive) ought of itself alone to have competency to ignore those institutions, and thus practically to annihilate them. A refutation of this theory will not be required. I will only call attention to the practical difficulty of determining the existence and limits of those atrocities and turpitudes, since possibly the subjective opinions of the depositaries of the three political powers might not be quite in harmony. Among these there might also be consistent communists, who would rank the whole institution of property among the atrocities.

If, therefore, we admit, as is here done, two classes of rules of law, which are governed by quite different principles, nothing is more important than the establishment of clear and certain boundaries between the two classes.

In many cases there is no doubt as to their limits; particularly in the case of those laws by which a legal institution is completely abolished. But there may be doubt in the case of laws which do not abolish a legal institution, but only modify it (*d*). Then everything will depend on the unbiassed examination of the matter and the purpose of the law. A very certain,

(*c*) Struve, pp. 150–152, 274–276.

(*d*) I have already called attention in a general manner to these doubts (§ 384). Particular cases of a doubtful character have occurred, § 390, Nos. 3, 4, § 393, No. 6.

and in most cases sufficient, means of demarcation, consists in inquiring whether a new enactment is one of those laws so often mentioned of a strictly positive and coercitive nature, which have their roots beyond the proper region of law (p. 361). In this case we have undoubtedly to rank it among the laws as to the existence of rights, to which the principle of non-retroactivity has no application.

Sect. LVI.—(§ 399.)

B. EXISTENCE OF RIGHTS.—APPLICATIONS. EXCEPTIONS.

The applications of the principle stated in § 398 will be divided, as was done in considering the laws relative to the acquisition of rights, according to certain classes of legal relations; but here a different classification is required from that before used.

I. The *first* class, and also the most important, consists of certain legal relations which by their nature extend beyond the duration of human life, nay, are destined for an unlimited continuance, and only perish accidentally in particular cases. They may commonly be described as restrictions of personal freedom, or of the freedom of immoveable property, and are often compounded of real and obligatory rights. Most of them (not all) have a historical existence, in so far as their origin falls within different epochs, and belongs to a national condition which no longer exists. These are therefore to be regarded as definitively closed, and are not like other legal relations constantly produced afresh (*a*). The laws by which such legal institutions are abolished or modified are always of a strictly positive and coercitive nature, because they have their roots beyond the domain of pure law (§ 398).

In Roman law, slavery, which has long since disappeared from modern Europe, belongs to this order.

The following institutions of this kind partly still exist in one modern law, and partly have been preserved at least until our days :—

(*a*) Comp. above, § 392, *e*.

Predial slavery (villenage).
Real burdens of all kinds, consisting of prestations of money, fruits, services (Frohnden, Robotten = Corvées). Especially the right of tithe.
Feudal tenures.
Family fideicommissa (entails).
Predial servitudes.
Emphyteusis (*b*).

The relation of old and new laws to one another can here hardly be the object of doubt.

II. The *second* class consists of some legal institutions concerning the relation of the sexes. The laws as to these institutions belong to this place, because they do not rest purely on juridical reasons, but on moral (partly moral and religious) grounds. The particular cases are these:—

1. *Divorce.*—If divorce in general is introduced or abolished by a new law, or if an alteration is made in the grounds of divorce, the question arises: What is the influence of the new law on subsisting marriages?

If such a law is regarded from the abstract juridical point of view, it appears similar in its nature to laws as to the alienation of property. By this divorce each party loses the rights previously arising from the marriage, and each acquires freedom from the claims of the other, as well as all the advantages of celibacy (possibility of a new marriage). Accordingly it might be supposed that the laws as to divorce stand in exactly the same position as those relative to matrimonial rights of property (§ 396). Then each spouse would have acquired, by the conclusion of the marriage, an immutable right to be judged in any future divorce according to the law existing at the beginning of the marriage.

This view, however, must be rejected, because the laws as to divorce have moral grounds and aims, are therefore of a coercitive nature, and so belong to the laws as to the existence of marriage (*c*). This is equally true, whether the new law

(*b*) The two last mentioned classes have not, like the others, a historical character pointing to a past order of things, but the modifying laws relating to them are in their grounds and purposes quite similar to those concerning tithes and services.

(*c*) It may be thought one-sided and unfounded that this character is here attributed only to divorce, not to the whole purely personal law of

children. By extending the claims of the children, it may be attempted both to alleviate this condition and to counteract the levity and incontinence of men. On the other hand, by limiting or taking away these claims, it may be attempted to check the levity and misconduct of women, and to hinder the peace of many marriages from being disturbed by claims preferred by strange women. In both tendencies of modern laws a moral aim is unmistakeably present, and it may be immaterial which of these tendencies is better founded in itself, or in an enlarged experience.

If this be admitted, the new law as to illegitimate children must have instantaneous application, irrespective of the law which existed at the date of the conception or birth of the child. The same rule has already been established in reference to local collisions (§ 374, Notes *aa*, *bb*).

In conformity with these opinions is the French law, which forbids even *inquiry* as to paternity (*i*), and thus cuts off even the possibility of securing to an illegitimate child, except where there is voluntary recognition, any claims against the father. This law has been unjustly censured, as if it involved an improper retroaction (*k*). It has been vindicated, just as erroneously, as having for its object a matter of personal status (*l*). The true justification of it is, that it is a coercitive law.

To the same effect is the Prussian transitory law, which, in different terms from the French, ordains that illegitimate children, even if they are born under a foreign law, shall henceforward be able to make good the rights granted to them by the Landrecht (*m*).

III. A third class, finally, is composed of many laws as to purely juridical institutions, either entirely abolishing or fundamentally changing them. Such laws, therefore, are instantaneously applicable to existing legal relations.

Among these is the law by which Justinian abolished the two kinds of property before existing (*ex jure quiritium* and *in bonis*), and substituted a simple right of property, including in

(*i*) *Code Civil*, art. 340: 'La recherche de la paternité est interdite.'
(*k*) Struve, p. 233.
(*l*) Weber, pp. 79–82. The French jurists take the same view.
(*m*) *Provinces beyond the Elbe*, § 11; *West Prussia*, § 14; *Posen*, § 14. (See above, § 383.)

itself all the rights hitherto capable of separation (*n*). Such also is the French law, which refuses the action of vindication to the proprietor of a moveable. If it should be introduced anywhere instead of the Roman law, it would take effect instantaneously on all moveable property; as would also the converse change in the law of property.

To this class belong also new laws introducing legal servitudes as natural restrictions of property, or, conversely, laws abolishing such servitudes when they have previously existed (§ 390, No. 2).

The change of the Roman right of pledge into the Prussian hypothec is of a like nature; the two systems cannot co-exist, but the one must be forthwith ejected by the other (§ 390, No. 3). What measures are to be taken in order to effect this change without violating existing rights, will be shown immediately (§ 400).

Finally, we have to add the case in which testamentary succession is abolished by a new law, in a state which formerly allowed it (§ 393, No. 6).

Exceptions to the principle laid down for this class of new laws are just as conceivable as in regard to laws concerning the acquisition of rights (§ 397). But here they never occur with the effect of extending the operation of the new law, since it is extended as far as possible by the principle itself. They can only tend to limit the efficacy of the new law by way of indulgence.

An instance of this kind from a Prussian transitory law has already occurred (§ 399, II. 1). The Prussian law of divorce was immediately to take effect, yet with the exception of many facts affording reasons for divorce.

Another exception occurs in the law of the kingdom of Westphalia, which abolished feudal tenures and fideicommissa, that is, changed them into free property. This law was naturally held not merely to prevent the constitution of new fiefs (Lehen) and entails, but to change the condition of existing tenures. It did so, however, with this favourable exception,

(*n*) *L. un. C. de nudo j. Quir. toll.* (7. 25). The peculiar character of the *fundus Italicus* and the *res mancipi* then ceased of itself. *L. un. C. de usuc. transform.* (7. 31).

that the next case of succession should still be treated according to the previous law (o).

Sect. LVII.—§ 400.

B. EXISTENCE OF RIGHTS.—EQUITABLE CONSIDERATIONS.

I now revert to the question above reserved as to the justice and equity of the class of laws under consideration (p. 361).

It has been shown that these laws, at least in the most numerous and most important cases, cannot possibly be understood except as affecting vested rights, since they either annihilate the legal institutions themselves, and therefore the legal relations subject to them (a), or at least essentially modify them, in either case without respect to the will of the parties interested.

It is possible, while admitting this, to add to the admission the plausible objection, that just for this reason such laws must be regarded as utterly unjust and inadmissible. Those who make this objection evidently proceed on the assumption, that every violation of an acquired right, without the assent of the person interested, is simply impossible from the standpoint of moral right, and they regard this impossibility as a supreme and absolute principle. But this assumption cannot be admitted for the following reasons:—

In the first place, because it is incompatible with the general nature and origin of law. Law has its root in the common consciousness of the nation. This is, on the one hand, entirely different from the easily and quickly changing, the accidental and momentary consciousness of the individual man; but, on the other hand, it is subject to the law of progressive development, and cannot therefore be conceived as fixed and immoveable (b). Hence we cannot possibly admit for any single epoch

(o) The Prussian law of 11th March 1818 afterwards added to this exception that all Lehen and fideicommissa, in which the next case of succession so reserved had not yet occurred, should be held as restored for ever. *Gesetzsammlung*, 1818, p. 17.

(a) Comp. above, vol. i. §§ 4, 5, as to the notions of legal relation and legal institution.

(b) Vol. i. § 7.

the power of throwing a spell and exercising a domination over every future age by its own sense of right. Some examples will make this clear.

Throughout all antiquity the status of slavery was regarded as a kind of natural necessity, and no one imagined the possibility of a civilised people living without slaves. In modern Christian Europe, in the same way, this status is regarded as totally impossible, and utterly contrary to all sense of right (*c*). The transition from one of these conditions into the other, in consequence of the very gradual operation of Christian morals and circumstances, has been effected so slowly and imperceptibly, that we cannot fix with certainty the epoch of history at which the former state of things ceased. Suppose, then, this transition had not been so gradual, but had occurred within a brief space of time, in consequence, perhaps, of a powerful spiritual shock to the national conscience, we could not possibly refuse to such a new age the right of giving way to the present universal conviction, and repudiating all further recognition of slavery as a legal institution. At the same time, various ways may be imagined of effecting the change, and guarding against possible dangers.

The right of tithe may afford another example. In times of a hardly developed, stationary culture of the soil, this might be a simple, natural, convenient legal institution, and receive great extension; but with the lively development of commercial activity, the conviction necessarily arose, that by such a tax on the gross produce, all progress in agriculture is checked, and often rendered impossible. Those subject to it suffered by the burden, and through them the whole state; but not those entitled to it, who therefore opposed a change in the tithes, by which they profited. When, therefore, the conviction of the disadvantages connected with this state of things became

(*c*) Many writers have sought to obscure or to weaken this contrast by comparing the status connected with those severe punishments of modern times which consist of deprivation of freedom, with the mild and often friendly condition of the slaves of antiquity. But the true relations of things are thus altered. In order to keep the contrast before our eyes in all its clearness, two things must be remembered: First, the origin of slavery by birth; secondly, the legal position of the slave in the same line with domestic animals, as a kind of merchandise. (Ulpian, xix. 1.) Modern slavery in the East, as well as the totally different slavery of America, are not here taken into account.

general, the legislative change of the hitherto irredeemable tithes into a redeemable charge was justified, because a great and evident benefit was thus obtained for the state and those burdened, without any loss to the creditors, who had full indemnification.

The first argument which I have developed against the assumption of the absolute iniquity of laws which, by destroying or modifying legal institutions, interfere with vested rights, was derived from the origin of law, and therefore from the contemplation of the nation in whose sense of right the law itself has its root. A second argument, which leads to the same result, relates to the individual man as the possessor of acquired rights. They who assert the absolute inviolability of acquired rights by new laws, merely protest against the compulsion involved in such violations, and allow the fairness and justice of the change as soon as the assent of the party interested is given to the abolition or modification of his acquired right. But let us examine a little more closely the character of those who are the possessors of acquired rights. Such a right appears as an extension of the power of an individual man, and is always of a more or less accidental nature (*d*); but the individual man has a limited and transient existence. If, therefore, on account of their interference with vested rights, open war is declared against laws which abolish or alter legal institutions, such opposition ought at least, in consideration of the finite character of the possessors of such rights, to be confined within narrow limits on two sides.

At the most, their legitimate effect may be denied to new laws as long as the possessor of a real right lives. If he leaves heirs, these have, at the time when the new law appears, no vested right that can be injured. In other words, all succession is purely positive; and if a new law imposes on it restrictions and conditions, no violation of acquired rights can be found in this. We shall apply this to the case above cited as an example. If the new law which was enacted to abolish slavery declared that in future no heir could acquire by succession property in slaves, this would certainly be no violation of an acquired right.

This view is founded on the nearness of the end of every

(*d*) See vol. i. §§ 4, 52, 53.

human life. But if we look to its beginning, we are led to the same result. Every man must recognise the state of the law which he finds determined and settled at his birth. If, therefore, a legal institution is abolished or altered by a new law before his birth, for him at least no acquired right can be thus injured (*e*).

Still these reasons avail to refute only the notion of the absolute injustice and unrighteousness of all laws of this kind. I am very far from desiring to allow unrestricted and arbitrary influence to such laws. The whole question should rather be withdrawn from the province of absolute right, and transferred to that of legislative policy, which is its true place, and where many ruinous errors may be avoided by caution, prudence, and moderation. The principal points that should be kept in view are perhaps the following:—

The first care must be, not to proceed inconsiderately, not lightly to admit the necessity of laws of this kind; and therefore to be distrustful of any assertions, derived from mere theories and supported by alleged public opinion, that the general welfare demands innovation.

In the second place, the utmost tenderness and fairness must be used in the practical execution of details. In the most important laws of this class, which concern legal relations of a permanent character (§ 399, I.), this must consist in the circumstance that a legal institution is not abolished, but modified, that the legal relation is made capable of being dissolved. If in this way a true and complete indemnification of the parties interested is effected, the law has attained its end. This is not difficult in the numerous cases of real burdens of every kind, in which only two persons are generally concerned. Every political or economical end is fully attained by redemption with indemnity, without enriching the one party at the expense of the other, which can by no means be justified by the nature of such laws.

A noble example of such indemnification was afforded in modern times by the English emancipation of slaves, when the state indemnified the owners of slaves at its own cost for the loss they sustained.

(*e*) Meyer, pp. 34, 35. Comp. above, § 395, *b*. Hence, a law abolishing feudal tenures (Lehen) or fideicommissa certainly does not injure the rights of those who are born after its promulgation.

It is very difficult to solve this problem in abolishing fiefs (Lehen) and fideicommissa, because the claims and expectations of the persons interested in the succession are extremely uncertain. It may be attempted to diminish the disadvantages by delaying the execution of the measure (§ 399, *o*).

In many cases no compensation is necessary; but it is enough to effect such a transition as will avert every possible injustice. This was done in the numerous instances in which the Prussian system of hypothecs was substituted for the right of pledge of the common law. It was only necessary to preserve to creditors holding a pledge their right and their priority. This was done by summoning them publicly to intimate their claims within a specified period, in order to be registered in the new books of hypothecs in the rank which their former right assigned to them.

There was no need for such a precaution, still less for an indemnity, when Justinian abolished the double property which had hitherto existed (§ 399, *n*). For by this change no one lost a right or an advantage; and it only effected the end declared by the lawgiver himself, namely, to free the minds of the studious youth from the terror which the useless learning preserved in this doctrine had hitherto inspired.

I. INDEX OF CASES.

II. INDEX OF SUBJECTS.

THE END.